Office® 2008
for the Mac
1 2 3 4 5 6 7 **on Demand**

Steve Johnson

Perspection, Inc.

 Que Publishing, 800 East 96th Street, Indianapolis, IN 46240 USA

Office® 2008 for the Mac On Demand

Copyright © 2009 by Perspection, Inc.

Library of Congress Cataloging-in-Publication data is on file

ISBN-10 0-7897-3923-2

ISBN-13 978-0-7897-3923-0

Printed and bound in the United States of America

First Printing: September 2008

11 10 09 08   4 3 2 1

Que Publishing offers excellent discounts on this book when ordered in quantity for bulk purchases or special sales.

For information, please contact: U.S. Corporate and Government Sales

    1-800-382-3419 or corpsales@pearsontechgroup.com

For sales outside the U.S., please contact: International Sales

    1-317-428-3341 or International@pearsontechgroup.com

Trademarks

All terms mentioned in this book that are known to be trademarks or service marks have been appropriately capitalized. Que cannot attest to the accuracy of this information. Use of a term in this book should not be regarded as affecting the validity of any trademark or service mark.

Microsoft and the Microsoft Office logo are registered trademarks of Microsoft Corporation in the United States and/or other countries.

Warning and Disclaimer

Every effort has been made to make this book as complete and as accurate as possible, but no warranty or fitness is implied. The authors and the publishers shall have neither liability nor responsibility to any person or entity with respect to any loss or damage arising from the information contained in this book.

Publisher
Paul Boger

Associate Publisher
Greg Wiegand

Acquisitions Editor
Laura Norman

Managing Editor
Steve Johnson

Author
Steve Johnson

Technical Editor
Holly Johnson

Page Layout
James Teyler
Beth Teyler

Interior Designers
Steve Johnson
Marian Hartsough

Indexer
Katherine Stimson

Proofreader
Holly Johnson

Team Coordinator
Cindy Teeters

Acknowledgements

Perspection, Inc.

Office 2008 for the Mac On Demand has been created by the professional trainers and writers at Perspection, Inc. to the standards you've come to expect from Que publishing. Together, we are pleased to present this training book.

Perspection, Inc. is a software training company committed to providing information and training to help people use software more effectively in order to communicate, make decisions, and solve problems. Perspection writes and produces software training books, and develops multimedia and Web-based training. Since 1991, we have written more than 90 computer books, with several bestsellers to our credit, and sold over 5 million books.

This book incorporates Perspection's training expertise to ensure that you'll receive the maximum return on your time. You'll focus on the tasks and skills that increase productivity while working at your own pace and convenience.

We invite you to visit the Perspection Web site at:

www.perspection.com

Acknowledgements

The task of creating any book requires the talents of many hard-working people pulling together to meet impossible deadlines and untold stresses. We'd like to thank the outstanding team responsible for making this book possible: the writer, Steve Johnson; the production team, James Teyler and Beth Teyler; the editor and proofreader, Holly Johnson; and the indexer, Katherine Stimson. Also, a special thanks to Earl Todd for helping out in crunch time.

At Que publishing, we'd like to thank Greg Wiegand and Laura Norman for the opportunity to undertake this project, Cindy Teeters for administrative support, and Sandra Schroeder for your production expertise and support.

Perspection

About The Author

Steve Johnson has written more than 45 books on a variety of computer software, including Adobe Photoshop CS3 and CS2, Adobe Flash CS3, Dreamweaver CS3, Microsoft Office 2007 and 2003, Microsoft Windows Vista and XP, and Apple Mac OS X Leopard. In 1991, after working for Apple Computer and Microsoft, Steve founded Perspection, Inc., which writes and produces software training. When he is not staying up late writing, he enjoys playing golf, gardening, and spending time with his wife, Holly, and three children, JP, Brett, and Hannah. Steve and his family live in Pleasanton, California, but can also be found visiting family all over the western United States.

We Want To Hear From You!

As the reader of this book, *you* are our most important critic and commentator. We value your opinion and want to know what we're doing right, what we could do better, what areas you'd like to see us publish in, and any other words of wisdom you're willing to pass our way.

As an associate publisher for Que, I welcome your comments. You can email or write me directly to let me know what you did or didn't like about this book—as well as what we can do to make our books better.

Please note that I cannot help you with technical problems related to the topic of this book. We do have a User Services group, however, where I will forward specific technical questions related to the book.

When you write, please be sure to include this book's title and author as well as your name, email address, and phone number. I will carefully review your comments and share them with the author and editors who worked on the book.

Email: feedback@quepublishing.com

Mail: Greg Wiegand
Que Publishing
800 East 96th Street
Indianapolis, IN 46240 USA

For more information about this book or another Que title, visit our Web site at *informit.com/register*. Type the ISBN (excluding hyphens) or the title of a book in the Search field to find the page you're looking for.

Contents

Introduction

Welcome to *Office 2008 for the Mac On Demand*, a visual quick reference book that shows you how to work efficiently with Microsoft Office. This book provides complete coverage of basic to advanced Office skills.

How This Book Works

You don't have to read this book in any particular order. We've designed the book so that you can jump in, get the information you need, and jump out. However, the book does follow a logical progression from simple tasks to more complex ones. Each task is presented on no more than two facing pages, which lets you focus on a single task without having to turn the page. To find the information that you need, just look up the task in the table of contents or index, and turn to the page listed. Read the task introduction, follow the step-by-step instructions in the left column along with screen illustrations in the right column, and you're done.

What's New

If you're searching for what's new in Office 2008, just look for the icon: **New!**. The new icon appears in the table of contents and throughout this book so you can quickly and easily identify a new or improved feature in Office 2008. A complete description of each new feature appears in the New Features guide in the back of this book.

Keyboard Shortcuts

Most menu commands have a keyboard equivalent, such as ⌘+P, as a quicker alternative to using the mouse. A complete list of keyboard shortcuts is available on the Web at *www.perspection.com*.

How You'll Learn

How This Book Works

What's New

Keyboard Shortcuts

Step-by-Step Instructions

Real World Examples

Workshop

Get More on the Web

Step-by-Step Instructions

This book provides concise step-by-step instructions that show you "how" to accomplish a task. Each set of instructions includes illustrations that directly correspond to the easy-to-read steps. Also included in the text are time-savers, tables, and sidebars to help you work more efficiently or to teach you more in-depth information. A "Did You Know?" provides tips and techniques to help you work smarter, while a "See Also" leads you to other parts of the book containing related information about the task.

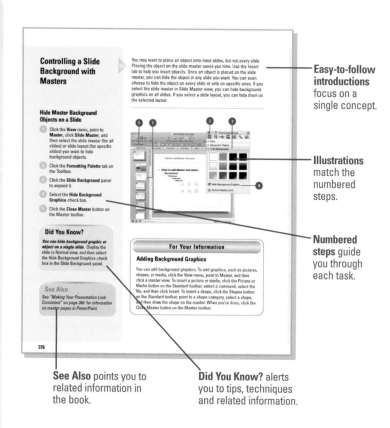

Easy-to-follow introductions focus on a single concept.

Illustrations match the numbered steps.

Numbered steps guide you through each task.

See Also points you to related information in the book.

Did You Know? alerts you to tips, techniques and related information.

Real World Examples

This book uses real world examples files to give you a context in which to use the task. By using the example files, you won't waste time looking for or creating sample files. You get a start file and a result file, so you can compare your work. Not every topic needs an example file, such as changing options, so we provide a complete list of the example files used through out the book. The example files that you need for project tasks along with a complete file list are available on the Web at *www.perspection.com*.

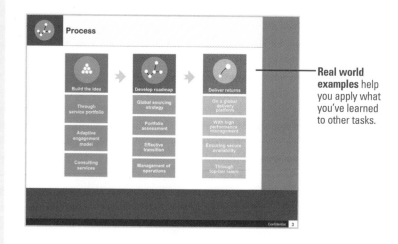

Real world examples help you apply what you've learned to other tasks.

Workshop

This book shows you how to put together the individual step-by-step tasks into in-depth projects with the Workshop. You start each project with a sample file, work through the steps, and then compare your results with project results file at the end. The Workshop projects and associated files are available on the Web at *www.perspection.com*.

Workshop

Introduction

The Workshop is all about being creative and thinking outside of the box. These workshops will help your right-brain soar, while making your left-brain happy, by explaining why things work the way they do. Exploring possibilities is great fun; however, always stay grounded with knowledge of how things work.

Getting and Using the Project Files

Each project in The Workshop includes a start file to help you get started with the project, and a final file to provide you with the results of the project so you can see how well you accomplished the task.

Before you can use the project files, you need to download them from the Web. You can access the files at *www.perspection.com* in the software downloads area. After you download the files from the Web, uncompress the files into a folder on your hard drive to which you have easy access from your Microsoft Office program.

Project 1: Creating a Drop-Down List

Skills and Tools: Create a drop-down list

Entering data in a worksheet can be tedious and repetitive. To make the job easier and get consistent accurate data, you can create a drop-down list of entries you define. To create a drop-down list, you create a list of valid entries in a single column or row without blanks, define a name, and then use the List option in the Data Validation dialog box. To enter data using a drop-down list, click the cell with the defined drop-down list, click the list arrow, and then click the entry you want.

The Project

In this project, you'll learn how to create a drop-down list from a named range of cells for use in conditional formatting.

The Process

1. Open Excel 2008, open DropDown_start.xlsm, and then save it as DropDown.xlsm.
2. Click the **Numbers** tab.

483

The **Workshop** walks you through in-depth projects to help you put Microsoft Office to work.

Get More On The Web

In addition to the information in this book, you can also get more information on the Web to help you get up to speed faster with Office 2008. Some of the information includes:

Transition Helpers

◆ **Only New Features.** Download and print the new feature tasks as a quick and easy guide.

Productivity Tools

◆ **Keyboard Shortcuts.** Download a list of keyboard shortcuts to learn faster ways to get the job done.

Keyboard Shortcuts

Microsoft Office 2008 Common Tasks

If a command on a menu includes a keyboard reference, known as a **keyboard shortcut**, in a ScreenTip or next to the command name, you can perform the action by pressing and holding the first key, and then pressing the second key to perform the command quickly. In some cases, a keyboard shortcut uses three keys. Simply press and hold the first two keys, and then press the third key. For keyboard shortcuts in which you press one key immediately followed by another key, the keys to press are separated by a comma (,). Keyboard shortcuts provide an alternative to using the mouse and make it easy to perform repetitive commands.

Finding a Keyboard Shortcut

To help you find the keyboard shortcut you're looking for, the shortcuts are organized in categories and listed with page numbers.

Common Tasks

Dialog Boxes, 4
Element Gallery, 5
Find and Replace, 5
Format, 5
Language bar, 6
Tables, 6
Toolbox, 3
Undo and Redo, 6

Dialog Boxes: Open and Save As, 4
File, 6
Font, 5
Help, 2
Smart Tags, 6
Text or Cells, 3
Windows, 3

Function Keys

⌨+Function, 8
Functions, 7
Control+Function, 7
Control+⌨+Functions, 8

⌨+Shift+Function, 8
Shift+Function, 7
Control+Shift+Function, 8

If you're searching for new keyboard shortcuts in Microsoft Office 2008, just look for the letter: N. The N appears in the Keyboard Shortcuts table so you can quickly and easily identify new or changed shortcuts.

Additional content is available on the Web. You can download keyboard shortcuts.

More Content

◆ **Photographs.** Download photographs and other graphics to use in your Office documents.

◆ **More Content.** Download new content developed after publication. For example, you can download additional chapters on Word 2008, Excel 2008, PowerPoint 2008, and Microsoft Messenger.

You can access these additional resources on the Web at *www.perspection.com.*

Chatting Online with Messenger

Introduction

Office 2008 makes communicating with other computers over the Internet easier than ever with Microsoft Messenger for Mac (version 6). This chapter describes version 6; your down-loaded version may differ slightly. You can talk to others over the Internet (like you do on a telephone), use video to see and be seen by others while you converse, share programs and files, collaborate on documents, share graphical content, and ask for or get remote online assistance from a contact.

You can use Microsoft Messenger (New!) to exchange instant messages with a designated list of contacts over the Internet. An **instant message** is an online typewritten conver-sation in real-time between two or more contacts. Unlike an e-mail message, instant messages require both parties to be online, and the communication is instantaneous. With Messenger, you can send instant messages to any of your contacts who are online; have conversations with a group of friends; see the latest information about your contacts; see and hear your contacts; send and receive text messages with a mobile device; send a voice clip to express yourself person-ally; and save your conversations. In addition, you can make computer to telephone or computer to computer calls, share and update files with your friends using the Sharing folder, and connect with your friends who use Yahoo Messenger.

Messenger uses different services to exchange messages, files, and other information. The default service is .NET Messenger Service, which individuals mostly use. For those working in a corporate environment, Messenger supports Communications Service for networks that use SIP-server technology and Exchange Instant Messaging for networks that use Microsoft Exchange Server. You can set up Messenger to access more than one type of messaging service.

What You'll Do

Prepare for Messenger

Start and View Messenger

Change My Status

Personalize Messenger

Add Online Contacts

Manage Contacts and Groups

Send and Receive Instant Messages

Block a Contact

Send a File During an Instant Message

Share Files Using Shared Folders

Make a Video and Voice Call

Send a Message to a Mobile Device

Get Remote Assistance

Customize Messenger

1

Additional content is available on the Web. You can download a chapte on Microsoft Messenger.

Getting Started with Office

Introduction

As you manage your business and personal worlds, you continually need to accomplish more, and do it better and faster. Microsoft Office 2008 for the Macintosh provides you with the tools to do all this and more. Each of its programs—Word, Excel, PowerPoint, and Entourage—has a special function, yet they all work together.

Word 2008 is a word processing program you can use to create documents, such as letters, manuals, and reports. Excel 2008 is a spreadsheet program you can use to organize, analyze, and present data, such as a budget or expense report. PowerPoint 2008 is a presentation program you can use to create and deliver professional presentations. Entourage 2008 is a communication and information management program you can use to manage e-mail messages, appointments, contacts, tasks, and notes.

Each Office program uses a similar structure of windows, ribbons, menus, toolbars, and dialog boxes, so you can focus on creating the best document in the least amount of time. Office programs (Word, Excel, PowerPoint, and Entourage) are set up with toolbars, an Element Gallery (**New!**), and a Toolbox (**New!**). You can perform your most basic actions the same way in every program. For example, in each Office program, you open, save, and close documents with the same buttons or commands. When you have a question, the identical help feature is available throughout the Office programs.

Office 2008 also makes communicating with other computers over the Internet easier than ever with Microsoft Messenger for the Macintosh. You can use Messenger to exchange instant messages with a designated list of contacts over the Internet. An instant message is an online typewritten conversation in real-time between two or more contacts.

What You'll Do

Start an Office Program

Use the Project Gallery

View an Office Program Window

Choose Commands

Work with Toolbars

Work with the Elements Gallery

Create a Blank Office Document

Create a Document Using a Template

Open an Existing Office Document

Manage Windows

Switch Views

Use the Toolbox

Check Compatibility

Save an Office Document

Save an Office Document with Different Formats

Creating a Template

Recover an Office Document

Get Updates on the Web

Get Help While You Work

Close a Document and Quit Office

Starting an Office Program

The two quickest ways to start a Microsoft Office program are to select it on the Dock or double-click an alias icon on the desktop. However, you can also start a program from the Office 2008 folder located in the Applications folder. By providing different ways to start a program, you can work the way you like and start programs with a click of a button. When you start an Office program, the Project Gallery appears—depending on your preferences—or a program window opens, displaying a blank document, where you can begin working immediately.

Start an Office Program

◆ **Dock**. Click the program icon in the Dock.

◆ **Microsoft Office 2008 folder**. Open the Applications folder, double-click the Microsoft Office 2008 folder, and then double-click the program icon.

◆ **Project Gallery New Tab**. Start (from the Finder) or display (in an Office program) the Project Gallery, click the New tab, click a category, click a project, and then click Open.

◆ **Alias**. Double-click an alias for the Office program.

If an alert appears relating to network connections, click the **Deny** or **Always Allow** to decline or accept incoming network connections. If you click Deny, it may limit the application's functionality.

Microsoft Office 2008 folder   Alias of Microsoft Word

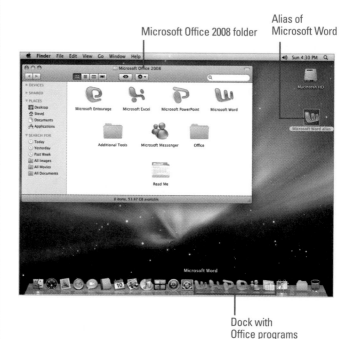

Dock with Office programs

Project Gallery New tab

Start an Office Program and Open One or More Documents

◆ **Single Document**. Double-click an Office document icon or document alias; or drag an Office document icon onto a compatible Office program icon.

◆ **Multiple Documents**. Select one or more document icons, Control-click one of them, and then select an Office program from the Open With submenu.

◆ **Email Attachment**. Within Entourage or other mail program, such as Mail, double-click or open the Office document attached to an email message.

Did You Know?

You can open items in Entourage. Simply, double-click a scheduled event, to do item or task in My Day, or the reminder in Office Reminders to start and open the item in Entourage.

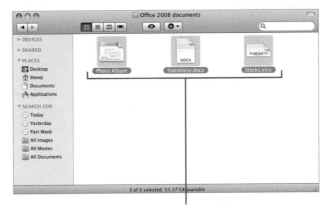

Start an Office program and open documents

Using the Project Gallery

The Project Gallery provides easy access to blank documents, templates, wizards, existing or recently opened documents, and projects. You can open the Project Gallery from the Dock in the Finder or from any of the Office programs. The Project Center uses tabs—New, Recent, Project Center, and Settings—to group commands. The Settings tab allows you to set preferences that apply to all Office programs, such as Show Project Gallery at startup, or that change the display of the Project Gallery.

Use the Project Gallery

1 Start Project Gallery.

- ◆ **From the Finder.** Click the **Microsoft Project Gallery** icon in the Dock.

- ◆ **From an Office Program.** Click the **File** menu, and then click **Project Gallery**.

    TIMESAVER *To open the Project Gallery from an Office program, press Shift+⌘+P.*

    The Project Gallery dialog box appears.

2 Click a tab or button to create or open a document, or set preferences.

- ◆ **Create a new document.** Click the **New** tab, select **Blank Document** from the Category list, select a document type, and then click **Open**.

- ◆ **Open a recent document.** Click the **Recent** tab, select a time period from the Date pane, select a document, and then click **Open** or **Open a Copy**.

- ◆ **Open a project file.** Click the **Project Center** tab, select a document, and then click **Open**.

- ◆ **Open an existing document.** Click the **Open Other** button, select a document from the Open dialog box, and then click **Open**.

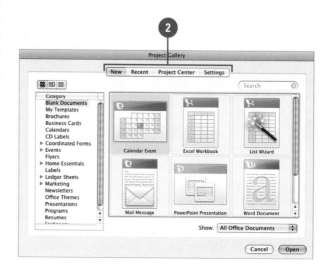

Set Project Gallery Preferences

1. Click the **Microsoft Project Gallery** icon in the Dock, or open an Office program, click the **File** menu, and then click **Project Gallery**.

2. Click the **Settings** tab.

3. Specify any of the following options:

   ◆ **Show Project Gallery at startup.** Display the Project Gallery when you start an Office program.

   ◆ **Confirm before opening other programs.** Display an alert before opening other programs.

   ◆ **Open on.** Display the Project Gallery with a specific tab or the last selection.

   ◆ **Show this number of recently opened files.** Display the specified number of recent documents in the Recent tab.

   ◆ **Documents and Wizards.** Select the document types and wizards you want to view.

   ◆ **File Locations.** Click the link to change the default file location for local templates or workgroup templates.

   ◆ **Restore Defaults.** Click the Restore Defaults button to change the preference options back to the original settings.

4. Click **OK**.

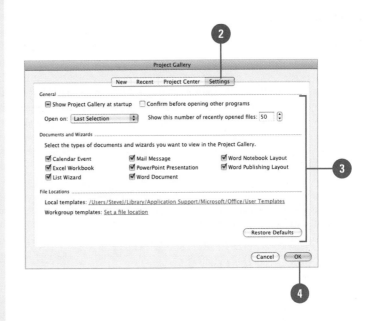

See Also

See "Creating a Document Using a Template" on page 12 for information on using templates and wizards.

Viewing an Office Program Window

Standard Toolbar
Click to access command comments
on the toolbar.

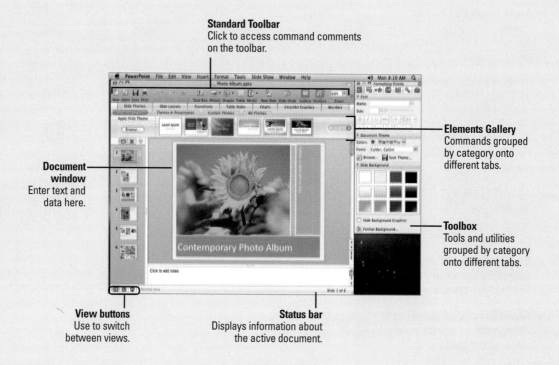

Elements Gallery
Commands grouped
by category onto
different tabs.

Document window
Enter text and
data here.

Toolbox
Tools and utilities
grouped by category
onto different tabs.

View buttons
Use to switch
between views.

Status bar
Displays information about
the active document.

Choosing Commands

The Office commands are organized in groups on menus and toolbars. Menus display commands organized in groups, while the Standard toolbar displays frequently used buttons that you may be already familiar with from previous versions of Office. In addition to menus, you can also display a **shortcut menu** with a group of related commands by right-clicking or Control-clicking a program element.

Choose a Command from a Menu

1. Click a menu name.

2. Click the command you want.

   If the command is followed by an arrow, point to the arrow to see a list of related options, and then click the option you want.

   TIMESAVER *You can use a shortcut key to choose a command. Press and hold down the first key and then press the second key. For example, press and hold the ⌘ key and then press S (or ⌘+S) to select the Save command.*

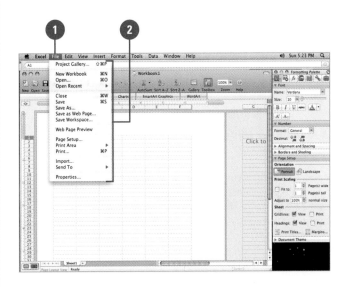

Choose a Command from a Shortcut Menu

1. Right-click or Control-click an object (a cell or graphic element).

2. Click a command on the shortcut menu. If the command is followed by an arrow, point to the command to see a list of related options, and then click the option you want.

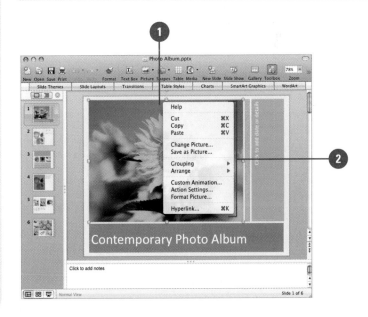

Working with Toolbars

When an Office program starts, the Standard toolbar appears at the top of the window, unless you've changed your settings. Office includes its most common commands, such as Save and Undo, on the Standard toolbar. Click a toolbar button to choose a command. If you are not sure what a toolbar button does, point to it to display a ScreenTip. You can customize the toolbar by adding command buttons or groups to it. You can also display toolbars designed for specific tasks, such as drawing pictures, importing data, or creating charts. If you're not using a toolbar or want to position it in another place, you can hide or move it. When you move a toolbar, you can dock it to the document window or allow it to float (undock) in a separate window. The toolbars are personalized as you work, showing only the buttons you use most often. Additional toolbar buttons are available by clicking the double-arrow on the right-edge of the toolbar.

Choose a Command Using a Toolbar

◆ **Get command help**. If you're not sure what a button does, point to it to display a ScreenTip. If the ScreenTip includes *Press F1 for more help*, press F1.

◆ **Choose a command**. Click the button, or button arrow, and then click a command or option.

Choose a command

Did You Know?

You can turn off or change ScreenTips. Click the View menu, click Customize Toolbars and Menus, click the Toolbars and Menus tab, clear the Show ScreenTips For Toolbar Commands check box, and then click OK.

You can display toolbar buttons without the name. Click the View menu, click Customize Toolbars and Menus, click the Toolbars and Menus tab, clear the Show Icon and Text check box, and then click OK. You can also Control-click a toolbar, and then click Icon and Text or Icon Only.

Show and Hide a Toolbar

1 Control-click any visible toolbar, or click the **View** menu, and then point to **Toolbars**.

2 Click the name of the toolbar you want to display or hide.

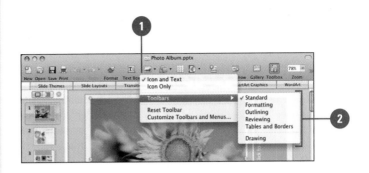

Work with Toolbars

◆ **Dock.** To dock a toolbar, click the View menu, click **Customize Toolbars and Menus**, click the **Toolbars and Menus** tab, select the **Dock** check box next to the undocked toolbar, and then click **OK**.

◆ **UnDock.** To undock a toolbar (except for the Standard toolbar), Control-click the toolbar, and then click **Dock Toolbar in Window**.

◆ **Move.** To move an undocked toolbar, click the gray edge bar on the left edge of the toolbar, and then drag it to a new location.

◆ **Close.** To close an undocked toolbar, click the Close button on the gray edge bar.

◆ **Resize.** To change the size of an undocked toolbar, drag to bottom right-corner until the toolbar is the shape you want.

◆ **Collapse/Expand.** To collapse or expand a docked toolbar, click the button in the upper-right corner of the Standard toolbar.

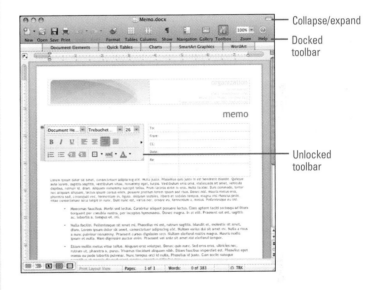

Collapse/expand

Docked toolbar

Unlocked toolbar

For Your Information

Using a Dialog Box

A **dialog box** is a window that opens when you click a toolbar button, such as Open, or click a menu command followed by an ellipsis (...). A dialog box allows you to supply more information before the program carries out the command you selected. After you enter information or make selections in a dialog box, click the OK button to complete the command. Click the Cancel button to close the dialog box without issuing the command. In many dialog boxes, you can also click an Apply button to apply your changes without closing the dialog box.

Working with the Elements Gallery

The Elements Gallery (**New!**) is a new look for Word, PowerPoint, and Excel that provides a visual way to quickly make document design and formatting changes. You can apply built-in layouts and other common design features to documents, such as a cover pages in Word, ledger sheets in Excel, and themes in PowerPoint. The Elements Gallery is located above the document window and is comprised of tabs (**New!**) that are organized by tasks or objects. The controls on each tab are organized into groups. The controls in each group execute a command, or display a menu of commands or a thumbnail gallery. In preferences, you can change how the Elements Gallery opens and appears.

Work with the Elements Gallery

◆ **Show.** Click the **Elements Gallery** button on the Standard toolbar or click an Elements Gallery tab.

◆ **Hide.** Click the **Elements Gallery** button on the Standard toolbar.

TIMESAVER *Click the current Elements Gallery tab to hide it.*

When the Elements Gallery is hidden, a row of tabs remains below the Standard toolbar.

   ◆ You can also click the **View** menu, and then click **Elements Gallery**.

◆ **Use.** Select an item or object, and then do the following:

   ◆ Click an Elements Gallery tab.

   ◆ Click a group name.

   ◆ Click the design or formatting style you want.

◆ **Preferences.** Click the **<Program>** menu, click **Preferences**, click the **Gallery** icon, and then specify any of the following:

   ◆ Open Elements Gallery when application opens.

   ◆ Magnify element thumbnails.

   ◆ Color and Transparency.

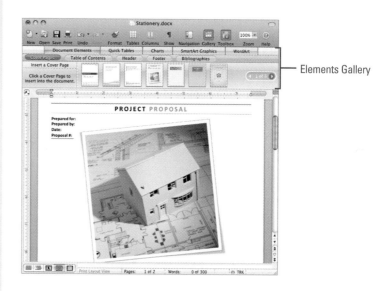
Elements Gallery

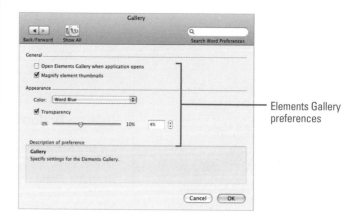
Elements Gallery preferences

Creating a Blank Office Document

When you start an Office program, the program window opens with a new blank Office document—a Word document, Excel workbook, or PowerPoint presentation—so that you can begin working in it. If preferences are set to display the Project Gallery, you can create a blank new document using the You can also start as many new Office documents as you want whenever an Office program is running. Each new document displays a default name—such as Document1, Book1, or Presentation1—numbered according to how many new documents you have started during the work session until you save it with a more meaningful name. The document name appears on the title bar.

Create a Blank Office Document

- **Toolbar.** Do any of the following to use a toolbar to create a new document:

  - **All.** Click the **New** button on the Standard toolbar.

  - **Word.** Click the **New** button drop-down to select different types of new blank documents.

- **Menu.** Do any of the following to use a menu to create a new document:

  - **Word.** Click the **File**, and then click **New Blank Document**.

  - **Excel.** Click the **File**, and then click **New Workbook**.

  - **PowerPoint.** Click the **File**, and then click **New Presentation**.

  TIMESAVER *To create a blank Office document, press* ⌘+*N.*

- **Project Gallery.** Click the **File** menu, click **Project Gallery**, click the **New** tab, select **Blank Document** from the Category list, select a document type, and then click **Open**.

  A new blank document appears in the Office program window.

New button   New command   New blank document

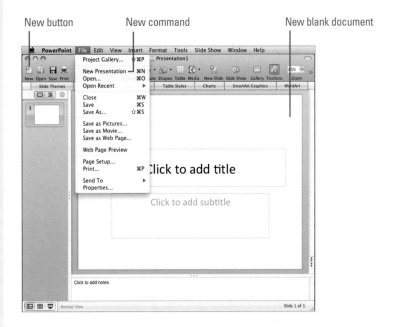

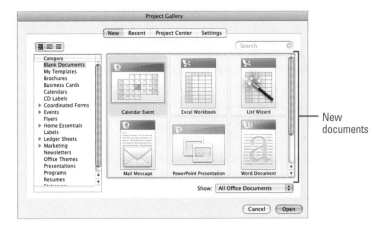

New documents

Creating a Document Using a Template

Office provides a collection of professionally designed templates that you can use to help you create documents. Start with a template when you have a good idea of your content but want to take advantage of a template's professional look. A **template** is an Office program file that provides you with a unified document design, which includes themes, so you only need to add text and graphics. When you start an Office program, a blank document opens based on a default template. The default template defines the page margins, default font, and other settings. When you create a document from a template, Office uses a copy of the template, not the original template. A **wizard** walks you through the steps to create a finished document tailored to your preferences. First the wizard asks you for information, and then when you click Finish, the wizard creates a completely formatted document based on the options and content you entered. If you can't find the template you want on your computer, you can check the Mactopia Office Online web site for more.

Create an Office Document with a Template

1. Click the **File** menu, and then click **Project Gallery**.

2. Click the **New** tab.

3. Select a category from the Category list.

   ◆ Click the **Blank Documents** category to create a blank document.

   ◆ Click the **My Templates** category to open the Project Gallery where you can select a saved template.

   ◆ Click a document type category, and then click a template from the Spotlight section.

4. Click the **Show** drop-down, and then select an Office program to narrow down the available templates.

5. Select the template you want.

6. Click **Open**.

7. Edit and format the template content.

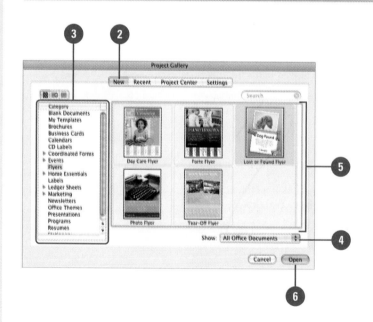

Create an Office Document with a Wizard

1 Click the **File** menu, and then click **Project Gallery**.

2 Click the **New** tab.

3 Select a category from the Category list.

4 Click the **Show** drop-down, and then select an Office program to narrow down the available templates and wizards.

5 Select the wizard you want; not every wizard has the word Wizard in it's name.

6 Click **Open**.

7 Follow the step-by-step instructions. Click **Next** to move to the next wizard dialog box.

8 When you reach the last wizard dialog box, click **Finish**, **Save & Exit**, or **OK**. (Button names vary.)

Did You Know?

You can download template packs on the web. Go to *www.microsoft.com /mac*, and then search for Office Templates.

You can create a new document based on a recent document. In the Project Gallery, click the Recent tab, select a document, and then click Open a Copy. Office uses the document template to create the new document.

You can display the Project Gallery at startup for an Office program. Click the <Program> menu, click Preferences, click the General icon, select the Show Project Gallery at Startup check box, and then click OK.

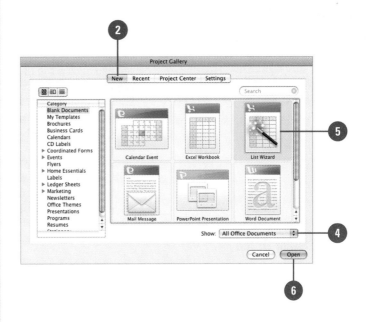

Opening an Existing Office Document

You can open an Office document and start Office simultaneously, or you can open an Office document or file created in another program after you start an Office program. You can open an existing Office document by using the File menu or the Standard toolbar. On the File menu, you can choose the Open command to locate and select the document you want in the Open dialog box or choose a recently used document from the Open Recent submenu list. If the Open Recent list gets too long, you can set preferences to specify the number of documents you want to display. In the Open dialog box, you can open Office documents based on the current or older versions, or other document types, such as text files and web pages. When you open an Office document from 97-2004, Office 2008 goes into compatibility mode (**New!**)—indicated on the title bar—where it disables new features that cannot be displayed or converted well by previous versions.

Open an Existing Office Document

1. Click the **Open** button on the Standard toolbar, or click the **File** menu, and then click **Open**.

2. If you want to open a specific file type, click the **Enable** drop-down, and then click a file type.

3. If the file is located in another folder, click the **Where** drop-down, and then navigate to the file.

4. Select the Office file you want to open.

5. Click the **Open** drop-down, and then click one of the following options:

   - **Original** to open the selected file.

   - **Read-Only** to open the selected file with protection.

   - **Copy** to open a copy of the selected file.

6. Click **Open**.

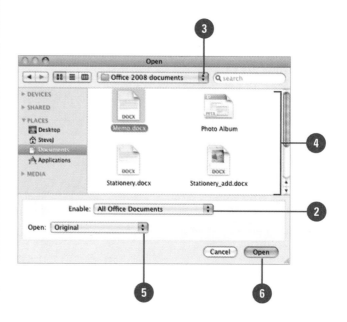

Open a Recently Opened Documents

1. Click the **File** menu, and then point to **Open Recent**.

2. Click the Office document you want to open.

   ◆ To clear the Open Recent menu, click **Clear Recent**.

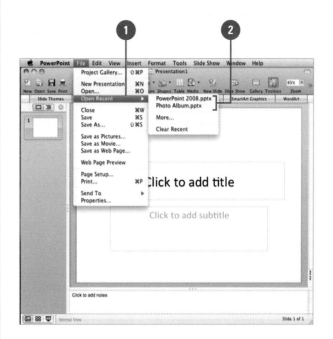

For Your Information

Changing the Default File Location

When you display the Open dialog box, the default file folder location appears. If you prefer a different folder location, you can change the default file location using program preferences. In Word, click the Word menu, click Preferences, click the File Locations icon, select the file location you want to change, such as Documents, Clip art pictures, or User templates, click Modify, navigate to the new folder location, click Choose, and then click OK. In Excel, click the Excel menu, click Preferences, click the General icon, click Select for the Preferred file location or At startup option, navigate to the new folder location, click Choose, and then click OK. In PowerPoint, click the PowerPoint menu, click Preferences, click the Advanced icon, click Select for the Default file location option, navigate to the new folder location, click Choose, and then click OK.

Managing Windows

Every Office program and document opens inside a **window**, which contains a title bar and work area. This is where you create and edit your data. Most often, you'll probably fill the entire screen with one window. But when you want to move or copy information between programs or documents, it's easier to display several windows at once. You can arrange two or more windows from one program or from different programs on the screen at the same time. However, you must make the window active to work in it. You can also click the document buttons on the Dock to switch between open documents.

Resize and Move a Window

◆ **Close.** Click the red button to shut a window.

◆ **Minimize.** Click the yellow button to shrink a window to the Dock, or click the **Window** menu, and then click **Minimize Window**. To restore the window to its previous size, click the icon on the Dock.

TIMESAVER *Press ⌘+M.*

◆ **Zoom.** Click the green button to restore a window to its full size and position, or click the **Window** menu, and then click **Zoom Window**.

◆ **Move.** Move the mouse over the title bar, and then drag to move the window.

◆ **Resize.** Move the mouse over bottom right corner of the window, and then drag to move the window.

◆ **New.** Opens a new window containing a view of the current document. Click the **Window** menu, and then click **New Window**.

◆ **Arrange All.** Displays and resizes all open windows to fit on the screen at the same time. Open the windows, click the **Window** menu, and then click **Arrange All**.

◆ **Switch.** Click anywhere in the window, or click the **Window** menu, and then select it's name.

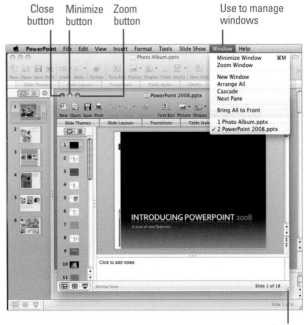

Close button   Minimize button   Zoom button   Use to manage windows

Drag to resize

Switching Views

Each Office program provides different views to help you work with and display information. To quickly switch between views—such as Normal, Page Layout, and Print Layout—you can use buttons on the view selector in the lower-left corner of the document window. **Normal view** is the main view in PowerPoint and Excel. It lets you focus on entering, modifying, and managing your data. **Page Layout view** and **Print Layout view** are the printout-related views in Excel and Word respectively. They let you focus on how your document is going to look when you print it. In addition to the view selector, you can also use view buttons on the View menu to switch between views.

Switch Between Views

◆ **Use the View Selector.** On the right-side of the Status bar, click any of the view buttons.

 ◆ **Word.** Draft, Outline, Publishing Layout, and Print Layout, Notebook Layout.

 ◆ **Excel.** Normal and Page Layout.

 ◆ **PowerPoint.** Normal, Slide Sorter, and Slide Show.

◆ **Use the View menu.** Click the View menu, and then click any of the view buttons.

 ◆ **Word.** Draft, Web Layout, Outline, Print Layout, Notebook Layout, and Publishing Layout.

 ◆ **Excel.** Normal, Page Layout, Page Break Preview, and Full Screen.

 ◆ **PowerPoint.** Normal, Slide Sorter, Notes Pages, Presenter Tools, and Slide Show.

View menu

View Selector buttons

Using the Toolbox

The Toolbox (**New!**) provides a variety of tools organized on tabs and grouped into panels all in one central location. Some tabs are available in all of the Office programs, such as Formatting Palette, Object Palette, Scrapbook and Compatibility Report, while others are program-specific, such as Formula Builder (Excel) and Custom Animation (PowerPoint). The Toolbox is a floating window that you can move around the screen for easy access. In addition, you can customize the Toolbox to specify which panels and tools to show and how to the Toolbox appears.

Use the Toolbox

◆ **Open.** Click the **Toolbox** button on the Standard toolbar, or click the **View** menu, and then select a Toolbox tab (nonchecked).

   ◆ **Entourage.** Click the **View** menu, point to **Toolbox**, and then select a Toolbox tab.

◆ **Switch.** Click a Toolbox tab.

◆ **Close.** Click the **Toolbox** button on the Standard toolbar again, or click the **View** menu, and then select the current (checked) Toolbox tab.

◆ **Move.** Drag the Toolbox title bar.

◆ **Collapse or Expand.** Click the Zoom button (green) on the Toolbox title bar.

◆ **Collapse or Expand a Panel.** Click the triangle next to the section name.

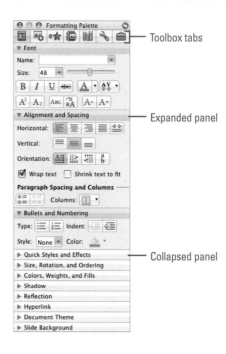

Toolbox tabs

Expanded panel

Collapsed panel

Customize the Toolbox

1. Click the **Toolbox Settings** button on the Toolbox title bar.

   The Toolbox flips to display Toolbox settings.

2. Click the **Close Effect** drop-down, and then select an effect: **Genie**, **Scale**, or **None**.

3. Select the **When inactive for** check box to specify how you want to show the Toolbox when not in use, and then specify any of the following:

   ◆ Inactive Interval. Drag the slider.

   ◆ Inactive Action. Click the **Collapse**, **Fade**, or **Close**.

4. Click the Palette drop-down, and then select the tab you want to customize.

5. Specify the options you want for the selected tab; options vary depending on the tab.

6. Click **OK**.

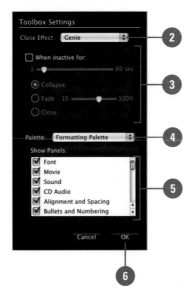

Checking Compatibility

The Compatibility Report (**New!**) identifies the potential loss of functionality when you want to save an Office document for use in a previous version of Office on the Macintosh or in Windows. The Compatibility Report generates a report that provides a summary of the potential losses in the document. Use the report information to determine what caused each message and for suggestions on how to change it. If the loss is due to a new feature in Office 2008—such as custom layouts or styles applied to shapes, pictures, and WordArt—you might be able to simply remove the effect or feature. In other cases, you might not be able to do anything about it. To maintain a visual appearance, SmartArt graphics are converted to bitmaps to preserve their overall look and cannot be edited.

Check Compatibility

1. Open the Toolbox, if necessary.

2. Click the **Compatibility Report** tab on the Toolbox.

3. Click the **Check compatibility with** drop-down, and then select the Office version in which you want to check against.

4. Click **Check Document**.

   Office checks compatibility and displays issues and the button changes to Recheck Document.

5. Select each numbered issue that appears in the Results box.

6. View the compatibility summary information for each issue, so you can make changes, as necessary.

7. For each selected issue, click one of the following:

   ◆ Fix issues. Click **Fix** (once), or click the **Fix** drop-down, and then click **Fix Once**, **Fix All**, or **Don't Show Again**.

   ◆ Ignore issues. Click **Ignore** (once), or click the **Ignore** drop-down, and then click **Ignore Once**, **Ignore All**, or **Don't Show Again**.

8. Click **OK**, if prompted.

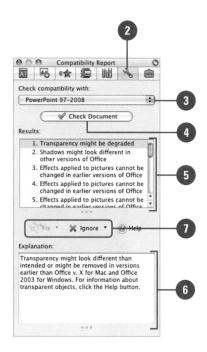

Set Compatibility Preferences

1. Click the **<Program>** menu, and then click **Preferences**.

2. Click the **Compatibility** icon.

3. Select the **Check documents for compatibility** check box to use the Compatibility Report on the Toolbox.

4. To check for compatibility issues previously ignored, use either of the following buttons:

   ◆ **Reset Ignored Issues.** Checks the current document for issues previously ignored.

   ◆ **Reset All Issues.** Checks all documents for issues previously ignored.

5. In Word, click the **Recommended option for** drop-down, select word processing program you want to display compatibility options for, and then select the ones you want.

6. Click **OK**.

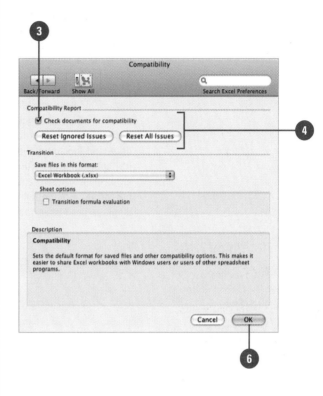

Saving an Office Document

When you create an Office document, save it as a file on your computer so you can work with it later. When you save a document for the first time or if you want to save a copy of a file, use the Save As command. When you want to save an open document, use the Save button on the Standard toolbar. When you save a document, Office 2008 saves 97-2004 files in an older format using compatibility mode (**New!**) and new 2008 files in an XML (Extensible Markup Language) based file format (**New!**), which is the same as Office 2007 files for Windows. The XML format significantly reduces file sizes, makes it easier to recover damaged files, and allows for increased compatibility, sharing, and transportability. An Office 97-2004 document stays in compatibility mode—indicated on the title bar—until you convert it to the new 2008 file format. Compatibility mode disables new features that cannot be displayed or converted well by previous versions.

Save a Document for Office 2008

1. Click the **Save** button on the Standard toolbar, or click the **File** menu, and then click **Save**.

    TIMESAVER *Press ⌘+S.*

    If the Office document is new, the Save As dialog box appears, where you can save the document.

2. Type a document file name.

3. Click the **Where** drop-down, and then click the drive or folder where you want to save the file.

4. Click the **Format** drop-down, and then select the Office 2008 file format, such as Word Document (.docx), or Excel Workbook (.xlsx).

5. Select the **Append file extension** check box to append and display the file extension, which is useful for cross-platform compatibility.

6. To check compatibility, click **Compatibility Report**, and then work through any issues.

7. Click **Save**.

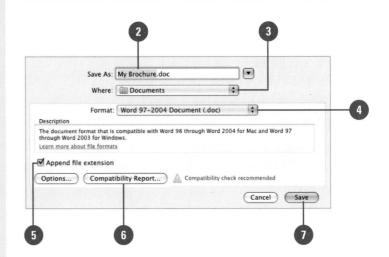

Save an Office 97-2004 Document

1. Open the Office 97-2004 document you want to continue to save in the 97-2004 format.

   The 97-2004 document opens in compatibility mode.

2. Click the **Save** button on the Standard toolbar, or click the **File** menu, and then click **Save**.

   The Office program stays in compatibility mode.

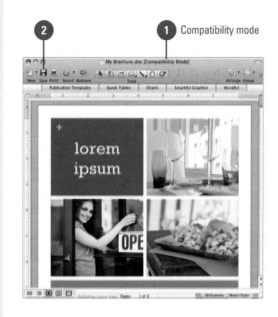

Compatibility mode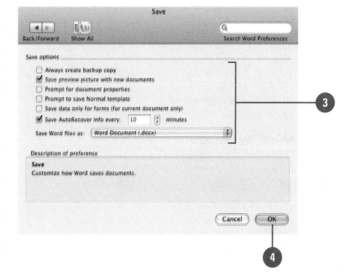

Set Save Options

1. Click the **<Program>** menu, and then click **Preferences**.

2. Click the **Save** icon.

   TIMESAVER *In Word and PowerPoint, click Options in the Save As dialog box to display the Save Preferences dialog box.*

3. Set the save options you want; options vary depending on the Office program.

   ◆ **Not sure about an option?** Point to an option to display a description at the bottom of the Preferences dialog box.

4. Click **OK**.

Saving an Office Document with Different Formats

Office 2008 is a versatile suite of programs that allow you to save your documents in a variety of different formats—see the table on the following page for a list and description. For example, you might want to save your document as a Web page that you can view in a Web browser. Or you can save a document in an earlier 97-2004 version in case the people you work with have not upgraded to Office 2008. If you save a document to 97-2004, some new features and formatting are converted to uneditable pictures or not retained. In this case, it's important to run a Compatibility Report to check for any issues. In addition to the new XML-based file format for Office 2008 (**New!**), Excel 2008 also allows you to save a workbook in a binary file format (or BIFF12), which is based on the segmented compressed file format (**New!**). This file format is most useful for large or complex workbooks, and optimized for performance and backward compatibility.

Save an Office Document with Another Format

1. Click the **File** menu, and then click **Save As**.

2. Type a document file name.

3. Click the **Where** drop-down, and then click the drive or folder where you want to save the file.

4. Click the **Format** drop-down, and then select a file format.

   See the table on the following page for a description of different formats.

5. Select the **Append file extension** check box to append and display the file extension, which is useful for cross-platform compatibility.

6. Click **Save**.

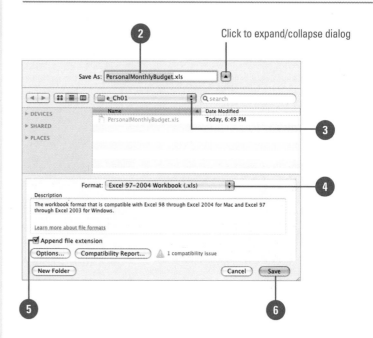

Click to expand/collapse dialog

See Also

See "Creating a PDF Document" on page 492 information on using and saving a file with different formats.

Common Office 2008 Save File Formats

Save As file type	Extension	Used to save
Word Document (**New!**)	.docx	Word 2008 document
Word 97-2004 Document	.doc	Word 97 to Word 2004 document
Word Template (**New!**)	.dotx	Word 2008 template
Word 97-2004 Template	.dot	Excel 97-2004 template
Word Macro-Enabled Document (**New!**)	.docm	Word 2008 document that includes macros
Word Macro-Enabled Template (**New!**)	.dotm	Word 2008 template that includes macros
Excel Workbook (**New!**)	.xlsx	Excel 2008 workbook
Excel 97-2004 Workbook	.xls	Excel 97 to Excel 2004 workbook
Excel Binary Workbook (**New!**)	.xlsb	Excel 2008 workbook with a binary compressed file format for large or complex workbooks
Excel Template (**New!**)	.xltx	Excel 2008 template
Excel 97-2004 Template	.xlt	Excel 97-2004 template
Excel Macro-Enabled Workbook (**New!**)	.xlsm	Excel workbook that preserves VBA and Excel 4 macro sheets
Excel Macro-Enabled Template (**New!**)	.xltm	Excel template that preserves VBA and Excel 4 macro sheets
PowerPoint Presentation (**New!**)	.pptx	PowerPoint 2008 presentation
PowerPoint 97-2004	.ppt	PowerPoint 97 to PowerPoint 2004 presentation
PowerPoint Template (**New!**)	.potx	PowerPoint 2008 template
PowerPoint 97-2004 Template	.pot	PowerPoint 97 to PowerPoint 2004 template
PowerPoint Show (**New!**)	.pps; .ppsx	PowerPoint 2008 presentation that opens in Slide Show view
PowerPoint 97-2004 Show	.ppt	PowerPoint 97-2004 presentation that opens in Slide Show view
PowerPoint Macro-Enabled Presentation (**New!**)	.pptm	PowerPoint 2008 presentation that preserves VBA code
PowerPoint Macro-Enabled Template (**New!**)	.potm	PowerPoint 2008 template that includes macros
PowerPoint Macro-Enabled Show (**New!**)	.ppsm	PowerPoint 2008 show that includes macros
Rich Text Format	.rtf	Text document with formatting
Plain Text	.txt	Plain text without any formatting
PDF (**New!**)	.pdf	Fixed-layout electronic file format that preserves document formatting developed by Adobe
Single File Web Page	.mht	Web page as a single file with an .htm file
Web Page	.htm	Web page as a folder with an .htm file

Creating a Template

You can create your own template as easily as you create a document. Like those that come with Office, custom templates can save you time. Perhaps each month you create an inventory document in which you enter repetitive information; all that changes is the actual data. By creating your own template, you can have a custom form that is ready for completion each time you take inventory. A template file saves all the customization you made to reuse in other Office documents. Although you can store your template anywhere you want, you may find it handy to store it in the Templates folder that Microsoft Office uses to store its templates. If you store your design templates in the Templates folder, those templates appear as options when you choose the Project Gallery command on the File menu, and then click My Templates.

Create a Template

1. Enter all the necessary information in a new document—including formulas, labels, graphics, and formatting.

2. Click the **File** menu, and then click **Save As**.

3. Click the **Format** list arrow, and then select a template format.

   ◆ **<Program> Template**. Creates a template for Office 2008.

   ◆ **<Program> Macro-Enabled Template**. Creates a template for Office 2007 with macros.

   ◆ **<Program> 97-2004 Template**. Creates a template for Office 97-2004.

   The folder changes to My Templates.

4. Type a name for your template.

5. Click **Save**.

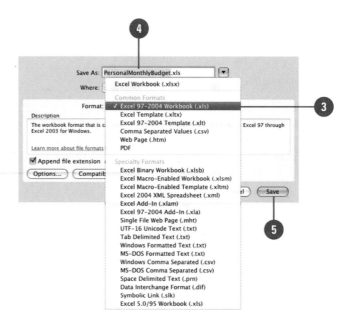

Modify an Existing Template

1 Click the **File** menu, and then click **Open**.

2 Navigate to the Templates folder, and then open the folder with the template you want to change.

The Templates folder is typically located in the Applications: Microsoft Office 2008:Office: Media:Templates folder.

3 Click the **Enable** drop-down, and then click **<Program> Templates**.

4 Select a template.

5 Click **Open**.

6 Make the changes you want to the template.

7 Click the **File** menu, and then click **Save As**.

◆ **Replace Template.** Click the **Save** button on the Standard toolbar.

8 Type a new name for your template.

9 Navigate to the My Templates folder.

The My Templates folder is typically located in the Users: <UserName>:Library:Application Support:Microsoft:Office:user Templates:My Templates folder.

10 Click **Save**.

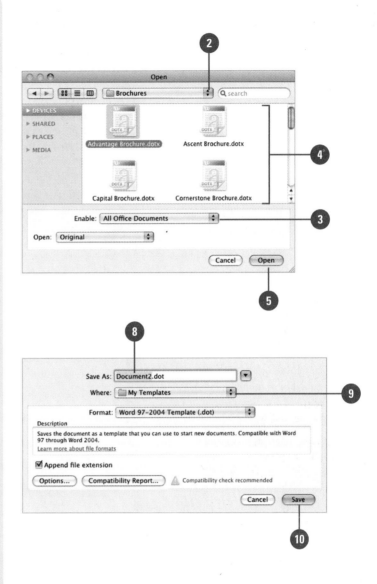

Recovering an Office Document

AutoRecover saves your current Office document at preset intervals into a separate AutoRecover file. If an Office program encounters a problem and stops responding, the program automatically opens the AutoRecover file—a temporary copy of your current file. If you want to keep the file, save it with a new name and you're good to go again. AutoRecover runs in the background as you work. If the AutoRecover save interval is set to run frequently, it can slow down your computer. However, if it's set to run at a longer interval, you could lose valuable information. It's a balance you need to determine.

Recover an Office Document

1. Click the **<Program>** menu, and then click **Preferences**.

2. Click the **Save** icon.

3. Do one of the following:

   ◆ **Word and PowerPoint.** Select the **Save AutoRecover info every _x_ minutes** check box.

   ◆ **Excel.** Select the **Save AutoRecover information after this number of minutes** check box.

4. Enter the number of minutes, or click the **Up** and **Down** arrows to adjust the minutes.

5. Click **OK**.

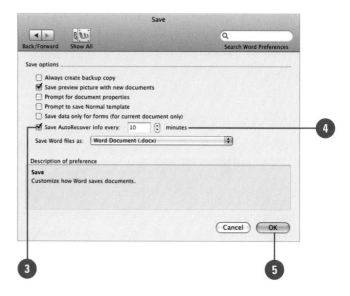

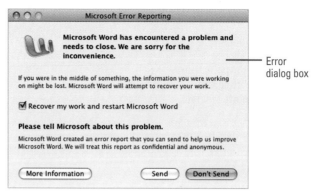

Error dialog box

Getting Updates on the Web

Office offers a quick and easy way to update an Office program with any new software downloads that improve the stability and security of the program. Simply, select the Check for Updates command on the Help menu to use Microsoft AutoUpdate, which scans your computer for necessary updates, and then choose which Office updates you want to download and install.

Get Updates on the Web

1. Click the **Help** button, and then click **Check for Updates**.

   The Microsoft AutoUpdate dialog box appears.

2. Select an update option.

   ◆ **Manual.** Select to check for updates when you want.

   ◆ **Automatically.** Select an interval to automatically check for updates: Daily, Weekly, or Monthly.

3. Click **Check for Updates**.

   IMPORTANT *You will need to close any open Office programs.*

4. Select an install check box to specify which updates you want to download and install.

5. Click **OK** when no updates are available or click **Install**, and then follow the setup wizard instructions.

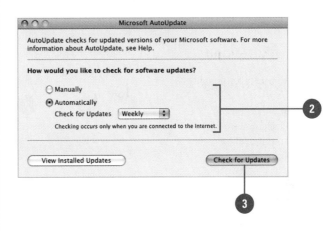

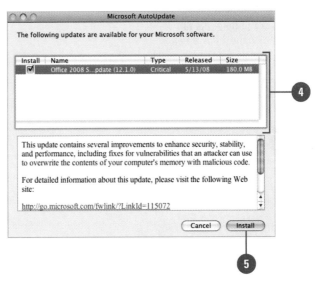

Did You Know?

You can participate in the Microsoft Customer Improvement Program. Click the <Program> menu, click Preferences, click the Feedback icon, click the Yes, I am willing to participate anonymously in the Customer Improvement Program. (Recommended) option, and then click OK.

Getting Help While You Work

At some time, everyone has a question or two about the program they are using. Each Office program provides answers and resources you need, including feature help, articles, and tips. By connecting to Microsoft Online Help, you not only have access to standard product help information stored on your computer (Offline Help), but you also have access to updated information over the Web (Online Help) without leaving the Help Viewer. The Help Viewer allows you to browse a catalog of topics using a table of contents to locate information or enter phrases to search for specific information. When you use any of these help options, a list of possible answers is shown to you with the most likely answer or most frequently-used at the top of the list.

Browse for Help Information

1. Click the **Help** button on the Standard toolbar, or click the **Help** menu, and then click **<Program> Help**.

2. Locate the Help topic you want.

   ◆ Click a link on the Help Home page.

   ◆ Click the **Topics** button on the toolbar, click the **Contents tab** on the Topics pane, click a help category (triangle icon) and then click a topic (doc icon).

3. Read the topic, and then click any links to get additional help information.

4. Use the Help toolbar to navigation help topics:

   ◆ Click the **Home** button to return to the first page of the help.

   ◆ Click the **Back** and **Forward** button to view previously viewed topics.

   ◆ If you want to print the topic, click the **Print** button on the toolbar.

5. When you're done, click the **Close** button to quit Help.

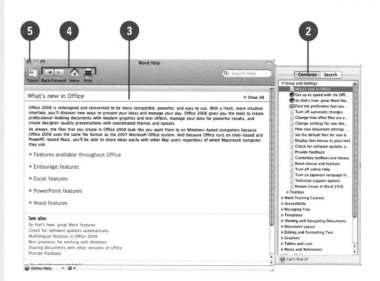

Search for Help

1 Click the **Help** button on the Standard toolbar, or click the **Help** menu, and then click **<Program> Help**.

2 Type one or more keywords in the Search box, and then press Return.

The Topics pane appears with a list of topics that meet your search criteria.

4 Click a topic.

5 Read the topic, and then click any links to get information on related topics or definitions.

◆ To restart a search, click the Close button (x) in the Search box, type new keywords, and then press Return.

6 When you're done, click the **Close** button.

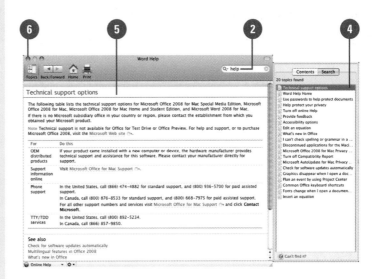

For Your Information

Getting Help Online

You can contact Microsoft for product information and provide feedback. You can find out more about Microsoft Office 2008 or send feedback to Microsoft concerning a program online at the mactopia web site. Click the Help menu, and then click Visit the Product Web Site or Send Feedback about <Program>.

Closing a Document and Quitting Office

After you finish working on a document, you can close it. Closing a document makes more computer memory available for other activities. Closing a document is different from quitting a program; after you close a document, the program is still running. When you're finished using the program, you should quit it. To protect your files, always save your documents and quit before turning off the computer.

Close an Office Document

1. Click the **Close** button on the Document window, or click the **File** menu, and then click **Close**.

   TIMESAVER Press ⌘+W.

2. If you have made changes to any open files since last saving them, a dialog box opens, asking if you want to save changes. Click **Save** to save any changes, or click **Don't Save** to ignore your changes.

Close command

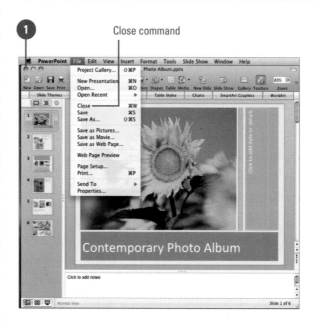

Quit an Office Program

1. Click the **<Program>** menu, and then click **Quit <Program>**.

   For example, for Word, click the Word menu, and then click Quit Word.

   TIMESAVER Press ⌘+Q.

2. If you have made changes to any open files since last saving them, a dialog box opens asking if you want to save changes. Click **Save** to save any changes, or click **Don't Save** to ignore your changes.

Using Shared Office Tools

2

Introduction

The Microsoft Office 2008 programs are designed to work together so you can focus on what you need to do, rather than how to do it. In fact, the Office programs share tools and features for your most common tasks so you can work more seamlessly from one program to another. All the Office programs work with text and objects in the same way. As a result, once you learn how to move, find, correct, and format text in one program, you can perform these tasks in every program. If you know how to perform a task in Word, you already know (for the most part) how to perform the same task in Excel, PowerPoint, and Entourage.

Office offers a Find and Replace feature that allows you to look for text and values and make changes as necessary. When you need to spell check your document, Office can check and suggest spelling corrections. You can even customize the spelling dictionary by adding company specific words into AutoCorrect so that the spell checker doesn't think it's a misspelled word. Additional language tools area available to build up the content of your documents. If you accidentally make a change, you can use the Undo feature to remove, or "undo," your last change.

Not everyone has an eye for color, and pulling it all together can be daunting, so Office provides you with designed themes, which you can apply to any document. A **theme** is a set of unified design elements that provides a consistent look for a document by using color themes, fonts, and effects, such as shadows, shading, and animations.

After you finish your document you can preview and print it. In addition, you can add a password to protect it, which is not only a good idea for security purposes, it's an added feature to make sure that changes to your document aren't made by unauthorized people. You can protect all or part of a worksheet or an entire document.

What You'll Do

Edit and Format Text

Copy and Move Text

Use the Scrapbook

Find and Replace Text

Correct Text Automatically

Check Spelling

Change Spelling Options

Find the Right Words

Research Words

Translate Text to Another Language

Use Multiple Languages

Insert Symbols

Undo and Redo an Action

Zoom the View In and Out

Use the Format Painter

Add Custom Colors

Understand Themes

View and Apply a Theme

Apply Theme Colors and Fonts

Create and Apply a Custom Theme

Preview and Print a Document

Protect a Document

Modify Document Properties

Editing Text

Before you can edit text, you need to highlight, or select, the text you want to modify. Then you can delete, replace, move (cut), or copy text within one document or between documents even if they're from different programs. In either case, the steps are the same. Text you cut or copy is temporarily stored in the Clipboard. When you paste the text, the Paste Options button appears below it. When you click the button, a menu appears with options to specify how Office pastes the information in the document. To copy or move data without using the Clipboard, you can use a technique called **drag-and-drop**. Drag-and-drop makes it easy to copy or move text short distances.

Select and Edit Text

1. Move the I-beam pointer to the left or right of the text you want to select.

2. Drag the pointer to highlight the text, or click in the document to place the insertion point where you want to make a change.

   TIMESAVER *Double-click a word to select it; triple-click a paragraph to select it.*

3. Perform one of the following editing commands:

   ◆ To replace text, type your text.

   ◆ To delete text, press the Backspace key or the Delete key.

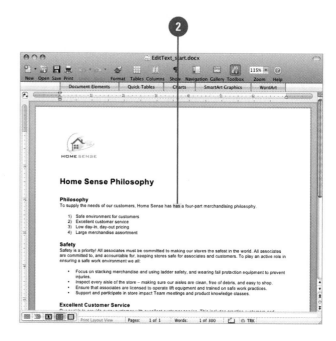

Insert and Delete Text

1 Click in the document to place the insertion point where you want to make the change.

◆ To insert text, type your text.

◆ To delete text, press the Backspace key or the Delete key.

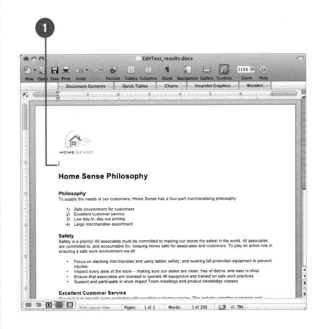

Copy or Move Text Using Drag-and-Drop

1 If you want to drag text between programs or documents, display both windows.

2 Select the text you want to move or copy.

TIMESAVER *You can also select objects and other elements.*

3 Point to the selected text, and then click and hold the mouse button.

If you want to copy the text, also press and hold ⌘. A plus sign (+) appears in the pointer box, indicating that you are dragging a copy of the selected text.

4 Drag the selection to the new location, and then release the mouse button and keyboard.

5 Click anywhere in the document to deselect the text.

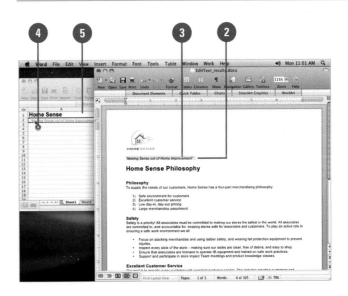

Formatting Text

A **font** is a collection of alphanumeric characters that share the same typeface, or design, and have similar characteristics. You can format text and numbers with font attributes—such as bolding, italics, or underlining—to enhance data to catch the reader's attention. The basic formats you apply to text are available in the Font panel on the Formatting Palette tab on the Toolbox, in the Font dialog box, and on the Formatting toolbar. Some of the formats available in the Font dialog box include strikethrough, and single or double normal and accounting underline.

Format Text Quickly

1 Select the text you want to format.

2 Click the **Formatting Palette** tab on the Toolbox.

3 Click the **Font** panel to expand it.

4 To change fonts, click the **Font** drop-down, and then click the font you want, either a theme font or any available fonts.

- In Word, click the **Font** menu, and then select a font. If necessary, select a font.

To change the font size, click one or more of the font size buttons:

- Click the **Font Size** drop-down, and then click the font size you want, or drag the slider.

- Click the **Increase Font Size** button or **Decrease Font Size** button.

To apply other formatting, click one or more of the formatting buttons:

- **Bold**

- **Italic**

- **Strikethrough**

- **Font Color**

- **Character Spacing** (Word and PowerPoint)

- **Superscript** or **Subscript**

- **Small Caps** or **All Caps** (Word and PowerPoint)

Format Text Using the Format Dialog Box

1. Select the text you want to format.

2. Click the **Format** menu, and then click **Font** or **Cell** (Excel).

   The Format dialog box opens.

3. Click the **Font** tab, if necessary.

4. Select the font, font style, and font size you want.

5. If you want, click **Underline** drop-down, and then click a style.

6. If you want, click **Font color**, and then click a color.

7. Select or clear the effects you want or don't want: **Strikethrough**, **Superscript**, and **Subscript**.

   - Additional options, such as Shadow, Outline, Small caps, All caps, are available depending on the Office program.

8. Click **OK**.

Did You Know?

What is a point? The size of each font character is measured in points (a point is approximately 1/72 of an inch). You can use any font that is installed on your computer on a document, but the default is 10-point Arial.

Each computer has different fonts installed. Users with whom you share files may not have all the fonts you've used in a document installed on their computers.

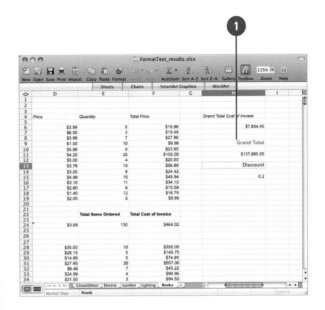

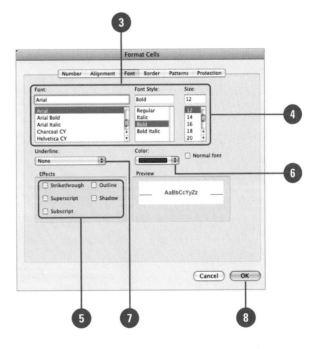

Copying and Moving Text

You can **copy** and **move** text or data from one location to another on any Office document. When you copy data, a duplicate of the selected information is placed on the Clipboard. When you move text, the selected information is removed and placed on the Clipboard. To complete the copy or move, you must **paste** the data stored on the Clipboard in another location. When you paste an item, the Paste Options button appears below it. When you click the button, a menu appears with options to specify how Office pastes the information in the document. With the Paste Special command, you can control what you want to paste and even perform mathematical operations in Excel.

Copy or Move Using the Clipboard

1. Select the item that you want to copy or move.

2. Click the **Edit** menu, and then click **Copy** or **Cut**.

   TIMESAVER *Press ⌘+C (Copy). Press ⌘+X (Cut).*

   ◆ If available, you can also click the **Copy** or **Cut** button on the Standard toolbar.

3. Click the location where you want to paste the data.

4. Click the **Edit** menu, and then click **Paste**.

   TIMESAVER *Press ⌘+V.*

   ◆ If available, you can also click the **Paste** button on the Standard toolbar.

   The data remains on the Clipboard, available for further pasting until you replace it with another selection.

5. If you want to change the way the data pastes into the document, click the **Paste Options** button, and then select the option you want.

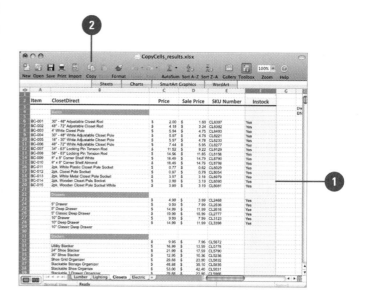

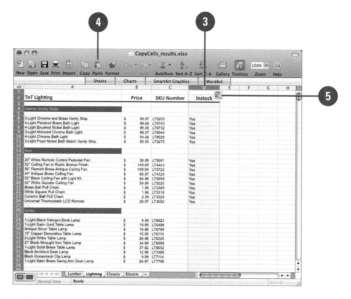

Paste Data with Special Results

1. Select the text or data that you want to copy.

2. Click the **Edit** menu, and then click **Copy**.

   ◆ If available, you can also click the **Copy** button on the Standard toolbar.

3. Click the location where you want to paste the text or data.

4. Click the **Edit** menu, and then click **Paste Special**.

5. Click the option buttons with the paste results you want.

6. Click **OK**.

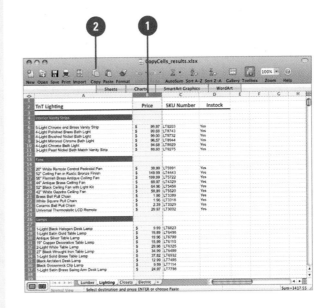

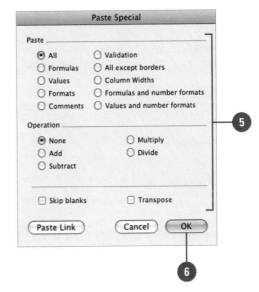

Using the Scrapbook

With the Scrapbook, you can store multiple pieces of information from several different sources in one storage area shared by other programs. You can add items—such as text, a graphic, an object, or a cell range—to the Scrapbook, known as **clips**, from the current selection, the Clipboard, or a existing file. You can paste these pieces of information into any program using different formats, including plain text and picture. The clips in the Scrapbook remains in the Scrapbook until you delete it. As your list of clips grows in the Scrapbook, you can organize the them by category and delete the one you no longer use.

Use the Scrapbook

1. Open the Toolbox, and then click the **Scrapbook** tab.

2. Select the item that you want to copy to the Scrapbook.

3. Click the **Edit** menu, and then click **Copy to Scrapbook**, or drag the item to the Scrapbook.

   ◆ **File.** In the Scrapbook, click the **Add** drop-down, click **Add File**, select the file, and then click **Choose**.

   ◆ **Clipboard.** In the Scrapbook, click the **Add** drop-down, click **Add from Clipboard**.

4. Click the location where you want to paste the item.

5. Select the clip that you want to paste from the Scrapbook.

6. Click the **Edit** menu, and then click **Paste from Scrapbook**, or drag the clip to the Scrapbook.

   ◆ **Plain Text.** In the Scrapbook, click the **Paste** drop-down, click **Paste as Plain Text**.

   ◆ **Picture.** In the Scrapbook, click the **Paste** drop-down, click **Paste as Picture**.

7. If you want to change the way the clip pastes into the document, click the **Paste Options** button, and then select the option you want.

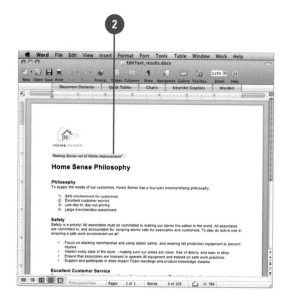

Organize Scrapbook Clips

1 Open the Toolbox, and then click the **Scrapbook** tab.

2 To change the view of clips in the Scrapbook, do any of the following:

◆ **View.** Click the **View** button, and then select an option: **List**, **Detail**, or **Large Preview**.

◆ **Filter.** Click the **Filter** drop-down, and then select the filter criteria you want.

3 To organize the clips in the Scrapbook, do any of the following:

◆ **Rename a Clip.** Double-click the clip, type a new name, and then press Return.

◆ **Assign to a Category.** Select the clips, click the **Categories** drop-down, and then select a category from the list.

◆ **Assign Keywords to Clips.** Select the clips, and then type keywords in the Keywords box.

4 To remove the clips in the Scrapbook, do any of the following:

◆ **Delete Clips.** Select the clips, click the **Delete** drop-down, and then click the Delete button.

◆ **Delete Visible Clips.** Display the clips you want to delete, select a clip, click the **Delete** drop-down, and then click **Delete Visible**.

◆ **Delete All Clips.** Select a clip, click the **Delete** drop-down, and then click **Delete All**.

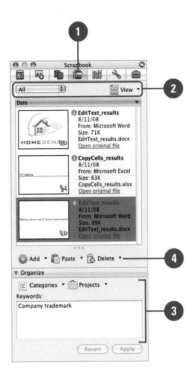

Finding and Replacing Text

The Find and Replace commands make it easy to locate or replace specific text or formulas in a document. For example, you might want to find each figure reference in a long report to verify that the proper graphic appears. Or you might want to replace all references to cell A3 in your Excel formulas with cell G3. The Find and Replace dialog boxes vary slightly from one Office program to the next, but the commands work essentially in the same way.

Find Text

1. Click at the beginning of the Office document.

2. Click the **Edit** menu, and then click **Find**.

   TIMESAVER *Press ⌘+F.*

3. Type the text you want to find.

4. Select the find options you want. Click the **Expand** button to display options, if available.

5. Click **Find Next** until the text you want to locate is highlighted.

   You can click **Find Next** repeatedly to locate each instance of the item.

6. To find all cells with the contents you want, click **Find All**.

7. If a message box opens when you reach the end of the document, click **OK**.

8. Click **Close**.

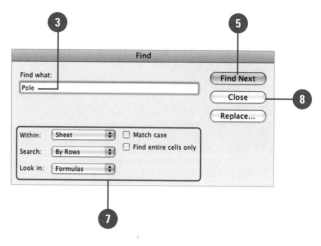

Did You Know?

You can go to different locations in Word. Click the Edit menu, click Go To, select the Go to what option you want, specify a location, and then click Next or Previous. When you're done, click Close.

Replace Text

1. Click at the beginning of the Office document.

2. Click the **Edit** menu, and then click **Replace**.

   TIMESAVER *Press Shift+⌘+H (Word).*

3. Type the text you want to search for.

4. Type the text you want to substitute.

5. Select the find options you want. Click the **Expand** button to display options, if necessary.

6. Click **Find Next** to begin the search, and then select the next instance of the search text.

7. Click **Replace** to substitute the replacement text, or click **Replace All** to substitute text throughout the entire document.

   You can click **Find Next** to locate the next instance of the item without making a replacement.

8. If a message box appears when you reach the end of the document, click **OK**.

9. Click **Close**.

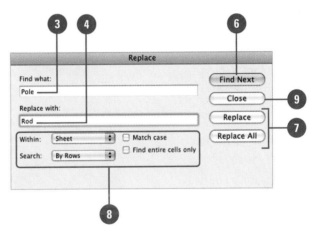

Did You Know?

You can format text that you find and replace. In a Word document, you can search for and replace text with specific formatting features, such as a font and font size. Click Expand in the Find And Replace dialog box, click Format, click the formatting options you want, and then complete the corresponding dialog box.

Correcting Text Automatically

Office's **AutoCorrect** feature automatically corrects common capitalization and spelling errors as you type. AutoCorrect comes with hundreds of text and symbol entries you can edit or remove. You can add words and phrases to the AutoCorrect dictionary that you misspell, or add often-typed words and save time by just typing their initials. You can use AutoCorrect to quickly insert symbols. For example, you can type (c) to insert ©. Use the AutoCorrect Exceptions dialog box to control how Office handles capital letters. When you point to a word that AutoCorrect changed, a small blue box appears under the first letter. When you point to the small blue box, the AutoCorrect Options button appears, which gives you control over whether you want the text to be corrected. You can also display the AutoCorrect dialog box and change AutoCorrect settings.

Turn On AutoCorrect

1. Click the **Tools** menu, and then click **AutoCorrect**.

   ◆ You can also open program preferences, and then click the **AutoCorrect** icon.

2. Select the **Show AutoCorrect smart button** (Word) or **Show AutoCorrect Options Buttons** (PowerPoint) check box to display the button to change AutoCorrect option when corrections arise.

3. Select the **Replace text as you type** check box.

4. Select the capitalization related check boxes you want AutoCorrect to change for you.

5. To change AutoCorrect exceptions, click **Exceptions**, click the **First Letter** or **INitial CAps** tab, make the changes you want, and then click **OK**.

6. Click **OK**.

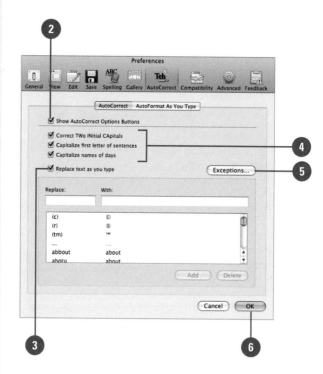

Add or Edit an AutoCorrect Entry

① Click the **Tools** menu, and then click **AutoCorrect**.

◆ You can also open program preferences, and then click the AutoCorrect icon.

② Do one of the following:

◆ **Add.** Type a misspelled word or an abbreviation.

◆ **Edit.** Select the one you want to change.

③ Type the replacement entry.

④ Click **Add** or **Replace**. If necessary, click **Yes** to redefine entry.

⑤ Click **OK**.

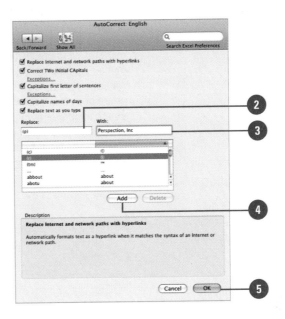

Replace Text as You Type

◆ To correct capitalization or spelling errors automatically, continue typing until AutoCorrect makes the required correction.

Point to the small blue box under the corrected text, and then click the AutoCorrect Options button drop-down to view your options. Click an option, or click a blank area of the document to deselect the AutoCorrect Options menu.

◆ To create a bulleted or numbered list, type 1. or * (for a bullet), press Tab or Spacebar, type any text, and then press Return. AutoCorrect inserts the next number or bullet. To end the list, press Backspace to erase the extra number or bullet.

Examples of AutoCorrect Changes

Type of Correction	If You Type	AutoCorrect Inserts
Capitalization	cAP LOCK	Cap Lock
Capitalization	TWo INitial CAps	Two Initial Caps
Capitalization	thursday	Thursday
Common typos	can;t	can't
Common typos	windoes	windows
Superscript ordinals	2nd	2nd
Stacked fractions	1/2	½
Smart quotes	" "	" "
Em dashes	Madison--a small city in Wisconsin--is a nice place to live.	Madison—a small city in Wisconsin—is a nice place to live.
Symbols	(c)	©
Symbols	(r)	®

Checking Spelling

A document's textual inaccuracies can distract the reader, so it's important that your text be error-free. Each Office program provides a spelling checker so that you can check the spelling in an entire document for words not listed in the dictionary (such as misspellings, names, technical terms, or acronyms) or duplicate words (such as *the the*). You can correct these errors as they arise or after you finish the entire document. You can use the Spelling button on the Review tab to check the entire document using the Spelling dialog box, or you can avoid spelling errors on a document by enabling the AutoCorrect feature to automatically correct words as you type.

Check Spelling All at Once

1. Click the **Tools** menu, and then click **Spelling** (PowerPoint and Excel) or **Spelling and Grammar** (Word).

   TIMESAVER *Press Option+ ⌘+L (Word and PowerPoint).*

2. If the Spelling dialog box opens, choose an option:

   ◆ Click **Ignore Once** to skip the word, or click **Ignore All** to skip every instance of the word.

   ◆ Click **Add** to add a word to your dictionary, so it doesn't show up as a misspelled word in the future.

   ◆ Click a suggestion, and then click **Change** or **Change All**.

   ◆ Select the correct word, and then click **AutoCorrect** to add it to the AutoCorrect list.

   ◆ If no suggestion is appropriate, click in the document and edit the text yourself. Click **Resume** to continue.

3. The Office program will prompt you when the spelling check is complete, or you can click **Close** to end the spelling check.

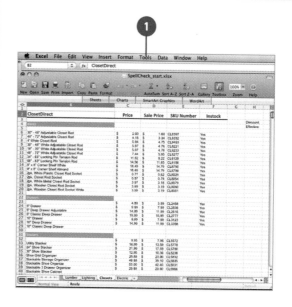

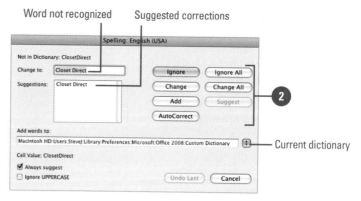

Word not recognized   Suggested corrections

Current dictionary

Changing Spelling Options

You can customize the way each Office program spell checks a document by selecting spelling settings in program preferences. Some spelling options are common to all Office programs, such as Always suggest and Ignore UPPERCASE, while others are tailored to specific Office programs, such as Check spelling as you type and Ignore Internet and file addresses (**New!**). If you have ever mistakenly used *their* instead of *there*, you can use contextual spelling to fix it. While you work in a document, you can can set options to have the spelling checker search for mistakes in the background.

Change Spelling Options

① Click the **Word** or **PowerPoint** menu, and then click **Preferences**.

② Click the **Spelling & Grammar** (Word) or **Spelling** (PowerPoint) icon.

◆ Excel's spelling options are available in the Spelling dialog box. Click the **Tools** menu, and then click **Spelling**.

③ Select or clear the spelling options you want.

◆ **Check spelling as you type**.

◆ **Hide spelling errors in this document**.

◆ **Always suggest corrections**.

◆ **Suggest from main dictionary only** (Word).

◆ **Ignore words in UPPERCASE**.

◆ **Ignore words with numbers**.

◆ **Ignore Internet and file addresses (New!)** (Word).

◆ **Use German post-reform rules**.

◆ **French Modes**.

◆ **Custom Dictionary** (Word). Select to exclude your custom dictionary.

④ Click **OK**.

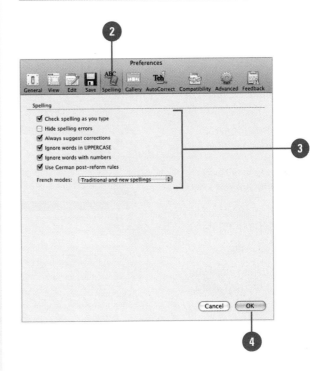

Finding the Right Words

Repeating the same word in a document can reduce a message's effectiveness. Instead, replace some words with synonyms or find antonyms. If you need help finding exactly the right words, use the Thesaurus to look up synonyms quickly. Not sure of the meaning of a word. Use the Dictionary to look up the definition. If you're bilingual, you can even look up words from different language perspectives. These features can save you time and improve the quality and readability of your documents. The Thesaurus and Dictionary can be accessed under Reference Tools on the Toolbox.

Use the Thesaurus

1. Click the **Tools** menu, and then click **Thesaurus**.

   The Reference Tools tab appears on the Toolbox with the Thesaurus panel expanded.

2. Type a word or phrase into the Word or Phrase box, and then press Return.

3. Select the meaning you want for the text.

4. Select the synonym you want.

5. Click one of the following:

   ◆ **Insert** to replace the word you looked up with the new word.

   ◆ **Look Up** to look up the word for other options.

Reference Tools

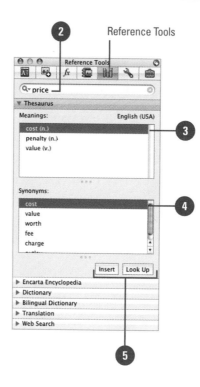

Use the Dictionary

1. Click the **Tools** menu, and then click **Dictionary**.

   The Reference Tools tab appears on the Toolbox with the Dictionary panel expanded.

2. Type a word or phrase into the Word or Phrase box, and then press Return.

3. Click the **Language** drop-down, and then select the language you want.

4. Click triangles to expand or collapse parts of the definition.

5. To use the Bilingual Dictionary, do the following.

   ◆ Click the **Bilingual Dictionary** panel to expand it.

   ◆ Click the **From** drop-down, and then select a language.

   ◆ Click the **To** drop-down, and then select a language.

   ◆ Click triangles or panel name to expand or collapse parts of the definition.

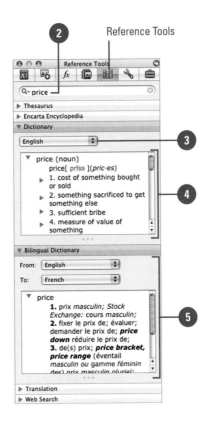

Reference Tools

Researching Words

Office 2008 provides access to Microsoft Encarta Encyclopedia content and Web Search results to research a word or phrase. Encarta Encyclopedia is an online web site that provides a wide-range of information in a variety of media types, while Web Search generates a list of search results to related web sites. You can read information and click links in the Encarta Encyclopedia and Web Search panels under the Reference Tools tab on the Toolbox to open web sites with your default web browser.

Use the Encarta Encyclopedia and Web Search

1. Click the **Reference Tools** tab on the Toolbox.

2. Type a word or phrase into the Word or Phrase box, and then press Return.

3. Click the **Encarta Encyclopedia** and **Web Search** panels to expand them.

4. Click the **Language** drop-down, and then select the language you want.

5. Read the information provided in the Encarta Encyclopedia or Web Search, and then click a link to find out more.

   Your default web browser opens, displaying the web site.

6. Read the information provided on the web site, and then quit your web browser.

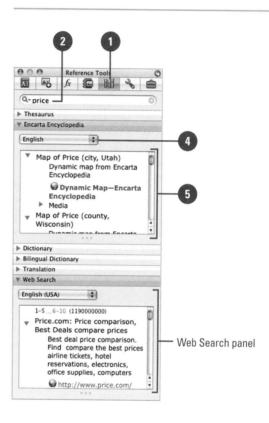

Web Search panel

50

Translating Text to Another Language

With Reference Tools, you can translate single words or short phrases into different languages by using bilingual dictionaries. The Reference Tools tab on the Toolbox provides you with different translations and allows you to incorporate it into your work. If you need to translate an entire document for basic subject matter understanding, Web-based machine translation services are available. A machine translation is helpful for general meaning, but may not preserve the full meaning of the content.

Translate Text

1. Click the **Reference Tools** tab on the Toolbox.

2. Type a word or phrase into the Word or Phrase box, and then press Return.

3. Click the **Translation** panel to expand it.

4. Click the **From** drop-down, and then select the language of the selected text.

5. Click the **To** drop-down, and then select the language you want to translate into.

6. Read the information provided in the Translation panel, and then click any link to get more information.

7. When you're done, click the Translation panel to collapse it.

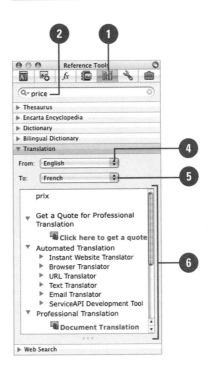

Using Multiple Languages

International Microsoft Office users can change the language that appears on their screens by changing the default language settings. Users around the world can enter, display, and edit text in all supported languages—including European languages, Japanese, Chinese, Korean, Hebrew, and Arabic—to name a few. You'll probably be able to use Office programs in your native language. If the text in your document is written in more than one language, you can designate the language of selected text so the spelling checker uses the right dictionary.

Mark Text as a Language

1 In Word or PowerPoint, select the text you want to mark.

2 Click the **Tools** menu, and then click **Language**.

3 Click the language you want to assign to the selected text.

4 Click **OK**.

Did You Know?

You can check spelling based on a language in Excel. Click the Tools menu, click Language, select a language, and then click OK.

You can check your keyboard layout. After you enable editing for another language, such as Hebrew, Cyrillic, or Greek, you might need to install the correct keyboard layout so you can enter characters for that language. In the System Preferences, click International, click the Input Menu, check your keyboard layout for the language you want, and then click the Close button.

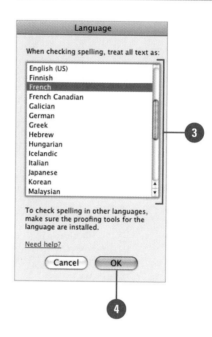

Inserting Symbols

All of the Office 2008 programs come with a host of symbols and special characters for every need. Insert just the right one to keep from compromising a document's professional appearance with a hand-drawn arrow («) or missing mathematical symbol (å). You can insert symbols and special characters by using the Object Palette (**New!**) on the Toolbox.

Insert Symbols

1. Click the document where you want to insert a symbol or character.

2. Click the **Object Palette** tab on the Toolbox.

3. Click the **Symbols** tab on the Object Palette.

4. Click the category drop-down, and then select the symbol category you want.

5. Drag the **Zoom** slider to change the view percentage for the symbols.

6. Click a symbol or character.

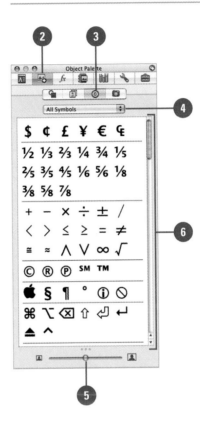

See Also

See "Inserting Symbols and Special Characters" on page 168 for information on inserting symbols in Word.

Undoing and Redoing an Action

You may realize you've made a mistake shortly after completing an action or a task. The Undo feature lets you "take back" one or more previous actions, including data you entered, edits you made, or commands you selected. For example, if you were to enter a number in a cell, and then decide the number was incorrect, you could undo the entry instead of selecting the data and deleting it. A few moments later, if you decide the number you deleted was correct after all, you could use the Redo feature to restore it to the cell.

Undo or Redo an Action

◆ **Undo button.** Click the **Undo** button on the Standard toolbar to reverse your most recent action, such as typing a word, formatting a paragraph, or creating a chart.

   TIMESAVER *Press Ctrl+Z to undo.*

◆ **Redo button.** Click the **Redo** button on the Standard toolbar to restore the last action you reversed.

   TIMESAVER *Press Ctrl+Y to redo your undo.*

◆ **Undo list.** Click the **Undo** button arrow on the Standard toolbar, and then select the consecutive actions you want to reverse.

◆ **Redo list.** Click the **Redo** button arrow on the Standard toolbar, and then select the consecutive actions you want to restore.

Undo button   Undo list

Redo button   Redo list

Zooming the View In and Out

Working with the Zoom tools gives you one more way to control exactly what you see in an Office document. The Zoom tools are located on the Standard toolbar. Large documents, presentations, or worksheets can be difficult to work with and difficult to view. Many Office documents, when viewed at 100%, are larger than the maximized size of the window. When this happens, viewing the entire document requires reducing the zoom.

Change the View

1 Click the **Zoom** drop-down on the Standard toolbar, and then select any of the following zoom options:

- ◆ **%**. Select the zoom percentage you want.

- ◆ **Fit** (PowerPoint). Select to zoom to fit the window.

- ◆ **Selection** (Excel). Select to zoom to the current selection.

- ◆ **One Page** (Excel). Select to zoom to the current page.

- ◆ **Page Width** (Word). Select to zoom to the current page width.

- ◆ **Whole Page** (Word). Select to zoom to the current page.

- ◆ **Two Pages** (Word). Select to zoom to the current two pages.

2 To set a custom zoom percentage, click the **View** menu, click **Zoom**, specify a custom zoom percentage, and then click **OK**.

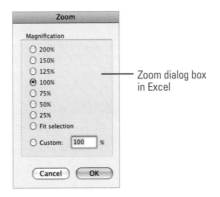

Zoom dialog box in Excel

Using the Format Painter

After formatting text or a cell in a document, you might want to apply those same formatting changes to other cells on the document. For example, you might want each subtotal on your document to be formatted in italic, bold, 12-point Times New Roman, with a dollar sign, commas, and two decimal places. Rather than selecting each subtotal and applying the individual formatting to each cell, you can **paint** (that is, copy) the formatting from one cell to others. The Format Painter lets you "pick up" the style of one section and apply, or "paint," it to another. To apply a format style to more than one item, double-click the Format Painter button on the Standard toolbar instead of a single-click. The double-click keeps the Format Painter active until you want to press Esc to disable it, so you can apply formatting styles to any text or object you want in your document.

Apply a Format Style Using the Format Painter

1 Select a cell or range containing the formatting you want to copy.

2 Click the **Format Painter** button on the Standard toolbar.

If you want to apply the format to more than one item, double-click the Format Painter button.

3 Drag to select the text or click the object to which you want to apply the format.

4 If you double-clicked the Format Painter button, drag to select the text or click the object to which you want to apply the format, and then press Esc when you're done.

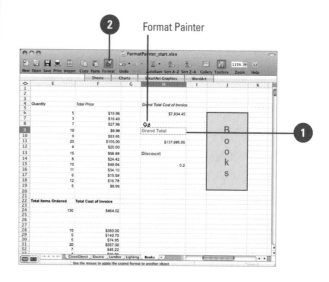

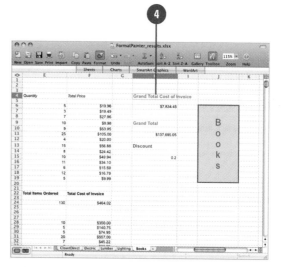

56

Adding Custom Colors

In addition to the standard and theme colors, Office allows you to add more colors to your document. These additional colors are available on each color palette, which you can access using Mores Colors on a Color button, such as the Fill Color or Font Color button. These colors are useful when you want to use a specific color, but the document color theme does not have that color. Colors that you add to a document appear in all color palettes and remain in the palette even if the color theme changes.

Add a Color to the Menus

1. Click the **Formatting Palette** tab on the Toolbox.

2. Click the **Font** panel to expand it.

3. Click the **Font Color** button, and then click **More Colors**.

   This is one method. You can also use other color menus to access the Colors dialog box.

4. Click one of the color buttons at the top: **Color Wheel**, **Color Sliders**, **Color Palettes**, **Image Palettes**, or **Crayons**.

5. Select a custom color using one of the following methods:

   ◆ Drag across the palette until the pointer is over the color you want. Drag the black arrow to adjust the amount of black and white in the color.

     The new color appears above the current color at the bottom right.

6. Drag the custom color from the color box to the blank boxes at the bottom of the Colors dialog box.

   The new color is available for use in documents using the Colors dialog box.

7. Click **OK**.

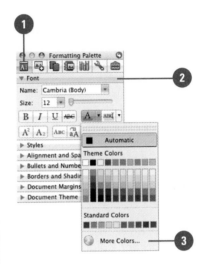

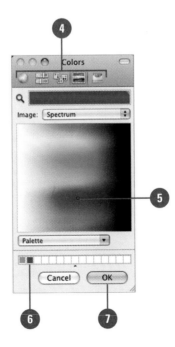

Understanding Themes

A theme helps you create professional-looking documents that use an appropriate balance of color for your document content. You can use a default color theme (**New!**) or create a custom one. All Office documents have a theme. If you don't apply one, Office applies the default Office theme.

Themes in Office are made up of a palette of twelve colors (**New!**). These colors appear on color palettes when you click a color-related button, such as Fill Color or Font Color button on the Font or Colors, Weights, and Fills panel or in a dialog box. These twelve colors correspond to the following elements in a document:

Four Text and Background. The two background colors (light and dark combinations) are the canvas, or drawing area, color of the document. The two text colors (light and dark combinations) are for typing text and drawing lines, and contrast with the background colors.

Six Accent. These colors are designed to work as a complementary color palette for objects, such as shadows and fills. These colors contrast with both the background and text colors.

One hyperlink. This color is designed to work as a complementary color for objects and hyperlinks.

One followed hyperlink. This color is designed to work as a complementary color for objects and visited hyperlinks.

The first four colors in the Theme Colors list represent the document text and background colors (light and dark for each). The remaining colors represent the six accent and two hyperlink colors for the theme. When you apply another theme or change any of these colors to create a new theme, the colors shown in the Theme Colors dialog box and color palettes change to match the current colors.

Accent 5   Accent 4   Accent 6   Accent 1   Accent 3

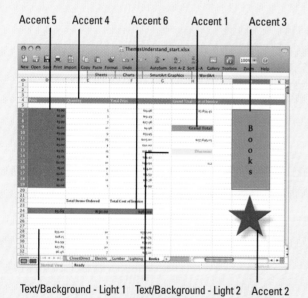

Text/Background - Light 1   Text/Background - Light 2   Accent 2

Twelve theme colors

Sample color themes: Dark and Light

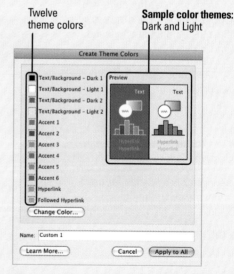

Viewing and Applying a Theme

A document theme (**New!**) consists of theme colors, fonts, and effects. You can quickly format an entire document with a professional look by applying a theme. When you apply a theme, the background, text, graphics, charts, and tables all change to reflect the theme. You can choose from one or more standard themes. When you add new content, the document elements change to match the theme ensuring all of your material will look consistent. You can even use the same theme in other Microsoft Office 2008 programs, such as Word and PowerPoint, so all your work matches. Can't find a theme you like? Search Microsoft Office Online.

View and Apply a Standard Theme

1. Open the document you want to apply a theme.

2. Do either of the following:

   ◆ **PowerPoint.** Click the **Slide Themes** tab in the Elements Gallery, and then select a tab (**Built-in Themes**, **Themes in Presentation**, **Custom Themes**, **All Themes**) with the category you want.

   ◆ **Excel and Word.** Click the **Document Theme** panel on the Formatting Palette tab to expand it.

3. Click the scroll arrows to see additional styles.

4. Click the theme you want to apply to the active document.

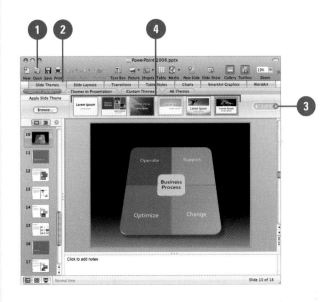

Themes in Word

Applying and Creating Theme Colors

You may like a certain color theme except for one or two colors. You can change an existing color theme (**New!**) and apply your changes to the entire document. In PowerPoint, you can create your own custom theme colors (**New!**) by using the standard Apple Color dialog box, where you can select colors from a color wheel, color sliders, color palettes, image palettes, or crayons. You can accomplish this by using sliders, dragging on a color-space, or entering a numeric value that corresponds to a specific color. Once you create this new color theme, you can add it to your collection of color themes so that you can make it available to any Office program.

Apply Theme Colors

1. Open the document you want to apply a color theme.

2. Click the **Formatting Palette** tab on the Toolbox.

3. Click the **Document Theme** panel to expand it.

4. Click the **Theme Colors** button, and then click a color theme.

   A check mark indicates the currently applied color theme.

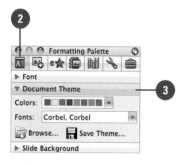

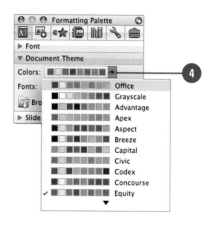

Create Theme Colors

1. In PowerPoint, open a new document or one with a color theme you want to use as the basis of a new a color theme.

2. Click the **Format** menu, and then click **Theme Colors**.

3. Click the Theme Colors buttons (Text/Background, Accent, or Hyperlink, etc.) for the colors you want to change. Repeat steps 5 - 8 for each color that you want to change.

4. Click **Change Color**.

5. Select a color from the different color tabs.

6. Click **OK**.

7. Type a new name for the color theme.

8. Click **Apply to All**.

   PowerPoint applies the custom theme colors to all of your slides and adds the custom theme color to the Theme Colors drop-down on the Formatting Palette in all Microsoft Office programs.

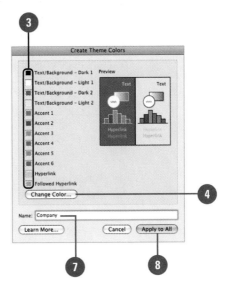

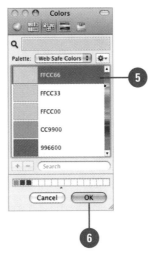

For Your Information

Deleting a Custom Theme Color

If you no longer want to use a custom theme color, you can remove it. In the Mac OS X Finder, drag the file with your custom theme color to the Trash. The custom theme color file is located in the following folder: /*Username*/Library/Application Support/Microsoft/Office/User Template/My Themes/Theme Colors. The deleted theme color remains in the Theme Colors drop-down list until you quit and then reopen the Office program.

Applying Theme Fonts

A document theme consists of theme colors, fonts, and effects. Theme fonts (**New!**) include heading and body text fonts. Each document uses a set of theme fonts. When you click the Theme Fonts drop-down on the Document Theme panel, the name of the current heading and body text font appear highlighted in the gallery menu. If you want to apply the theme, click it on the menu. You can apply a set of theme fonts to another theme.

Apply Theme Fonts

1. Open the document you want to apply theme fonts.

2. Click the **Formatting Palette** tab on the Toolbox.

3. Click the **Document Theme** panel to expand it.

4. Click the **Theme Fonts** button, and then click a font theme.

   A check mark indicates the currently applied color fonts.

Did You Know?

You can apply theme fonts using the Font Name drop-down. To apply a theme font to normal text, select it, and then click the Font Name drop-down on the Font panel, and then select the theme font indicated near the top.

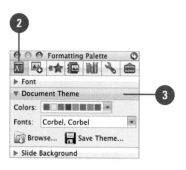

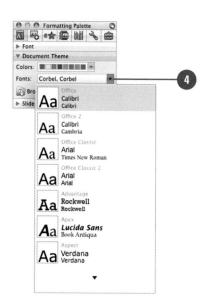

Creating a Custom Theme

If you have special needs for specific colors, fonts, and effects, such as a company sales or marketing document, you can create your own theme by customizing theme colors and theme fonts, and saving them as a theme file (.thmx) (**New!**), which you can reuse. You can apply the saved theme to other documents. When you save a custom theme, the file is automatically saved in the My Themes folder and added to the list of custom themes used by Office 2008 programs. When you no longer need a custom theme, you can delete it from the My Themes folder.

Create a Custom Theme

1. Click the **Formatting Palette** tab on the Toolbox.

2. Click the **Document Theme** panel to expand it.

3. Create a theme by customizing theme colors and theme fonts.

4. Click **Save Theme**.

5. Type a name for the theme file.

6. Click **Save**.

   In PowerPoint, the custom theme appears under the Custom Themes tab, which is available in the Elements Gallery under Slide Themes.

   In Word and Excel, the custom theme appears at the top of the themes list in the Document Theme panel.

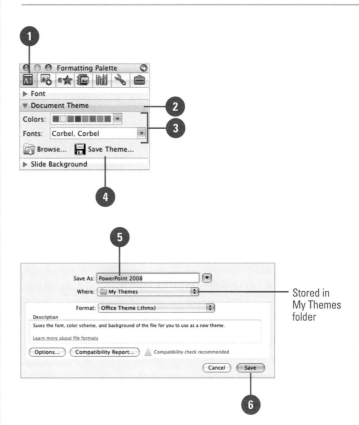

Stored in My Themes folder

For Your Information

Deleting a Custom Theme

If you no longer want to use a custom theme, you can remove it. In the Mac OS X Finder, drag the file with your custom theme color to the Trash. The custom theme color file is located in the following folder: /*Username*/Library/Application Support/Microsoft/Office/User Template/My Themes. The deleted theme remains in the Theme list until you quit and then reopen the Office program.

Applying a Custom Theme

When you can create your own theme by customizing theme colors and theme fonts, and saving them as a theme file (.thmx) (**New!**), you can apply the saved theme to other Office documents. When you save a custom theme file in the My Themes folder, you can choose the custom theme from the Themes gallery. If you save a custom theme file in another folder location, you can use the Browse for Themes button on the Document Theme panel to locate and select the custom theme file you want to reuse.

Apply a Custom Theme

1. Open the document you want to apply a custom theme.

2. Click the **Formatting Palette** tab on the Toolbox.

3. Click the **Document Theme** panel to expand it.

4. To apply a custom theme from a file, click **Browse for Themes**.

   The Choose Theme or Themed Document dialog box opens, displaying the My Themes folder, which is the default location for Office themes.

5. If the file is located in another folder, navigate to the file.

6. Click the theme file you want to use.

7. Click **Apply**.

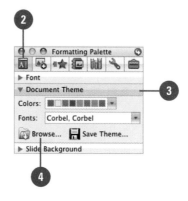

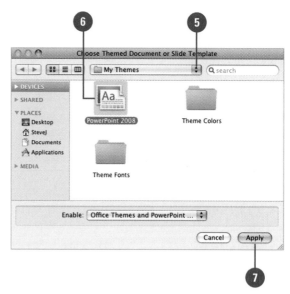

Previewing a Document

Before printing, you should verify that the page looks the way you want. You save time, money, and paper by avoiding duplicate printing. **Preview** shows you the exact placement of your text, graphics, or data on each printed page. Preview temporarily converts your Office document to a PDF for viewing purposes; your original document remains unchanged. You can use Preview to view PDF and image files as well as alter them, convert them, add your own comments with a note, and insert links to web sites or other pages. You can view all or part of your document as it will appear when you print it, which is known as WYSIWYG (What You See Is What You Get). Preview makes it easy to zoom in and out to view page content more comfortably. You can access Preview from the Applications folder or from an Office program's Print dialog box.

Preview a Document

1. Open a document.

2. Click the **File** menu, and then click **Print**.

3. In the Print dialog box, click **Preview**.

   The Preview Utility launches.

4. Select from the following options:

   ◆ **Next/Previous**. Click to move between pages in the document.

   ◆ **Zoom In or Zoom Out**. Click to increase or decrease the viewing size of the image.

   ◆ **Move**. Click to move around the current page.

   ◆ **Text**. Click to select text on the current page.

   ◆ **Select**. Click to select a portion of the current page.

   ◆ **Sidebar**. Click to expand or collapse the thumbnail page view of the images.

5. Click **Cancel** to close or **Print** to print the document.

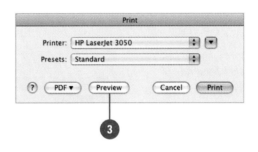

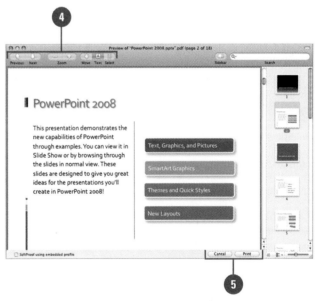

Printing a Document

When you're ready to print your Office document, you can choose several printing options. You can print all or part of any document and control the appearance of many features, such as whether gridlines are displayed, whether column letters and row numbers are displayed, and whether to include print titles, which are the columns and rows that repeat on each page. You can quickly print a copy of your document to review it by clicking the Print button on the Standard toolbar. You can also use the Print dialog box to specify several print options, such as choosing a new printer, selecting the number of pages in the document you want printed, and specifying the number of copies.

Print All or Part of a Document

1. Open a document.

2. Click the **File** menu, and then click **Print**.

   TIMESAVER To print without the Print dialog box, click the Print button on the Standard toolbar.

3. Click the **Printer** pop-up, and then select an available printer.

4. Click the **Presets** pop-up, and then select a user-defined print setting.

5. Click the **Expand/Collapse** arrow, if necessary, to expand the Print dialog box.

6. Specify the following standard print options:

   ◆ **Preview Image.** Click the arrows below the preview image to view the document.

   ◆ **Copies.** Type the number of copies you want. Select or clear the **Collated** check box. Selected prints 1, 2, 3, 1, 2, 3. Cleared prints 1, 1, 2, 2, 3, 3.

   ◆ **Pages.** Click the **All** option or the **From** option, and then enter the print range you want.

   ◆ **Paper Size.** Select the paper size you want.

   ◆ **Orientation.** Select the portrait or landscape option you want.

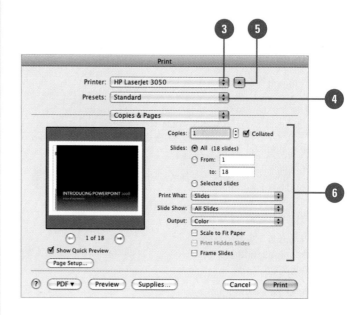

7 Click the **Options** pop-up, and then select from the available options:

- **Application Specific Options.** If you're using Microsoft Word, this option lists specific options for that specific application.

- **Layout.** When printing large documents, allows you to select how many pages per sheet, the layout direction, border options, and two-sided printing.

- **Color Matching.** Gives you access to Macintosh's ColorSync management system, and the ability to apply the new Quartz Filters to the printed document.

- **Paper Handling.** Select to print in reverse order (page 1 prints last), whether to print all, odd, or even pages, and scale a document to fit the paper.

- **Paper Feed.** Select the paper tray for all pages or a different paper tray for the first and remaining pages.

- **Cover Page.** Lets you select options to print a cover page, such as standard, classified, unclassified, or confidential.

- **Scheduler.** Lets you schedule a time for printing the document.

- **Summary.** Shows a summary of all the printer options that have been selected.

IMPORTANT *The print settings on the Options pop-up vary depending on the selected printer.*

8 To save your print settings, click the **Presets** pop-up, click **Save As**, type a name, and then click **OK**.

9 Click **Print**.

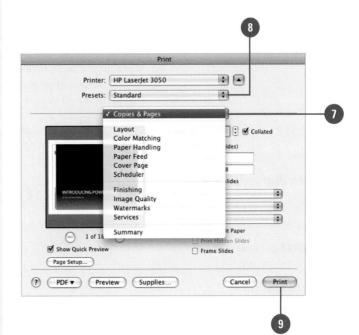

Protecting a Document

In Word and Excel, you can assign a password and other security options so that only those who know the password can open the document, or to protect the integrity of your document as it moves from person to person. At times, you will want the information to be used but not changed; at other times, you will want only specific people to be able to view the document. Setting a document as read-only is useful when you want a document, such as a company-wide bulletin, to be distributed and read, but not changed. Password protection takes effect the next time you open the document.

Add Password Protection

1. In Word and Excel, open the document you want to protect.

2. Click the **Word** or **Excel** menu, and then click **Preferences**.

3. Click the **Security** icon.

4. Type a password in the Password to open box or the Password to modify box.

   IMPORTANT *It's critical that you remember your password. If you forget your password, Microsoft can't retrieve it.*

5. Select or clear the **Read-only recommended** check box.

6. To set options to protection for, click **Protect Document** (Word), **Protect Sheet** (Excel), or **Protect Worksheet** (Excel), select the options you want, and then click **OK**.

7. Click **OK**.

8. Type your password again.

9. Click **OK**.

10. If you entered passwords for Open and Modify, type your password again, and then click **OK**.

11. Click **Save**, and then click **Yes** to replace existing document.

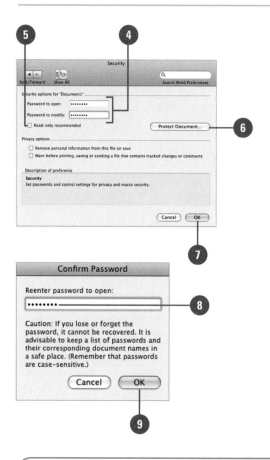

For Your Information

Using a Strong Password

Hackers identify passwords as strong or weak. A strong password is a combination of uppercase and lowercase letters, numbers, and symbols, such as Grea8t!, while a weak one doesn't use different character types, such as Hannah1. Be sure to write down your passwords and place them in a secure location.

Open a Document with Password Protection

1. In Word and Excel, click the **File** menu, click **Open**, navigate to a document with password protection, and then click **Open**.

2. Click **Read Only** if you do not wish to modify the document, or type the password in the Password dialog box.

3. Click **OK**.

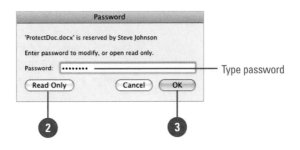

Type password

Change or Remove the Password Protection

1. In Word and Excel, click the **File** menu, click **Open**, navigate to a document with password protection, and then click **Open**.

2. Type the password in the Password dialog box.

3. Click **OK**.

4. Click the **Word** or **Excel** menu, and then click **Preferences**.

5. Click the **Security** icon.

6. Select the contents in the Password to modify box or the Password to open box, and then choose the option you want:

   ◆ **Change password.** Type a new password, click **OK**, and then retype your password.

   ◆ **Delete password.** Press Delete.

7. Click **OK**.

8. Click **Save**, and then click **Yes** to replace existing document.

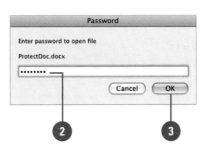

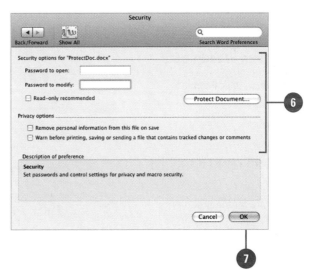

Modifying Document Properties

If you're not sure of the version of a document, or if you need statistical information about a document, such as the number of pages, paragraphs, lines, words, and characters to fulfill a requirement, you can use the Properties dialog box to quickly find this information. You can create custom file properties, such as client or project, to help you manage and track files. If you associate a file property to an item in the document, the file property updates when you change the item.

Display and Modify Document Properties

1 Click the **File** menu, and then click **Properties**.

2 Click the tabs (**General**, **Summary**, **Statistics**, or **Contents**) to view information about the document.

3 To add title and author information for the document, click the **Summary** tab.

4 To add and modify tracking properties, click the **Custom** tab.

5 When you are done changing your document properties, click **OK**.

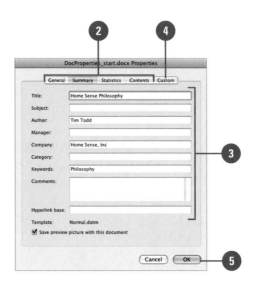

Customize Document Properties

1 Click the **File** menu, and then click **Properties**.

2 Click the **Custom** tab.

3 Type a name for the custom property or select a name from the list.

4 Click the data type for the property you want to add, and then type a value for the property that matches the type you selected in the Type box.

5 Click **Add**.

6 Click **OK**.

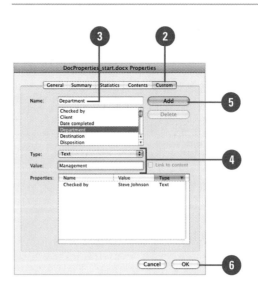

Adding Art to Office Documents

3

Introduction

Although well-illustrated documents can't make up for a lack of content, you can capture your audiences' attention if your documents are vibrant and visually interesting. Microsoft Office comes with a vast array of clip art, and there are endless amounts available through other software packages or on the Web. When going online to look at clips, you can categorize them so that it's easier to find the best choice for your Office document. You can use the Microsoft Online Web site to search for and download additional clip art.

You can easily enhance an Office document by adding a picture—one of your own or one of the hundreds that come with Microsoft Office. If you need to modify your pictures, you can resize them, compress them for storage, change their brightness or contrast, recolor them, or crop them.

WordArt is another feature that adds detail to your document. Available in other Office programs, WordArt can bring together your documents—you can change its color, shape, shadow, or size. Because WordArt comes with so many style choices, time spent customizing your documents is minimal.

In Office programs, you can insert SmartArt graphics (**New!**) to create diagrams that convey processes or relationships. Office provides a wide-variety of built-in SmartArt graphic types from which to choose, including graphical lists, process, cycle, hierarchy, relationship, matrix, and pyramid. Using built-in SmartArt graphics makes it easy to create and modify charts without having to create them from scratch.

Instead of adding a table of dry numbers, insert a chart. Charts add visual interest and useful information represented by lines, bars, pie slices, or other markers. Office uses Microsoft Excel (**New!**) to embed and display the information in a chart.

What You'll Do

Locate and Insert Clip Art

Insert a Picture

Add a Quick Style to a Picture

Apply a Shape and Border to a Picture

Apply Picture Effects

Modify Picture Brightness and Contrast

Recolor a Picture

Modify Picture Size

Crop, Rotate and Recolor a Picture

Create and Format WordArt Text

Modify WordArt Text Effects

Create and Format SmartArt Graphics

Modify a SmartArt Graphic

Create and Modify an Organization Chart

Insert and Create a Chart

Change a Chart Type and Layout Style

Change Chart Titles and Labels

Edit Chart Data

Save a Chart Template

Share Information Between Programs

Link and Embedding Objects

Flag Documents for Follow Up

Locating and Inserting Clip Art

To add a clip art image to a document, you can use the Clip Gallery or the Clip Art tab on the Toolbox. The Clip Gallery helps you search for clip art and access additional clip art available on Office Online, a clip gallery that Microsoft maintains on its Web site. The Clip Art tab on the Toolbox provides easy access to a subset of the clip art available in the Clip Gallery. You can limit search results to specific keywords with the Search box, a clip art category, or a type of media file. If you have your own images, you can import them into the Clip Gallery, and then modify their properties for search purposes. After you find the clip art you want, you can insert it.

Insert Clip Art from the Clip Gallery

1. Do either of the following to start the Clip Gallery:

   - In Word and Excel, click the **Insert** menu, point to **Picture**, and then click **Clip Art**.

   - In PowerPoint, click the **Insert** menu, and then click **Clip Art**.

2. To narrow your search, do one of the following:

   - **Category.** Click a category with the type of clip art you are looking for.

   - **Search.** Type the keyword(s) associated with the clip you are looking for, and then click **Search**.

     Clips matching the keywords appear in the Results list.

   - **Online.** Click **Online**. Search and download images from the Office Online Web site.

3. Select the clip art you want.

4. To preview the clip art before you insert it, select the **Preview** check box.

5. Click **Insert** to insert the selected clip art and close the Clip Gallery.

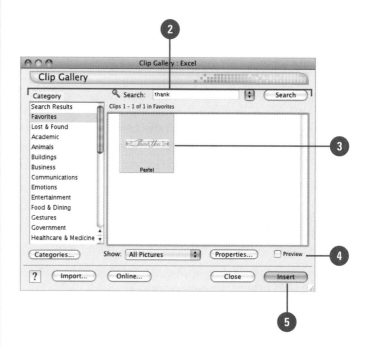

For Your Information

Understanding Clip Art Objects

Clip art objects (pictures and animated pictures) are images made up of geometric shapes, such as lines, curves, circles, squares, and so on. These images, known as vector images, are mathematically defined, which makes them easy to resize and manipulate. A picture in the Microsoft Windows Metafile (.wmf) file format is an example of a vector image. Clip Gallery also includes sounds or motion clips, which you can insert into a document. A **motion clip** is an animated picture—also known as an animated GIF—frequently used in Web pages. When you insert a sound, a small icon appears representing the sound file.

Work with the Clip Gallery

1. Start the Clip Gallery.

2. Do any of the following:

    ◆ **Categories.** Click **Categories**, click **New Category** to create a category or click **Delete** to remove a selected category, and then **OK**.

    ◆ **Properties.** Select a clip art image, click **Properties**, and then use the Description, Categories, and Keywords tabs to modify properties for search purposes, and then click **OK**.

    ◆ **Import.** Click **Import**, select the images you want, select an import option, and then click **Import**.

3. Click **Close**.

Insert Clip Art from the Toolbox

1. Click the **Object Palette** tab on the Toolbox.

2. Click the **Clip Art** tab on the Object Palette.

3. Click the **Categories** drop-down, and then select the clip art category you want.

4. Drag the **Zoom** slider to change the view percentage for the clip art.

5. Drag the clip art image to the location where you want it.

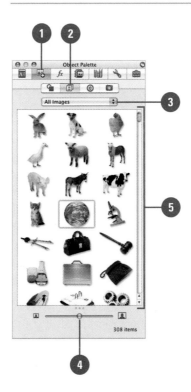

Inserting a Picture

Office makes it possible for you to insert pictures, graphics, scanned photographs, art, photos, or artwork from a CD, DVD, online source, iPhoto library or other program into a document. You can insert pictures from files or insert photos from your iPhoto library. When you insert pictures from files on your hard disk drive, scanner, digital camera, or Web camera, Office allows you to select multiple pictures, view thumbnails of them, and insert them all at once, which speeds up the process. If you want to insert photos from an iPhoto library, you can access them using the Photos tab under the Object Palette tab on the Toolbox. After you select the picture or photo you want, you can insert it.

Insert a Picture from a File

1. Do either of the following to start the Clip Gallery:

   ◆ In Word and Excel, click the **Insert** menu, point to **Picture**, and then click **From File.**

   ◆ In PowerPoint, click the **Insert** menu, and then click **Picture**.

2. Navigate to the location on the drive and folder that contain the file you want to insert.

3. To display specific file types, click the **Enable** drop-down, and then select an option.

4. Click the file you want to insert.

5. Specify any of the following:

   ◆ To link a picture file, select the **Link to File** check box.

   ◆ To save the picture with the document, select the **Save with Document** check box.

   ◆ If the picture contains layers and you want to keep them separate, select the **Treat picture layers as separate objects** check box.

6. Click **Insert**.

   TROUBLE? *If you see a red "x" instead of a picture or motion clip in your document, then you don't have a graphics filter installed on your computer for that clip.*

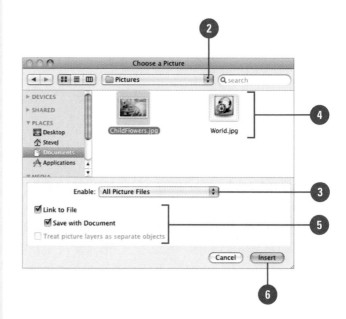

Insert Photos from the Toolbox

1. Click the **Object Palette** tab on the Toolbox.

2. Click the **Photos** tab on the Object Palette.

3. Click the **Categories** drop-down, and then select the iPhoto library category you want.

4. To locate a specific photo, enter a keyword in the Search box, and then press Return.

5. Drag the **Zoom** slider to change the view percentage for the photos.

6. Drag the photo to the location where you want it.

Did You Know?

You can replace the picture. If you want to replace a picture you have already inserted, select the picture, click the Replace button in the Picture panel on the Formatting Palette tab on the Toolbox, select the picture you want to replace the current one, and then click Insert.

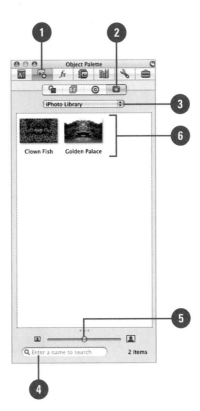

Adding a Quick Style to a Picture

Instead of changing individual attributes of a picture—such as shape, border, and effects—you can quickly add them all at once with the Picture Quick Style gallery. The Picture Quick Style gallery (**New!**) provides a variety of different formatting combinations. When you select a picture, the the Picture Quick Style gallery appears on the Quick Styles tab in the Quick Styles and Effects panel on the Formatting Palette tab on the Toolbox.

Add a Quick Style to a Picture

1. Click the picture you want to change.

2. Click the **Formatting Palette** tab on the Toolbox.

3. Click the **Quick Styles and Effects** panel to expand it, and then click the **Quick Styles** tab.

4. Click the scroll up or down arrows to see additional styles.

   The current style appears highlighted in the gallery.

5. Click the style you want from the gallery to apply it to the selected picture.

6. To specify additional picture options, click **More Options**, select the options you want, and then click **OK**.

Did You Know?

You can save a shape as a picture in the PNG format. Option-click the shape, click Save as Picture, type a name, and then click Save.

You can quickly return a picture back to its original form. Select the picture, click the Formatting Palette tab on the Toolbox, and then click the Reset button.

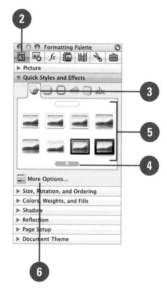

Applying a Shape to a Picture

After you insert a picture into your document, you can select it and apply one of Office's shapes to it (**New!**). The picture appears in the shape just like it has been cropped. The Picture Shape gallery makes it easy to choose the shape you want to use. The Picture Shape gallery is organized into categories—including rectangles, basic shapes, block arrows, equation shapes, flowchart, stars and banners, callouts, and action buttons—to make it easier to find the shape you want. You can try different shapes to find the one you want.

Apply a Shape to a Picture

1. Click the picture you want to change.

2. Click the **Formatting Palette** tab on the Toolbox.

3. Click the **Shape** button on the Picture panel, and then point to the type of shape you want to apply.

4. Select the shape you want to apply to the selected picture.

Did You Know?

You can quickly return a picture back to its original form. Select the picture, click the Formatting Palette tab on the Toolbox, and then click the Reset button.

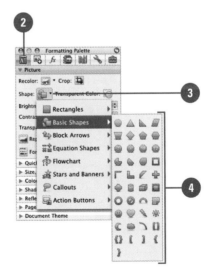

Applying Picture Effects

You can change the look of a picture by applying effects (**New!**), such as shadows, glow, reflections, 3-D rotations, and text transformation. You can also apply effects to a shape by using the Picture Shape gallery for quick results, or by using the Format Picture dialog box for custom results. From the Quick Styles and Effects gallery, you can apply a built-in combination of 3-D effects or individual effects to a picture. If you don't care for the results, you can use undo to remove it.

Add an Effect to a Picture

1. Click the picture you want to change.

2. Click the **Formatting Palette** tab on the Toolbox.

3. Click the **Quick Styles and Effects** panel to expand it.

4. Click the one of the following sub-tabs to display an effect:

   ◆ **Quick Styles** to select one of the styles.

   ◆ **Shadows** to select one of the shadow types.

   ◆ **Glows** to select one of the glow variations.

   ◆ **Reflections** to select one of the reflection variations.

   ◆ **3-D Effects** to select one of the 3-D variations.

   ◆ **Text Transformations** to select one of the WordArt variations.

5. Click the scroll up or down arrows to see additional styles.

6. Click the effect you want from the gallery to apply it to the selected picture.

7. To specify additional picture options, click **More Options**, select the options you want, and then click **OK**.

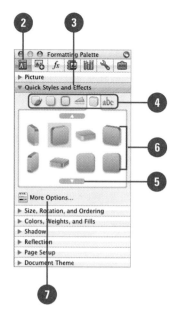

Customize a Shadow or Reflection

1 Click the picture with the shadow you want to change.

2 Click the **Formatting Palette** tab on the Toolbox.

3 To customize a shadow, click the **Shadows** panel to expand it, and then specify any of the following options:

- ◆ **Shadow.** Clear the check box to remove the shadow.

- ◆ **Angle.** Drag the dial or specify a degree to adjust the shadow angle.

- ◆ **Style.** Select a shadow style: Inner, Outer, or Perspective.

- ◆ **Color.** Select a color for the shadow.

- ◆ **Distance.** Select a distance (in points) for the shadow.

- ◆ **Blur.** Select a distance (in points) to blur the shadow.

- ◆ **Transparency.** Select an percentage to make the shadow transparent.

4 To customize a reflection, click the **Reflections** pane to expand it, and then specify any of the following options:

- ◆ **Reflection.** Clear the check box to remove the reflection.

- ◆ **Transparency.** Select a percentage to make the reflection transparent.

- ◆ **Size.** Select a percentage size for the reflection.

- ◆ **Distance.** Select a distance (in points) for the reflection.

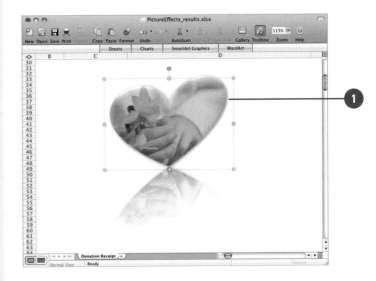

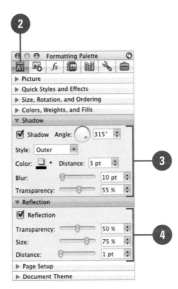

Applying a Border to a Picture

After you insert a picture, you can add and modify the picture border by changing individual outline formatting using the the Colors, Weights, and Fills panel on the Formatting Palette on the Toolbox. The Colors, Weights, and Fills panel provides options to add a border, select a border color, and change border width and style. You can try different border combinations to find the one you want. If you don't care for the results, you can use undo to remove it.

Apply a Border to a Picture

1. Click the picture you want to change.

2. Click the **Formatting Palette** tab on the Toolbox.

3. Click the **Colors, Weights, and Fills** panel to expand it.

4. Specify any of the following options under the Line section of the panel:

   ◆ **Color.** Click the Color button arrow, and then select a color or other color related option.

   ◆ **Style.** Click the Style button, and then select a line style, or click Line Effects for additional options in the Format Picture dialog box.

   ◆ **Dashed.** Click the Dashed button, and then select a dashed line style.

   ◆ **Weight.** Select a line thickness (in points) for the line.

   ◆ **Transparency.** Select an percentage to make the line transparent.

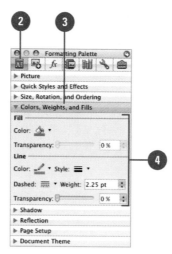

Modifying Picture Brightness and Contrast

Once you have inserted a picture, you can control the image's colors, brightness, and contrast using Picture tools on the Formatting Palette tab on the Toolbox. The brightness and contrast controls let you make simple adjustments to the tonal range of a picture. The brightness and contrast controls change a picture by an overall lightening or darkening of the image pixels. You can experiment with the settings to get the look you want. If you don't like the look, you can use the Reset Picture button to return the picture back to its original starting point.

Change Brightness

1. Click the picture whose brightness you want to increase or decrease.

2. Click the **Formatting Palette** tab on the Toolbox.

3. Click the **Picture** panel to expand it.

4. Drag the **Brightness** slider to a positive brightness to lighten the object colors by adding more white, or to a negative brightness to darken the object colors by adding more black.

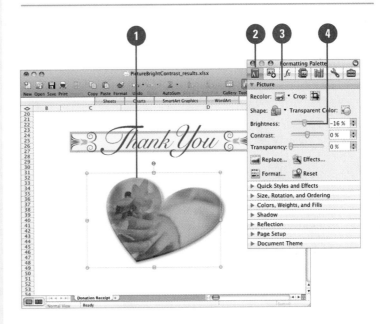

Change Contrast

1. Click the picture whose contrast you want to increase or decrease.

2. Click the **Formatting Palette** tab on the Toolbox.

3. Click the **Picture** panel to expand it.

4. Drag the **Contrast** slider to a positive contrast to increase intensity, resulting in less gray, or to a negative contrast to decrease intensity, resulting in more gray.

Recoloring a Picture

You can recolor clip art and other objects to match the color scheme of your document. For example, if you use a flower clip art as your business logo, you can change shades of pink in the spring to shades of orange in the autumn. The Picture Recolor gallery (**New!**) provides a variety of different formatting combinations. You can also use a transparent background in your picture to avoid conflict between its background color and your document's background. With a transparent background, the picture takes on the same background as your document.

Recolor a Picture

1 Click the picture whose color you want to change.

2 Click the **Formatting Palette** tab on the Toolbox.

3 Click the **Picture** panel to expand it.

4 Click the **Recolor** button.

5 Click one of the Color options.

- ◆ **Color Modes.** Click an option to apply a color type:

  Grayscale. Converts colors into whites, blacks and shades of gray between black and white.

  Sepia. Converts colors into very light gold and yellow colors like a picture from the old west.

  Washout. Converts colors into whites and very light colors.

  Black and White. Converts colors into only white and black.

- ◆ **Dark and Light Variations.** Click an option to apply an accent color in light or dark variations.

- ◆ **More Variations.** Point to this option to select a specific color.

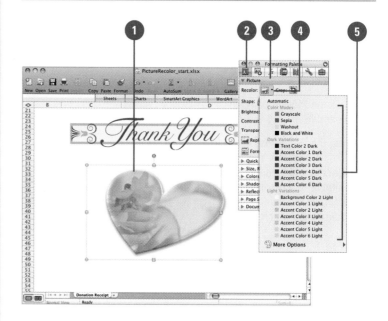

Dark Variations

Light Variations

Set a Transparent Background

1. Click the picture you want to change.

2. Click the **Formatting Palette** tab on the Toolbox.

3. Click the **Picture** panel to expand it.

4. Click the **Transparent Color** button.

5. Move the pointer over the object until the pointer changes shape.

6. Click the color you want to set as transparent.

7. Move the pointer over the picture where you want to apply the transparent color, and then click to apply it.

8. When you're done, click outside the image.

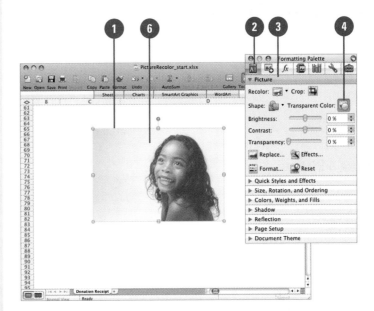

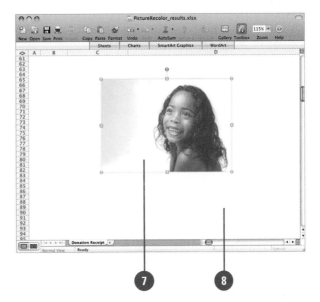

Did You Know?

Why is the Set Transparent Color command dimmed? Setting a color as transparent works only with bitmaps. If you are working with an object that is not a bitmap, you will not be able to use this feature.

You can't modify some pictures in Office. If the picture is a bitmap (.BMP, .JPG, .GIF, or .PNG), you need to edit its colors in an image editing program, such as Adobe Photoshop, Microsoft Paint, or Paint Shop Pro.

You can reset a picture back to its original state. Click the picture you want to reset, click the Formatting Palette tab on the Toolbox, expand the Picture panel, and then click the Reset button.

Modifying Picture Size

Once you have inserted a picture, clip art and other objects into your document, you can adapt them to meet your needs. Like any object, you can resize a picture. You can use the sizing handles to quickly resize a picture or use height and width options in the Size section on the Size, Rotation, and Ordering panel to resize a picture more precisely. If you want to set unique or multiple options at the same time, you can use the Format Picture dialog box. These options allow you to make sure your pictures keep the same relative proportions as the original and lock size proportions.

Resize a Picture

1 Click the object you want to resize.

2 Drag one of the sizing handles to increase or decrease the object's size.

◆ Drag a middle handle to resize the object up, down, left, or right.

◆ Drag a corner handle to resize the object proportionally.

Resize a Picture Precisely

1 Click the object you want to resize.

2 Click the **Formatting Palette** tab on the Toolbox.

3 Click the **Size, Rotation, and Ordering** panel to expand it.

4 Click the up and down arrows or enter a number (in inches) in the Height and Width boxes under Size (in), and then press Return.

If the **Lock aspect ratio** check box is selected, height or width automatically changes when you change one of them.

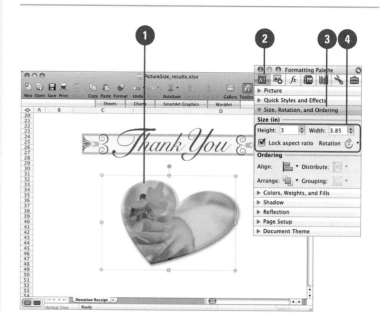

Precisely Scale a Picture

1 Click the object you want to resize.

2 Click the **Formatting Palette** tab on the Toolbox.

3 Click the **Picture** panel to expand it.

4 Click the **Format** button.

5 Click **Size** in the left panel.

6 To keep the picture proportional, select the **Lock aspect ratio** check box.

7 To keep the picture the same relative size, select the **Relative to original picture size** check box.

8 Click the up and down arrows or enter a number in the Height and Width boxes in one of the following:

- ◆ **Size.** Enter a height and width size in inches.

- ◆ **Scale.** Enter a percentage size.

If the Lock aspect ratio check box is selected, height or width automatically changes when you change one of them.

9 Click **OK**.

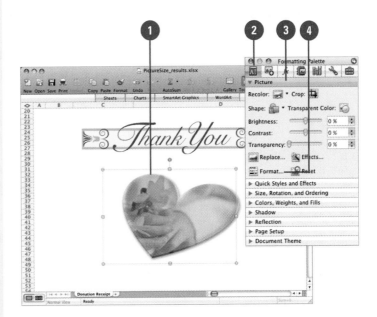

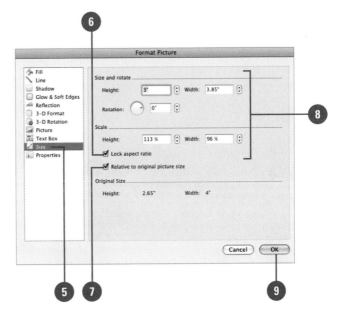

Did You Know?

Resizing bitmaps can cause distortion. Bitmap images are made up of dots, and do not lend themselves as easily to resizing because the dots can't expand and contract, which can lead to distortion. To avoid distortion, resize bitmaps proportionally and try to resize smaller instead of larger.

Cropping and Rotating a Picture

You can crop clip art to isolate just one portion of the picture. Because clip art uses vector image technology, you can crop even the smallest part of it and then enlarge it, and the clip art will still be recognizable. You can also crop bitmapped pictures, but if you enlarge the area you cropped, you lose picture detail. Use the Crop button to crop an image by hand. You can also crop using the Format Picture dialog box, which gives you precise control over the dimensions of the area you want to crop. You can also rotate a picture by increments or freehand.

Crop a Picture Quickly

1. Click the picture you want to crop.

2. Click the **Formatting Palette** tab on the Toolbox.

3. Click the **Picture** panel to expand it.

4. Click the **Crop** button.

5. Drag the sizing handles until the borders surround the area you want to crop.

6. Click outside the image when you are finished.

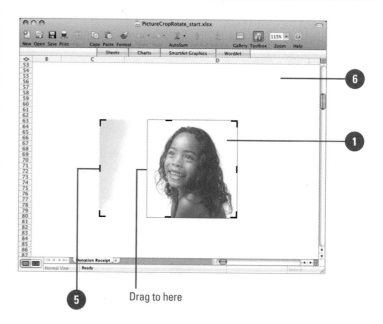

Drag to here

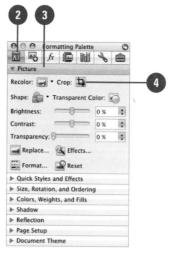

Rotate a Picture

1 Click the object you want to rotate.

2 Position the pointer (which changes to the Free Rotate pointer) over the green rotate lever at the top of the object, and then drag to rotate the object.

◆ You can also use the **Rotation** button on the Size, Rotation, and Ordering panel on the Formatting Palette tab, or click the **Format** button on the Picture panel and use the Rotation dial under Size in the Format Picture dialog box.

3 Click outside the object to set the rotation.

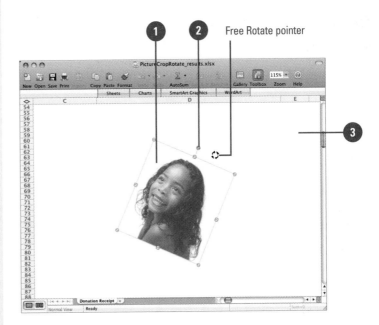

Free Rotate pointer

Creating WordArt Text

The WordArt feature lets you create stylized text to draw attention to your most important words. Most users apply WordArt to a word or a short phrase, such as *Make a Difference*. You should apply WordArt to a document sparingly. Its visual appeal and unique look requires uncluttered space. When you use WordArt, you can choose from a variety of text styles that come with the WordArt Style gallery (**New!**), or you can create your own using tools in the WordArt Styles group. You can also use the free angle handle (pink diamond) inside the selected text box to adjust your WordArt text angle.

Insert WordArt Text in Excel or PowerPoint

1. In Excel or PowerPoint, click the **WordArt** tab on the Elements Gallery.

2. Click the **2-D Styles** or **3-D Styles** button to display the type of WordArt style you want.

3. Click one of the WordArt styles.

   ◆ You can click the arrows on the right to display more styles.

   A WordArt text box appears on the document with selected placeholder text.

4. Type the text you want WordArt to use.

5. If applicable, use the Font and Paragraph options on the Font panel on the Formatting Palette tab to modify the text you entered.

6. To edit WordArt text, click to place the insertion point where you want to edit, and then edit the text.

Did You Know?

You can remove WordArt text. In Excel or PowerPoint, select the WordArt text you want to remove, click the WordArt tab on the Elements Gallery, click the Remove Style button.

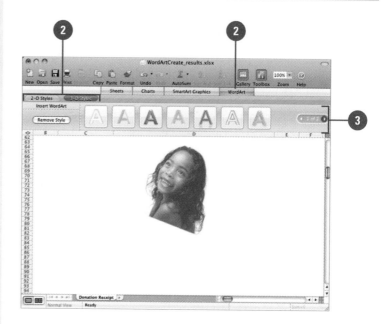

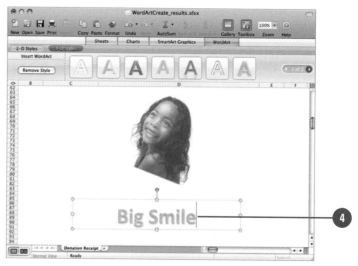

Insert and Format WordArt Text in Word

1 In Word, click the **WordArt** tab on the Elements Gallery.

2 Click one of the style buttons (**All**, **Simple**, **Bold**, **Enhanced**, or **Elegant**) to display the type of WordArt style you want.

3 Click one of the WordArt styles.

♦ You can click the arrows on the right to display more styles.

A WordArt text box appears on the document with selected placeholder text.

4 Double-click the WordArt text box to modify the text.

5 Type the text you want WordArt to use.

6 Click **OK**.

7 Use the WordArt options on the WordArt panel on the Formatting Palette tab to modify the text you entered.

♦ **Format as Shape.** Click the button, and then select a shape for the text.

♦ **Format WordArt.** Click the button to change colors, lines, size, and layout.

♦ **Equalize Character Height.** Click the button to toggle equalize character height on and off.

♦ **Stack Text Vertically.** Click the button to toggle vertical text on and off.

♦ **Align Text.** Click the button to align text in the text box.

♦ **Set Character Spacing.** Click the button to tighten or loosen character spacing.

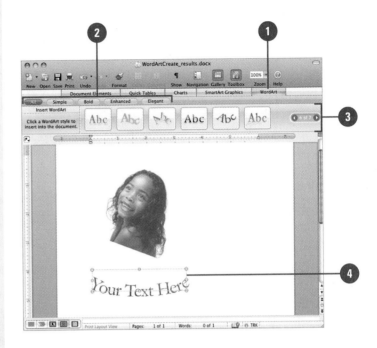

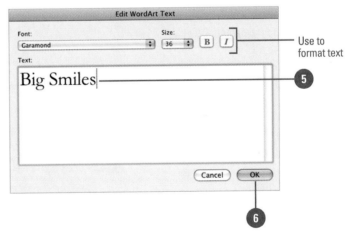

Use to format text

Formatting WordArt Text

You can change the look of WordArt text by applying effects (**New!**), such as shadows, glows, reflections, glows, 3-D rotations, and text transformations. You can apply effects to a shape by using the Quick Styles and Effects gallery for quick results. From the Quick Styles and Effects gallery you can apply a built-in combination of 3-D effects or individual effects to WordArt text. In addition to applying one of the pre-formatted WordArt styles, you can also create your own style by shaping your text into a variety of shapes, curves, styles, and color patterns. The Colors, Weights, and Fills panel on the Formatting Palette tab gives you tools for changing the fill and outline of your WordArt text.

Apply an Effect to WordArt Text

① In Excel or PowerPoint, click the WordArt object you want to change.

② Click the **Formatting Palette** tab on the Toolbox.

③ Click the **Quick Styles and Effects** panel to expand it.

④ Click the one of the following sub-tabs to display an effect:

◆ **Quick Styles** to select one of the styles.

◆ **Shadows** to select one of the shadow types.

◆ **Glows** to select one of the glow variations.

◆ **Reflections** to select one of the reflection variations.

◆ **3-D Effects** to select one of the 3-D variations.

◆ **Text Transformations** to select one of the WordArt style variations.

⑤ Click the scroll up or down arrows to see additional styles.

⑥ Click the effect you want from the gallery to apply it to the selected shape.

⑦ To specify additional picture options, click **More Options**, select the options you want, and then click **OK**.

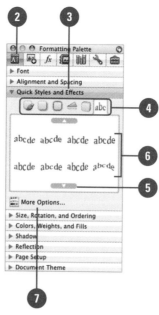

Apply a Fill or Line Color to WordArt Text

1. In Excel or PowerPoint, click the WordArt object you want to change.

2. Click the **Formatting Palette** tab on the Toolbox.

3. Click the **Colors, Weights, and Fills** panel to expand it.

4. Click the **Color Fill** button arrow, and then click one of the following:

   ◆ **No Fill** to remove a fill color.

   ◆ **Color** to select a theme or standard color.

   ◆ **Fill Effects** to select a solid fill color, picture file, gradient, or texture using the tabs on the Format Shape dialog box.

5. Click the **Line Color** button arrow, and then click one of the following:

   ◆ **No Fill** to remove a line color.

   ◆ **Color** to select a theme or standard color.

   ◆ **Line Effects** to select a solid fill color, gradient, or weights & arrows using the tabs on the Format Shape dialog box.

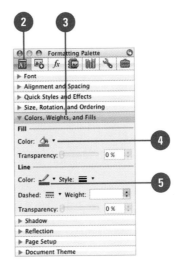

Modifying WordArt Text Position

You can apply a number of text effects to your WordArt objects that determine alignment and direction. The effects of some of the adjustments you make are more pronounced for certain WordArt styles than others. Some of these effects make the text unreadable for certain styles, so apply these effects carefully. You can apply effects to a shape by using the Format Shape dialog box for custom results. You can also use the free rotate handle (green circle) at the top of the selected text box to rotate your WordArt text. In addition, you can use the Rotation button on the Size, Rotation, and Ordering panel on the Formatting Palette tab to rotate your WordArt text left or right or flip it.

Change WordArt Text Direction

1. Option-click the WordArt object you want to change, and then click **Format Shape** or **Format WordArt**.

2. If necessary, click **Text Box** in the left pane.

3. Click the **Vertical alignment** or **Horizontal alignment** list arrow, and then select an option: **Top**, **Middle**, **Bottom**, **Top Center**, **Middle Center**, or **Bottom Center**.

4. Click the **Text direction** list arrow, and then select an option: **Horizontal, Rotate all text 90°, Rotate all text 270°**, or **Stacked**.

5. Click **OK**.

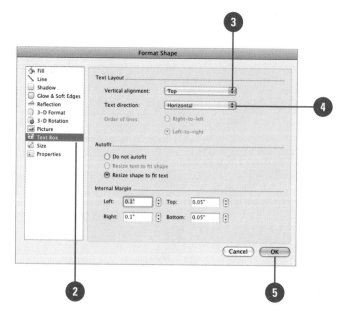

Rotate WordArt Text with Free Rotate

1. Click the WordArt object you want to change.

2. Drag the free rotate handle (green circle) to rotate the object in any direction you want.

3. When you're done, release the mouse button.

4. Click outside the object to deselect it.

Rotate or Flip WordArt Text

1. Click the WordArt object you want to change.

2. Click the **Formatting Palette** tab on the Toolbox.

3. Click the **Size, Rotation, and Ordering** panel to expand it.

4. Click the **Rotation** button arrow, and then click **Rotate Left**, **Rotate Right**, **Flip Horizontal**, or **Flip Vertical**.

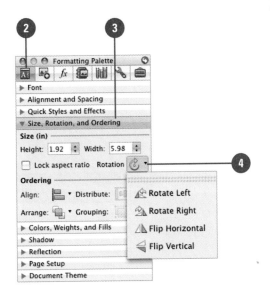

Creating SmartArt Graphics

SmartArt graphics (**New!**) allow you to create diagrams that convey processes or relationships. Office provides a wide variety of built-in SmartArt graphic types, including graphical lists, process, cycle, hierarchy, relationship, matrix, and pyramid. Using built-in SmartArt graphics makes it easy to create and modify charts without having to create them from scratch.

Create a SmartArt Graphic

1. Click the **SmartArt Graphics** tab on the Elements Gallery.

2. Click one of the buttons (All, Recently Used, List, Process, etc.) to display the type of SmartArt style you want.

3. Click one of the SmartArt styles.

   ◆ You can click the arrows on the right to display more styles.

   TIMESAVER *In a PowerPoint content placeholder, you can click the SmartArt icon to start.*

   The SmartArt graphic appears in the document.

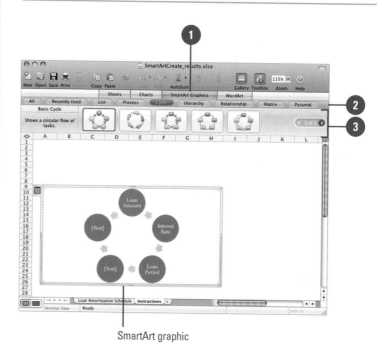

SmartArt graphic

Did You Know?

You can change a SmartArt diagram type. Select the SmartArt graphic, expand the SmartArt Graphics Styles panel, click the Styles tab, click the up or down arrow to display more styles, and then select a diagram type.

You cannot drag text into the Text pane. Although you can't drag text into the Text pane, you can copy and paste text.

You can create a blank SmartArt graphic. In the Text pane, press ⌘+A to select all the placeholder text, and then press Delete.

SmartArt Graphic Purposes

Type	Purpose
List	Show non-sequential information
Process	Show steps in a process or timeline
Cycle	Show a continual process
Hierarchy	Show a decision tree or create an organization chart
Relationship	Illustrate connections
Matrix	Show how parts relate to a whole
Pyramid	Show proportional relationships up and down

④ Click the **Text Pane** button, or click the control with two arrows along the left side of the selection to show the Text pane.

⑤ Label the shapes by doing one of the following:

◆ Type text in the [Text] box.

◆ You can use the arrow keys to move around the Text pane, or use the **Promote** or **Demote** buttons to indent.

◆ At the end of a line, press Return to insert a line (shape), or select line text, and then press Delete to remove a line (shape).

You can use the **Add** or **Delete** buttons to add or remove a line.

◆ Click a shape, and then type text directly into the shape.

⑥ When you're done, click outside of the SmartArt graphic.

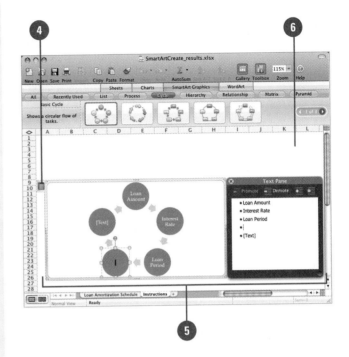

Convert Text to a SmartArt Graphic

① In PowerPoint, select the text box with the text you want to convert to a SmartArt graphic.

② Click the **SmartArt Graphics** tab on the Elements Gallery.

③ Click one of the buttons (All, Recently Used, List, Process, etc.) to display the type of SmartArt style you want.

④ Click one of the SmartArt styles to apply it to the selected text.

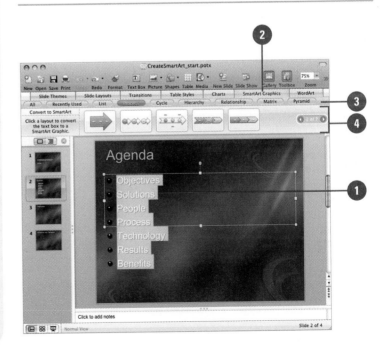

Formatting a SmartArt Graphic

If your current SmartArt graphics don't quite convey the message or look you want, you can change layouts by using the SmartArt Graphic Quick Styles (**New!**) on the Elements Gallery and selecting layout variations on the Styles tab (**New!**). If you only want to change the color, you can choose different color schemes using theme colors by using the Colors tab (**New!**). In addition to modifying shapes, you can also use familiar commands on the Font, and Alignment and Spacing panes on the Formatting Palette tab to format the text in a SmartArt graphic.

Apply a Quick Style to a SmartArt Graphic

1 Click the SmartArt graphic you want to modify.

2 Click the **SmartArt Graphics** tab on the Elements Gallery.

3 Click one of the buttons (All, Recently Used, List, Process, etc.) to display the type of SmartArt style you want.

4 Click the layout for the SmartArt graphic you want from the gallery.

◆ You can click the arrows on the right to display more styles.

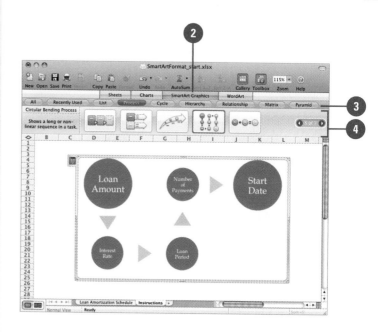

Did You Know?

You can quickly return a SmartArt graphic back to its original form. Select the SmartArt graphic, click the Formatting Palette tab on the Toolbox, expand the SmartArt Graphic Styles pane, and then click the Reset Graphic button.

You can format text in a SmartArt graphic like any other text. Select the text in the SmartArt graphic you want to format, click the Formatting Palette tab on the Toolbox, and then use the formatting options on the Font, and Alignment and Spacing panels.

Change a SmartArt Graphic Layout

1. Click the SmartArt graphic you want to modify.

2. Click the **Styles** tab on the SmartArt Graphics Styles panel.

3. Click the layout for the SmartArt graphic you want from the gallery.

   ◆ You can click the up or down arrow to display more styles.

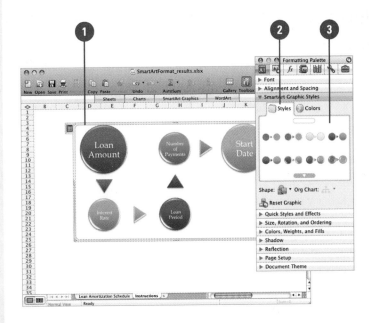

Change a SmartArt Graphic Colors

1. Click the SmartArt graphic you want to modify.

2. Click the **Colors** tab on the SmartArt Graphics Styles panel.

3. Click the color layout for the SmartArt graphic you want from the gallery.

   ◆ You can click the up or down arrow to display more styles.

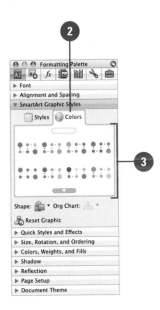

Modifying a SmartArt Graphic

After you create a SmartArt graphic, you can add, remove, change, or rearrange shapes to create a custom look. For shapes within a SmartArt graphic, you can change the shape from the Shape gallery and modify the shape text using familiar commands on the Font, and Alignment and Spacing panes on the Formatting Palette tab to create your own custom SmartArt graphic (**New!**). If you no longer want a shape you've added, simply select it, and then press Delete to remove it.

Add or Delete a Shape to a SmartArt Graphic

1. Select the shape in the SmartArt graphic you want to modify.

2. In the Text Pane, click to place the insertion point, and then click the **Add** or **Delete** button to insert or remove a shape.

   ◆ You can select a shape, and then press Delete to remove it.

   ◆ You can also use the **Promote** or **Demote** buttons to indent the text, which changes the shape position.

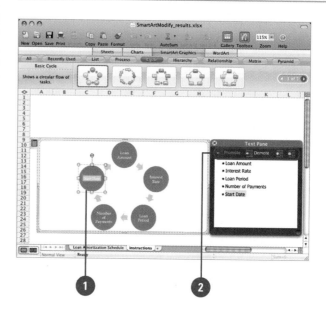

Change Shapes in a SmartArt Graphic

1. Select the shapes in the SmartArt graphic you want to modify.

2. Click the **SmartArt Graphics Styles** panel to expand it.

3. Click the **Shape** button, point to a category, and then click a shape.

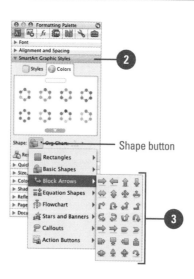

Shape button

Creating an Organization Chart

An organization chart shows the reporting relationships between individuals in an organization. For example, you can show the relationship between a manager and employees within a company. You can create an organization chart using a SmartArt graphic (**New!**) or using Microsoft Organization Chart (in Excel), which is available on the Picture submenu on the Insert. A SmartArt graphic organization chart makes it easy to add shapes using the graphic portion or the Text pane.

Create an Organization Chart Using a SmartArt Graphic

1. Click the **SmartArt Graphics** tab on the Elements Gallery.

2. Click the **Hierarchy** button on the SmartArt Graphics tab.

3. Click one of the SmartArt Hierarchy styles.

   The SmartArt graphic appears with a Text pane to insert text.

4. Label the shapes by doing one of the following:

   ◆ Type text in the [Text] box.

   You can use the arrow keys to move around the Text pane.

   ◆ Click a shape, and then type text directly into the shape.

5. To add shapes from the Text pane, place the insertion point at the beginning of the text where you want to add a shape, type the text you want, press Return, and then to indent the new shape, press Tab or to promote, press Shift+Tab.

   You can also click the **Org Chart** button on the **SmartArt Graphic Styles** panel, and then select the type of shape you want to add.

6. When you're done, click outside of the SmartArt graphic.

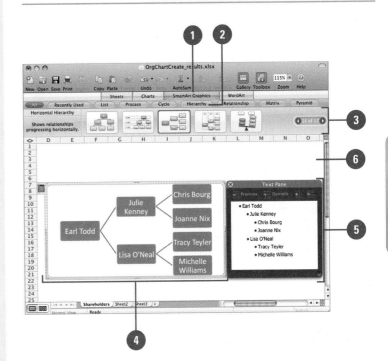

Modifying an Organization Chart

Like any SmartArt graphic, you can add special effects—such as soft edges, glows, or 3-D effects, and animation—to an organization chart. If your organization chart doesn't quite look the way you want, you can change layouts by using the SmartArt Graphic Quick Styles (**New!**) on the Elements Gallery and selecting layout variations on the Styles tab (**New!**). If you only want to change the color, you can choose different color schemes using theme colors by using the Colors tab (**New!**).

Change the Layout or Apply a Quick Style to an Organization Chart

1. Click the SmartArt graphic you want to modify.

2. Click the **Styles** tab on the SmartArt Graphics Styles panel.

3. Click the layout for the SmartArt graphic you want from the gallery.

   ◆ You can click the up or down arrow to display more styles.

4. Click the **Colors** tab on the SmartArt Graphics Styles panel.

5. Click the color layout for the SmartArt graphic you want from the gallery.

   ◆ You can click the up or down arrow to display more styles.

Did You Know?

You can change organization chart lines. Double-click the line you want to modify, click the Solid, Gradient, or Weights & Arrows tab, specify the options you want, such as color, transparency, weights, and dashes, and then click OK.

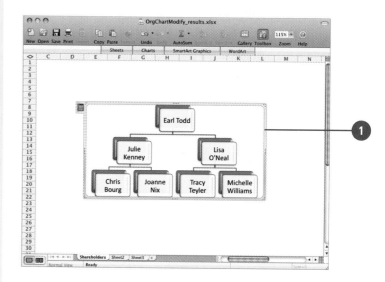

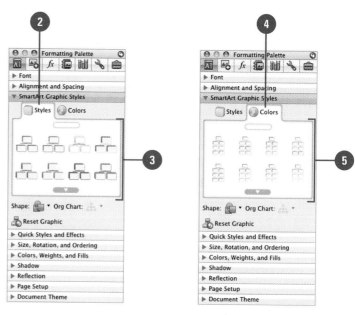

Inserting and Creating a Chart

A **chart** provides a visual, graphical representation of numerical data. Charts add visual interest and useful information represented by lines, bars, pie slices, or other markers. A group of data values from a worksheet row or column of data makes up a **data series**. Each data series has a unique color or pattern on the chart. Titles on the chart, horizontal (x-axis), and vertical (y-axis) identify the data. Gridlines are horizontal and vertical lines to help the reader determine data values in a chart. When you choose to place the chart on an existing sheet, rather than on a new sheet, the chart is called an **embedded object**. You can then resize or move it just as you would any graphic object. Office 2008 programs now use Microsoft Excel (**New!**) to embed and display a chart instead of Microsoft Graph.

Insert and Create a Chart

1. Select the data you want to use to create a chart (Excel).

2. Click the **Charts** tab on the Elements Gallery.

3. Click one of the tabs (**All, Area, Bar, Bubble, Column, Doughnut, Line, Pie, Radar, Stock, Surface, X Y (Scatter)**) to display the type of Chart style you want.

4. Click one of the Chart styles.

   ◆ You can click the arrows on the right to display more styles.

   Microsoft Excel opens (from Word or PowerPoint), displaying sample data, which you can change.

5. Use Excel commands to import or enter the chart data you want.

6. If you inserted the chart from Word or PowerPoint, switch back.

   A chart appears on the document as an embedded chart.

7. To delete the chart, select it, and then press Delete.

8. To create a chart sheet (Excel), click the **Insert** menu, point to **Sheet**, and then click **Chart Sheet**.

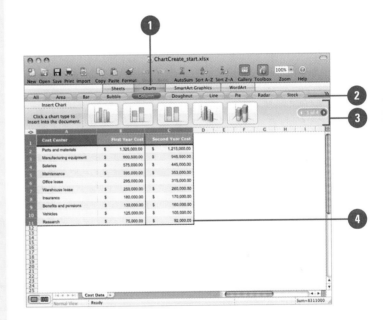

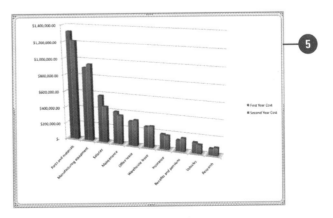

Changing a Chart Type

Your chart is what your audience sees, so make sure to take advantage of Office's pre-built chart layouts and styles (**New!**) to make the chart appealing and visually informative. Start by choosing the chart type that is best suited for presenting your data. There are a wide variety chart types, available in 2-D and 3-D formats, from which to choose. For each chart type, you can select a predefined chart layout and style to apply the formatting you want. If you want to format your chart beyond the provided formats, you can customize a chart. Save your customized settings so that you can apply that chart formatting to any chart you create. You can change the chart type for the entire chart, or you can change the chart type for a selected data series to create a combination chart.

Change a Chart Type for an Entire Chart

1. Select the chart you want to change.

2. Click the **Charts** tab on the Elements Gallery.

3. Click one of the tabs (**All**, **Area**, **Bar**, **Bubble**, **Column**, **Doughnut**, **Line**, **Pie**, **Radar**, **Stock**, **Surface**, **X Y (Scatter)**) to display the type of Chart style you want.

4. Click the layout for the chart you want from the gallery.

   ◆ You can click the arrows on the right to display more styles.

Did You Know?

You can delete a chart. Click the chart object, and then press Delete.

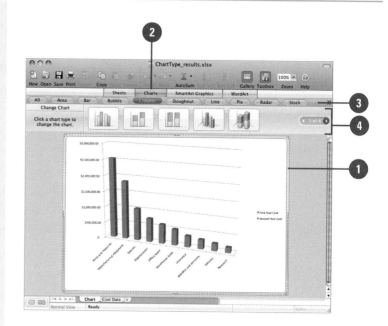

Changing a Chart Layout Style

Office's pre-built chart layout styles (**New!**) can make your chart more appealing and visually informative. Start by choosing the chart type that is best suited for presenting your data. There are a wide variety chart types, available in 2-D and 3-D formats, from which to choose. For each chart type, you can select a predefined chart layout style to apply the formatting you want. If you want to format your chart beyond the provided formats, you can customize a chart. Save your customized settings so that you can apply that chart formatting to any chart you create.

Change a Chart Layout or Chart Element Style

1. Select the chart you want to change.

2. Click the **Chart Style** panel to expand it.

3. Click the layout style for the chart you want from the gallery.

   ◆ You can click the up or down arrow to display more styles.

4. Select the chart element, such as a title or data series, you want to change.

5. Click the **Quick Styles and Effects** panel to expand it.

6. Click one of the tabs (Quick Styles, Shadows, Glows, Reflections, 3-D Effects, or text transformation).

7. Click the style for the chart element you want from the gallery.

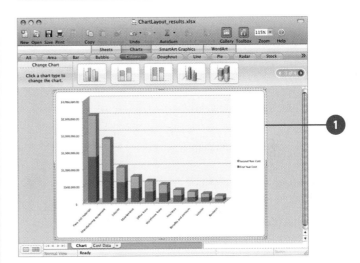

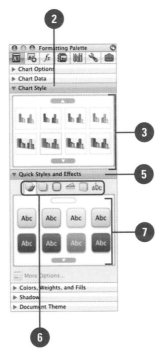

Changing Chart Titles

The layout of a chart typically comes with a chart title, axis titles, and a legend. However, you can also include other elements, such as data labels, and a data table. You can show, hide, or change the positions of these elements to achieve the look you want. The chart title typically appears at the top of the chart. However, you can change the title position to appear as an overlap text object on top of the chart. When you position the chart title as an overlay, the chart is resized to the maximum allowable size. In the same way, you can also reposition horizontal and vertical axis titles to achieve the best fit in a chart. If you want a more custom look, you can set individual options using the Format dialog box.

Change Chart Title

1. Select the chart you want to modify.

2. Click the **Chart Options** panel to expand it.

3. Click **Titles** drop-down, and then click one of the following:

   ◆ **Chart Title** to insert a title on the chart.

   ◆ **Horizontal (Category) Axis** to insert a title on the horizontal axis of the chart.

   ◆ **Vertical (Value) Axis** to insert a title on the vertical axis of the chart.

4. Click the text box to place the insertion point, and then modify the text.

Did You Know?

You can link a chart or axis title to a worksheet cell. On the chart, click the chart or axis title you want to link, click in the formula bar, type equal sign (=), select the worksheet cell that contains the data or text you want to display in the chart, and then press Return.

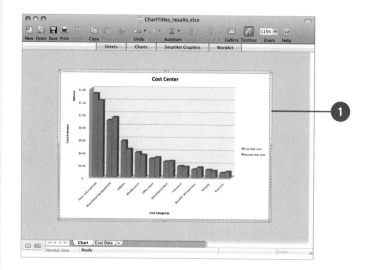

Changing Chart Labels

A **legend** is a set of text labels that helps the reader connect the colors and patterns in a chart with the data they represent. Legend text is derived from the data series plotted within a chart. You can rename an item within a legend by changing the text in the data series. If the legend chart location doesn't work with the chart type, you can reposition the legend at the right, left, top or bottom of the chart or overlay the legend on top of the chart on the right or left side. **Data labels** show data values in the chart to make it easier for the reader to see, while a Data table shows the data values in an associated table next to the chart. If you want a customized look, you can set individual options using the Format dialog box.

Change the Chart Legend, Labels, and Other Options

1. Select the chart you want to modify.

2. Click the **Chart Options** panel to expand it.

3. Click any of the following buttons to show axis: Primary Vertical Axis, Primary Horizontal Axis, Depth Axis, Secondary Vertical Axis, and Secondary Horizontal Axis.

4. Click any of the buttons for the major and minor gridlines.

5. Click **Labels** drop-down, and then click one of the following:

   ◆ **None** to hide the labels on the chart elements.

   ◆ **Value** to display labels on the vertical axis chart elements.

   ◆ **Category Name** to display labels on the horizontal axis chart elements.

6. Click **Legend** drop-down, and then click one of the following: **None**, **Bottom**, **Top Right**, **Top**, **Right**, and **Left**.

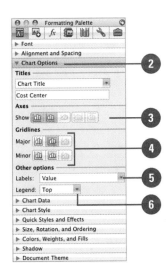

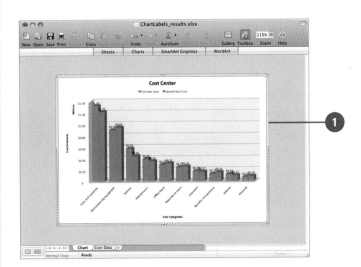

Editing Chart Data

You can edit chart data in a worksheet one cell at a time, or you can manipulate a range of data. If you're not sure what data to change to get the results you want, use the Edit Data Source dialog box to help you. You can work with data ranges by series, either row or column, which you can switch around. The Row series is the data range displayed on one axis, while the Column series is the data range displayed on the other axis. Use the Collapse Dialog button to temporarily minimize the dialog to select the data range you want. After you select your data, click the Expand Dialog button to return back to the dialog box.

Edit the Data Source

1 Click the chart you want to modify.

2 Click the **Chart Data** panel to expand it.

3 Click the **Edit in Excel** button.

4 In the Select Data Source dialog box, use any of the following:

- ◆ **Chart data range.** Displays the data range of the plotted chart.

- ◆ **Switch Row/Column.** Click to switch plotting the data series from rows or columns.

- ◆ **Add.** Click to add a new Legend data series to the chart.

- ◆ **Remove.** Click to remove the selected Legend data series.

5 Click **OK**.

Did You Know?

You can sort data by row or column. Select the chart, expand the Chart Data panel, and then click Row or Column button.

You can display a data table along with the chart. Select the chart, expand the Chart Data panel, and then click Data Table drop-down, and then select Data Table or Data Table with Legend Keys.

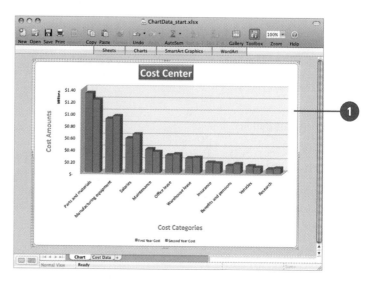

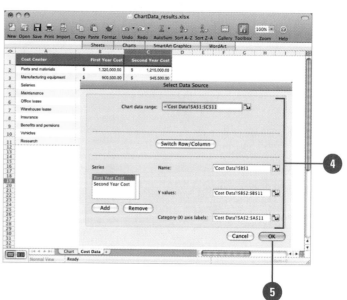

Sharing Information Between Programs

Office can convert data or text from one format to another using a technology known as **object linking and embedding (OLE)**. OLE allows you to move text or data between programs in much the same way as you move them within a program. The familiar cut and paste or drag and drop methods work between programs and documents just as they do within a document. In addition, all Office programs have special ways to move information from one program to another, including importing, exporting, embedding, linking, and hyperlinking.

Importing and Exporting

Importing and exporting information are two sides of the same coin. **Importing** copies a file created with the same or another program into your open file. The information becomes part of your open file, just as if you created it in that format. Some formatting and program-specific information such as formulas may be lost. **Exporting** converts a copy of your open file into the file type of another program. In other words, importing brings information into your open document, while exporting moves information from your open document into another program file.

Embedding

Embedding inserts a copy of a file created in one program into a file created in another program. Unlike imported files, you can edit the information in embedded files with the same commands and toolbar buttons used to create the original file. The original file is called the **source file**, while the file in which it is embedded is called the **destination file**. Any changes you make to an embedded object appear only in the destination file; the source file remains unchanged.

For example, if you place an Excel chart into a PowerPoint presentation, Excel is the source program, and PowerPoint is the destination program. The chart is the source file; the document is the destination file.

Linking

Linking displays information from one file (the source file) in a file created in another program (the destination file). You can view and edit the linked object from either the source file or the destination file. The changes are stored in the source file but also appear in the destination file. As you work, Office updates the linked object to ensure you always have the most current information. Office keeps track of all the drive, folder, and file name information for a source file. However, if you move or rename the source file, the link between files will break.

Once the link is broken, the information in the destination file becomes embedded rather than linked. In other words, changes to one copy of the file will no longer affect the other.

Embedding and Linking	
Term	**Definition**
Source program	The program that created the original object
Source file	The file that contains the original object
Destination program	The program that created the document into which you are inserting the object
Destination file	The file into which you are inserting the object

Linking and Embedding Objects

Information created using other Office programs can be shared among them. This means that data created in an Office document, and can be included in a Excel worksheet without being retyped. This makes projects such as annual or departmental reports simple to create. Information can be either **linked** or **embedded**. Data that is linked has the advantage of always being accurate because it is automatically updated when the linked document is modified.

Create a Link to Another File

1. Open the source file and any files containing information you want to link.

2. Select the information in the source file.

3. Click the **Edit** menu, and then click **Copy**.

4. Click the insertion point in the file containing the link.

5. Click the **Edit** menu, and then click **Paste Special**.

6. Click **Paste Link**.

Did You Know?

You can edit an embedded object. Edit an embedded object only if the program that created it is installed on your computer.

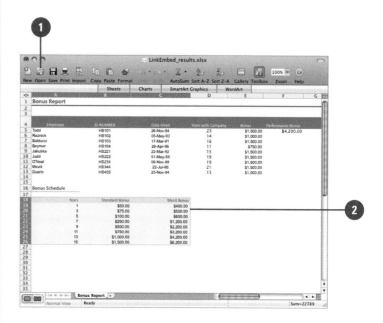

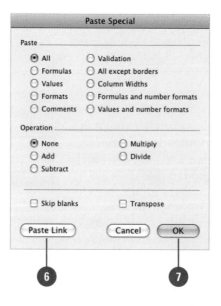

Embed a New Object

1. Click the **Insert** menu, and then click **Object**.

2. Click the object type you want to insert.

3. To display the object as an icon, select the **Display as icon** check box.

4. Click **OK**.

5. Follow the necessary steps to insert the object.

   The steps will vary depending on the object type.

Embed or Link to an Existing Object

1. Click the **Insert** menu, and then click **Object**.

2. Click **From File**.

3. Click the **Where** drop-down, and then select the location that contains the file you want.

4. Select the file that you want to link.

5. To create a link to the object, select the **Link to File** check box.

6. To display the object as an icon, select the **Display as icon** check box.

7. Click **OK**.

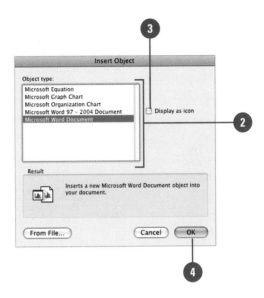

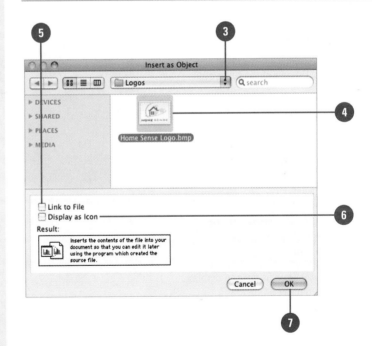

Flagging Documents for Follow Up

If you have an Office document that you need to work on later or get feedback from a co-worker, you can flag the document for follow up as an Entourage task. You can use the Office Reminder program to schedule a date and time for a pop-up reminder. When the date and time for the reminder takes place, the Office Reminder window appears—even if Office isn't running—displaying options to dismiss the reminder, dismiss all reminders, snooze the reminder for a short period of time, open the item, or do nothing.

Flag a Document for Follow Up

1. Open the Office document that you want to flag for follow up.

2. Click the **Tools** menu, and then click **Follow Up**.

3. Specify the date and time at which you want to get a reminder.

4. Click **OK**.

   The flagged document is setup for follow up as a new Entourage task.

5. At the designated date and time, the Office Reminder window appears. Do one of the following:

   ◆ **Complete.** Select the **Complete** check box to indicate the task is done or clear it to leave the task as incomplete.

   ◆ **Dismiss.** Click **Dismiss** to remove the reminder.

   ◆ **Dismiss All.** Click and hold **Dismiss**, and then click **Dismiss All** to remove all listed reminders.

   ◆ **Snooze.** Click **Snooze** to display the reminder again in the specified time.

   ◆ **Open the item.** Double-click the document name in the reminder to open and edit the item.

   ◆ **Do nothing.** Click the **Close** button to exit the Office Reminder window.

Select when follow up is complete

Adding Shapes to Office Documents

4

Introduction

When you want to add objects to a document, you can use Microsoft Office as a drawing package. Office provides a wide range of predesigned shapes, line options or freeform tools that allow you to draw, size, and format your own shapes and forms.

You can add several types of drawing objects to your Office documents—shapes, text boxes, lines, and freeforms. **Shapes** are preset objects, such as stars, circles, or ovals. **Text boxes** are objects with text, a shape without a border. **Lines** are simply the straight or curved lines (arcs) that can connect two points or are used as arrows. **Freeforms** are irregular curves or polygons that you can create as a free-hand drawing.

Once you create a drawing object, you can move, resize, nudge, copy or delete it on your documents. You can also change its style by adding color, creating a fill pattern, rotating it, and applying a shadow or 3-D effect. Take a simple shape and by the time you are done adding various effects, it could become an attractive piece of graphic art for your document. If you'd like to use it later, you can save it to the Clip Organizer.

Object placement on your documents is a key factor to successfully communicating your message. To save time and effort, multiple objects should be grouped if they are to be considered one larger object. Grouping helps you make changes later on, or copy your objects to another document. Office has the ability to line up your objects with precision—rulers and guides are part of the alignment process to help you. By grouping and aligning, you are assured that your drawing objects will be accurately placed.

Drawing and Resizing Shapes

Office supplies ready-made shapes, ranging from hearts to lightning bolts to stars. The ready-made shapes are available directly on the Shapes gallery on the Insert and Format tabs. Once you have placed a shape on a document, you can resize it using the sizing handles. Many shapes have an **adjustment handle**, a small yellow or pink diamond located near a resize handle that you can drag to alter the shape. For precision when resizing, use the Format AutoShape dialog box to specify the new size of the shape.

Draw a Shape

1. Click the **Object Palette** tab on the Toolbox.

2. Click the **Shapes** tab.

3. To narrow down the list of shapes, click the drop-down, and then select a category.

4. Click the shape you want to draw.

5. Drag the pointer on the document where you want to place the shape until the drawing object is the shape and size that you want.

   The shape you draw uses the line and fill color defined by the document's theme.

   TIMESAVER *To draw a proportional shape, hold down Shift as you drag the pointer.*

Did You Know?

You can quickly delete a shape. Click the shape to select it, and then press Delete.

You can draw a perfect circle or square. To draw a perfect circle or square, click the Oval or Rectangle button on the Shapes gallery, and then press and hold Shift as you drag.

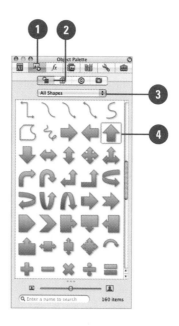

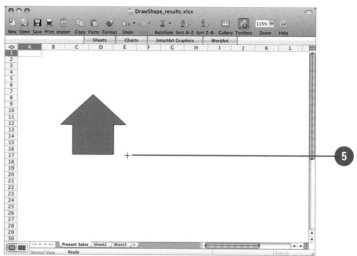

Resize a Shape

① Select the shape you want to resize.

② Drag one of the sizing handles.

◆ To resize the object in the vertical or horizontal direction, drag a sizing handle on the side of the selection box.

◆ To resize the object in both the vertical and horizontal directions, drag a sizing handle on the corner of the selection box.

◆ To resize the object with precise measurements, click the **Format** menu, click **AutoShape**, click the **Size** tab, specify exact height and width settings, and then click **OK**.

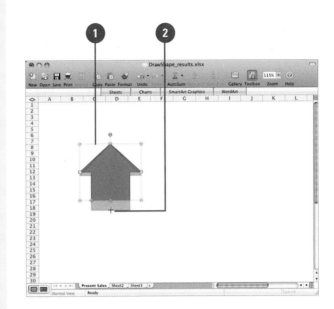

Adjust a Shape

① Select the shape you want to adjust.

② Click one of the adjustment handles (small yellow diamonds), and then drag the handle to alter the form of the shape.

Did You Know?

You can connect two shapes. Click the Object Palette tab on the Toolbox, click the Shadows tab, click a connector (located in the Lines and Connector category), position the pointer over an object handle (turns red), drag the connector to the object handle (turns red) on another object. An attached connector point appears as red circles, while an unattached connector point appears as light blue.

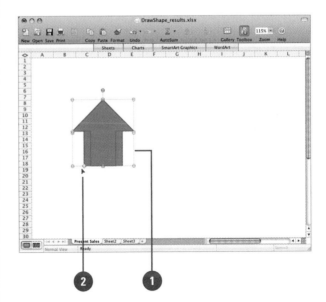

Creating and Editing Freeforms

When you need to create a customized shape, use the Office freeform tools. Choose a freeform tool from the Lines category in the list of shapes. Freeforms are like the drawings you make with a pen and paper, except that you use a mouse for your pen and a document for your paper. A freeform shape can either be an open curve or a closed curve. You can edit a freeform by using the Edit Points command to alter the vertices that create the shape.

Draw a Freeform Polygon

1. Click the **Object Palette** tab on the Toolbox.

2. Click the **Shapes** tab.

3. Click the drop-down, and then click **Lines and Connectors**.

4. Click the freeform connector shape you want.

5. Click the document where you want to place the first vertex of the polygon.

6. Move the pointer, and then click to place the second point of the polygon. A line joins the two points.

   ◆ To draw a line with curves, drag a line instead of clicking in steps 5 and 6.

7. Continue moving the mouse pointer and clicking to create additional sides of your polygon.

8. Finish the polygon. For a closed polygon, click near the starting point. For an open polygon, double-click the last point in the polygon.

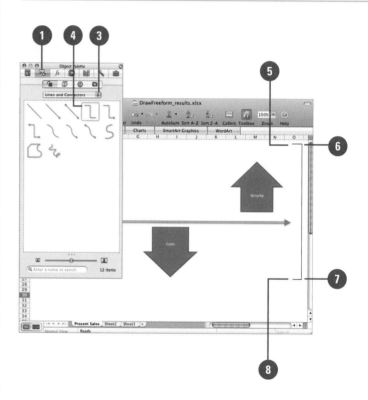

For Your Information

Modifying a Freeform Polygon

Each vertex indicated by a black dot (a corner in an irregular polygon and a bend in a curve) has two attributes: its position, and the angle at which the curve enters and leaves it. You can move the position of each vertex and control the corner or bend angles. You can also add or delete vertices as you like. When you delete a vertex, Office recalculates the freeform and smooths it among the remaining points. Similarly, if you add a new vertex, Office adds a corner or bend in your freeform. To edit a freeform, Control-click the freeform object, click Edit Points, modify any of the points (move or delete), and then click outside to set the new shape.

Adding Text to a Shape

You can add text to a shape in the same way you add text to a text box. Simply, select the shape object, and then start typing. Shapes range from rectangles and circles to arrows and stars. When you place text in a shape, the text becomes part of the object. If you rotate or flip the shape, the text rotates or flips too. You can use tools, such as an alignment button or Font Style, on the Font and Alignment and Spacing panels to format the text in a shape like the text in a text box.

Add Text to a Shape

1. Select the shape in which you want to add text.

2. Type the text you want.

3. To edit the text in a shape, click the text to place the insertion point, and then edit the text.

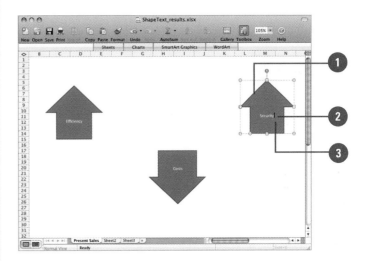

Adding a Quick Style to a Shape

Instead of changing individual attributes of a shape—such as shape fill, shape outline, and shape effects—you can quickly add them all at once with the Shape Quick Style gallery. The Shape Quick Style gallery (**New!**) provides a variety of different formatting combinations.

Add a Quick Style to a Shape

1. Select the shapes you want to modify.

2. Click the **Formatting Palette** tab on the Toolbox.

3. Click the **Quick Styles** tab on the Quick Styles and Effects panel.

4. Click the scroll up or down arrows to see additional styles.

   The current style appears highlighted in the gallery.

5. Click the style you want from the gallery to apply it to the selected shape.

Did You Know?

You can add a Quick Style to a text box. A shape is a text box without a fill and outline (border), so you can apply a Quick Style to a text box using the same steps.

See Also

See "Adding Other Effects to a Shape" on page 118 for information on applying other effects using the Quick Styles and Effects panel.

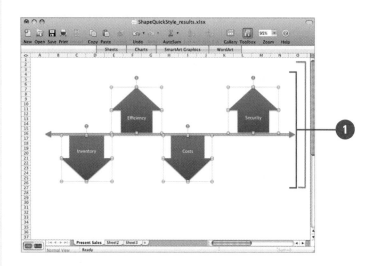

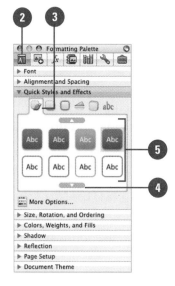

Adding a Quick Style to Shape Text

Instead of changing individual attributes of text in a shape, such as text fill, text outline, and text effects, you can quickly add them all at once with the WordArt Quick Style gallery. The WordArt Quick Style gallery (**New!**) provides a variety of different formatting combinations.

Add a Quick Style to Shape Text

1 Select the shapes with the text you want to modify.

2 In Excel or PowerPoint, click the **WordArt** tab on the Elements Gallery.

3 Click the **2-D Styles** or **3-D Styles** button to display the type of WordArt style you want.

4 Click one of the WordArt styles.

◆ You can click the arrows on the right to display more styles.

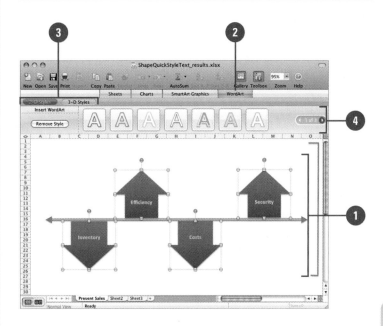

Adding Other Effects to a Shape

You can change the look of a shape by applying effects (**New!**), like shadows, reflections, glow, soft edges, bevels, and 3-D rotations. Apply effects to a shape by using the Shape Effects gallery for quick results, or by using the Format Shape dialog box for custom results. From the Shape Effects gallery you can apply a built-in combination of 3-D effects or individual effects to a shape. If you no longer want to apply a shape effect to an object, you can use undo to remove it.

Add Individual Effects to a Shape

1. Select the shape you want to modify.

2. Click the **Formatting Palette** tab on the Toolbox.

3. Click the **Quick Styles and Effects** panel to expand it.

4. Click the one of the following sub-tabs to display an effect:

   ◆ **Shadows** to select one of the shadow types.

   ◆ **Glows** to select one of the glow variations.

   ◆ **Reflections** to select one of the reflection variations.

   ◆ **3-D Effects** to select one of the 3-D variations.

   ◆ **Text Transformations** to select one of the WordArt variations.

See Also

See "Adding a Quick Style to a Shape" on page 116 for information on applying a quick style using the Quick Styles and Effects panel.

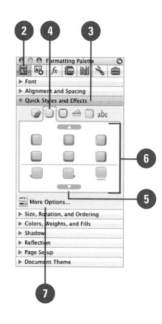

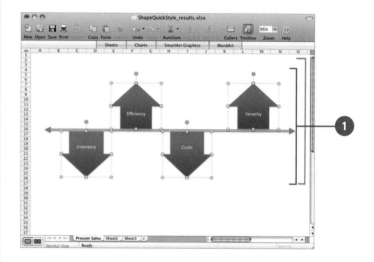

5 Click the scroll up or down arrows to see additional styles.

6 Click the effect you want from the gallery to apply it to the selected shape.

7 To specify additional shape options, click **More Options**, select the options you want, and then click **OK**.

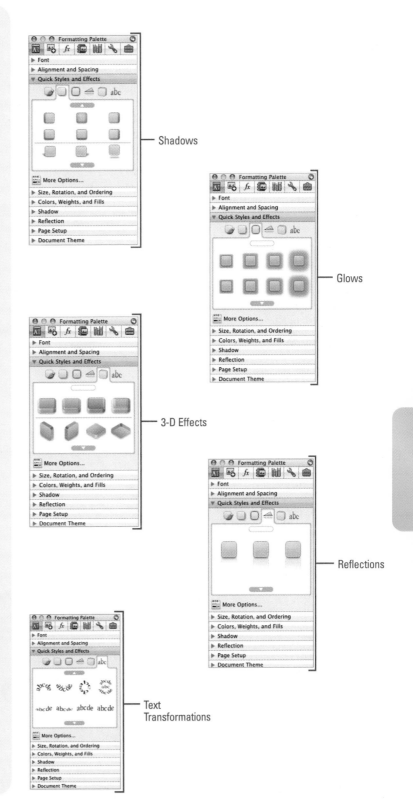

Shadows

Glows

3-D Effects

Reflections

Text Transformations

Applying Color Fills

When you create a closed drawing object such as a square, it applies the Fill color to the inside of the shape, and the Line color to the edge of the shape. A line drawing object uses the Line color. You can set the Fill to be a solid, gradient, texture or picture, and the Line can be a solid or pattern. If you want to make multiple changes to a shape at the same time, the Format AutoShape or Shape Format dialog box allows you to do everything in one place. If the solid color appears too dark, you can make the color fill more transparent. If you no longer want to apply a shape fill to an object, you can remove it.

Apply a Fill Color to a Shape

1. Select the shape you want to modify.

2. Click the **Formatting Palette** tab on the Toolbox.

3. Click the **Colors, Weights, and Fills** panel to expand it.

4. Click the **Fill Color** button.

5. Select the fill color option you want.

6. To remove a color fill, click the **Fill Color** button, and then click **No Fill**.

Did You Know?

You can set the color and line style for an object as the default. Control-click the object, and then click Set AutoShape Defaults. Any new objects you create will use the same styles.

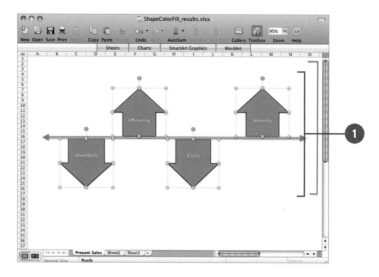

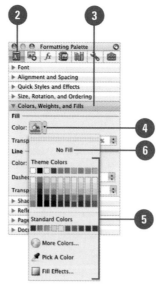

Apply a Shape Fill Color with a Transparency

1. Select the shape you want to modify.

2. Click the **Formatting Palette** tab on the Toolbox.

3. Click the **Colors, Weights, and Fills** panel to expand it.

4. For the Fill or Line color, drag the **Transparency** slider or enter a number from 0 (fully opaque) to 100 (fully transparent).

   All your changes are instantly applied to the shape.

   TROUBLE? *To cancel changes, click the Undo button on the Standard toolbar.*

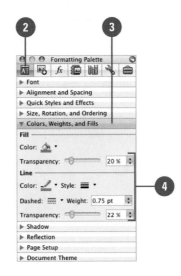

Apply a Line Color to a Shape

1. Select the shape you want to modify.

2. Click the **Formatting Palette** tab on the Toolbox.

3. Click the **Colors, Weights, and Fills** panel to expand it.

4. Click the **Line Color** button.

5. Select the line color option you want.

6. To format a line, click the **Style** or **Dashed** button, select a line style, and then specify the Weight you want for the line.

7. To remove a color fill, click the **Line Color** button, and then click **No Line**.

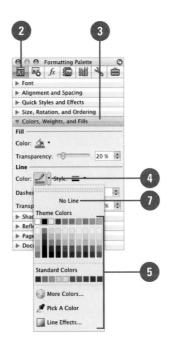

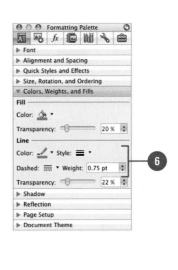

Applying Picture or Texture Fills

Applying a shape fill to a drawing object can add emphasis or create a point of interest in your document. You can insert a picture or texture into a shape. You can insert a picture from a file, or paste one in from the Clipboard. Stretch a picture or texture to fit across the selected shape or repeatedly tile it horizontally and vertically to fill the shape. If the image appears too dark, you can make the picture more transparent. You can also set an option to have the picture or texture rotate with the shape.

Apply a Picture or Texture Fill to a Shape

1. Select the shape you want to modify.

2. Click the **Formatting Palette** tab on the Toolbox.

3. Click the **Colors, Weights, and Fills** panel to expand it.

4. Click the **Fill Color** button, and then click **Fill Effects**.

5. Select the fill color option you want.

   ◆ Click the **Picture** tab, click **Choose a Picture**, locate and select a picture file you want, and then click **Insert**.

   ◆ Click the **Texture** tab, and then select a texture.

6. Drag the **Transparency** slider or enter a number from 0 (fully opaque) to 100 (fully transparent).

7. To have the picture or texture rotate with the shape, either select the **Rotate picture with shape** check box, or select the **Rotate texture with shape** check box.

   ◆ For picture, select the **Tile** check box to tile the picture in the shape or clear it to stretch the picture in the shape.

8. Click **OK**.

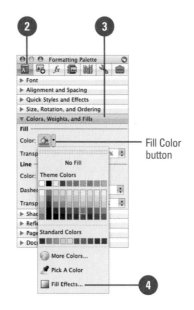

Fill Color button

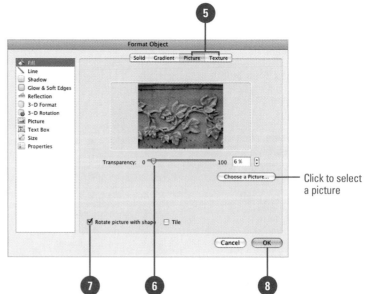

Click to select a picture

Applying Gradient Fills

Gradients are made up of two or more colors that gradually fade into each other. They can be used to give depth to a shape or create realistic shadows. Apply a gradient fill to a shape by using a gallery or presets for quick results, or by using the Format Shape dialog box for custom results. A gradient is made up of several gradient stops, which are used to create non-linear gradients. If you want to create a gradient that starts blue and goes to green, add two gradient stops, one for each color. Gradient stops consist of a position, a color, and a transparency percentage.

Apply a Gradient Fill to a Shape

1. Select the shape you want to modify.

2. Click the **Formatting Palette** tab on the Toolbox.

3. Click the **Colors, Weights, and Fills** panel to expand it.

4. Click the **Fill Color** button, and then click **Fill Effects**.

5. Click the **Gradient** tab.

6. Click the **Style** drop-down, and then select a gradient style: linear (parallel bands), radial (radiate from center), rectangle (radiate from corners), and path (radiate along path).

   ◆ If available, click the **Direction** drop-down, and then select a gradient direction.

7. To add another color to the gradient, click the **Color** drop-down, and then select a gradient color.

   ◆ Click **Add Color** or **Delete Color** to add or delete the selected color.

8. Drag the triangle slider to adjust the gradient.

9. Drag the **Transparency** slider or enter a number from 0 (fully opaque) to 100 (fully transparent).

10. Click **OK**.

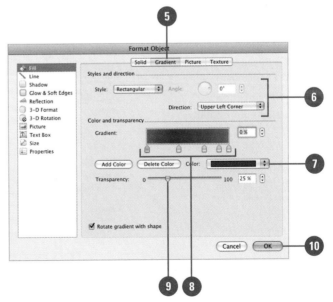

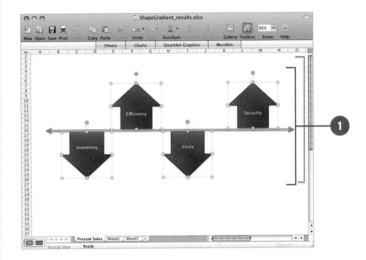

Aligning and Distributing Objects

In addition to using grids and guides to align objects to a specific point, you can align a group of objects to each other. The Align and Distribute commands make it easy to align two or more objects relative to each other or to the page. To evenly align several objects to each other across the document, either horizontally or vertically, select them and then choose a distribution option. Before you select an align command, specify how you want Office to align the objects. You can align the objects in relation to the document or to the selected objects.

Distribute Objects

1. Select the objects you want to distribute.

2. Click the **Formatting Palette** tab on the Toolbox.

3. Click the **Size, Rotation, and Ordering** panel to expand it.

4. Click the **Distribute** button.

5. On the Distribute menu, click the alignment method you want.

   ◆ Click **Align to Page** (Word) or **Align to Slide** (PowerPoint) to check the item if you want the objects to align relative to the page or slide. Click the command to uncheck the item if you want the objects to align related to each other.

6. On the Distribute submenu, click the distribution command you want.

   ◆ Click **Distribute Horizontally** to evenly distribute the objects horizontally.

   ◆ Click **Distribute Vertically** to evenly distribute the objects vertically.

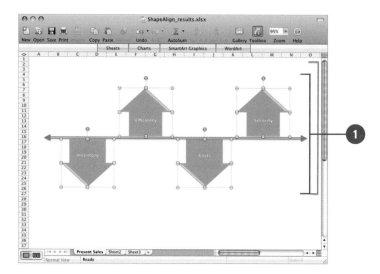

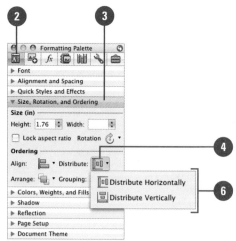

Align Objects with Other Objects

1. Select the objects you want to align.

2. Click the **Formatting Palette** tab on the Toolbox.

3. Click the **Size, Rotation, and Ordering** panel expand it.

4. Click the **Align** button.

5. On the Align menu, click the alignment method you want.

   ◆ Click **Align to Page** (Word) or **Align to Slide** (PowerPoint) to check the item if you want the objects to align relative to the page or slide. Click the command to uncheck the item if you want the objects to align related to each other.

6. On the Align menu, click the alignment command you want.

   ◆ Click **Align Left** to line up the objects with the left edge of the selection or document.

   ◆ Click **Align Center** to line up the objects with the center of the selection or document.

   ◆ Click **Align Right** to line up the objects with the right edge of the selection or document.

   ◆ Click **Align Top** to line up the objects with the top edge of the selection or document.

   ◆ Click **Align Middle** to line up the objects vertically with the middle of the selection or document.

   ◆ Click **Align Bottom** to line up the objects with the bottom of the selection or document.

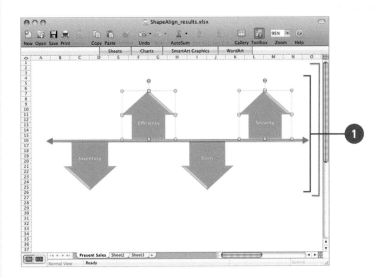

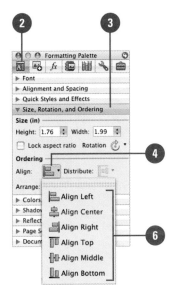

Aligning Objects to Grids and Guides

PowerPoint guides can align an individual object or a group of objects to a vertical or horizontal guide. Using guides makes it easier to create, modify, and align a shape. You can use dynamic or static guides. Dynamic guides (**New!**) appear as you need them when you drag an object, while static guides appear when you enable them. You can select from a variety of options, such as snapping objects to the grid or to other objects and displaying drawing guides on-screen. To align several objects to a guide, you first turn the guides on. Then you adjust the guides and drag the objects to align them to the guide.

Turn On or Turn Off Guides and Set Objects to Snap into Place

1. In PowerPoint, click the **View** menu, and then point to **Guides**.

2. On the menu, click the guide command you want.

   ◆ **Dynamic Guides.** A check mark indicates the guide is turned on; no check mark indicates the guide is turned off.

   ◆ **Static Guides.** A check mark indicates the guide is turned on; no check mark indicates the guide is turned off.

   TIMESAVER *To quickly turn the static guide on and off, press* ⌘+G.

3. On the menu, click the snap to method you want.

   ◆ **Snap to Grid.** Snaps an object to an invisible grid on the slide.

   ◆ **Snap to Shape.** Snaps an object to another shape.

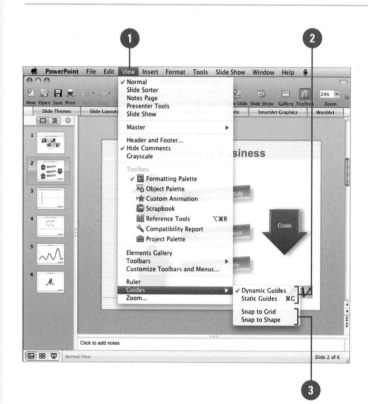

Add, Move, or Remove a Static Guide

◆ To move a guide, drag it.

◆ To add a new guide, press and hold the Option key, and then drag the line to the new location. You can place a guide anywhere on the slide.

◆ To remove a guide, drag the guide off the slide. You cannot remove the original guides, they must be turned off.

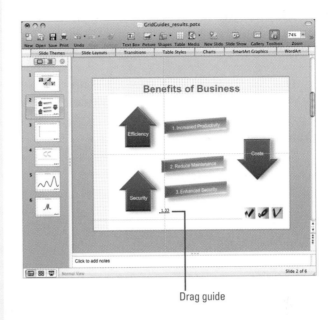

Drag guide

Align an Object to a Guide

1. If necessary, enable (to display) static guides on the screen (horizontal and vertical), or enable dynamic guides.

2. Drag the object's center or edge near the guide. PowerPoint aligns the center or edge to the guide.

Did You Know?

You can use the keyboard to override grid settings. To temporarily override settings for the grids and guides, press and hold the Option key as you drag an object.

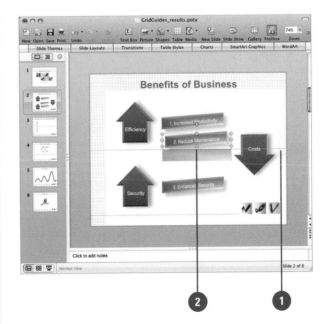

Changing Stacking Order

Multiple objects on a document appear in a stacking order, like layers of transparencies. Stacking is the placement of objects one on top of another. In other words, the first object that you draw is on the bottom and the last object that you draw is on top. You can change the order of this stack of objects by using Bring to Front, Send to Back, Bring Forward, and Send Backward commands on the Arrange button on the Size, Rotation, and Ordering panel.

Arrange a Stack of Objects

1. Select the objects you want to arrange.

2. Click the **Formatting Palette** tab on the Toolbox.

3. Click the **Size, Rotation, and Ordering** panel expand it.

4. Click the **Arrange** button.

5. On the Arrange menu, click the stacking method you want.

   ◆ **Bring to Front.** Moves a drawing to the top of the stack.

   ◆ **Bring to Back.** Moves a drawing to the bottom of the stack.

   ◆ **Send Forward.** Moves a drawing up one location in the stack.

   ◆ **Send Backward.** Moves a drawing down one location in the stack.

Did You Know?

You can view a hidden object in a stack. Press the Tab key or Shift+Tab to cycle forward or backward through the objects until you select the object you want.

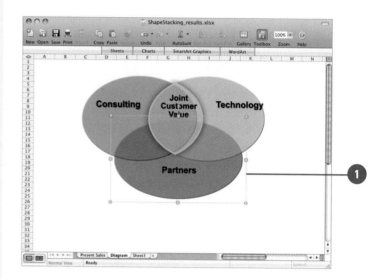

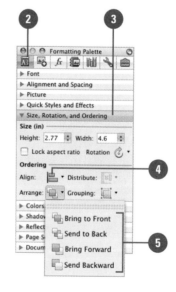

Rotating and Flipping Objects

After you create an object, you can change its orientation on the document by rotating or flipping it. Rotating turns an object 90 degrees to the right or left; flipping turns an object 180 degrees horizontally or vertically. For a more freeform rotation, which you cannot achieve in 90 or 180 degree increments, drag the green rotate lever at the top of an object. You can also rotate and flip any type of picture—including bitmaps—in a document. This is useful when you want to change the orientation of an image, such as changing the direction of an arrow.

Rotate an Object to any Angle

1. Select the object you want to rotate.

2. Position the pointer (which changes to the Free Rotate pointer) over the green rotate lever at the top of the object, and then drag to rotate the object.

3. Click outside the object to set the rotation.

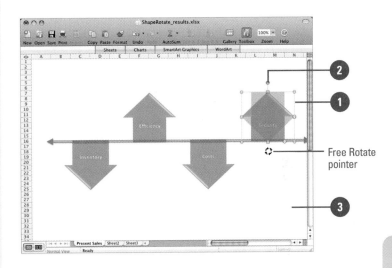

Free Rotate pointer

Rotate or Flip an Object Using Preset Increments

1. Select the object you want to rotate or flip.

2. Click the **Formatting Palette** tab on the Toolbox.

3. Click the **Size, Rotation, and Ordering** panel expand it.

4. Click the **Rotation** button, and then click the option you want.

   - **Rotate.** Click **Rotate Right** or **Rotate Left**.

   - **Flip.** Click **Flip Vertical** or **Flip Horizontal**.

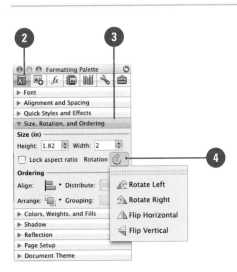

Grouping and Ungrouping Objects

Objects can be grouped, ungrouped, and regrouped to make editing and moving them easier. Rather than moving several objects one at a time, you can group the objects and move them all together. Grouped objects appear as one object, but each object in the group maintains its individual attributes. You can change an individual object within a group without ungrouping. This is useful when you need to make only a small change to a group, such as changing the color of a single shape in the group. You can also format specific shapes, drawings, or pictures within a group without ungrouping. Simply select the object within the group, change the object or edit text within the object, and then deselect the object. However, if you need to move an object in a group, you need to first ungroup the objects, move it, and then group the objects together again. After you ungroup a set of objects, Office remembers each object in the group and regroups those objects in one step when you use the Regroup command. Before you regroup a set of objects, make sure that at least one of the grouped objects is selected.

Group Objects Together

① Select the shapes you want to group together.

② Click the **Formatting Palette** tab on the Toolbox.

③ Click the **Size, Rotation, and Ordering** panel to expand it.

④ Click the **Grouping** button, and then click **Group**.

Did You Know?

You can use the Tab key to select objects in order. Move between the drawing objects on your document (even those hidden behind other objects) by pressing the Tab key.

You can use the shortcut menu to select Group related commands. Control-click the objects you want to group, point to Grouping, and then make your selections.

You can no longer ungroup tables. Due to the increased table size and theme functionality, tables can no longer be ungrouped.

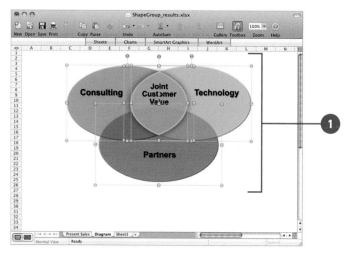

Ungroup Objects

1. Select the grouped object you want to ungroup.

2. Click the **Formatting Palette** tab on the Toolbox.

3. Click the **Size, Rotation, and Ordering** panel to expand it.

4. Click the **Grouping** button, and then click **Ungroup**.

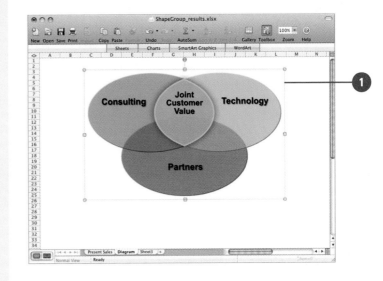

Regroup Objects

1. Select one of the objects in the group of objects you want to regroup.

2. Click the **Formatting Palette** tab on the Toolbox.

3. Click the **Size, Rotation, and Ordering** panel to expand it.

4. Click the **Grouping** button, and then click **Regroup**.

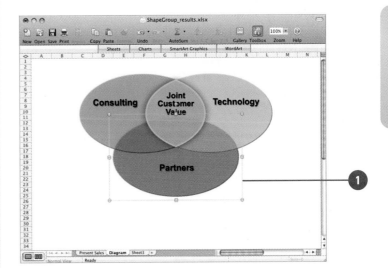

Did You Know?

You can troubleshoot the arrangement of objects. If you have trouble selecting an object because another object is in the way, you can use the Selection pane to help you select it.

Creating a Text Box

If you want to add text outside one of the standard places, such as a paragraph, cell, or placeholder, you can create a text box. A text box is an object container for text. After you create a text box, you can edit the size, shape, color, and other aspects of a text box, just as you can with a graphic. You can also format the text, just as you can with other text.

Create a Text Box

1. Click the **Insert** menu, and then click **Text Box**.

2. Click and drag to draw a text box.

   ◆ To add text that wraps, drag to create a box, and then start typing. Hold down Shift as you draw to create a square text box.

   ◆ To add text that doesn't wrap, click and then start typing.

3. Type or paste text into the box.

4. To change formatting in the text box, select the text box, and then do any of the following:

   ◆ **Format Text dialog box.** Click the **Format** menu, click **Text Box**, or double-click one of the text box's sides, set the options you want, and then click **OK**.

   ◆ **Colors, Weights, and Fills panel.** Click the **Formatting Palette** tab, expand the Colors, Weights, and Fills panel, and then select the options you want.

5. To delete a text box, select it, and then press Delete.

6. Click outside the selection box to deselect the text box.

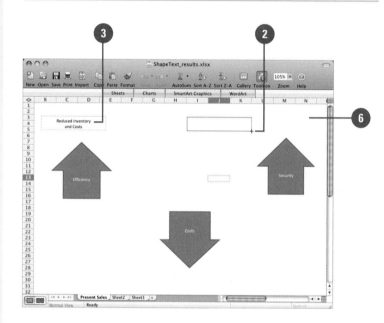

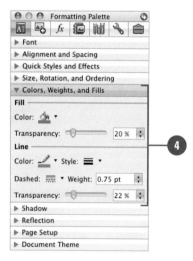

Creating a Document with Word

5

Introduction

Whether you're typing a carefully worded letter, creating a professional resume, or producing a can't-miss promotional newsletter for your business or neighborhood group, Microsoft Word 2008 is the program for you. Word contains all the tools and features you need to produce interesting documents that say exactly what you mean and that have the look to match.

Microsoft Word is designed especially for working with text, so it's a snap to create and edit letters, reports, mailing lists, tables, or any other word-based communication. What makes Word perfect for your documents is its editing capabilities combined with its variety of views. For example, you can jot down your ideas in Outline view. Then switch to Draft view to expand your thoughts into complete sentences and revise them without retyping the entire page. When you're done revising the document, switch to Print Layout view to read and proof your work. Tools such as the Spelling and Grammar Checker help you present your thoughts accurately, clearly, and effectively. Finally, in Print Layout view you can quickly add formatting elements, such as bold type and special fonts, to make your documents look professional.

What You'll Do

View the Word Window

Create a New Word Document

Move Around in a Document

Navigate a Document

Change Document Views

Create a Notebook

Create and Add to a Publication

Create an Outline

Set Up the Page and Page Margins

Select Text

Show Characters

Check Spelling and Grammar

Use Custom Dictionaries

Set Hyphenation

Insert AutoText and New Pages

Control the Way Pages Break

Insert New Sections

Arrange Text in Columns

Add Headers and Footers

Insert Page Numbers and the Date and Time

Insert Symbols and Special Characters

Viewing the Word Window

Standard Toolbar
Click to access command comments
on the toolbar.

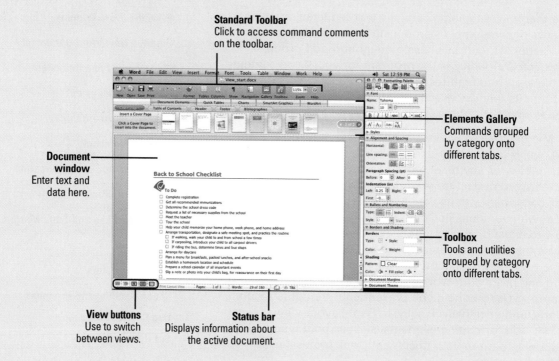

**Document
window**
Enter text and
data here.

Elements Gallery
Commands grouped
by category onto
different tabs.

Toolbox
Tools and utilities
grouped by category
onto different tabs.

View buttons
Use to switch
between views.

Status bar
Displays information about
the active document.

Creating a New Word Document

In Word, you can create three types of documents: Word Document, Word Notebook Layout, and Word Publishing Layout. Even though each document type uses the standard .docx extension, the internal layout format is different. When you create a new document in Word, you need to decide what type of document you want to create. The Word Document type, also known as normal, is the typical document format you have always used in Word. The Word Notebook Layout is a format like a conventional paper notebook or ring binder, which makes it easier to take notes in a meeting or lecture, organize information by using tabs, use flags to highlight information, handwrite annotations, and event record and play back audio notes. The Word Publishing Layout (**New!**) is a format for creating desktop publishing document, such as newsletters, brochures, and flyers. You can create a new Word document using the New button on the Standard toolbar or the Project Gallery under the Blank Documents category.

Create a New Word Document

◆ **Toolbar.** Click the **New** button drop-down on the Standard toolbar, and then select one of the following document commands:

  ◆ **New Blank Document.**

  ◆ **New Blank Notebook Layout Document.**

  ◆ **New Blank Publishing Layout Document.**

◆ **Project Gallery.** Click the **File** menu, click **Project Gallery**, click **Blank Document** from the Category list, select a Word document type, and then click **Open**.

  ◆ **Word Document.**

  ◆ **Word Notebook Layout.**

  ◆ **Word Publishing Layout.**

  A new blank document appears in the Office program window.

New blank documents types

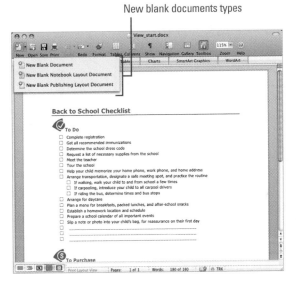

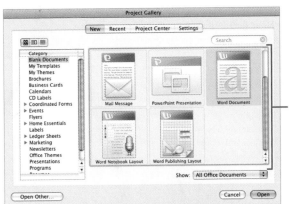

Project Gallery with new blank document types

Moving Around in a Document

As your document gets longer, some of your work shifts out of sight. You can easily move any part of a document back into view. **Scrolling** moves the document line by line. **Paging** moves the document page by page. **Browsing** moves you through your document by the item you specify, such as to the next word, comment, picture, table, or heading. The tools described here move you around a document no matter which document view you are in.

Scroll, Page, and Browse Through a Document

◆ To scroll through a document one line at a time, click the up or down scroll arrow on the vertical scroll bar.

◆ To quickly scroll through a document, click and hold the up or down scroll arrow on the vertical scroll bar.

◆ To scroll to a specific page or heading in a document, drag the scroll box on the vertical scroll bar until the page number or heading you want appears in the yellow box.

◆ To page through the document one screen at a time, press Page Up or Page Down on the keyboard.

◆ To browse a document by page, edits, headings, or other items, click the **Select Browse Object** button, and then click that item. If a dialog box opens, enter the name or number of the item you want to find, and then click the **Previous** or **Next** button to move from one item to the next.

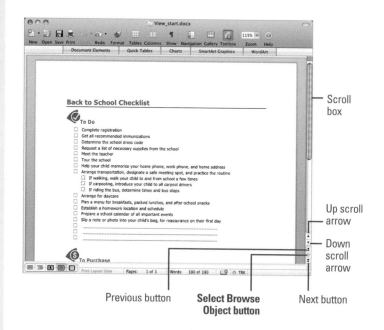

Scroll box

Up scroll arrow

Down scroll arrow

Previous button   **Select Browse Object button**   Next button

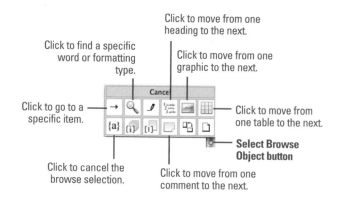

Click to move from one heading to the next.

Click to find a specific word or formatting type.

Click to move from one graphic to the next.

Click to go to a specific item.

Click to move from one table to the next.

Select Browse Object button

Click to cancel the browse selection.

Click to move from one comment to the next.

Navigating a Document

You can use the navigation pane to jump to any page or heading in a document. If you have a long document, such as a manual or report, this become very useful. With the navigation pane, you can display the Document Map or the Thumbnail view to quickly jump to different parts of your document. The Document Map view displays defined headings in the document, while the Thumbnail view displays a miniature representation of document pages.

Use the Navigation Pane

1. Click the **Navigation** button on the Standard toolbar.

2. Click the **Display** drop-down, and then select one of the following options:

   ◆ **Thumbnail.** Click to display miniature representations of document pages.

   ◆ **Document Map.** Click to display headings in the document.

3. To navigate to a new location in a document, do one of the following:

   ◆ **Thumbnail.** Click a page thumbnail.

   ◆ **Document Map.** Click a heading.

4. Click the **Navigation** button on the Standard toolbar again to close the navigation pane.

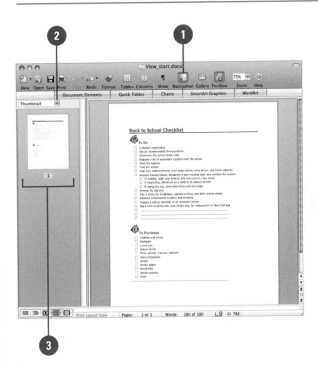

Did You Know?

You can change the width of the navigation pane. Drag the blue divider bar between the navigation pane and the document window to the left or right.

You can change the heading levels that appear in Document Map. In the Document Map display, Control-click in the navigation pane, and then select a Show Heading or the All command. You can also expand or collapse heading levels as needed.

Changing Document Views

Word displays the contents of a document in different ways to help you work efficiently with your content. The available views include Print Layout, Full Screen Reading, Web Layout, Outline, and Draft. You can change the window view from the View tab, or you can click a Document view button at the bottom right corner of the Word window.

Draft view displays the document as a single, long piece of "paper," divided into pages by perforation marks. This view is fine for composition but inadequate for editing or previewing your work prior to printing or other publication.

Web Layout view displays the document as it will appear on the Web. You can save documents as HTML code to make Web content creation easy.

Outline view displays the document as an outline with headings and subheadings. When you shift to Outline view, each heading has a clickable plus or minus sign next to it to expand or collapse the content under the heading. You can drag a plus, or minus sign to move the heading and all of its associated text.

Print Layout view displays a gray gap between each page to clearly delineate where each actual page break occurs. Word displays each new document in Print Layout view by default. This view is best for previewing your work before printing, and it works well with the Zoom feature on the View tab to increase and decrease the page view size and display multiple pages of the same document simultaneously onscreen.

Notebook Layout view displays the document in a format like a conventional paper notebook or ring binder. You can take notes in a meeting or lecture, create an outline, write down your thoughts, organize information by using section tabs, use flags to highlight information, handwrite annotations, assign an Entourage task as an action item, and event record and play back audio notes. Notebook layout view uses a unique format, so it's a good idea to use this layout from scratch. If you convert an existing document with another layout to notebook layout view, some formatting might change, including the placement of graphics.

Publishing Layout view (**New!**) displays the document in a specialized view for desktop publishing. In this view, you can create professional-looking newsletters, brochures, flyers, and calendars. Instead of using viewing text flowing down a page in a normal Word document, text appears in text boxes in a publication, which makes them easy to format and move around on a page. You can also use an image drop zone to quickly drag and drop pictures into a publication. You can start from an existing publication template by using the Project Gallery or create one of your own. Publishing layout view uses a unique format, so it's a good idea to use this layout from a template or scratch. If you convert an existing document with another layout to publishing layout view, some formatting might change, including the placement of graphics.

Draft view

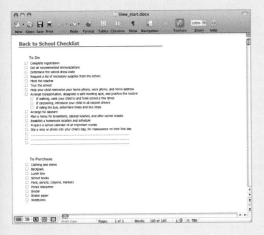

Web Layout view

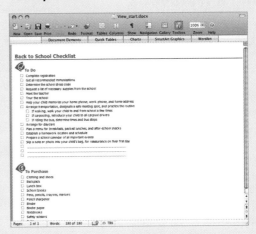

Outline view

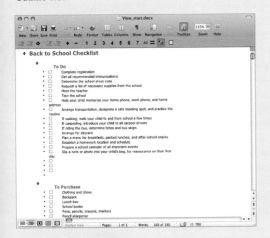

Print Layout view

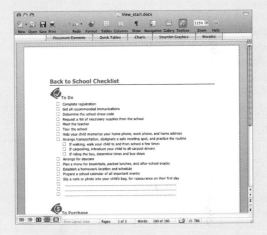

Notebook Layout view

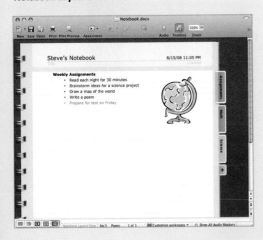

Publishing Layout view

Creating a Notebook

Notebook Layout view displays the document in a format like a conventional paper notebook or ring binder. You can take notes, create an outline, organize information by using section tabs, add drawings, pictures, and movies, and event record and play back audio notes. Notebook layout view uses a unique format, so it's a good idea to use this layout from scratch. If you convert an existing document with another layout to notebook layout view, some formatting might change, including the placement of graphics.

Work in Notebook Layout View

◆ **Create a new notebook.** Open the **Project Gallery**, click the **New** tab, click the **Word Notebook Layout** icon in the Blank Document category, and then click **Open**; or create a new document, and then click the **Notebook Layout View** button.

◆ **Convert an existing document.** Open or create a document, click the **Notebook Layout View** button, and then click **Convert**. To create a new one, click **Create New**.

◆ **Add a title.** Type the title on the Title line at the top. To change the text to the right, click the button under it, and then click **Author**, **Created**, or **Modified**.

◆ **Change the section tabs.** Click the plus (+) section tab to add a new section; Control-click a tab to rename, delete, or select a new color; or drag a tab up or down to change its order.

◆ **Change a notebook's appearance.** Click the **Appearance** button on the toolbar and then select an option; or click the **Customize Workspace** icon on the status bar to select a different background.

◆ **Enter notes.** Type text as you do in a normal document. Text automatically wraps to the next line as needed. Press Return to start a new note.

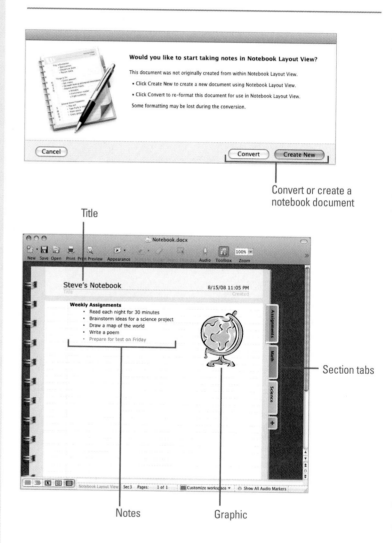

Convert or create a notebook document

Title

Section tabs

Notes

Graphic

140

- ◆ **Delete notes or objects.** Select the note, and then press Delete, or use the **Erase** tool on the toolbar.

- ◆ **Format notes.** Similar to other views, you can format text by using the Font command on the Format menu or the buttons on the Font panel.

- ◆ **Set indent levels.** Similar to Outline view, you can indent text by using the Tab key or the **Demote** or **Promote** button on the Note Levels panel.

- ◆ **Move notes around.** Similar to Outline view, you can move a note using by dragging the symbol to the left or using the **Move Up** or **Move Down** button on the Note Levels panel.

- ◆ **Search for text in notes.** Type search text in the Quick Search box, and then press Return.

- ◆ **Add images, movies, or music.** Click the **Insert** menu, point to **Picture**, and then select a command, or click the **Insert** menu, and then click **Movie**. Double-click the image to adjust the wrapping style in the Layout pane.

- ◆ **Add drawings.** Click the **Scribble** button on the toolbar and then draw. To set a new pen color or line width, click the **Scribble** button arrow, and then select the options you want.

- ◆ **Record audio.** With a microphone attached to your computer, click to place the insertion point, click the **Audio** button on the toolbar, click the **Start Recording** button, and then speak into the microphone. Click the **Stop** button to end the recording. Click the speaker icon in the note's margin to playback the recording.

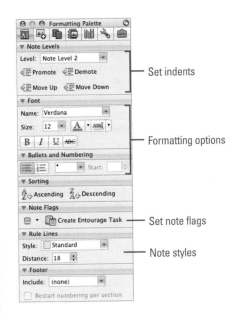

Set indents

Formatting options

Set note flags

Note styles

Flags   Drawing tools

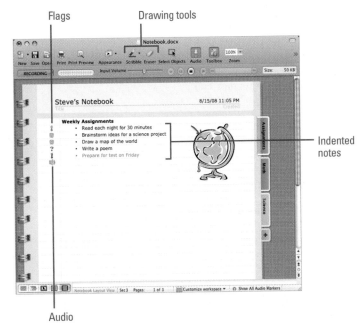

Indented notes

Audio

Creating a Publication

Publishing Layout view (**New!**) displays the document in a specialized view for desktop publishing. In this view, you can create professional-looking newsletters, brochures, flyers, and calendars. You can start from an existing publication template by using the Project Gallery, Publication Templates tab (**New!**) in the Elements Gallery, or create one of your own. Publishing layout view uses a unique format, so it's a good idea to use this layout from a template or scratch. Each publication page in Publishing Layout view contains two layers: a content layer on top and a master layer on the bottom. A content page holds unique elements, such as text and images, that you want to appear on that page, while a master page holds static elements, such as headers, footers, page numbers, and logos, that you want to appear on every page. A publication can have one master page or different master pages for even and odd pages, and a master page for the first page. Instead of using viewing text flowing down a page in a normal Word document, text appears in text boxes in a publication, which makes them easy to format and move around on a page. You can also use an image drop zone to quickly drag and drop pictures into a publication.

Create a Publication

- ◆ **Create a new blank publication.** Open the **Project Gallery**, click the **New** tab, click the **Word Publication Layout** icon in the Blank Document category, and then click **Open**.

  Create a new document, and then click the **Publication Layout View** button.

- ◆ **Create a new publication from a template.** Open the **Project Gallery**, click the **New** tab, select a template icon from a publication category, and then click **Open**.

  Create a blank publication, click the **Publication Templates** tab in the Elements Gallery, click a category tab, and then click a template thumbnail.

- ◆ **Convert an existing document.** Open or create a document, click the **Publishing Layout View** button, and then click **Convert**. To create a new one, click **Create New**.

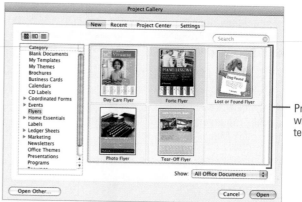

Project Gallery with publication templates

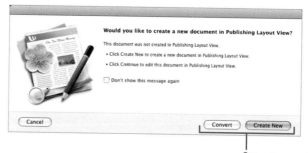

Convert or create a publication document

Work with Content and Master Pages

◆ **View a master page.** Scroll to a specific master page, click the **Master Pages** tab. To view other master pages, scroll using the vertical scroll bar.

◆ **View a content page.** Scroll to a specific page, click the **All Contents** tab. To view other pages, scroll using the vertical scroll bar.

◆ **Insert a content page.** Click the **All Contents** tab, display the page before where you want to insert a new page, click the **Insert** button arrow on the toolbar, and then click **New Page**.

◆ **Insert a master page.** Click the **All Contents** tab, display the page before where you want to insert a new master page, click the **Insert** button arrow on the toolbar, and then click **New Master**.

   A new content page along with a new master page appears.

◆ **Change master page types.** Click the **Master Pages** tab, and then select the check boxes in the Master Pages panel you want: **Different First Page**, **Different Odd and Even Pages**, or **Same As Previous**.

◆ **Delete a content page.** Click the **All Contents** tab, display the page you want to delete, and then click the **Remove** button on the toolbar.

◆ **Move a content page.** Click the **Navigation** button on the toolbar, and then drag a thumbnail up or down in the page list.

Insert or remove pages

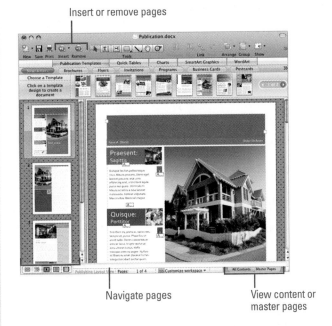

Navigate pages

View content or master pages

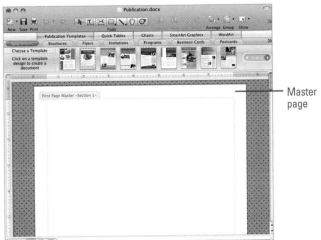

Master page

Master page options

Adding to a Publication

After you create a publication (**New!**), you can add text boxes, drawings, lines, and other images. Each of these elements is a distinct object, which you can move around. When you create a publication from a template, the document often includes placeholders for text, pictures, and other elements, which you can use to add content, as well as resize, modify, and format. Before you can add text to a publication, you need to create a text box, which you can also link together to flow text from one box to another (known as a story) on the same or different page. A number appears in the corner of each linked box to indicate its linking order in the story. An arrow appears in the link handles to indicate the flow of text, and an overflow indicator at the bottom of the last linked text box means there is additional text for you to place.

Add Content to Publication

◆ **Add text in a template.** Click the text placeholder to select the object, click the text, and then type your own text.

◆ **Replace a picture in a template.** Click the image to select it, click the **Replace** button on the Picture panel, select a picture, and then click **Insert**.

◆ **Create a normal or vertical text box.** Click the **Text Box** button (normal) or **Vertical Text Box** button on the toolbar, display the page where you want the text box, drag to create the rectangle box, and then type or paste your text into the box. Text automatically wraps as needed to fit within the text box.

◆ **Link to a new text box.** Click to select the source text box, click the box's forward or backwards link handle, and then draw a new text box.

◆ **Link to an existing text box.** Click to select the source text box, click the **Link** button on the toolbar, and then click the empty text box to which you want to link.

Publication tools

Graphic

Text box

- **Break a link.** Select the text box that you want to be the last link in the story, and then click the **Break** button on the toolbar. All boxes following the selected one will now be empty.

- **Remove a link.** Select the text box, and then press Delete. Only the text box is deleted. The story text remains.

- **Add drawings and lines.** Click the **Draw Shape** or **Draw Line** button on the toolbar, select a shape or line, and then draw it on the page.

- **Group objects.** Select the individual objects, click the **Group** button on the toolbar, and then click **Group**.

- **Ungroup objects.** Select the grouped object, click the **Group** button on the toolbar, and then click **Ungroup**.

- **Arrange objects.** Select one or more objects, click the **Arrange** button on the toolbar, and then click **Bring to Front**, **Send to Back**, **Bring Forward**, or **Send Backward**.

- **Move objects.** Drag it on the page. With dynamic guides on, you can align objects as you drag.

- **Add static guides.** Display the content or master page, point to the horizontal or vertical ruler, and then drag to place the guide. As you drag, a screentip displays the guide's position.

- **Remove static guides.** Drag it off the page.

- **Show or hide guides.** Click the **Show** button on the toolbar, and then select a command: **Static Guides**, **Dynamic Guides**, or **Margin Guides**. Shown guides are checked, while hidden guides are unchecked.

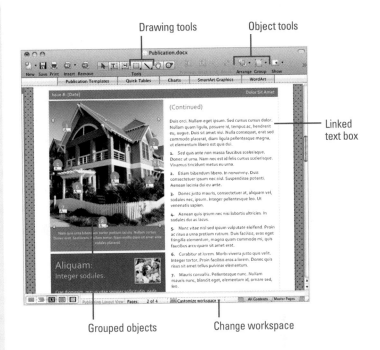

Drawing tools   Object tools

Linked text box

Grouped objects   Change workspace

For Your Information

Exploring Guides in a Publication

Guides are nonprinting lines that make it easier to align and place objects, such as text boxes, pictures, and shapes, in a publication. There are three types of guides: margin, static, and dynamic. **Margin guides** show the page margins as a blue rectangle around the edge of the page. You can change margin guides in the Document Margins panel on the Formatting Palette tab. **Static guides** are manually positioned vertical or horizontal lines that you can add to content (in blue) or master (in pink) pages. When you drag an object to a guide, the element snaps to the guide for easy alignment. **Dynamic guides** appear as you drag an object to align it with other items on the page.

Creating an Outline

Outlines are useful for organizing information, such as topics in an essay. An outline typically consists of main headings and subheadings. You can create an outline from scratch in Outline view or change a bulleted or numbered list into an outline using the bullets and numbering commands on the Outlining toolbar. In Outline view, you can use buttons in the Outlining toolbar or drag the mouse pointer to move headings and subheadings to different locations or levels.

Create an Outline from Scratch

1 In a new document, click the **Outline View** button.

2 Type a heading, and then press Return.

3 To assign a heading to a different level and apply the corresponding heading style, place the insertion point in the heading, and then click the **Promote** or **Demote** button until the heading is at the level you want, or click **Promote to Heading** or **Promote to Body** button.

To move a heading to a different location, place the insertion point in the heading, and then click the **Move Up** or **Move Down** button until the heading is moved where you want it to go.

The subordinate text under the heading moves with the heading.

4 To show text formatting or the first line only, click the **Show Formatting** or **Show First Line Only** button.

To show a specific level, click the **Show Level** button for the level you want, or click the **Show All Headings** button.

5 When you're done, click another view button to exit Outline view.

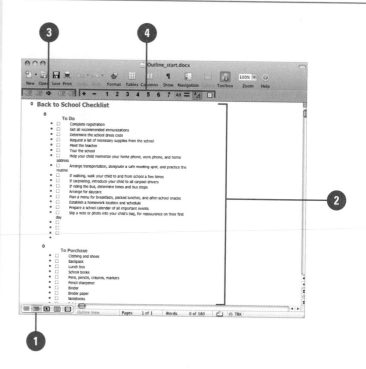

Working Together

Sending Text to a PowerPoint Presentation

You can send any Word document into PowerPoint, although only paragraphs tagged with heading styles become part of the slides. Each Heading 1 style in a Word document becomes the title of a separate PowerPoint slide. Heading 2 becomes the first level of indented text, and so on. If a document contains no styles, PowerPoint uses the paragraph indents to determine a slide structure. To send heading text to a PowerPoint presentation, click the File menu, point to Sent To, and then click PowerPoint.

Setting Up the Page

Every document you produce and print might need a different page setup. You can achieve the look you want by printing on a standard paper size (such as letter, legal, or envelope), international standard paper sizes, or any custom size that your printer accepts. The default setting is 8.5 x 11 inches, the most common letter and copy size. You can also print several pages on one sheet. You can also select the page orientation (portrait or landscape) that best fits the entire document or any section. **Portrait** orients the page vertically (taller than it is wide) and **landscape** orients the page horizontally (wider than it is tall).

Set Custom Page Size Options

1. Click the **File** menu, and then click **Page Setup**.

2. Click the **Settings** drop-down, and then click **Page Attributes**.

3. Click the **Format for** drop-down, and then select a printer to which you want to print the document.

4. Click the **Paper Size** drop-down, and then select the paper size you want, or specify a custom size.

5. Select the **Portrait** or **Landscape** icon.

6. Specify a scale percentage for the page; the default size is 100%.

7. Click the **Settings** drop-down, and then click **Microsoft Word**.

8. Click the **Apply Page Setup settings to** drop-down, and then click **This section**, **This point forward**, or **Whole document**.

9. To make your changes the default settings for all new documents, click **Default**, and then click **Yes**.

10. Click **OK**.

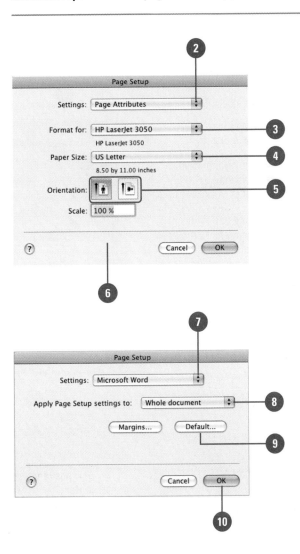

Setting Up the Page Margins

Margins are the blank space between the edge of a page and the text. The default setting for Word documents is 1.25 inches on the left and right, and 1 inch on the top and bottom. You can use the mouse pointer to adjust margins visually for the entire document, or you can use the Page Setup dialog box to set precise measurements for an entire document or a specific section. When you shift between portrait and landscape page orientation, the margin settings automatically change. If you need additional margin space for binding pages into a book or binder, you can adjust the left or right gutter settings. Gutters allow for additional margin space so that all of the document text remains visible after binding. Unless this is your purpose, leave the default settings in place.

Adjust Margins Visually

1. Click the **Print Layout** view button.

2. If necessary, click the **View** menu, and then click **Ruler** to display it.

3. Position the pointer over a margin boundary on the horizontal or vertical ruler.

4. Press and hold Option, and then click a margin boundary to display the measurements of the text and margin areas as you adjust the margins.

5. Drag the left, right, top, or bottom margin boundary to a new position.

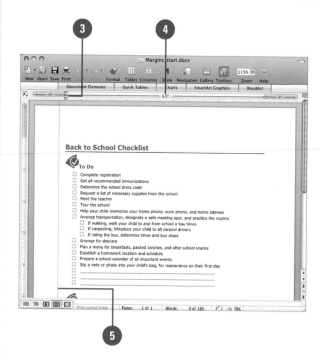

Change Margins Using the Document Margins Panel

1. Click the **Formatting Palette** tab on the Toolbox.

2. Click the **Document Margins** panel to expand it.

3. Specify the margin settings you want:

   ◆ Type new margin measurements (in inches) in the Top, Bottom, Left, or Right boxes.

   ◆ Type new header and footer (in inches) in the Header and Footer boxes.

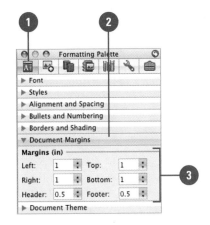

Change Margins Using Page Setup

1. Click the **Format** menu, and then click **Document**.

   The Page Setup dialog box opens.

2. Click the **Margins** tab.

3. Type new margin measurements (in inches) in the Top, Bottom, Left, or Right boxes, and Gutter boxes.

4. Type new header and footer (in inches) in the Header and Footer boxes.

5. Click the **Apply to** drop-down, and then click **Selected Text**, **This Point Forward**, or **Whole Document**.

6. To make the new margin settings the default for all new Word documents, click **Default**, and then click **Yes**.

7. Click **OK**.

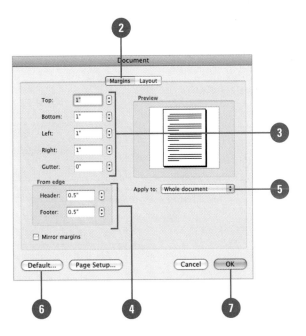

Selecting Text

The first step in working with text is to highlight, or **select**, the text you want. Once you've selected it, you can copy, move, format, and delete words, sentences, and paragraphs. When you finish with or decide not to use a selection, you can click anywhere in the document to **deselect** the text.

Select Text

1 Position the pointer in the word, paragraph, line, or part of the document you want to select.

2 Choose the method that accomplishes the selection you want to complete in the easiest way.

Refer to the table for methods to select text.

Did You Know?

AutoComplete finishes your words. As you enter common text, such as your name, months, today's date, and common salutations and closings, Word provides the rest of the text in a ScreenTip. Press Enter to have Word complete your words.

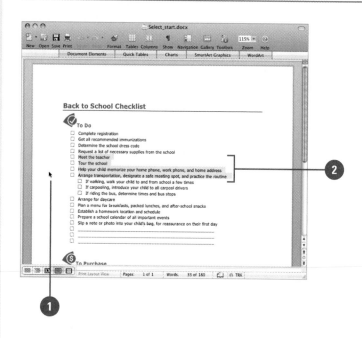

Selecting Text

To select	Do this
A single word	Double-click the word.
A single paragraph	Triple-click a word within the paragraph.
A single line	Click in the left margin next to the line.
Any part of a document	Click at the beginning of the text you want to highlight, and then drag to the end of the section you want to highlight.
A large selection	Click at the beginning of the text you want to highlight, and then press and hold Shift while you click at the end of the text that you want to highlight.
The entire document	Triple-click in the left margin.
An outline heading or subheading in Outline view	Click the bullet, plus sign, or minus sign.

Showing Characters

When you're selecting, editing, proofing, and working with text, it can be useful to see the nonprinting invisible characters in a document, such as spaces, tabs, returns, and line breaks. When you're proofing a document for incorrect punctuation, such as extra spaces between words and sentences and blank paragraph lines, it can be hard to see them without showing nonprinting characters. However, showing nonprinting characters while you write can be distracting. You can show/hide nonprinting characters by using the Show button on the Standard toolbar, which works like a toggle switch.

Show and Hide Nonprinting Characters

1. Click the **Show** button on the Standard toolbar to show or hide nonprinting characters.

   Refer to the table for common nonprinting characters.

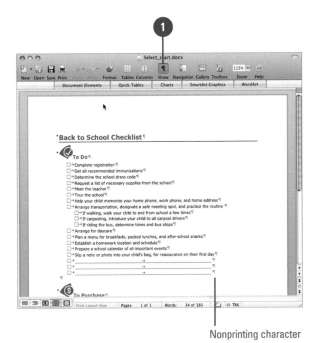

Nonprinting character

Common Nonprinting Characters

Symbol	Character
. (dot)	Space
→ (right arrow)	Tab
↵ (curved arrow)	Line break (new line, same paragraph)
¶	End of paragraph

Checking Spelling and Grammar

As you type, a red wavy line appears under words not listed in Word's dictionary (such as misspellings or names) or duplicated words (such as *the the*). A green wavy underline appears under words or phrases with grammatical errors. You can correct these errors as they arise or after you finish the entire document. Before you print your final document, use the Spelling and Grammar checker to ensure that your document is error-free.

Correct Spelling and Grammar as You Type

1. Control-click a word with a red or green wavy underline.

2. Click a substitution, or click **Ignore All** (or Grammar) to skip any other instances of the word.

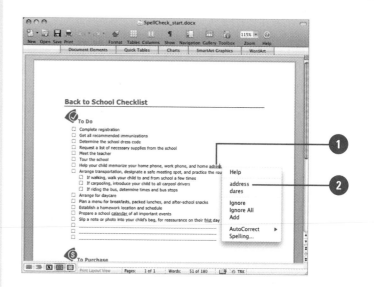

Change Spelling and Grammar Options in Word

1. Click the **Word** menu, button, and then click **Preferences**.

2. Click the **Spelling and Grammar** icon.

3. Select or clear the spelling and grammar option check boxes you want. Point to each option to display a description.

4. Click **OK**.

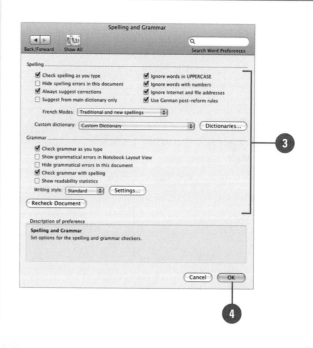

Correct Spelling and Grammar

1. Click at the beginning of the document or select the text you want to correct.

2. Click the **Tools** menu, and then click **Spelling and Grammar**.

   As it checks each sentence in the document, Word provides alternatives for misspelled words or problematic sentences.

3. To check spelling only, clear the **Check grammar** check box.

4. Choose an option:

   ◆ Click **Ignore** to skip the word or rule, or click **Ignore All** or **Ignore Rule** to skip every instance of the word or rule.

   ◆ Click **Add** to add a word to your dictionary, so it doesn't show up as a misspelled word in the future.

   ◆ Click a suggestion, and then click **Change** to make a substitution or click **Change All** to make all substitutions.

   ◆ If no suggestion is appropriate, click in the document and edit the text yourself. Click **Resume** to continue.

5. Click **OK** to return to the document.

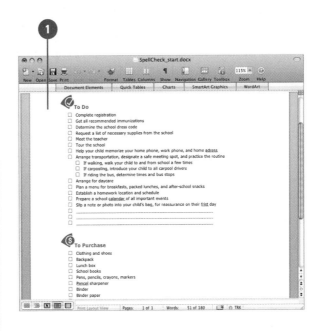

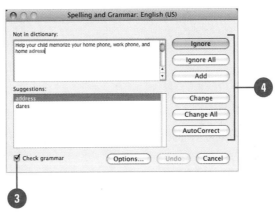

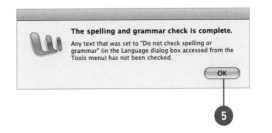

Did You Know?

You can add a familiar word to your dictionary. Control-click the wavy line under the word in question, and then click Add.

Using Custom Dictionaries

Before you can use a custom dictionary, you need to enable it first. You can enable and manage custom dictionaries by using the Custom Dictionaries dialog box. In the dialog box, you can change the language associated with a custom dictionary, create a new custom dictionary, or add or remove an existing custom dictionary. If you need to manage dictionary content, you can also change the default custom dictionary to which the spelling checker adds words, as well as add, delete, or edit words. When you use a language for the first time, Office automatically creates an exclusion dictionary. This dictionary forces the spelling checker to flag words you don't want to use.

Use a Custom Dictionary

1. Click the **Word** menu, button, and then click **Preferences**.

2. Click the **Spelling and Grammar** icon.

3. Click **Dictionaries**.

4. Select the check box next to **Custom Dictionary**.

5. Click the **Language** drop-down, and then select a language for a dictionary.

6. Click the options you want:

   ◆ Click **New** to create a new dictionary.

   ◆ Click **Edit** to add, delete, or edit words.

   ◆ Click **Add** to insert an existing dictionary.

   ◆ Click **Remove** to delete a dictionary.

7. Click **OK** to close the Custom Dictionaries dialog box.

8. Click **OK**.

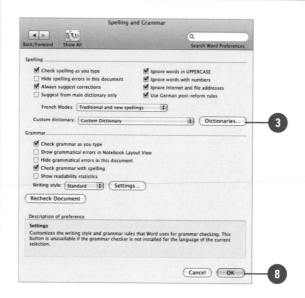

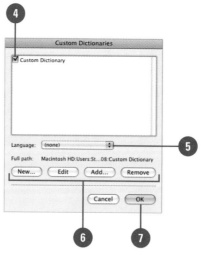

Setting Hyphenation

If a word doesn't fit at the end of a line, you can set hyphenation options to hyphenate the word to display partly on one line and partly on the next line, or move the word to the beginning of the next line. You can set options to automatically or manually hyphenate words in a document, and to specify the maximum amount of space allowed between a word and the right margin without hyphenating the word. When you manually hyphenate a document, Word searches the text for words to hyphenate and asks if you want to insert a hyphen in the text. You can also manually insert an optional or nonbreaking hyphen. An **optional hyphen** is a hyphen that you specify where you want a word to break if it falls at the end of a line. A **nonbreaking hyphen** prevents a hyphenated word from breaking if it falls at the end of a line.

Customize Hyphenation

1. Click the **Tools** menu, and then click **Hyphenation**.

2. Select or clear the **Automatically hyphenate document** check box.

   If you clear it, you can click **Manual** to check hyphenation.

3. Select or clear the **Hyphenate words in CAPS** check box.

4. In the Hyphenation zone box, specify the maximum amount of space between the word and the right margin you want.

5. Specify the limit for hyphens on consecutive lines you want.

6. Click **OK**.

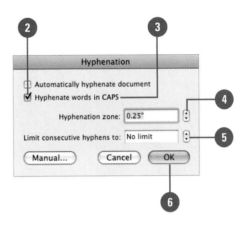

Did You Know?

You can remove manual hyphens. Click the Edit menu, click Replace, click Expand if necessary, click Special, and then click Optional Hyphen to remove manual hyphens or Nonbreaking Hyphen to remove nonbreaking hyphens. Leave the Replace with box empty, click Replace All.

Inserting AutoText

AutoText stores text and graphics you want to reuse, such as a company logo, boilerplate text, or formatted table. For example, you can use AutoText to quickly insert the text *To Whom It May Concern* or a graphic of your signature. You can use the AutoText entries that come with Word, or create your own. You can insert an AutoText entry as you type or use the AutoText submenu on the Insert menu. If you no longer want to use an AutoText entry, you can remove it using the AutoCorrect dialog box.

Insert AutoText

1. Click where you want to insert AutoText.

2. Click the **Insert** menu, and then point to **AutoText**.

3. Point to an AutoText category.

4. Click the AutoText entry you want.

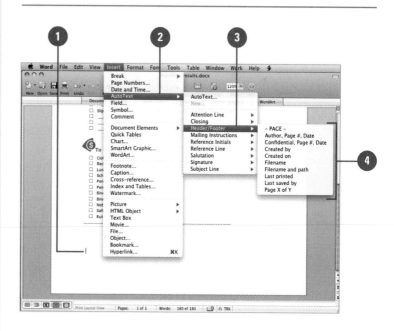

Insert AutoText As You Type

1. Start to type the beginning of the AutoText entry.

   After you type four characters that are a possible AutoText entry, a yellow box containing the AutoText entry's name appears.

2. Press Return to insert the AutoText entry, or keep typing something else to ignore it.

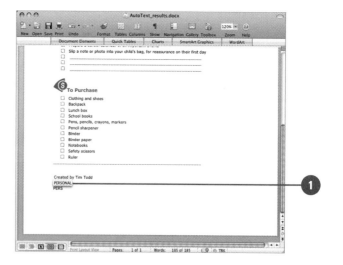

Create AutoText

1. Select the text or graphic in which you want to create an AutoText entry.

2. Click the **Insert** menu, point to **AutoText**, and then click **New**.

3. Type an AutoText name, or use the suggested one.

4. Click **OK**.

Delete an AutoText Entry

1. Click the **Insert** menu, point to **AutoText**, and then click **AutoText**.

2. Select the AutoText entry you want to delete.

3. Click **Delete**.

4. Click **OK**.

Did You Know?

You can use the AutoText toolbar for quick access. Click the View menu, point to Toolbars, and then click AutoText.

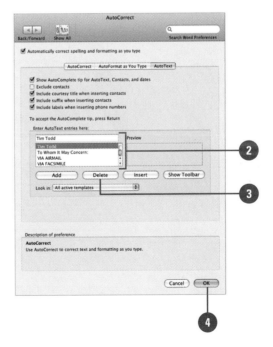

Inserting New Pages

When you fill a page, Word automatically inserts a page break, known as a **soft page break**, and starts a new page. As you add or delete text, this soft page break moves. A soft page break appears as a blue line in Draft view. To start a new page before the current one is filled, insert a **hard page break** that doesn't shift as you edit text. A hard page break appears as a blue line with the text Page Break centered in Draft view.

Insert and Delete a Hard Page Break

1. Click where you want to insert a hard page break.

2. Click the **Insert** menu, point to **Break**, and then click **Page Break**.

3. To delete a page break, click the page break in Draft view, and then press the Delete key.

   To move a page break, drag it to a new location in Draft view.

Did You Know?

You can opt to start a new line, but not a new paragraph. Insert a text wrapping break to force text to the next line in the same paragraph—the perfect tool to make a phrase fall on one line. Press Shift+Return where you want to insert a text wrapping break.

You can display and delete page breaks lines in Print Layout view. Click the Show button on the Standard toolbar. After you show the page break line, you can select and delete it.

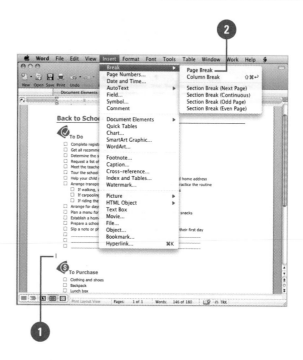

Page break in Draft view

Controlling the Way Pages Break

When you're creating a document, sometimes a line of text, known as a widow or orphan, in a paragraph doesn't fit on a page and looks out of place on the next page. A **widow** is the last line of a paragraph printed by itself at the top of a page. An **orphan** is the first line of a paragraph printed by it self at the bottom of a page. You can use the Widow/Orphan Control option to automatically correct the problem. If a widow or orphan occurs, Word adjusts the paragraph to make sure at least two lines appear together on the next page. When two paragraphs need to remain grouped to maintain their impact, regardless of where the normal page break would have occurred, you can keep paragraphs together on a page or in a column. If you need to start a paragraph at the top of a page, you can automatically generate a page break before a paragraph.

Control Pagination

1. Select the paragraph in which you want to control.

2. Click the **Format** menu, and then click **Paragraph**.

3. Click the **Line and Page Breaks** tab.

4. Select any of the following options:

   ◆ Select the **Widow/Orphan control** check box to avoid paragraphs ending with a single word on a line or a single line at the top of a page.

   ◆ Select the **Keep with next** check box to group paragraphs together.

   ◆ Select the **Keep lines together** check box to keep paragraph lines together.

   ◆ Select the **Page break before** check box to precede a paragraph with a page break.

5. Click **OK**.

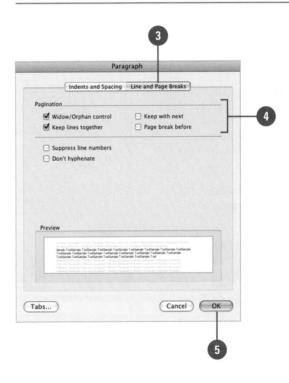

Inserting New Sections

A **section** is a mini-document within a document that stores margin settings, page orientation, page numbering, and so on. A section break appears as a double blue line with the text Section Break centered in Draft view. You can insert different types of section breaks depending on your needs. You can insert a section break with a new page, at the current location, or at the next even or odd page. After you create a section within a document, you can change margin and layout options for one or more sections.

Insert and Delete a Section Break

1. Click where you want to insert a section break.

2. Click the **Insert** menu, point to **Break**, and then select the type of section break you want:

   ◆ **Section Break (Next Page).** Starts the section on a new page.

   ◆ **Section Break (Continuous).** Starts the section wherever the point is located.

   ◆ **Section Break (Even Page).** Starts the section on the next even-numbered page.

   ◆ **Section Break (Odd Page).** Starts the section on the next odd-numbered page.

3. To delete a section break, click the section break in Draft view, and then press Delete.

Did You Know?

You can display and delete section breaks lines in Print Layout view. Click the Show button on the Standard toolbar. After you show the selection break line, you can select and delete it.

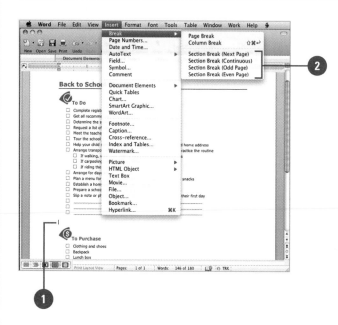

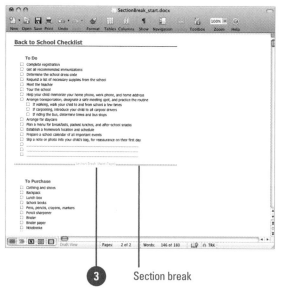

Section break

Change Document Options for One or More Sections

1. Click the text in the section where you want to change options.

2. Click the **Format** menu, and then click **Document**.

3. Click the **Margins** or **Layout** tab.

4. Change the margins and layout options that you want.

5. Click the **Apply to** drop-down, and then click **This section** or **Selected section**.

6. Click **OK**.

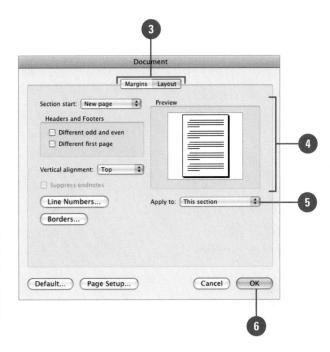

Arranging Text in Columns

Newspaper-style columns can give newsletters and brochures a more polished look. You can format an entire document, selected text, or individual sections into columns. You can create one, two, or three columns of equal size. You can also create two columns and have one column wider than the other. Word fills one column with text before the other, unless you insert a column break. **Column breaks** are used in two-column layouts to move the text after the insertion point to the top of the following column. You can also display a vertical line between the columns. To view the columns side by side, switch to print layout view.

Create Columns

1. Select the text you want to arrange in columns.

2. Click the **Columns** button on the Standard toolbar.

3. Select the number of columns you want.

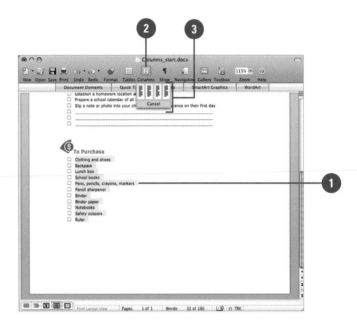

Did You Know?

You can remove columns quickly. Select the columns, click the Columns button on the Standard toolbar, and then click the first column.

You can align text in a column. Click the Align Left, Center, Align Right, or Justify button on the Alignment and Spacing panel on the Formatting Palette tab to align paragraphs in columns.

Modify Columns

1. Click in the columns you want to modify.

2. Click the **Format** menu, and then click **Columns**.

3. Click a column preset format.

4. If necessary, enter the number of columns you want.

5. Enter the width and spacing you want for each column.

6. To place a vertical line between columns, select the **Line between** check box.

7. Click the **Apply to** drop-down, and then select an option.

8. Click **OK**.

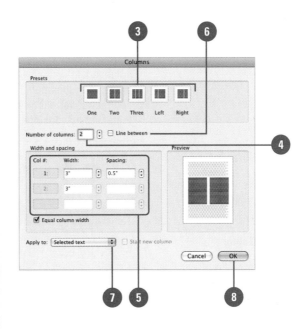

Insert a Column Break

1. Click where you want to insert a column break.

2. Click the **Insert** menu, point to **Break**, and then click **Column Break**.

   TIMESAVER *Press Shift+⌘+Return.*

3. To delete a column break, click the column break dotted line in Draft view or select lines above and below the break, and then press the Delete key.

Adding Headers and Footers

Most books, including this one, use headers and footers to help you keep track of where you are. A **header** is text printed in the top margin of every page within a document. **Footer** text is printed in the bottom margin. Commonly used headers and footers contain your name, the document title, the filename, the print date, and page numbers. If you divide your document into sections, you can create different headers and footers for each section. Word makes it easy to add headers and footers to any document using Document Elements (**New!**).

Create and Edit Headers and Footers

1. Click the **Document Elements** tab in the Elements Gallery.

2. Click the **Header** or **Footer** tab.

3. Click the **Insert as** drop-down, and then click **Odd Pages**, **Even Pages**, or **All Pages**.

4. Click the style you want from the gallery to apply it to the document.

   ◆ Click the scroll up or down arrows to see additional styles.

5. To edit a header or footer, double-click it.

6. Click the header or footer box, and then type the text you want. Edit and format header or footer text as usual.

7. To insert common items in a header or footer, click the **Insert** menu, and then select a command (**Page Numbers**, **Date and Time**, or **Picture**).

8. When you're done, click the **Close** button on the header or footer.

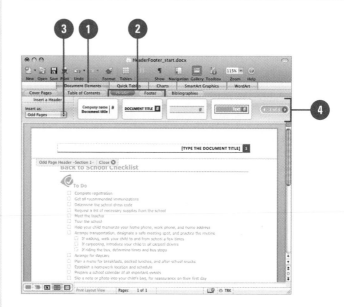

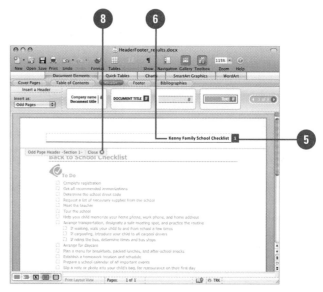

Did You Know?

You can remove a header or footer. Double-click the header or footer, select all the text and other elements, and then press Delete.

Work with Headers and Footers

1 Double-click a header or footer.

The Header and Footer panel opens on the Formatting Palette tab on the Toolbox.

2 To navigate headers and footers, click any of the following buttons on the Header and Footer panel: **Show Previous**, **Show Next**, **Switch Between Header and Footer**, or **Go To**

3 Select any of the following options:

- ◆ Select the **Different Odd & Even Pages** check box to create different headers or footers for odd and even pages.

- ◆ Select the **Different First Page** check box to create a unique header or footer for the document's first page.

- ◆ Select the **Hide Body Text** check box to hide document text.

4 To change header and footer position, adjust the **Header from Top** or **Footers from Bottom** settings.

5 When you're done, click the **Close** button on the header or footer.

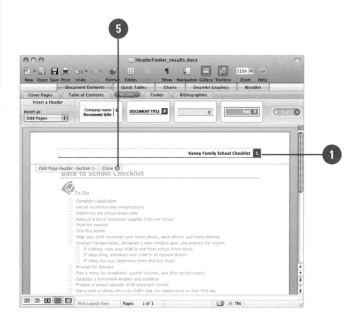

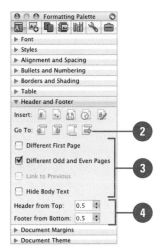

Did You Know?

There are default tab stops used to align header and footer text. Typically, headers and footers have two default tab stops. The first, in the middle, centers text. The second, on the far right, aligns text on the right margin. To left align text, don't press Tab. You can add and move the tab stops as needed. In addition, you can use the alignment buttons on the Alignment and Spacing panel on the Formatting Palette tab.

Inserting Page Numbers and the Date and Time

Page numbers help you keep your document in order or find a topic from the table of contents. Number the entire document consecutively or each section independently; pick a numbering scheme, such as roman numerals or letters. When you insert page numbers, you can select the position and alignment of the numbers on the page. The date and time field ensures you know which printout is the latest. Word uses your computer's internal calendar and clock as its source. You can insert the date and time for any installed language. Add page numbers and the date in a footer to conveniently keep track of your work.

Insert and Format Page Numbers

1. Click the **Insert** menu, and then click **Page Numbers**.

2. Click the **Position** drop-down, and then select a position.

3. Click the **Alignment** drop-down, and then select an alignment.

4. Select the **Show number on first page** check box to show it, or clear it to show it on page 2.

5. To set or change page formatting, click **Format**.

6. Click the **Number format** drop-down, and then select a scheme.

7. Select the starting number.

8. Click **OK**.

9. Click **OK**.

Did You Know?

You can quickly insert page numbers. Click the Insert Page Number button in the Header and Footer panel on the Formatting Palette tab.

You can quickly insert the number of pages. Click the Insert Number of Pages button in the Header and Footer panel on the Formatting Palette tab.

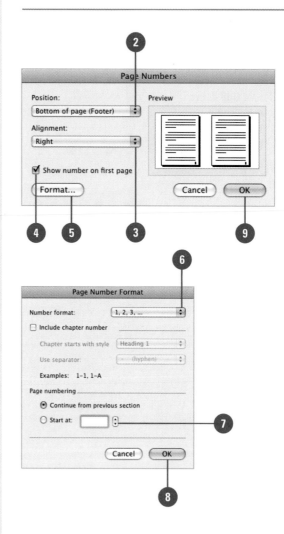

Insert the Date or Time

1. Do either of the following:

   ◆ To place the date or time on every page, display or insert a header or footer.

   ◆ To insert the date or time on a single page, display the page.

2. Click to place the insertion point where you want to insert the date or time.

3. Click the **Insert** menu, and then click **Date and Time**.

4. To have the date or time automatically update, select the **Update automatically** check box.

5. Click the date and time format you want.

6. To set the current date and time (based on your computer clock) as the default, click **Default**, and then click **Yes**.

7. Click **OK**.

Did You Know?

You can remove a page number or the date and time. Double-click the header or footer, select all the text and other elements, and then press Delete.

You can quickly insert date or time numbers. Click the Insert Date or Insert Time button in the Header and Footer panel on the Formatting Palette tab.

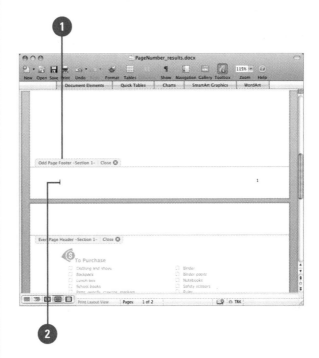

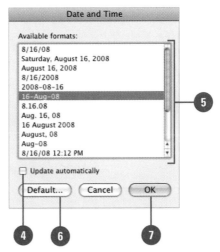

Inserting Symbols and Special Characters

Word comes with a host of symbols and special characters for every need. Insert just the right one to keep from compromising a document's professional appearance with a hand-drawn arrow («) or missing mathematical symbol (å). In Word, you can insert symbols and special characters by using the Symbol command on the Insert menu or by using the Object Palette (**New!**) on the Toolbox, which is also available in all Office 2008 programs.

Insert Symbols and Special Characters

① Click the document where you want to insert a symbol or character.

② Click the **Insert** menu, and then click **Symbol**.

③ Click the **Symbols** tab or the **Special Characters** tab.

④ To see other symbols, click the **Font** drop-down, and then click a new font.

⑤ Click a symbol or character.

⑥ Click **Insert**.

Did You Know?

You can assign a shortcut key to insert a symbol within the document. Click the Insert menu, click Symbol, click a symbol, click Keyboard Shortcut, enter the shortcut key information requested, and then click OK.

See Also

See "Inserting Symbols" on page 53 for information on inserting symbols in all Office programs.

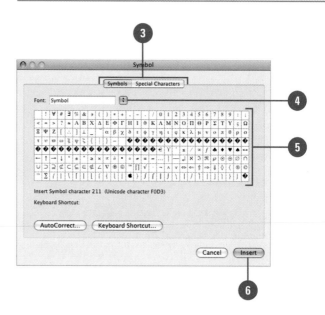

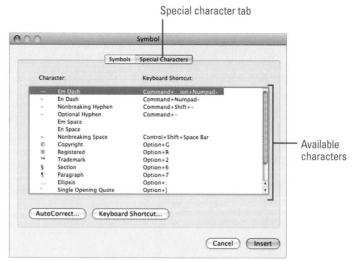

Special character tab

Available characters

Formatting a Document with Word

6

Introduction

The text of your document is complete, but now you want others to think your document is fun, professional, interesting, dynamic, and extraordinary. Try Microsoft Word 2008 to use extensive formatting features in order to lay out the information in your documents and create the exact look and mood you want.

Word documents are based on templates, which are pre-designed and preformatted files that serve as the foundation of the documents. Each template is made up of styles that have common design elements, such as coordinated fonts, sizes, and colors, as well as, page layout designs. Start with a Word template for memos, reports, fax cover pages, Web pages, and so on. Apply the existing styles for headings, titles, body text, and so forth. Then modify the template's styles, or create your own to better suit your needs. Make sure you get the look you want by adding emphasis using italics, boldface, and underline, changing text alignment, adjusting line and paragraph spacing, setting tabs and indents, and creating bulleted and numbered lists. When you're done, your document is sure to demand attention and convey your message in its appearance.

What You'll Do

Format Text for Emphasis

Use Automatic Formatting

Find and Replace Formatting

Change Paragraph Alignment

Change Line Spacing

Display Rulers

Set Paragraph Tabs

Set Paragraph Indents

Create Bulleted and Numbered Lists

Change Character Spacing

Change Text Direction

Apply a Style

Reveal Formatting Styles

Create and Modify Styles

Hide Text

Formatting Text for Emphasis

You'll often want to format, or change the style of, certain words or phrases to add emphasis to parts of a document. In addition to the standard formatting options—**Bold**, *Italic*, <u>Underline</u>, etc.—Word provides additional formatting effects to text, including Strikethrough, Double Strikethrough, Superscript, Subscript, Shadow, Outline, Emboss, Engrave, Small Caps, All Caps, and Hidden. To help you format sentences correctly and change capitalization, you can change text case.

Change Text Case

1. Select the text you want to format.

2. Click the **Format** menu, and then click **Change Case**.

3. Click the option you want:

   ◆ Sentence case.

   ◆ lowercase

   ◆ UPPERCASE

   ◆ Capitalize Each Word

   ◆ tOGGLEcASE

4. Click **OK**.

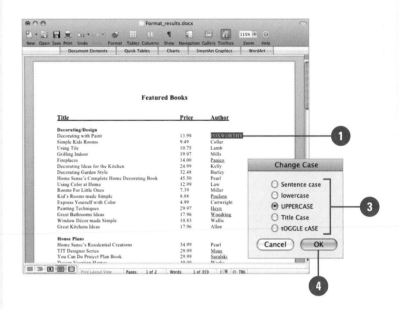

Highlight Text

1. Select the text you want to format.

2. Click the **Formatting Palette** tab on the Toolbox.

3. Click the **Font** panel to expand it.

4. Click the **Highlight** button arrow, and then click the color you want.

   ◆ Add highlight. Click a color.

   ◆ Remove highlight. Click **None**.

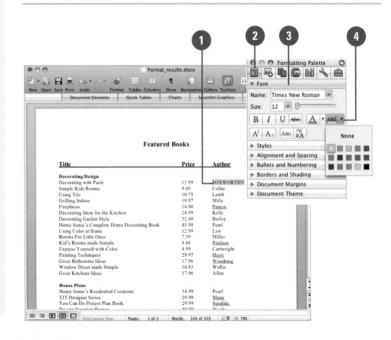

Apply Formatting Effects to Text

① Select the text you want to format.

② Click the **Format** menu, and then click **Font**.

③ Click the **Font** tab.

④ Click the formatting (**Font**, **Font Style**, **Size**, **Font color**, **Underline style**, and **Underline color**) you want.

⑤ Click to select the effects (**Strikethrough**, **Double strikethrough**, **Superscript**, **Subscript**, **Shadow**, **Outline**, **Emboss**, **Engrave**, **Small caps**, **All caps**, and **Hidden**) you want.

⑥ Check the results in the Preview box.

⑦ Select the **Enable all ligatures in document** check box to display ligatures, which are joined or decorative characters. This improves text style and readability.

Office 2008 can display ligatures (**New!**), while Office 2007 for Windows or older version cannot.

⑧ To make the new formatting options the default for all new Word documents, click **Default**, and then click **Yes**.

⑨ Click **OK**.

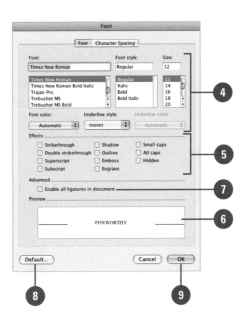

Did You Know?

You can use ligatures in fonts. You can use ligatures in Apple Advanced Typography (AAT) fonts, in Mac OS X v10.4 Tiger and both AAT and OpenType fonts in Mac OS X v10.5 (Leopard).

Using Automatic Formatting

Word can automatically perform some formatting functions for you as you type a document. For example, you can change straight quotation marks to smart (curly) quotes, hyphens to en-dashes or em-dashes, an asterisk before and after text to bold text, or an underscore before and after text to italic text. You can also type a number and text or a bullet and text to start a numbered or bulleted list. If you had AutoFormat disabled when you created the document, you still have the option of using the feature to find and correct errors in formatting.

Set Up Automatic Formatting As You Type

1. Click the **Tools** menu, and then click **AutoCorrect**.

2. Click the **AutoFormat As You Type** tab.

3. Select or clear the AutoFormat check boxes you want to use. Point to the option to display a description.

4. Click **OK**.

   Your choices take effect, but they only apply to text you will be entering subsequently. In this case, AutoFormat does not correct errors retroactively.

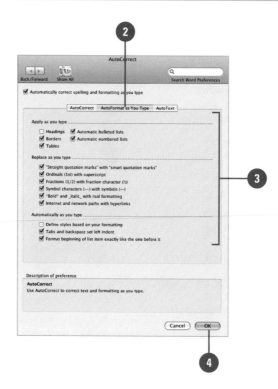

Change Document Formatting with AutoFormat

1. Click the **Format** menu, and then click **AutoFormat**.

2. Click **Options,** select the formatting options you want, and then click **OK**.

3. Click the **AutoFormat now** option to have Word automatically format the document, or click the **AutoFormat and review each change** option to review, and then accept or reject each change.

4. Click **OK**.

   If you chose the AutoFormat and review each change option, then continue.

5. Click **Review Changes** to look at changes individually.

6. Click **Style Gallery** if you want to preview your document, and then click **OK**.

7. Use the Accept and Reject buttons to accept or reject the review changes.

8. Click **Close** or **Cancel**.

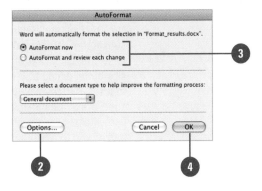

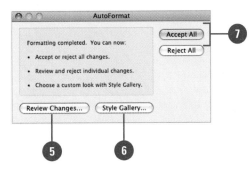

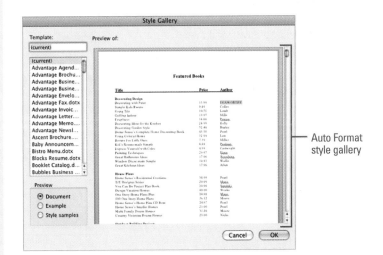

Auto Format style gallery

Finding and Replacing Formatting

Suddenly you realize all the bold text in your report would be easier to read in italics. Do you spend time making these changes one by one? No. The Find and Replace feature locates the formatting and instantly substitutes new formatting. If your search for a formatting change is an easy one, click Less in the Find and Replace dialog box to decrease the size of the dialog box. If your search is a more complex one, click More to display additional options. With the Match Case option, you can specify exact capitalization. The Highlight all items found in option highlights items found to make them easier to read. The Go To tab quickly moves you to a place or item in your document.

Find Formatting

1 Click the **Edit** menu, and then click **Find**.

2 To clear any previous settings, click **No Formatting**.

3 If you want to locate formatted text, type the word or words.

4 Click the **Format** drop-down, and then click the formatting option you want to find.

5 To highlight located items, click **Highlight all items found in** check box, click the drop-down, and then click **Main Document** or **Headers and Footers**.

6 Click **Find Next** to select the next instance of the formatted text.

7 Click **OK** to confirm Word finished the search.

8 Click **Close** or **Cancel**.

Did You Know?

You can find an item or location.
In Word, you can search for an item, such as bookmark or comment, or location, such as a page or section. Click the Edit menu, click Go To, click an item to find, enter an item number or name, click Next, or Previous, and then click Close.

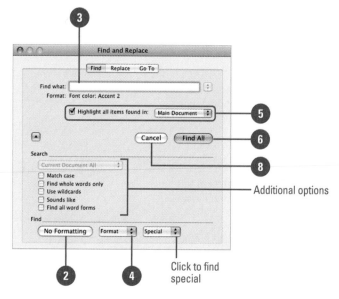

Additional options

Click to find special

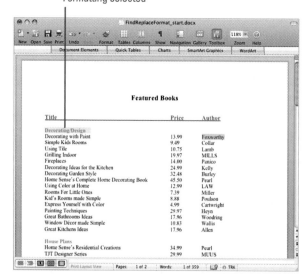

Formatting selected

Replace Formatting

1. Click the **Edit** menu, and then click **Replace**.

2. Click in the Find What box. If you want to locate formatted text, type the word or words.

3. Click the **Format** drop-down, and then click the formatting you want to find. When you're done, click **OK**.

4. Click in the Replace with box, and then type any text you want to substitute.

5. Click the **Format** drop-down, and then click the formatting you want to substitute. When you're done, click **OK**.

6. To substitute every instance of the formatting, click **Replace All**.

   To substitute the formatting one instance at a time, click **Find Next**, and then click **Replace**.

   If you want to cancel the replace, click **Cancel**.

7. If necessary, click **Yes** to search from the start of the document.

8. Click **OK** to confirm completion.

9. Click the **Close** button or **Cancel**.

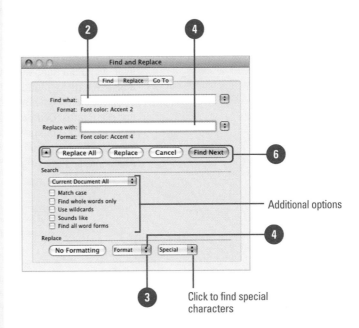

Additional options

Click to find special characters

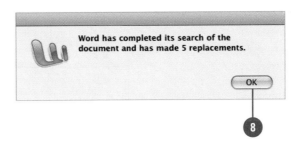

Did You Know?

You can find and replace special characters and document elements.
In Word, you can search for and replace special characters (for example, an em dash) and document elements (for example, a tab character). Click More in the Find and Replace dialog box, click Special, and then click the item you want from the menu.

Changing Paragraph Alignment

Text starts out positioned evenly along the left margin, and uneven, or **ragged**, at the right margin. Left-aligned text works well for body paragraphs in most cases, but other alignments vary the look of a document and help lead the reader through the text. **Right-aligned text**, which is even along the right margin and ragged at the left margin, is good for adding a date to a letter. **Justified text** spreads text evenly between the margins, creating a clean, professional look, often used in newspapers and magazines. **Centered text** is best for titles and headings. You can use Click-And-Type to quickly center titles or set different text alignment on the same line, or you can use the alignment buttons on the Alignment and Spacing panel to set alignment on one or more lines.

Align New Text with Click-And-Type

◆ Position the I-beam at the left, right, or center of the line where you want to insert new text.

When the I-beam shows the appropriate alignment, double-click to place the insertion point, and then type your text.

Click-And-Type Text Pointers

Pointer	Purpose
I≡	Left-aligns text
≡I	Right-aligns text
I	Centers text
I⁺≡	Creates a new line in the same paragraph
▣ I	Creates a text around a picture

Align Existing Text

1 Position the I-beam, or select at least one line in each paragraph to align.

2 Click the **Formatting Palette** tab.

3 Click the **Alignment and Spacing** panel to expand it.

4 Click the alignment button you want:

◆ **Align Text Left**

◆ **Align Center**

◆ **Align Text Right**

◆ **Justify**

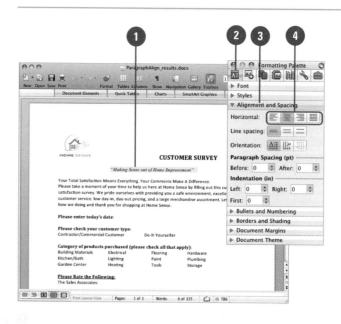

Changing Line Spacing

The lines in all Word documents are single-spaced by default, which is appropriate for letters and most documents. But you can easily change your document line spacing to double or 1.5 lines to allow extra space between every line. This is useful when you want to make notes on a printed document. Sometimes, you'll want to add space above and below certain paragraphs, for headlines, or indented quotations to help set off the text.

Change Line Spacing

1. Select the text you want to change.

2. Click the **Formatting Palette** tab.

3. Click the **Alignment and Spacing** panel to expand it.

4. To quickly change line spacing, click a line spacing button: **Single Space**, **1.5 Space**, or **Double Space**.

    TIMESAVER *Press* ⌘+1 *for single-spacing,* ⌘+5 *for 1.5 spacing, or* ⌘+2 *for double-spacing.*

5. To quickly change spacing before or after a paragraph spacing, specify a number in the **Before** or **After** boxes.

6. To enter precise parameters, click the **Format** menu, click **Paragraph**, click the **Indents and Spacing** tab, specify the line or paragraph settings you want, and then click **OK**.

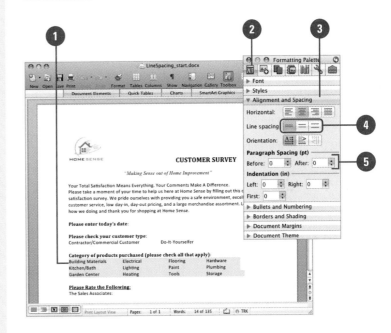

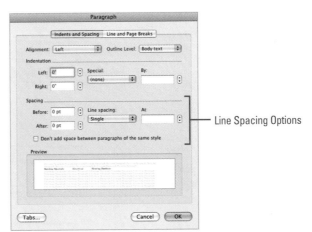

Line Spacing Options

Displaying Rulers

Word rulers do more than measure. The **horizontal ruler** above the document shows the length of the typing line and lets you quickly adjust left and right margins and indents, set tabs, and change column widths. The **vertical ruler** along the left edge of the document lets you adjust top and bottom margins and change table row heights. You can hide the rulers to get more room for your document. As you work with long documents, use the document map to jump to any heading in your document. Headings are in the left pane and documents in the right.

Show and Hide the Rulers

1. Click the **View** menu, and then click **Ruler**.

   ◆ To view the horizontal ruler, click the **Web Layout View** or **Draft View** button.

   ◆ To view the horizontal and vertical rulers, click the **Print Layout View** button.

2. When the rulers are hidden, you can move your mouse over the horizontal or vertical ruler area to display them as you need it.

Did You Know?

You can change the ruler measurements. Change the ruler to show inches, centimeters, millimeters, points, or picas. Click the Word menu, click Preferences, click General, click the Measurement units drop-down, and then select the measurement you want, and then click OK.

You can set your text to be hyphenated. Hyphenation prevents ugly gaps and short lines in text. Click the Tools menu, click Hyphenation, and then select the Automatically hyphenate document check box for automatic use or clear it and click Manual for manual use. Click Options to set the hyphenation zone and limit the number of consecutive hyphens (usually two), and then click OK.

Vertical ruler   Horizontal ruler

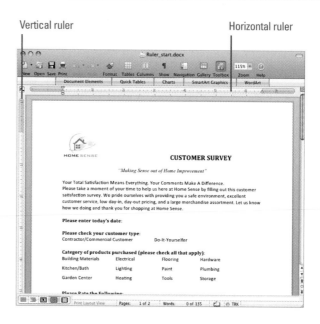

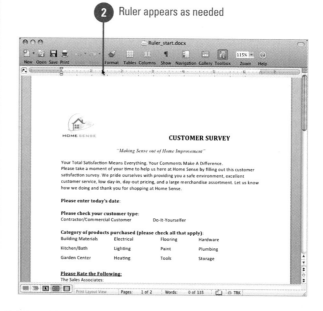

Ruler appears as needed

Setting Paragraph Tabs

In your document, **tabs** set how text or numerical data aligns in relation to the document margins. A **tab stop** is a predefined stopping point along the document's typing line. Default tab stops are set every half-inch, but you can set multiple tabs per paragraph at any location. Choose from four text tab stops: left, right, center, and decimal (for numerical data). The bar tab inserts a vertical bar at the tab stop. You can use the Tab button on the horizontal ruler to switch between the available tabs.

Create and Clear a Tab Stop

1 Select one or more paragraphs in which you want to set a tab stop.

2 Click the **Tab** button on the horizontal ruler, and then select the type of tab stop you want.

3 Click the ruler where you want to set the tab stop.

4 If necessary, drag the tab stop to position it where you want.

To display a numerical measurement in the ruler where the tab is placed, press and hold Alt as you drag.

5 To clear a tab stop, drag it off the ruler.

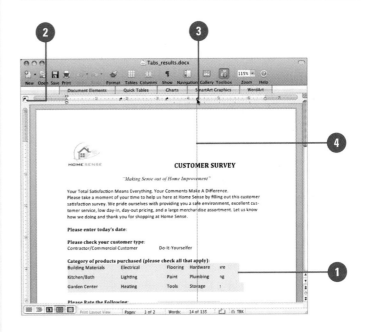

Did You Know?

You can view formatting marks.
Sometimes it's hard to see the number of spaces or tabs between words. You can change the view to display formatting marks, a period for space and an arrow for tabs. Click Show button on the Standard toolbar to toggle on and off.

Tab Stops	
Tab Stop	**Purpose**
└	Aligns text to the left of the tab stop
┘	Aligns text to the right of the tab stop
┴	Centers text on the tab stop
┷	Aligns numbers on the decimal point
I	Inserts a vertical bar at the tab stop

Setting Paragraph Indents

Quickly indent lines of text to precise locations from the left or right margin with the horizontal ruler. Indent the first line of a paragraph (called a **first-line indent**) as books do to distinguish paragraphs. Indent the second and subsequent lines of a paragraph from the left margin (called a **hanging indent**) to create a properly formatted bibliography. Indent the entire paragraph any amount from the left and right margins (called **left indents** and **right indents**) to separate quoted passages. You can indent the first line of a paragraph by clicking at the beginning of the paragraph, and then pressing Tab. You can indent the entire paragraph by selecting it, and then pressing Tab.

Indent Paragraph Lines Precisely

1. Click the **View** menu, and then click **Ruler** to display the Ruler.

2. Click the paragraph or select multiple paragraphs to indent:

   ◆ To change the left indent of the first line, drag the First-line Indent marker.

   ◆ To change the indent of the second and subsequent lines, drag the Hanging Indent marker.

   ◆ To change the left indent for all lines, drag the Left Indent marker.

   ◆ To change the right indent for all lines, drag the Right Indent marker.

   As you drag a marker, the dotted guideline helps you accurately position the indent. You can also press and hold Control to see a measurement in the ruler.

   ◆ To set precise parameters for left, right, and first-line indents, expand the **Alignment and Spacing** panel on the Formatting Palette tab, and then specify measurements in the **Left**, **Right**, and **First** boxes.

Hanging Indent marker

First-line Indent marker

Left Indent marker

Right Indent marker

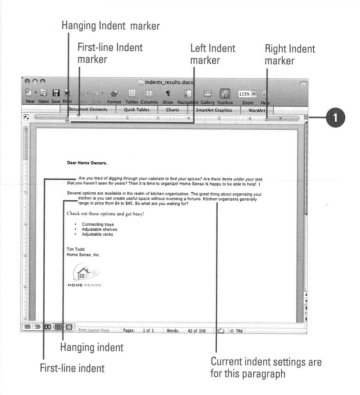

Hanging indent

First-line indent

Current indent settings are for this paragraph

Indent a Paragraph

1. Click the paragraph, or select multiple paragraphs to indent.

2. Click the **Formatting Palette** tab.

3. Click the **Bullet and Numbering** panel to expand it.

4. Click the **Increase Indent** button or **Decrease Indent** button to move the paragraph right or left one-half inch.

Did You Know?

You can add line numbers to a document or page. Click the Format menu, click Document, click the Layout tab, click Line Numbers, select the Add line numbering check box, set numbering options, click Restart Each Page, Restart Each Section, or Continuous, click OK, and then click OK.

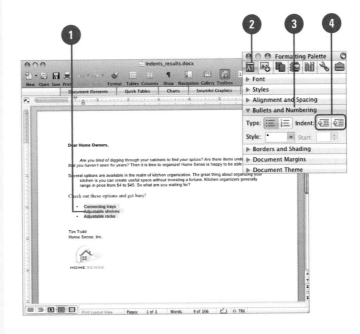

Set Indentation Using the Tab Key

1. Click the **Word** menu, and then click **Preferences**.

2. Click the **AutoCorrect** icon.

3. Click the **AutoFormat as You Type** tab.

4. Select the **Tabs and backspace set left indent** check box.

5. Click **OK**.

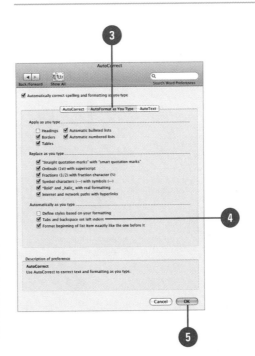

Creating Bulleted and Numbered Lists

The best way to draw attention to a list is to format the items with bullets or numbers. You can even create multi-level lists. For different emphasis, change any bullet or number style to one of Word's many predefined formats. For example, switch round bullets to check boxes or Roman numerals to lowercase letters. You can also customize the list style or insert a picture as a bullet. If you move, insert, or delete items in a numbered list, Word sequentially renumbers the list for you.

Create a Bulleted or Numbered List

1. Click where you want to create a bulleted or numbered list.

2. Click the **Formatting Palette** tab.

3. Click the **Bullet and Numbering** panel to expand it.

4. Click the **Bullets** or **Numbering** button.

5. Click the **Style** drop-down, and then select a style.

6. For a numbered list, enter a start value for the numbered list.

7. Type the first item in your list, and then press Return.

8. Type the next item in your list, and then press Return.

9. Click the **Bullets** or **Numbering** button again, or press Return to end the list.

Did You Know?

You can quickly create a numbered list. Click to place the insertion point at the beginning of a line, type 1., press the Spacebar, type the first item, and then press Return. Press Return or Backspace to end the list.

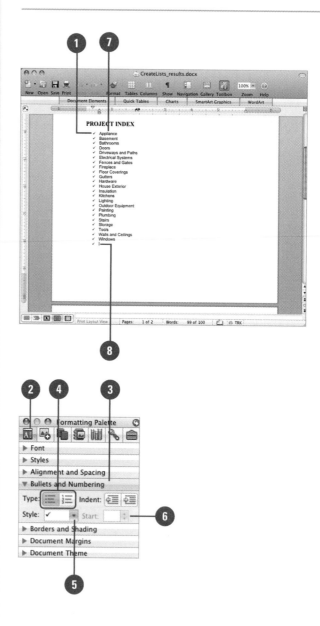

Change Bullet or Number Styles

1 Select the list, click the **Format** menu, and then click **Bullets and Numbering**.

2 Click the **Bulleted** tab or the **Numbered** tab.

3 Click a predefined format.

4 Click **Customize** to change the format style, and then click **OK**. You can change the Bullet (or Number) Position and Text Position options to specify where you want the bullet (or number) to appear and how much to indent the text.

5 Click the **Restart numbering** or **Continue previous list** option.

6 Click **OK**.

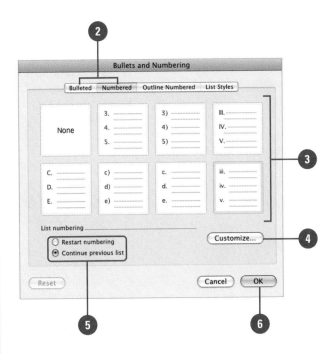

Create a Multi-Level Bulleted or Numbered List

1 Start the list as usual.

2 Press Tab to indent a line to the next level bullet or number, type the item, and then press Return to insert the next bullet or number.

3 Press Shift+Tab to return to the previous level bullet or number.

4 End the list as usual.

5 To format the multi-level list, select the list, click the **Format** menu, click the **Bullets and Numbering**, click the **Outline Numbered** tab, select a format, and then click **OK**.

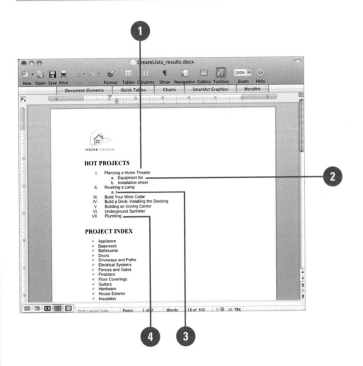

Changing Character Spacing

Kerning is the amount of space between each individual character that you type. Sometimes the space between two characters is larger than others, which makes the word look uneven. You can use the Font dialog box to change the kerning setting for selected characters. Kerning works only with TrueType or Adobe Type Manager fonts. You can expand or condense character spacing to create a special effect for a title, or re-align the position of characters to the bottom edge of the text—this is helpful for positioning the copyright or trademark symbols.

Change Character Spacing

1. Select the text you want to format.

2. Click the **Format** menu, and then click **Font**.

3. Click the **Character Spacing** tab.

4. Click the **Spacing** drop-down, click an option, and then specify a point size to expand or condense spacing by the amount specified.

5. Click the **Position** drop-down, click an option, and then specify a point size to raise or lower the text in relation to the baseline (bottom of the text).

6. Select the **Kerning for fonts** check box, and then specify a point size.

7. Check the results in the Preview box.

8. To make the new formatting options the default for all new Word documents, click **Default**, and then click **Yes**.

9. Click **OK**.

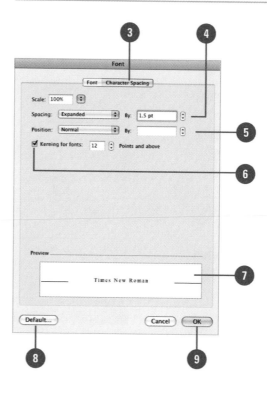

Changing Text Direction

When you create a document in Word, the default text direction, also known as orientation, is horizontal across the page. If you want to create a different type of document, such as a flyer, you can change the text direction to vertical right or vertical left. You can change text direction by using the Alignment and Spacing panel on the Formatting Palette tab or the Text Direction command on the Format menu.

Change Text Direction Using the Alignment and Spacing Panel

1. Select the text you want to align.

2. Click the **Formatting Palette** tab on the Toolbox.

3. Click the **Alignment and Spacing** panel to expand it.

4. Click any of the **Change Text Direction** buttons on the panel.

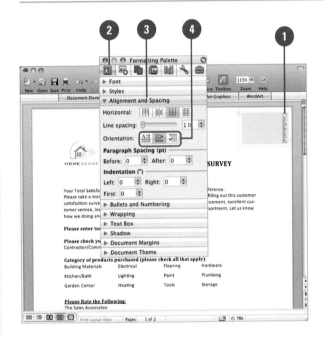

Change Text Direction

1. Click the **Format** menu, and then click **Text Direction**.

2. Click any of the text direction icons.

3. Click **OK**.

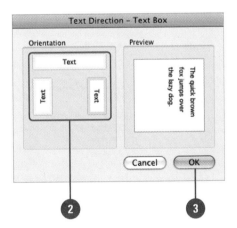

Applying a Style

The Format Painter copies and pastes formatting from one batch of selected text to another without copying the text. When you want to apply multiple groupings of formatting, save each as a style. A **style** is a collection of formatting settings saved with a name in a document or template that you can apply to text at any time. If you modify a style, you make the change once, but all text tagged with that style changes to reflect the new format. Each style set consists of a variety of different formatting style combinations, which you can view using the styles available in the Styles panel on the Formatting Palette tab. The Styles panel allows you to view the current style of the selected text, create or modify a style, view available or all styles, and clear formatting.

Apply a Style

1. Select the text to which you want to apply a style.

2. Click the **Formatting Palette** tab.

3. Click the **Styles** panel to expand it.

4. Click the scroll up or down arrow in the Styles panel to see additional styles.

5. Click the style you want to apply from the styles list.

Did You Know?

You can clear style formatting. Select the text you want to clear, click the Formatting Palette tab, click the Style panel to expand it, and then click Clear Formatting at the top of the styles list.

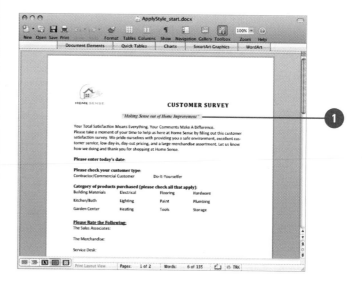

Current style

Revealing Formatting Styles

Text within a document is based on a style, which you can view using the Style panel or the Reveal Formatting command. If you want to view the style for one piece of text, the Style panel is quick and easy. You can open the Styles panel to display the format of selected text, such as its font and font effects. However, if you want to view the style for multiple pieces of text, the Reveal Formatting command is the best way to go, where you can turn it on, view text styles, and then turn it off.

Reveal Formatting Styles

1. Click the **View** menu, and then click **Reveal Formatting**.

   The cursor changes to a comment bubble with text.

2. Select the text you want to reveal.

   A screen appears, displaying paragraph and font formatting styles with specific details.

3. To dismiss the screen, move your mouse.

4. When you're done, click the **View** menu, and then click **Reveal Formatting**.

Formatting style revealed

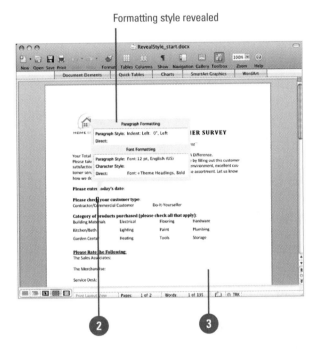

For Your Information

Selecting Text with Similar Formatting

A quick way to select text with similar formatting is to use the Select Text with Similar Formatting command. After you select the text with the formatting you want to find, click the Select button on the Styles panel on the Formatting Palette tab. Word highlights all the text with similar formatting in the document. With the text selected, you can change the text formatting.

Creating and Modifying Styles

Word provides a variety of styles to choose from. But sometimes you need to create a new style or modify an existing one to get the exact look you want. When you create a new style, specify if it applies to paragraphs or characters, and give the style a short, descriptive name that describes its purpose so you and others recall when to use that style. A **paragraph style** is a group of format settings that can be applied only to all of the text within a paragraph (even if it is a one-line paragraph), while a **character style** is a group of format settings that is applied to any block of text at the user's discretion. To modify a style, adjust the formatting settings of an existing style.

Create a New Style

1. Select the text whose formatting you want to save as a style.

2. Click the **Formatting Palette** tab, and then click the **Styles** panel to expand it.

   ◆ You can also click the **Format** menu, and then click **Styles**.

3. Click **New Style**.

4. Type a short, descriptive name.

5. Click the **Style type** drop-down, and then click **Paragraph** to include the selected text's line spacing and margins in the style, or click **Character** to include only formatting, such as font, size, and bold, in the style.

6. Click the **Style for following paragraph** drop-down, and then click the name of style you want to be applied after a paragraph with the new style.

7. To add the style to the document template, select the **Add to template** check box.

8. To automatically update the style, select the **Automatically update** check box.

9. Click **OK**.

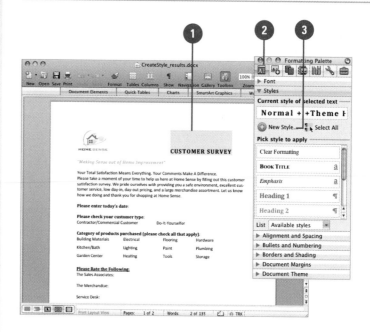

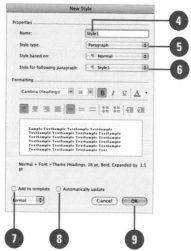

Modify a Style

1. Click the **Format** menu, and then click **Styles**.

2. Select the style you want to modify.

   - You can also point to a style in the Styles panel on the **Formatting Palette** tab, click the list arrow, and then click **Modify**.

3. Click **Modify**.

4. Click **Format**, and then click the formatting type you want:

   - To change character formatting, such as font type and boldface, click **Font**.

   - To change line spacing and indents, click **Paragraph**.

5. Select the properties and formatting options you want.

6. Check the Preview box, and review the style description. Make any formatting changes necessary.

7. Click **OK**.

8. Click **Apply**.

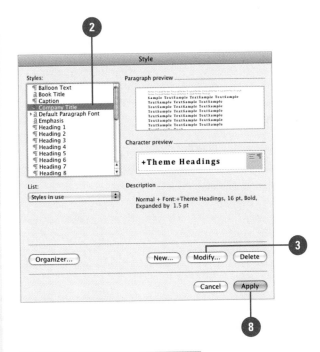

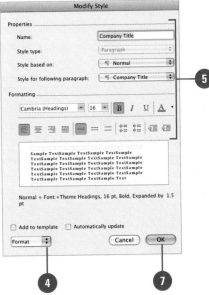

Did You Know?

You can save time by using the Styles feature. Once you format a document with styles, you can try different looks quickly. Modify each style, and then watch all text tagged with that style change automatically.

You can view different style lists. When looking at the list of styles in the Styles panel, you can select what types of styles to view from the List drop-down: Available Formatting, Formatting In Use, Available Styles, and All Styles.

Hiding Text

If you have confidential information in a document or text that you don't want others to see, you can hide the text. When you hide text, you can't view or print the text unless you select the Hidden Text option in the Preferences dialog box. When you display or print hidden text, the characters appear with a dotted lined underneath. Hiding text does not protect your text from being seen, but it does conceal it from others.

Hide or Unhide Text

1. Select the text you want to hide or the hidden text.

2. Click the **Format** menu, and then click the **Font**.

3. Click the **Font** tab.

4. Select or clear the **Hidden** check box.

5. Click **OK**.

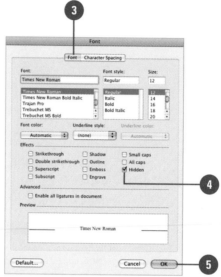

Display or Print Hidden Text

1. Click the **Word** button, and then click **Preferences**.

2. Click the **View** icon.

3. Select the **Hidden text** check box.

4. Click the **Back** button.

5. Click the **Print** icon.

6. Select the **Hidden text** check box.

7. Click **OK**.

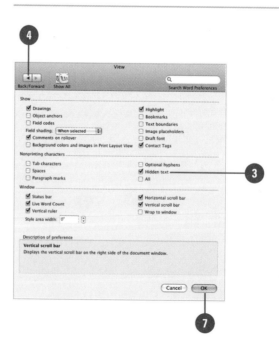

Enhancing a Document with Word

Introduction

Once you've mastered the basics, Microsoft Word 2008 has plenty of advanced features to enhance your documents. Whether it's a single-page flyer or a twenty-page report, you can arrange the text and add enhancements that make your document appealing and easy to read.

After you create your basic document, consider how you can improve its appearance and communicate its message more effectively. For example, if your document is a brochure or newsletter, arrange the text in columns and add an enlarged capital letter to the first word in each paragraph to add style and grab the readers attention. Or organize information in a table to draw attention to important data or clarify the details of a complicated paragraph.

Another way to impress clients, business associates, social groups, or even family members is to create personalized form letters for any occasion—an upcoming meeting, a holiday greeting, or a family announcement. Create a formatted document and enter text that doesn't change. Any data that changes from person to person (such as names) goes into another file, which you merge with the form letter. In a snap, you've got personalized letters that show you care.

What You'll Do

Add a Drop Cap

Add a Watermark

Add Page Backgrounds

Wrap Text Around an Object

Work with Text Boxes

Create and Modify a Table

Enter Text in a Table and Adjust Cells

Format a Table and Calculate a Value

Add a Quick Style to a Table

Create a Form Letter and Labels

Insert a Table of Contents

Create an Index and Captions

Create a Table of Figures

Create Footnotes or Endnotes

Create a Bookmark

Compare Documents

Use Track Changes

Address Envelopes and Labels

Use Print Preview

Add a Cover Page

Adding a Drop Cap

A few simple elements—drop caps, borders, and shading—make your newsletters and brochures look like a professional produced them. A **drop cap** is the enlarged first letter of a paragraph that provides instant style to a document. Instead of using a desktop publishing program to create a drop cap effect, you can quickly achieve the same thing in Word. You can change the drop cap position, font, and height, and then enter the distance between the drop cap and paragraph.

Add a Drop Cap

1. Click the paragraph with the drop cap.

2. Click the **Print Layout View** button.

3. Click the **Format** menu, and then click **Drop Cap**.

4. Click a drop cap position.

5. Change the drop cap font and height, and then enter the distance between the drop cap and text.

6. Click **OK**.

Did You Know?

You can remove a drop cap. In Print Layout view, select the paragraph with the drop cap, click the Format menu, click Drop Cap, click Remove, and then click OK.

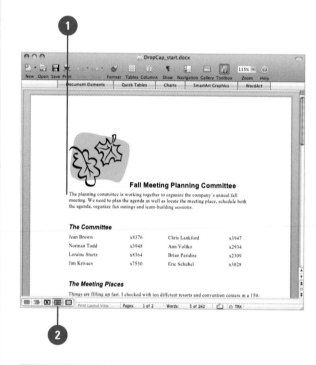

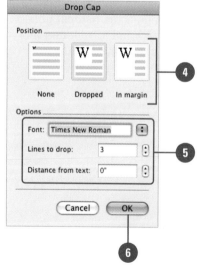

Adding a Watermark

A **watermark** is a background effect—some text or a graphic, that prints in a light shade behind your text on your document. You can use a washed out version of your company logo, or you can add text such as SAMPLE, DRAFT, PROPOSAL, or CONFIDENTIAL. If you decide to change your watermark, it's as easy as typing in some new text.

Add or Remove a Watermark

1. Click the **Print Layout View** button.

2. Click the **Insert** menu, and then click **Watermark**.

3. To remove a watermark, click the **No watermark** option.

4. To insert a picture as a watermark, click the **Picture watermark** option, click **Select Picture**, select a picture, and then click **OK**.

5. To customize watermark text, click the **Text watermark** option, select the settings you want.

6. Click **OK**.

Did You Know?

You can remove a watermark. In Print Layout view, select the paragraph with the drop cap, click the Insert menu, click watermark, click the No watermark option, and then click OK.

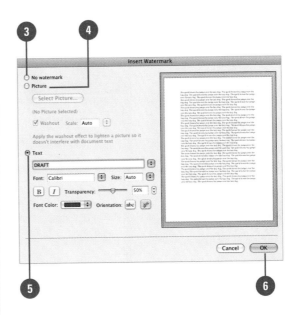

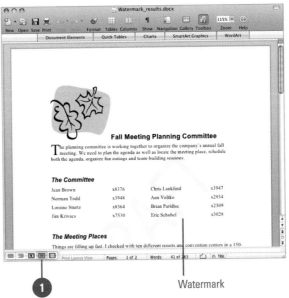

Watermark

Adding Page Backgrounds

Borders are lines or graphics that appear around a page, paragraph, selected text, or table cells. With borders, you can change the line style, width, and colors, and you can add shadows and 3D effects. In addition to a page border, you can also change the page color. If you apply a theme color as the page color, it changes if you change the document theme. **Shading** is a color that fills the background of selected text, paragraphs, or table cells. For more attractive pages, add clips or columns.

Add Borders and Shading

1 Select the text you want to have a border.

2 Click the **Print Layout View** button.

3 Click the **Format** menu, and then click **Borders and Shading**.

4 Click the **Borders** tab.

5 Do one of the following:

   ◆ Click a box setting to modify all border edges.

   ◆ Click the edge in the diagram to modify individual border edges.

6 Click a border style, color, and width.

7 Click the **Shading** tab.

8 Click the **Fill** list arrow, and then click a fill color.

9 Click **OK**.

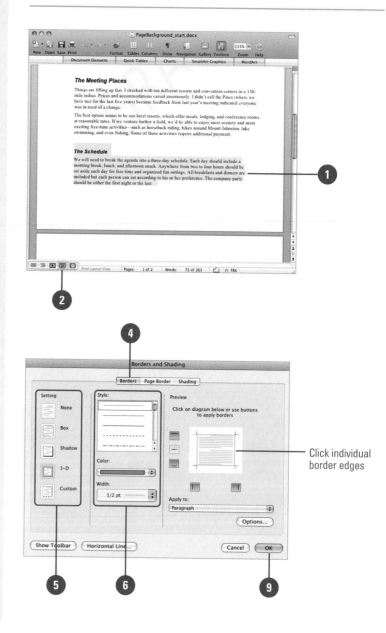

Click individual border edges

Add or Remove a Page Border

1. Click the page you want to have a border.

2. Click the **Print Layout View** button.

3. Click the **Format** menu, and then click **Borders and Shading**.

4. Click the **Page Border** tab.

5. Click a box setting.

6. Click a line style, or click the Art list arrow, and then select a line or art style.

7. Click a **Width** list arrow, and then select a width.

8. Click the **Apply to** list arrow, and then select the pages you want to have borders.

9. Click **OK**.

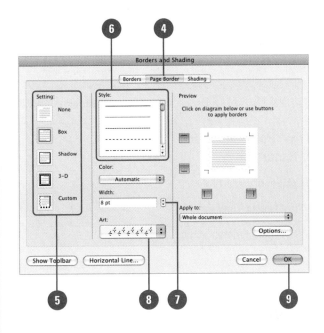

Change the Page Background Color

1. Click the page you want to have a border.

2. Click the **Format** menu, and then click **Background**.

3. Click the color you want to use as the page background.

4. To remove the color, click **No Fill**.

5. Click the **Close** button on the Background window.

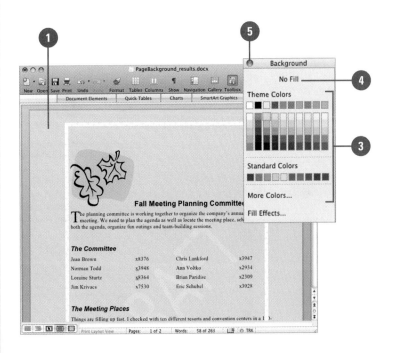

Wrapping Text Around an Object

When integrating pictures, charts, tables, or other graphics with your text, you need to wrap the text around the object regardless of where it is placed on the page. Rather than having to constantly reset margins and make other tedious adjustments, Word simplifies this task with the text wrapping feature. Unless your object or table is large enough to span the entire page, your layout will look more professional if you wrap your text around it instead of leaving excessive white space.

Change the Text Position Around an Object or Picture

1. Select the object or picture.

2. Click the **Print Layout View** button.

3. Click the **Formatting Palette** tab on the toolbox.

4. Click the **Wrapping** panel to expand it.

5. Click the **Style** button, and then click the text wrapping option you want.

6. Click the **Wrap to** button, and then click the text wrapping alignment option you want: **Both Sides**, **Left**, **Right**, **Largest Side**.

7. To customize distance from the text, specify the distance you want in the **Left**, **Right**, **Top**, and **Bottom** boxes.

Did You Know?

You can also use the Layout pane in the Format Picture dialog box to adjust text wrapping. Select the picture, click the Format menu, click Picture, click Layout, adjust the wrapping options you want, and then click OK.

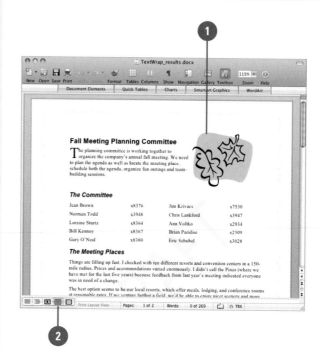

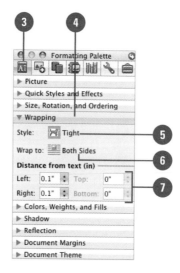

Wrap Text Tightly Around an Object or Picture

1. Select the object or picture.

2. Click the **Print Layout View** button.

3. Click the **Formatting Palette** tab on the toolbox.

4. Click the **Wrapping** panel to expand it.

5. Click the **Style** button, and then click **Tight**.

6. Click the **Style** button, and then click **Edit Wrap Boundary**.

7. Drag edit points around the object or picture to tighten text around it.

8. Click a blank area of the document to deselect the object or picture.

Did You Know?

You can wrap text around a table.
Select the table, click the Table menu, click Table Properties, click the Table tab, select the alignment and text wrapping options you want, click Positioning to set precise measurements, and then click OK.

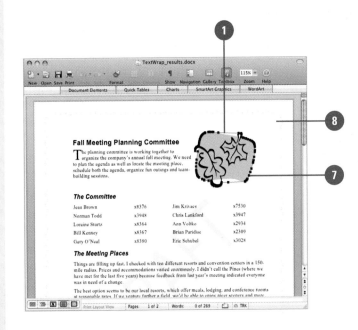

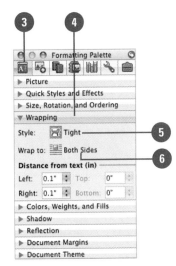

Working with Text Boxes

In addition to normal text on a page, you can also create independent text boxes to hold other types of information—such as titles, heading, side bars, and articles—similar to those found on a desktop publishing page. You can insert a text box with predefined information or you can create a blank text box. You can even link two or more text boxes together to have text flow to different parts of a document. If you no longer need the text boxes to link, you can quickly break the link.

Create a Text Box from Existing Text

1. Select the text you want to place in a text box.

2. Click the **Insert** menu, and then click **Text Box**.

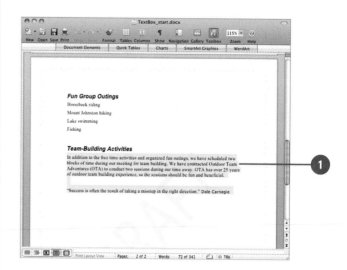

Create a Text Box

1. Click the **Insert** menu, and then click **Text Box**.

2. Point to where you want to place the text box, and then drag to create a text box the size you want.

3. If necessary, click the text box to select it.

4. Type the text you want.

5. To resize the text box, drag a size handle.

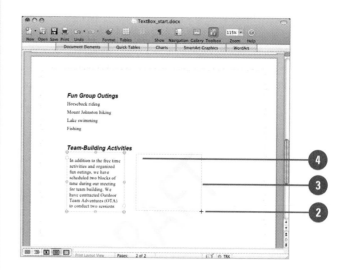

Link Text Boxes

1 Select the source text box.

2 Do either of the following:

◆ **Link to a new text box.** Click the box's forward or backwards link handle, and then draw a new text box.

◆ **Link to an existing empty text box.** Create an empty destination text box, Control-click the source text box, click **Create Text Box Link**, and then click the empty text box to which you want to link.

Did You Know?

You can remove a link. Select the text box, and then press Delete. Only the text box is deleted. The story text remains.

You can break a link. Control-click the text box that you want to be the last link in the story, and then click Break Forward Link. All boxes following the selected one will now be empty.

You can change text direction in a text box. Select the text box you want to modify, click the Formatting Palette tab, click the Alignment and Spacing panel to expand it, and then click one of the Orientation buttons.

See Also

See "Adding to a Publication" on page 144 for information on creating and linking text boxes in a publication.

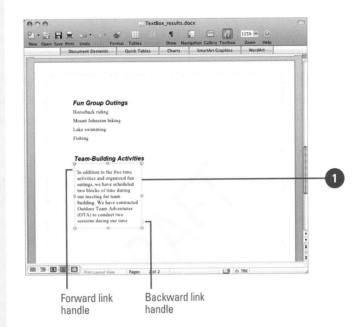

Forward link handle

Backward link handle

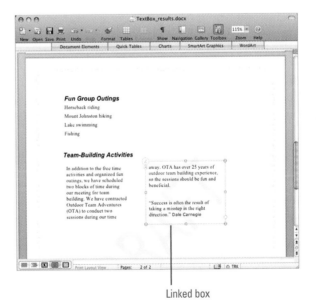

Linked box

Creating a Table

A **table** organizes information neatly into rows and columns. The intersection of a row and a column is called a **cell**. You can draw a custom table with various sized cells and then enter text, or you can create a table from existing text separated by paragraphs, tabs, or commas. In addition, now you can create **nested tables** (a table created within a table cell), **floating tables** (tables with text wrapped around them), or **side-by-side tables** (separate but adjacent tables). If you decide not to use a table, you can convert it to text.

Create a Table from Existing Text

1. Select the text for the table.

2. Click the **Table** menu, point to Convert, and then click **Convert Text to Table**.

3. Enter the number of columns.

4. Select an AutoFit column width option.

5. To format the table, click **Auto-Format**, select the formatting options you want, and then click **OK**.

6. Click a symbol to separate text into table cells.

7. Click **OK**.

Did You Know?

You can convert a table back to text. Select the table, click the Table menu, point to Convert, click Convert Table to Text, select the Separate text with option, typically Tabs, and then click OK.

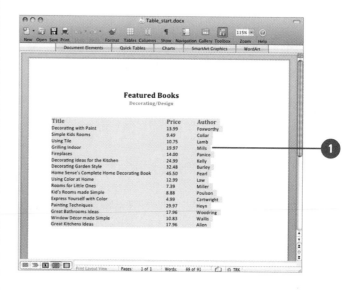

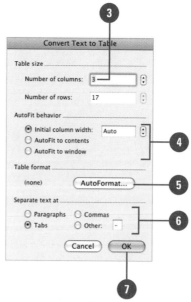

Entering Text in a Table

Once you create your table, you enter text into cells just as you would in a paragraph, except pressing Tab moves you from cell to cell. As you type in a cell, text wraps to the next line, and the height of a row expands as you enter text that extends beyond the column width. The first row in the table is good for column headings, whereas the left-most column is good for row labels. Before you can modify a table, you need to know how to select the rows and columns of a table.

Enter Text and Move Around a Table

1. The insertion point shows where text that you type will appear in a table. After you type text in a cell:

   ◆ Press Enter to start a new paragraph within that cell.

   ◆ Press Tab to move the insertion point to the next cell to the right (or to the first cell in the next row).

   ◆ Press the arrow keys or click in a cell to move the insertion point to a new location.

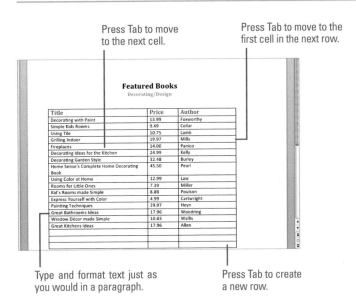

Press Tab to move to the next cell.

Press Tab to move to the first cell in the next row.

Type and format text just as you would in a paragraph.

Press Tab to create a new row.

Select Table Elements

Refer to this table for methods of selecting table elements, including:

   ◆ The entire table

   ◆ One or more rows and columns

   ◆ One or more cells

Did You Know?

You can delete contents within a cell. Select the cells whose contents you want to delete, and then press Delete.

Selecting Table Elements

To Select	Do This
The entire table	Click ⊞ next to the table, or click anywhere in the table, click the Table menu, point to Select, and then click Table.
One or more rows	Click in the left margin next to the first row you want to select, and then drag to select the rows you want.
One or more columns	Click just above the first column you want to select, and then drag with ↓ to select the columns you want.
The column or row with the insertion point	Click the Table menu, point to Select, and then click Column or Row.
A single cell	Drag a cell or click the cell with ➚
More than one cell	Drag with ➚ to select a group of cells.

Modifying a Table

As you begin to work on a table, you might need to modify its structure by adding more rows, columns, or cells to accommodate new text, graphics, or other tables. The table realigns as needed to accommodate the new structure. When you insert rows, columns, or cells, the existing rows shift down, the existing columns shift right, and you choose what direction the existing cells shift. Similarly, when you delete unneeded rows, columns, or cells from a table, the table realigns itself.

Insert Additional Rows or Columns

1. Select the row above which you want the new rows to appear, or select the column to the left of which you want the new columns to appear.

2. Drag to select the number of rows or columns you want to insert.

3. Click the **Formatting Palette** tab.

4. Click the **Table** panel to expand it.

5. Click the **Insert** button arrow, and then click an insert option:

   ◆ **Columns to the Left**.

   ◆ **Columns to the Right**.

   ◆ **Rows Above**.

   ◆ **Rows Below**.

Did You Know?

You can insert cells. Select the cell from where you want to insert new cells, click the Formatting Palette tab, click the Table panel to expand it, click the Insert button arrow, click Insert Cells, select a shift cell option, and then click OK.

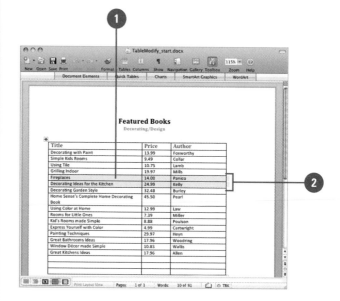

Insert options

202

Delete Table, Rows, Columns, or Cells

1. Select the rows, columns, or cells you want to delete.

2. Click the **Formatting Palette** tab.

3. Click the **Table** panel to expand it.

4. Click the **Delete** button arrow, and then click a delete option:

   - **Table**.

   - **Columns**.

   - **Rows**.

   - **Cells**. Select the direction in which you want the remaining cells to shift to fill the space, and then click OK.

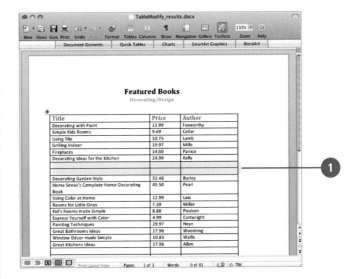

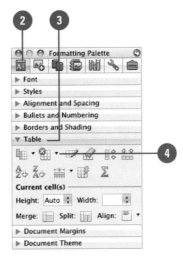

Adjusting Table Cells

Often there is more to modifying a table than adding or deleting rows or columns; you need to make cells just the right size to accommodate the text you are entering in the table. For example, a title in the first row of a table might be longer than the first cell in that row. To spread the title across the top of the table, you can merge (combine) the cells to form one long cell. Sometimes, to indicate a division in a topic, you need to split (or divide) a cell into two. You can also split one table into two at any row. Moreover, you can modify the width of any column and height of any row to better present your data.

Merge and Split Table Cells and Tables

- To merge two or more cells into a single cell, select the cells you want to merge, click the **Table** panel under the Formatting Palette tab, and then click the **Merge Cells** button.

- To split a cell into multiple cells, click the cell you want to split, click the **Table** panel under the Formatting Palette tab, and then click the **Split Cells** button. Enter the number of rows or columns (or both) you want to split the selected cell into, clear the **Merge cells before split** check box, and then click **OK**.

- To split a table into two tables separated by a paragraph, click in the row that you want as the top row in the second table, click the **Table** panel under the Formatting Palette tab, and then click the **Split Table** button.

- To merge two tables into button one, delete the paragraph between them.

The three cells in this row will merge into one.

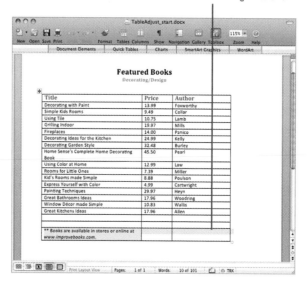

Split cells

Merge cells

Adjust Column Widths and Row Heights

① Select the columns or rows you want to change.

② Click the **Formatting Palette** tab.

③ Click the **Table** panel to expand it.

④ Change the Height and Width boxes:

- ◆ **Height.** To change the row height, enter a height in the Height box and then press Return, or use the Up and Down arrows.

- ◆ **Width.** To change the column width, enter a width in the Width box and then press Return, or use the Up and Down arrows.

Change Table Properties

① Click in the table you want to change.

② Click the **Table** menu, and then click **Table Properties**.

③ Click the **Table** tab.

④ Click an alignment option, and then specify an indent from the left (when you select the Left alignment option).

⑤ Click a text wrapping option.

⑥ Click **OK**.

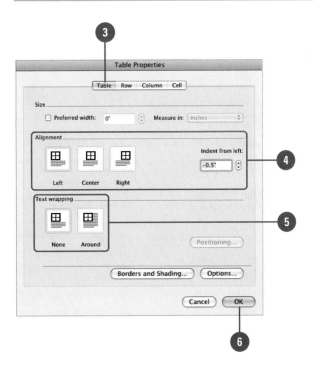

Formatting a Table

Tables distinguish text from paragraphs. In turn, formatting, alignment, and text direction distinguish text in table cells. Start by applying one of Word's predesigned table formats using AutoFormat. Then customize your table by realigning the cells' contents both horizontally and vertically, changing the direction of text within selected cells, such as the column headings, and resizing the entire table. You can modify borders and shading using the Tables panel or Tables and Borders toolbar to make printed tables easier to read and more attractive.

Format a Table Automatically

1. Select the table you want to format.

2. Click the **Table** menu, and then click **Table AutoFormat**.

3. Click a format.

4. Select the formatting options you want to apply.

5. Click **OK**.

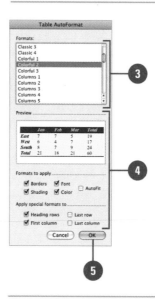

Align Text Within Cells

1. Select the cells, rows, or columns you want to align.

2. Click the **Formatting Palette** tab.

3. Click the **Table** panel to expand it.

4. Click the **Align** button arrow, and then select one of the alignment buttons.

Did You Know?

You can create nested tables. Select the table or cells, click the Edit menu, click Cut or Copy, Control-click the table cell, and then click Paste as Nested Table.

Sort the Contents of a Table

1. Click in the table or select the columns or rows you want to sort.

2. Click the **Table** menu, and then click **Sort**.

3. Click the **Sort by** list arrow, and then select how you want to sort the data.

4. Specify the type of data, how the table is using the data, and the direction of the sort.

5. To sort by multiple columns or rows, select Then by options.

6. Click **OK**.

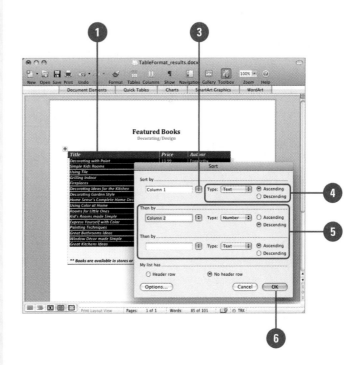

Did You Know?

You can quickly sort is ascending or descending order. Select the columns or rows you want to sort, click the Sort Ascending or Sort Descending button on the Table panel.

Change Text Direction Within Cells

1. Select the cells you want to change.

2. Click the **Formatting Palette** tab.

3. Click the **Alignment and Spacing** panel to expand it.

4. Click one of the **Change Text Direction** buttons.

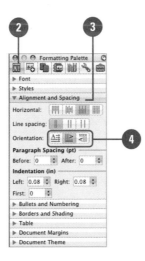

Adding a Quick Style to a Table

Instead of changing individual attributes of a table, you can quickly add them all at once with the Quick Tables style gallery on the Elements Gallery. The Quick Tables style gallery (**New!**) provides a variety of different formatting combinations, including colorful grids, calendars, directions, invoice, quarterly report. Using built-in table styles makes it easy to create and format tables without having to create them from scratch.

Add a Quick Style to a Table

1. Click to place the insertion point where you want to place the table.

2. Click the **Quick Tables** tab on the Elements Gallery.

3. Click **Basic** or **Complex** button to display the type of table style you want.

4. Click the layout for the table you want from the gallery.

   ◆ You can click the arrows on the right to display more styles.

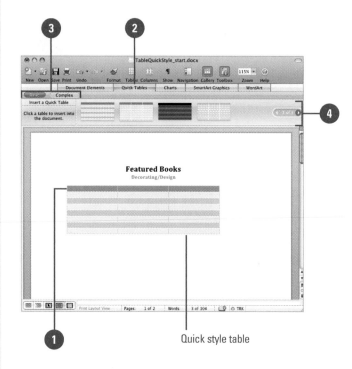

Quick style table

Calculating a Value in a Table

Sometimes the simple equations proposed by Word do not adequately cover what you are trying to calculate in the table. When that is the case, you need to create a custom equation to do the work. The Formula dialog box give you a choice of 18 paste functions to help you create your formula. Should you need help, you can activate Help to see examples of how to use each paste function, or for more complex formulas, try Microsoft's Online Community for advice from other users.

Calculate a Value

1. Click the cell in which you want the result to appear.

2. Click the **Table** menu, and then click **Formula**. If Word proposes a formula that you do not want to use, delete it.

3. Click the **Paste Function** list arrow, and then select a function.

4. To reference the contents of a table cell, type the cell references in the parentheses in the formula. For instance, to average the values in cells a1 through a4, the formula would read =Average(a1,a4). If you are doing the average of a row in the last column of the row, simplify this to =Average(left).

5. In the Number format box, enter a format for the numbers. For example, to display the numbers as a decimal percentage, click 0.00%. For now, enter 0 to display the average as the nearest whole number. To display a true average, enter 0.00 in the Number Format box.

6. Click **OK**.

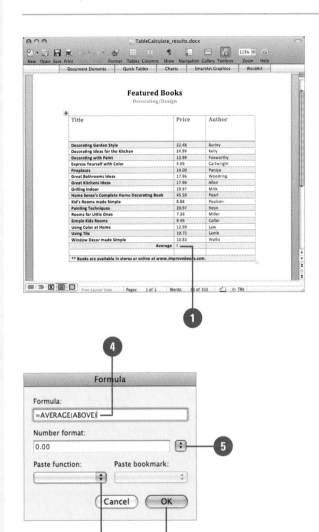

Did You Know?

You can quickly calculate a sum in a table. AutoSum suggests the range to sum. Click the cell where you want the result to appear, click the AutoSum button on the Table panel.

Creating a Form Letter

Did you ever send the same letter to several people and spend a lot of time changing personal information, such as names and addresses? If so, form letters will save you time. **Mail merge** is the process of combining names and addresses stored in a data file with a main document (usually a form letter) to produce customized documents using the Mail Merge Manager (**New!**). There are four main steps to merging. First, select the document you want to use. Second, create a data file with the variable information. Third, create the main document with the boilerplate (unchanging information) and merge fields. Each merge field corresponds to a piece of information in the data source and appears in the main document with the greater than and less than characters around it. For example, the <<Address Block>> merge field corresponds to name and address information in the data source. Finally, merge the main document with the data source to create a new document with all the merged information.

Create a Form Letter Using Mail Merge

1. Create or open the document you want to use as the main document.

2. Click the **Tools** menu, and then click **Mail Merge Manager**.

   The Mail Merge Manager opens.

3. In the Select Document Type panel, click **Create New**, and then select a document type option (such as Form Letters).

4. In the Select Recipients List panel, click **Get List**, and then select a recipient option:

   ◆ **New Data Source.** Click to create a data source from scratch.

   ◆ **Open Data Source.** Click to use data from an existing Word or Excel document.

   ◆ **Office Address Book.** Click to use contact information from your Address Book.

   ◆ **FileMaker Pro.** Click to import data from selected fields in an existing FileMaker Pro 7.0-9.0 database.

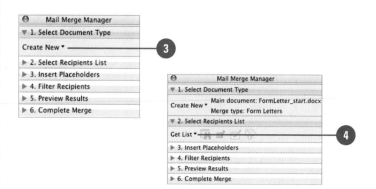

Open data source

Select data

5 In the Insert Placeholder panel, drag field items (such as Address Block or Greeting Line) from the Insert Placeholder into the main document, add spacing, text, and punctuation, and then format the text and field items.

6 In the Filter Recipients panel, click **Options** to specify the filtering options you want.

7 In the Preview Results pane, click the **View Merged Data** button, preview the data in the main document and make any changes. Click the arrow buttons to move from one data record to the next.

8 In the Complete Merge panel, click the **Merge Data Range** drop-down, and then select an option:

◆ **All.** Click to merge all records.

◆ **Current Record.** Click to merge only records selected in the Preview Results pane.

◆ **Custom.** Click to specify a range of records to merge.

9 In the Complete Merge panel, click the **Merge Data Range** drop-down, and then select a range option.

10 In the Complete Merge panel, click one of the following buttons:

◆ **Merge to Printer.** Click to send the merge to the printer.

◆ **Merge to New Document.** Click to create a Word document that you can edit and print.

◆ **Generate e-mail messages.** Click to send the merge document to the Outbox in Entourage.

11 When you're done, click the **Close** button on the Mail Merge Manager, and then save the form letter.

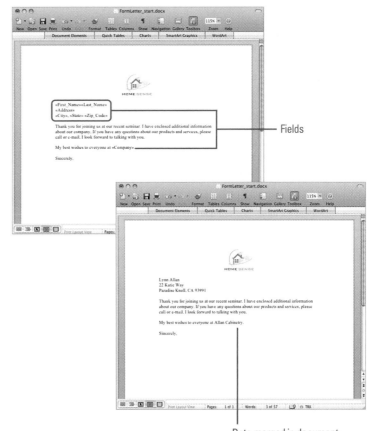

Fields

Data merged in document

Creating Labels

You can use a data document to create more than one kind of merge document using the Mail Merge Manager (**New!**). For example, you can use a data document to print mailing labels or envelopes to use with your mailing. The process for creating mailing labels is similar to the mail merge process for form letters, except that you insert the merge field into a main document that contains a table with cells in a specific size for labels. During the process for creating mailing labels, you can select brand-name labels in a specific size, such as Avery Standard 1529. After you merge the data into the main document with the labels, you can print the labels on a printer.

Create Labels Using Mail Merge

1. Create or open the document you want to use as the main document.

2. Click the **Tools** menu, and then click **Mail Merge Manager**.

   The Mail Merge Manager opens.

3. In the Select Document Type panel, click **Create New**, and then select a document type option (such as Labels).

4. Select which labels to print, any other options, and then click **OK**.

5. In the Select Recipients List panel, click **Get List**, and then select a recipient option:

   ◆ **New Data Source.** Click to create a data source from scratch.

   ◆ **Open Data Source.** Click to use data from an existing Word or Excel document.

   ◆ **Office Address Book.** Click to use contact information from your Address Book.

   ◆ **FileMaker Pro.** Click to import data from selected fields in an existing FileMaker Pro 7.0-9.0 database.

6. Use the **Insert Merge Field** drop-down to insert the fields you want in the label, and then click **OK**.

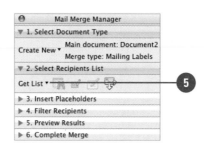

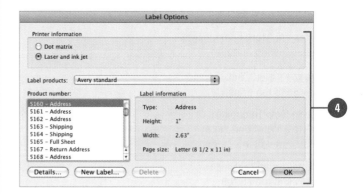

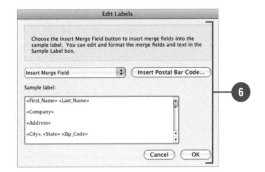

7. In the Insert Placeholder panel, drag field items (such as Address Block or Greeting Line) from the Insert Placeholder into the main document, add spacing, text, and punctuation, and then format the text and field items.

8. In the Filter Recipients panel, click **Options** to specify the filtering options you want.

9. In the Preview Results pane, click the **View Merged Data** button, preview the data in the main document and make any changes. Click the arrow buttons to move from one data record to the next.

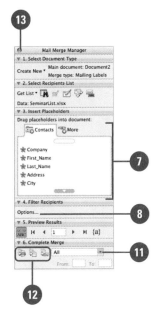

10. In the Complete Merge panel, click the **Merge Data Range** drop-down, and then select an option:

    ◆ **All.** Click to merge all records.

    ◆ **Current Record.** Click to merge only records selected in the Preview Results pane.

    ◆ **Custom.** Click to specify a range of records to merge.

11. In the Complete Merge panel, click the **Merge Data Range** drop-down, and then select a range option.

12. In the Complete Merge panel, click one of the following buttons:

    ◆ **Merge to Printer.** Click to send the merge to the printer.

    ◆ **Merge to New Document.** Click to create a Word document that you can edit and print.

    ◆ **Generate e-mail messages.** Click to send the merge document to the Outbox in Entourage.

13. When you're done, click the **Close** button on the Mail Merge Manager, and then save the form letter.

Field inserted into the labels

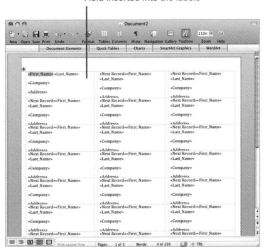

Inserting a Table of Contents

A **table of contents** provides an outline of main topics and page locations. Word builds a table of contents based on the styles in a document that you choose. By default, Heading 1 is the first-level entry, Heading 2 the second level, and so on. In a printed table of contents, a **leader**, a line whose style you select, connects an entry to its page number. In Web documents, entries become hyperlinks. Hide nonprinting characters before creating a table of contents so text doesn't shift to other pages as you print. Word makes it easy to add a table of contents to any document using the Document Elements (**New!**).

Insert a Table of Contents

1. Position the insertion point where you want the table of contents.

2. Click the **Document Elements** tab on the Elements Gallery.

3. Click the **Table of Contents** button.

4. Click the **Heading Styles** or **Manual Formatting** option.

5. Click the layout for the table of contents you want from the gallery.

   ◆ You can click the arrows on the right to display more styles.

6. To customize a table of contents, click the **Insert** menu, click **Index and Tables**, click the **Table of Contents** tab, select the format, levels, tab leader, and options you want, and then click **OK**.

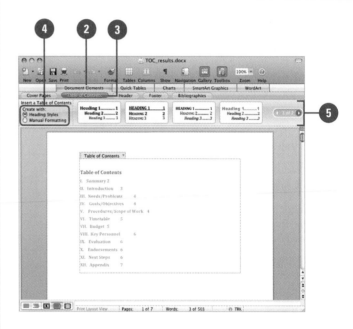

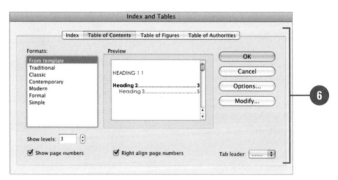

Creating an Index

An index appears at the end of a document and alphabetically lists the main topics, names, and items used in a long document. Each index listing is called an entry. You can create an index entry for a word, phrase, or symbol for a topic. In an index, a cross-reference indicates another index entry that is related to the current entry. There are several ways to create an index. Begin by marking index entries. Some index entries will refer to blocks of text that span multiple pages within a document.

Create an Index

1. To use existing text as an index entry, select the text. To enter your text as an index entry, click at the point where you want the index entry inserted.

2. Press ⌘+Option+Shift+X.

3. Type or edit the entry. The entry can be customized by creating a sub-entry or a cross-reference to another entry.

4. To format the text for the index, Control-click it in the Main Entry or Sub-entry box, click **Font**, select your formatting options, and then click **OK**.

5. To select a format for the index page numbers, select the **Bold** or **Italic** check boxes.

6. To mark the index entry, click **Mark** or **Mark All** for all similar text.

   Repeat steps 1-6 for additional index entries, and then click **Close**.

7. Go to the page where you want to display your Index.

8. Click the **Insert** menu, and then click **Index and Tables**.

9. Click the **Index** tab, and then select options for type, format, columns, and other settings.

10. Click **OK**.

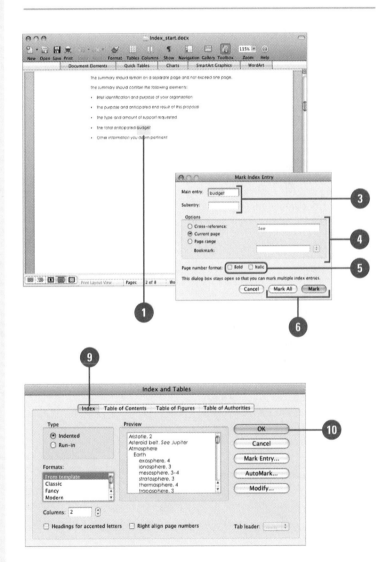

Creating Captions

Captions are helpful not only to associate images with the text that refers to them, but also to provide the reader with amplifying information about the figure, table, chart, or other illustration displayed. You can use preset captions provided, such as Figure, or you can create your own custom caption for your document.

Insert a Caption

1. Select the image that you want to caption.

2. Click the **Insert** menu, and then click **Caption**.

3. If you want to use a Label other than the default setting of Figure, which is appropriate for most art, click the **Label** list arrow, and then click **Equation** or **Table**.

4. If you want to use a numbering sequence other than the default setting of 1,2,3…, click **Numbering**, make your selections, and then click **OK**.

5. Click **OK**.

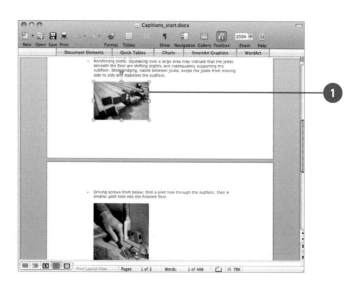

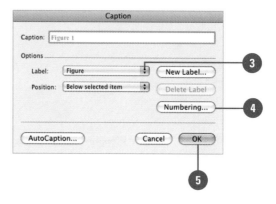

Did You Know?

You can have Word automatically add a caption field. Whenever you insert a particular type of file, such as a bitmapped image, click AutoCaption. In the Add Caption When Inserting list, click the check boxes to select the instances where you want the feature to apply, select the Label, Positioning and Numbering options you want, and then click OK.

You can add custom labels for captions. Click New Label, type the name of the New Label, and then click OK.

Creating Footnotes or Endnotes

Footnotes are used to provide additional information that is inappropriate for the body of the text, and to document your references for information or quotes presented in the body of the document. Footnotes are appropriate for academic, scientific, and, occasionally, business purposes. Footnotes appear at the bottom of the page on which the information is cited, and Word automatically inserts a reference mark at the insertion point to associate the information presented with the note at the bottom of the page. Creating and manipulating endnotes is identical to performing the same functions for footnotes. Endnotes differ from footnotes in that they appear at the end of the document or section (in the case of longer documents), not the bottom of the page on which the reference mark appears.

Create a Footnote or Endnote

1. Position the insertion point where you want to insert a footnote.

2. Click the **Insert** menu, and then click **Footnote**.

3. Click the **Footnote** or **Endnote** option.

4. Click the numbering option you want.

5. Click **Options**, select the location where you want to place the footnote or endnote, the number format, starting number, and numbering, and then click **OK**.

6. Click **OK** to insert a reference mark in the text. Word moves the insertion point to the bottom of the page corresponding to the number of the reference mark.

7. Type the text of your footnote or endnote.

8. Click in the document to continue with your work.

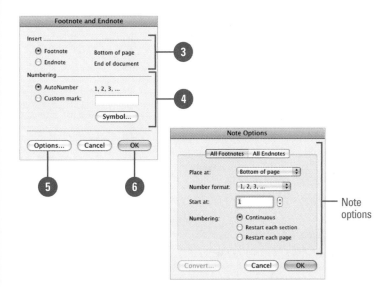

Creating a Bookmark

Instead of scrolling through a long document to find a specific word, phrase or section you can use bookmarks. **Bookmarks** are used to mark text so that you, or your reader, can quickly return to it. Using bookmarks as a destination make it easy to navigate through a long document. You can also navigate through documents with bookmarks by selecting a bookmark as a destination in the Go To dialog box.

Create a Bookmark

1. Click in your document where you want to insert a Bookmark.

2. Click the **Insert** menu, and then click **Bookmark**.

3. Type a one word descriptive name for your Bookmark.

4. Click **Add**.

Did You Know?

You can go to different locations in Word. Click the Edit menu, click Go To, select the Go to what option you want, specify a location, and then click Next or Previous. When you're done, click Close.

You can delete a bookmark. Click the Insert menu, click Bookmark, select the bookmark you want to remove, click Delete, and then click Close.

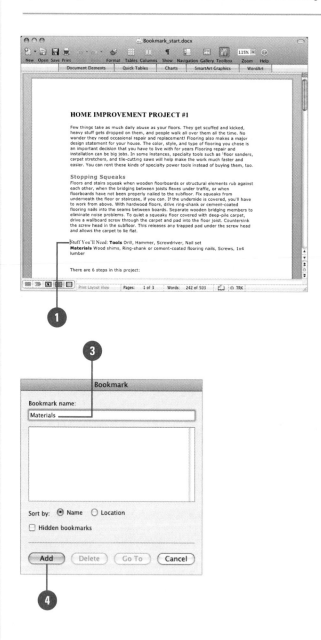

Comparing Documents

If you want to compare an earlier version of a document with the current version, or if you receive multiple edited versions of the original document back from the recipients, you can compare the documents and merge the changes into one document. The changes can be merged into one document or viewed for comparison. When you compare or merge documents, the text that differs between the two versions will be highlighted in a different color or with track reviewing marks.

Compare Documents

1. Open one of the two versions of the document you want to compare.

2. Click the **Tools** menu, point to **Track Changes**, and then click **Compare Documents**.

3. Select the document that you want to compare, and then click **Open**.

   A copy of your first version opens with revision marks inserted showing any differences from your second version.

4. Use the Reviewing toolbar to view, accept, or reject the differences between the documents.

Did You Know?

You can merge documents together.
Open the source document, click the Tools menu, click Merge Documents, select the document that you want to use as the merge, and then click Open.

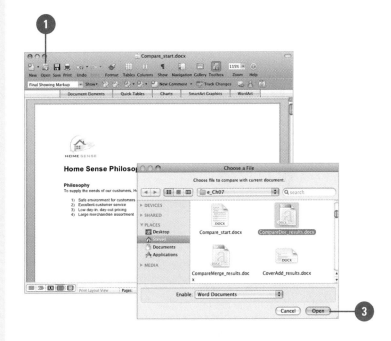

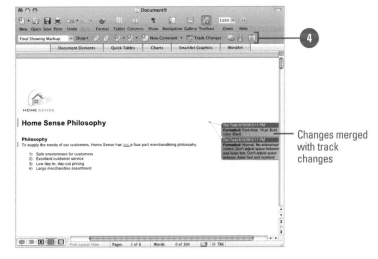

Changes merged with track changes

Using Track Changes

Tracking changes in a document allows you to make revisions to a document without losing the original text. Word shows changed text in a different color from the original text and uses revision marks, such as underlines, to distinguish the revised text from the original. You can review changes by using the Reviewing toolbar, which contains buttons that let you accept and reject changes and comments. If you compare and merge two documents, you can review the changes and accept or reject the results.

Track Changes as You Work

1. Open the document you want to edit.

2. Click the **View** menu, point to **Toolbars**, and then click **Reviewing** to display it.

3. Click the **Track Changes** button on the Review toolbar.

   TIMESAVER *Click Track Changes (TRK) on the Status bar or press Ctrl+Shift+E to turn tracking on or off.*

4. Make changes to your document. The changes are reflected using alternate color characters, along with comments in balloons at the side of the screen (if you are in Print Layout view) or displayed in a separate window at the bottom of the screen (if you are in Draft view).

5. Click the **Track Changes** button to turn off track changes.

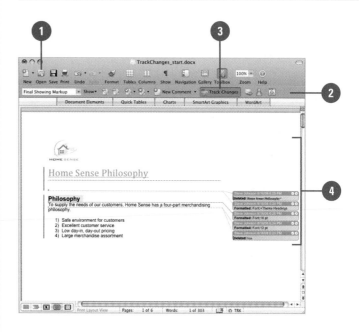

Did You Know?

You can show or hide balloons.
Click the Review tab, click the Balloons button, and then select Show Revisions in Balloons, Show Revisions Inline, or Show Only Comments and Formatting in Balloons.

Review Changes

1 Open the document you want to review.

2 Click the **View** menu, point to **Toolbars**, and then click **Reviewing** to display it.

3 Use the buttons on the Reviewing toolbar to review changes:

- Click the **Next** button or the **Previous** button to view changes one at a time.

- Click the **Accept Change** button or the **Reject Change/Delete Comment** button to respond to the revisions.

- Click the **Accept Change** button arrow, and then click **Accept All Changes in Document** to accept all changes at once.

- Click the **Reject Change/Delete Comment** button arrow, and then click **Reject All Changes in Document** to reject all changes at once.

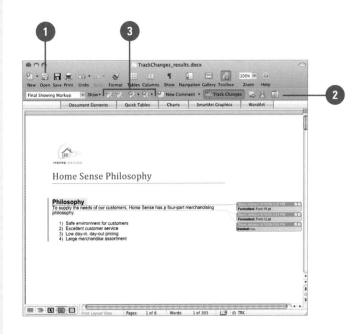

Did You Know?

You can display different versions of reviewing marks. Display the Review toolbar, click the Display for Review list arrow, and then select an option (Final Showing Markup, Final, Original Showing Markup, or Original).

You can show or hide individual reviewers. Display the Review toolbar, click the Show Markup button, point to Reviewers, and then click the reviewer you want to show or hide.

You can show or hide the Reviewing pane. The Reviewing pane shows a list of changes in a pane. Display the Review toolbar, click the Reviewing Pane button, and then click the option you want.

For Your Information

Adding and Removing Comments

Comments are useful when someone who is editing the document has questions pertaining to the document. When you insert a comment in Print Layout view, it opens a balloon where you want enter a comment. To insert a comment, click the View menu, point to Rulers, click Review to display the toolbar, place the insertion point where you want the comment, click the New Comment button, and then type a comment. To edit a comment, click in the comment balloon and edit normally. To remove a comment, Control-click it, and then click Delete, or use one of the delete commands on the Reject Change/ Delete Comment button arrow on the Review toolbar. Each comment includes the name and initials of the person who made the comment, which you can change in the Word Preferences dialog box. Click the Word menu, click Preferences, click the User Information icon, make any changes to the username and initials, and then click OK.

Addressing Envelopes and Labels

When you write a letter, you can use Word to print an address on an envelope or mailing label. Word scans your document to find a delivery address. You can use the one Word finds, enter another one, or select one from your Address Book. You can specify a return address, or you can omit it. Addresses can contain text, graphics, and bar codes. The POSTNET bar code is a machine-readable depiction of a U.S. zip code and delivery address; the FIM-A code identifies the front of a courtesy reply envelope. You can print a single label or multiple labels.

Address and Print Envelopes

1. Click the **Tools** menu, and then click **Envelopes**.

2. Type the recipients name and address, or click the **Insert Address** button to search for it.

3. Type your name and address.

4. Specify the options you want for bar code, font, size, position, and printing.

5. Click **OK**, or insert an envelope in your printer, and then click **Print**.

Address and Print Mailing Labels

1. Click the **Tools** menu, and then click **Labels**.

2. Type the recipients name and address, or the **Insert Address** button to search for it.

3. Click **Options**, select which labels to print, any other options, and then click **OK**.

4. Specify the options you want for number of labels and printing.

5. Click **OK**, or insert labels in your printer, and then click **Print**.

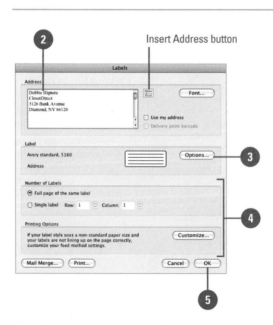

Using Print Preview

Before printing, you should verify that the page looks the way you want. You save time, money, and paper by avoiding duplicate printing. **Print Preview** shows you the exact placement of your data on each printed page. You can view all or part of your document as it will appear when you print it. Print Preview makes it easy to zoom in and out to view data more comfortably, preview page breaks, and print. If the text on a page in Word doesn't quite fit, you can use the One Page button and then Word tries to reduce the font and spacing size to make it fit. In Word, you can also edit text (**New!**) in Print Preview by turning the Magnifier off.

Use Print Preview

① Click the **File** menu, and then click **Print Preview**.

② Click the **Magnifier** button on the toolbar to select it, or position the Zoom pointer anywhere on the document, and then click it to enlarge a specific area of the page. Click again to reduce it.

◆ To change the view, click the **View** list arrow on the toolbar, and then select a view percentage, or Page Width, Whole Page, or Two Pages.

③ To edit text in Word, click the **Magnifier** button on the toolbar to deselect it.

④ If you do not want to print from Print Preview, click the **Close Print Preview** button on the toolbar to return to the document.

⑤ If you want to print from Print Preview, click the **Print** button on the toolbar.

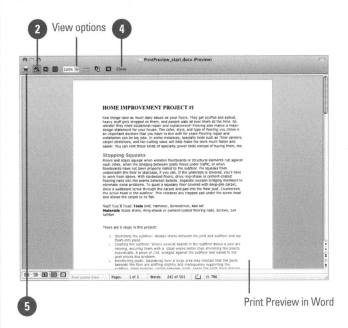

View options

Print Preview in Word

Did You Know?

You can preview your work from the Print dialog box. In the Print dialog box, click Preview. After previewing, you can click the Print button or the Close Print Preview button to return to your document.

Adding a Cover Page

A cover page provides an introduction to a report, or an important memo you want to circulate to others. Word makes it easy to add a cover page to any document using Document Elements (**New!**). You can quickly select one from a gallery of styles that fit your document. Each cover page includes text boxes sample text, which you can change, and defined fields, such as a title and author's name, that automatically get filled in with information from document properties.

Insert a Cover Page

1. Open the document to which you want to insert a cover page.

2. Click the **Document Elements** tab on the Elements Gallery.

3. Click the **Cover Page** button to display a gallery of cover pages.

4. Click the cover page you want.

   ◆ You can click the arrows on the right to display more styles.

   Word inserts a cover at the beginning of your document. You can click

5. To remove a cover page, click the **Cover Page** button at the top of the cover page, and then click **Remove Cover Page**.

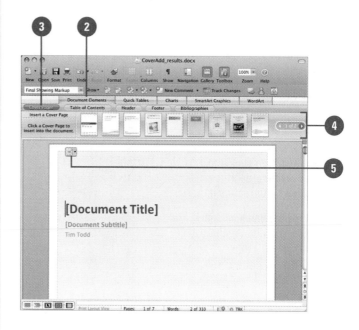

Creating a Worksheet with Excel

8

Introduction

At times, you'll need to reorganize a workbook by adding additional worksheets, moving their appearance order within the workbook, or even deleting an unused or outdated worksheet. You can rename worksheets to better show the theme of your workbook. When using your workbook, there may be times when you'll want to hide certain worksheets due to sensitive or confidential information. You can also freeze the column and row headings to ease viewing a long list of data.

On any worksheet, you can insert and delete cells, rows, and columns. You can adjust column width and row height so that you can structure the worksheet exactly the way you want. It's easy to make changes because Microsoft Office Excel updates cell references in existing formulas as necessary whenever you modify a worksheet and automatically recalculates formulas to ensure that the results are always up-to-date.

Perhaps each month you create an inventory worksheet in which you enter repetitive information; all that changes is the actual data. By creating your own template, you can have a custom form that is ready for completion each time you take inventory. Formatting, formulas and other settings are already set up, so that you can begin working on the task at hand. A template file saves all the customization you made to reuse in other workbooks. Microsoft Excel comes with a variety of pre-made templates that you can use for your own business and personal needs.

What You'll Do

View the Excel Window

Select Cells

Move Around the Workbook

Enter Labels and Values on a Worksheet

Enter Values Quickly with AutoFill

Edit and Clear Cell Contents

Insert and Delete Cell Contents

Select Rows, Columns, and Special Ranges

Select and Name a Worksheet

Insert and Delete a Worksheet

Move and Copy a Worksheet

Hide and Unhide a Worksheet

Hide and Unhide a Column or Row

Insert and Delete a Column or Row

Adjust Column Width and Row Height

Split a Worksheet into Panes

Freeze and Unfreeze a Column or Row

Show and Hide Workbook Elements

Viewing the Excel Window

Formula bar
Enter or build formulas here

Standard Toolbar
Click to access command comments on the toolbar.

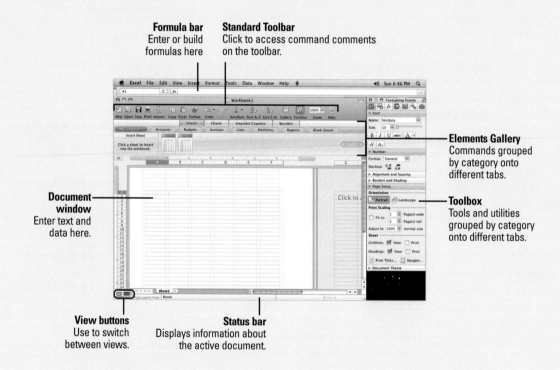

Elements Gallery
Commands grouped by category onto different tabs.

Toolbox
Tools and utilities grouped by category onto different tabs.

Document window
Enter text and data here.

View buttons
Use to switch between views.

Status bar
Displays information about the active document.

Selecting Cells

In order to work with a cell—to enter data in it, edit or move it, or perform an action—you **select** the cell so it becomes the active cell. When you want to work with more than one cell at a time—to move or copy them, use them in a **formula**, or perform any group action—you must first select the cells as a **range**. A range can be **contiguous** (where selected cells are adjacent to each other) or **non-contiguous** (where the cells may be in different parts of the worksheet and are not adjacent to each other). As you select a range, you can see the range reference in the Name box. A **range reference** contains the cell address of the top-left cell in the range, a colon (:), and the cell address of the bottom-right cell in the range.

Select a Contiguous Range

1. Click the first cell that you want to include in the range.

2. Drag the mouse to the last cell you want to include in the range.

   TIMESAVER *Instead of dragging, hold down the Shift key, and then click the lower-right cell in the range.*

   When a range is selected, the top-left cell is surrounded by the cell pointer, while the additional cells are selected.

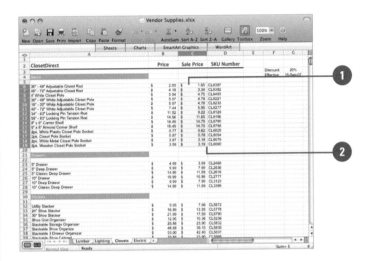

Select a Non-contiguous Range

1. Click the first cell you want to include in the range.

2. Drag the mouse to the last contiguous cell, and then release the mouse button.

3. Press and hold ⌘, and then click the next cell or drag the pointer over the next group of cells you want in the range.

   To select more, repeat step 3 until all non-contiguous ranges are selected.

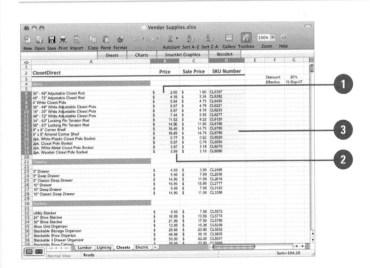

Moving Around the Workbook

You can move around a worksheet using your mouse or the keyboard. You might find that using your mouse to move from cell to cell is most convenient, while using various keyboard combinations is easier for quickly covering large areas of a worksheet. Or, you might find that entering numbers on the keypad and pressing Return is a better method. Certain keys on the keyboard—Home, End, and Delete to name a few—are best used as shortcuts to navigate in the worksheet. However, there is no right way; whichever method feels the most comfortable is the one you should use.

Use the Mouse to Navigate

Using the mouse, you can navigate to:

- Another cell
- Another part of the worksheet
- Another worksheet

Did You Know?

Microsoft IntelliMouse users can roll from cell to cell with IntelliMouse. If you have the new Microsoft IntelliMouse—with the wheel button between the left and right buttons—you can click the wheel button and move the mouse in any direction to move quickly around the worksheet.

You can quickly zoom in or out using IntelliMouse. Instead of scrolling when you roll with the IntelliMouse, you can zoom in or out. To turn on this feature, click the Office button, click Excel Options, click Advanced, select the Zoom on roll with IntelliMouse check box, and then click OK.

To move from one cell to another, point to the cell you what to move to, and then click.

When you click the wheel button on the IntelliMouse, the pointer changes shape. Drag the pointer in any direction to move to a new location quickly.

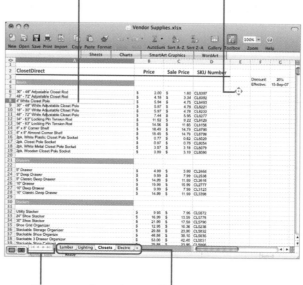

To see more sheet tabs without changing the location of the active cell, click a sheet scroll button

To move from one worksheet to another, click the tab of the sheet you want to move to.

Use the Keyboard to Navigate

Using the keyboard, you can navigate in a worksheet to:

◆ Another cell

◆ Another part of the worksheet

    Refer to the table for keyboard shortcuts for navigating around a worksheet.

Did You Know?

You can change or move cell selections after pressing Enter. When you press Return, the active cell moves down one cell. To change the direction, click the Excel menu, click Preferences, click the Edit icon, click the Direction drop-down, select a direction, and then click OK.

Keys For Navigating in a Worksheet

Press This Key	To Move
Left arrow	One cell to the left
Right arrow	One cell to the right
Up arrow	One cell up
Down arrow	One cell down
Enter	One cell down
Tab	One cell to the right
Shift+Tab	One cell to the left
Page Up	One screen up
Page Down	One screen down
End+arrow key	In the direction of the arrow key to the next cell containing data or to the last empty cell in current row or column
Home	To column A in the current row
Ctrl+Home	To cell A1
Ctrl+End	To the last cell in the worksheet containing data

Go To a Specific Location

1 Click the **Edit** menu, and then click **Go To**.

2 Select a location or type a cell address to where you want to go.

3 To go to other locations (such as comments, blanks, last cell, objects, formulas, etc.), click **Special**, select an option, and then click **OK**.

    TIMESAVER *To open the Special dialog box directly, click the Find & Select button, and then click Go To Special.*

4 Click **OK**.

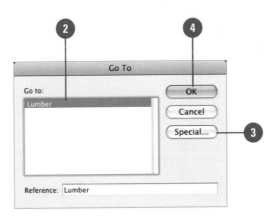

Entering Labels on a Worksheet

Labels turn a worksheet full of numbers into a meaningful report by identifying the different types of information it contains. You use labels to describe the data in worksheet cells, columns, and rows. You can enter a number as a label (for example, the year 2008), so that Excel does not use the number in its calculations. To help keep your labels consistent, you can use Excel's **AutoComplete** feature, which automatically completes your entries (excluding numbers, dates, or times) based on previously entered labels.

Enter a Text Label

① Click the cell where you want to enter a label.

② Type a label. A label can include uppercase and lowercase letters, spaces, punctuation, and numbers.

③ Press Return.

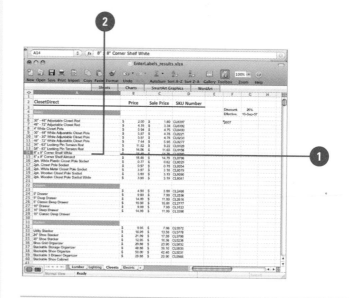

Enter a Number as a Label

① Click the cell where you want to enter a number as a label.

② Type ' (an apostrophe). The apostrophe is a label prefix and does not appear on the worksheet.

③ Type a number value.

④ Press Return.

If a green triangle appears, it indicates a smart tag. Select the cell to display the Error Smart Tag button, where you can select options related to the label.

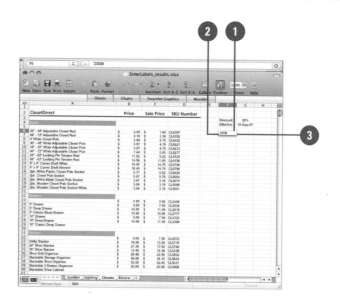

Enter a Label Using AutoComplete

1 Type the first few characters of a label.

If Excel recognizes the entry, AutoComplete completes it.

2 To accept the suggested entry, press Return.

3 To reject the suggested completion, simply continue typing.

Did You Know?

Excel doesn't recognize the entry.
The AutoComplete option may not be turned on. To turn on the feature, click the Excel menu, click Preferences, click the AutoComplete icon, select Enable AutoComplete for cell values check box, and then click OK.

Long labels might appear truncated.
When you enter a label that is wider than the cell it occupies, the excess text appears to spill into the next cell to the right—unless there is data in the adjacent cell. If that cell contains data, the label will appear truncated—you'll only see the portion of the label that fits in the cell's current width. Click the cell to see its entire contents displayed on the formula bar.

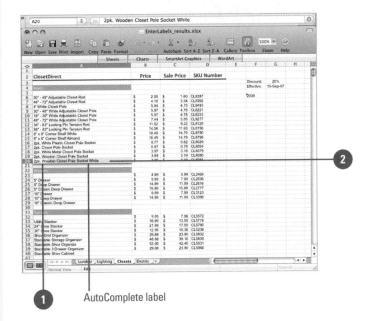

AutoComplete label

Entering Values on a Worksheet

You can enter values as whole numbers, decimals, percentages, or dates using the numbers on the top row of your keyboard, or by pressing your Num Lock key, the numeric keypad on the right. When you enter a date or the time of day, Excel automatically recognizes these entries (if entered in an acceptable format) as numeric values and changes the cell's format to a default date or time format. You can also change the way values, dates or times of day are shown.

Enter a Value

1. Click the cell where you want to enter a value.

2. Type a value.

3. Press Return.

Did You Know?

You can use the numeric keypad to enter numbers. Make sure NUM appears in the lower-right corner of the status bar. before you begin using the numbers.

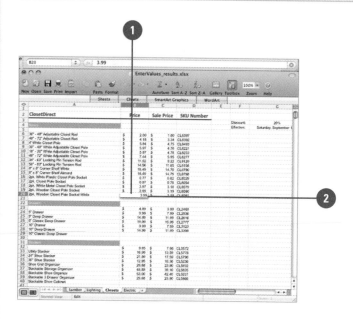

Enter a Date or Time

1. To enter a date, type the date using a slash (/) or a hyphen (-) between the month, day, and year in a cell or on the formula bar.

   To enter a time, type the hour based on a 12-hour clock, followed by a colon (:), followed by the minute, followed by a space, and ending with an "a" or a "p" to denote A.M. or P.M.

2. Press Return.

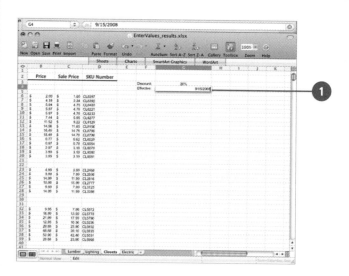

Entering Values Quickly with AutoFill

AutoFill is a feature that automatically fills in data based on the data in adjacent cells. Using the **fill handle**, you can enter data in a series, or you can copy values or formulas to adjacent cells. A single cell entry can result in a repeating value or label, or the results can be a more complex series. You can enter your value or label, and then complete entries such as days of the week, weeks of the year, months of the year, or consecutive numbering.

Enter Repeating Data or Series Using AutoFill

1. Select the first cell in the range you want to fill.

2. Enter the starting value to be repeated, or in a series.

3. Position the pointer on the lower-right corner of the selected cell. The pointer changes to the fill handle (a black plus sign).

4. Drag the fill handle over the range you want the value repeated.

5. To choose how to fill the selection, click the **AutoFill Options** button, and then click the option you want.

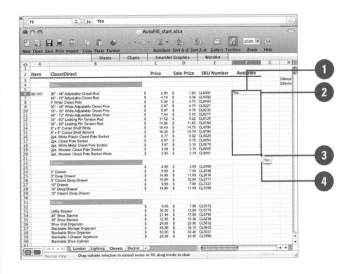

Create a Custom Fill

1. If you want to use an existing list, select the list of items.

2. Click the **Excel** menu, and then click **Preferences**.

3. Click the **Custom Lists** icon.

4. Click the option you want.

   - **New list.** Click **NEW LIST**, type the entries you want, press Return after each. Click **Add**.

   - **Existing list.** Verify the cell reference of the selected list appears in the Import list, and then click **Import**.

5. Click **OK**.

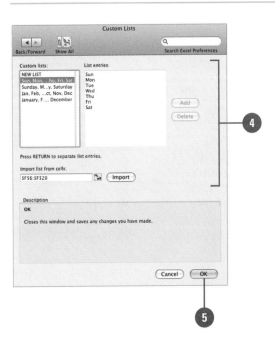

Editing Cell Contents

Even if you plan ahead, you can count on having to make changes on a worksheet. Sometimes it's because you want to correct an error. Other times it's because you want to see how your worksheet results would be affected by different conditions, such as higher sales, fewer units produced, or other variables. You can edit data just as easily as you enter it, using the formula bar or directly editing the active cell.

Edit Cell Contents

1. Double-click the cell you want to edit. The insertion point appears in the cell.

   The Status bar now displays Edit instead of Ready.

2. If necessary, use the Home, End, and arrow keys to position the insertion point within the cell contents.

3. Use any combination of the Backspace and Delete keys to erase unwanted characters, and then type new characters as needed.

4. Press Return to accept the edit, or press Esc to cancel the edit.

   The Status bar now displays Ready instead of Edit.

Did You Know?

You can change editing options. Click the Word menu, click Preferences, click the Edit icon, change the editing options you want, and then click OK.

You can edit cell contents using the formula bar. Click the cell you want to edit, click to place the insertion point on the formula bar, and then edit the cell contents.

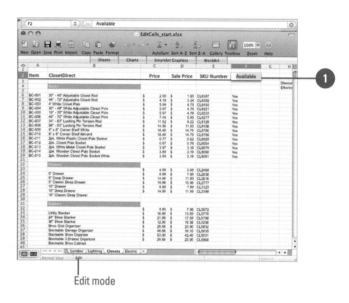

Edit mode

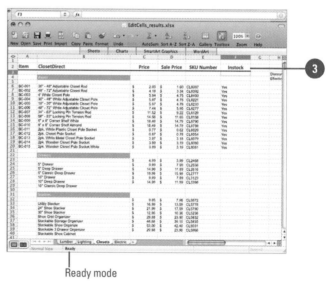

Ready mode

Clearing Cell Contents

You can clear a cell to remove its contents. Clearing a cell does not remove the cell from the worksheet; it just removes from the cell whatever elements you specify: data, comments (also called **cell notes**), or formatting instructions. When clearing a cell, you must specify whether to remove one, two, or all three of these elements from the selected cell or range.

Clear Cell Contents, Formatting, and Comments

① Select the cell or range you want to clear.

② Click the **Edit** menu, point to **Clear**, and then click any of the following options:

◆ **Clear All.** Clears contents and formatting.

◆ **Clear Formats.** Clears formatting and leaves contents.

◆ **Clear Contents.** Clears contents and leaves formatting.

◆ **Clear Comments.** Clears comments; removes purple triangle indicator.

TIMESAVER *To quickly clear contents, select the cell or range you want to clear, Control-click the cell or range, and then click Clear Contents, or press Delete.*

Did You Know?

You can find or replace cell contents. Click the cell or cells containing content you want to replace. Click the Edit menu, and then click Find. You can click the Replace tab for additional options to replace cell contents.

Inserting and Deleting Cell Contents

You can **insert** new, blank cells anywhere on the worksheet in order to enter new data or data you forgot to enter earlier. Inserting cells moves the remaining cells in the column or row in the direction of your choice, and Excel adjusts any formulas so they refer to the correct cells. You can also **delete** cells if you find you don't need them; deleting cells shifts the remaining cells to the left or up—just the opposite of inserting cells. When you delete a cell, Excel removes the actual cell from the worksheet.

Insert a Cell

1. Select the cell or cells where you want to insert the new cell(s).

2. Click the **Insert** menu, and then click **Cells**.

3. Click the option you want:

   ◆ **Shift cells right** to move cells to the right one column.

   ◆ **Shift cells down** to move cells down one row.

   ◆ **Entire row** to move the entire row down one row.

   ◆ **Entire column** to move entire column over one column.

4. Click **OK**.

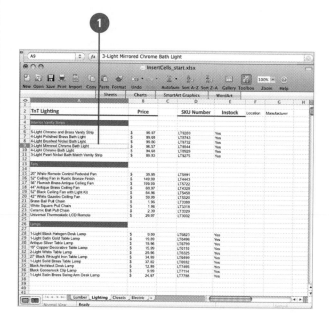

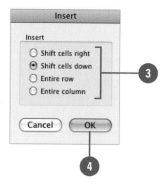

Delete a Cell

1. Select the cell or range you want to delete.

2. Click the **Edit** menu, and then click **Delete**.

3. Click the option you want.

   ◆ **Shift cells left** to move the remaining cells to the left.

   ◆ **Shift cells up** to move the remaining cells up.

   ◆ **Entire row** to delete the entire row.

   ◆ **Entire column** to delete the entire column.

4. Click **OK**.

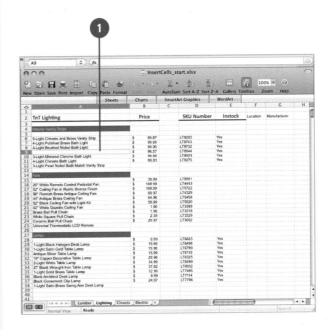

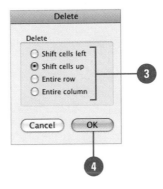

Selecting Rows, Columns, and Special Ranges

In addition to selecting a range of contiguous and non-contiguous cells in a single worksheet, you may need to select entire rows and columns, or even a range of cells across multiple worksheets. Cells can contain many different types of data, such as comments, constants, formulas, or conditional formats. Excel provides an easy way to locate these and many other special types of cells with the Go To Special dialog box. For example, you can select the Row Differences or Column Differences option to select cells that are different from other cells in a row or column, or select the Dependents option to select cells with formulas that refer to the active cell.

Select an Entire Rows or Columns

◆ To select a single row or column, click in the row or column heading, or select any cell in the row or column, and press Shift+spacebar.

◆ To select multiple adjacent rows or columns, drag in the row or column headings.

◆ To select multiple nonadjacent rows or columns, press ⌘ while you click the borders for the rows or columns you want to include.

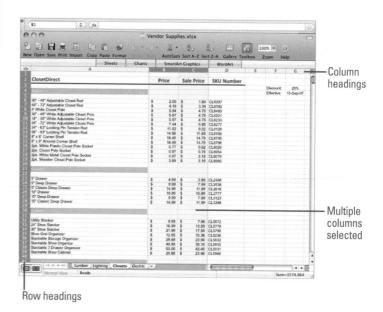

Column headings

Multiple columns selected

Row headings

Did You Know?

You can select the entire worksheet quickly. Click the Select All button located above the row number 1 and the left of column A.

Select Multisheet Ranges

1. Select the range in one sheet.

2. Select the worksheets to include in the range.

   To select contiguous worksheets, press Shift and click the last sheet tab you want to include. To select non-contiguous worksheets, press ⌘ and click the sheets you want.

   When you make a worksheet selection, Excel enters Group mode.

3. To exit Group mode, click any sheet tab.

Group selection

Make Special Range Selections

1. If you want to make a selection from within a range, select the range you want.

2. Click the **Edit** menu, and then click **Go To**.

   TIMESAVER *Press F5 to open the Go To dialog box.*

3. Click **Special**.

4. Click the option in which you want to make a selection. When you click the Formulas option, select or clear the formula related check boxes.

5. Click **OK**.

   If no cells are found, Excel displays a message.

Special range selection

Selecting and Naming a Worksheet

Each new workbook opens with three worksheets (or sheets), in which you store and analyze values. You can work in the active, or selected, worksheet. The default worksheet names are Sheet1, Sheet2, and Sheet3, which appear on the sheet tab, like file folder labels. As you create a worksheet, give it a meaningful name to help you remember its contents. The sheet tab size adjusts to fit the name's length, so using short names means more sheet tabs will be visible. If you work on a project that requires more than three worksheets, add additional sheets to the workbook so all related information is stored in one file.

Select a Worksheet

1. If necessary, click a sheet tab scroll button to display other tabs.

2. Click a sheet tab to make it the active worksheet.

3. To select multiple worksheets, press and hold ⌘ as you click other sheet tabs. When multiple worksheets are selected, [Group] appears in the title bar.

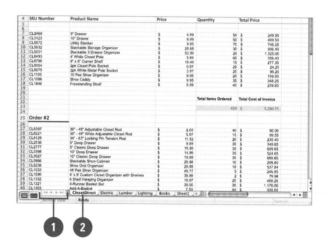

Name or Rename a Worksheet

1. Double-click the sheet tab you want to name.

   ◆ You can also click the **Format** menu, point to **Sheet**, and then click **Rename**.

2. Type a new name.

3. Press Return.

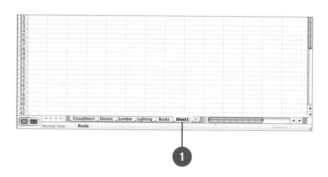

Did You Know?

You can select all worksheets. Control-click any sheet tab, and then click Select All Sheets.

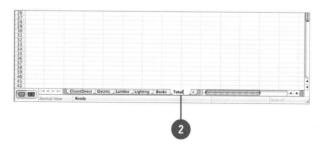

Inserting and Deleting a Worksheet

You can add or delete sheets in a workbook. If, for example, you are working on a project that requires more than three worksheets, you can insert additional sheets in one workbook rather than open multiple workbooks. You can insert as many sheets in a workbook as you want. On the other hand, if you are using only one or two sheets in a workbook, you can delete the unused sheets to save disk space. Before you delete a sheet from a workbook, make sure you don't need the data. You cannot undo the deletion.

Insert a Blank Worksheet

1 Click the sheet tab to the right of where you want to insert the new sheet.

2 Click the **Insert Worksheet** icon at the end of the sheet tabs (**New!**).

◆ You can also click the **Insert** menu, point to **Sheet**, and then click **Blank Sheet**.

A new worksheet is inserted to the left of the selected worksheet.

Delete a Worksheet

1 Click the sheet tab of the worksheet you want to delete.

2 Click the **Edit** menu, and then click **Delete Sheet**.

◆ You can also Control-click the sheet tab, and then click **Delete**.

3 Click **OK** to confirm the deletion.

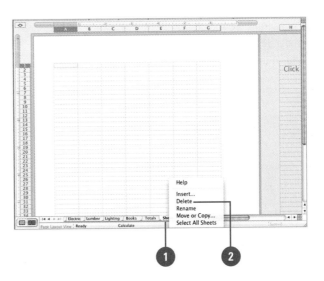

New sheet

Inserting a Worksheet from the Elements Gallery

When you insert a worksheet in Excel, you have several choice beyond the blank sheet. You can also insert a blank worksheet designed for creating a list or chart. If you don't want to start a worksheet from scratch, Excel provides a gallery of different styles from which to choose. From the Sheets tab in the Elements Gallery (**New!**), you can select a Quick Style worksheet from a variety of categories, such as Accounts, Budgets, Invoices, Lists, Portfolios, or Reports. The Quick Style worksheets are templates with all the layout, formatting, and formulas you need to get started quickly. All you need to do is add your own data.

Insert a Blank Worksheet from the Elements Gallery

1. Click the sheet tab to the right of where you want to insert the new sheet.

2. Click the **Sheets** tab on the Elements Gallery.

3. Click the **Blank Sheets** tab.

4. Click the type of blank worksheet you want to use:

   ◆ **Blank Sheet.** Inserts a blank worksheet.

   ◆ **List Sheet.** Inserts a blank worksheet designed for creating a list.

   ◆ **Chart Sheet.** Inserts a blank worksheet designed for creating a chart.

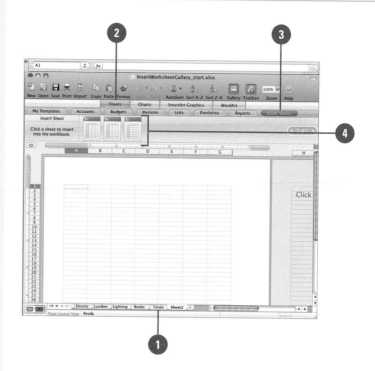

Insert a Quick Style Worksheet

1. Click the sheet tab to the right of where you want to insert the new sheet.

2. Click the **Sheets** tab on the Elements Gallery.

3. Click one of the tabs (**Accounts**, **Budgets**, **Invoices**, **Lists**, **Portfolios**, or **Reports**) with the type of the worksheet you want to insert.

4. Click the style you want from the gallery.

   - Click the scroll up or down arrows to see additional styles.

5. Click the **Formatting Palette** tab on the Toolbox.

6. Click the panel associated with the Quick Style worksheet. For example, click Ledger Sheet panel for the Inventory worksheet.

7. Change the settings you want for the worksheet.

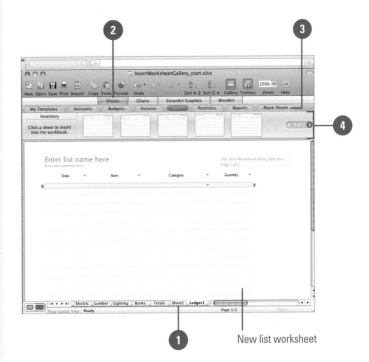

New list worksheet

Moving and Copying a Worksheet

After adding several sheets to a workbook, you might want to reorganize them. You can arrange sheets in chronological order or in order of importance. You can easily move or copy a sheet within a workbook or to a different open workbook. Copying a worksheet is easier and often more convenient then re-entering similar information on a new sheet. If you are moving or copying a worksheet a short distance, you should use the mouse. For longer distances, you should use the Move or Copy command.

Move a Worksheet Within a Workbook

1. Click the sheet tab of the worksheet you want to move, and then hold down the mouse button.

2. When the mouse pointer changes to a sheet of paper, drag it to the right of the sheet tab where you want to move the worksheet.

3. Release the mouse button.

Did You Know?

You can give your worksheet a different background. Click the tab of the sheet on which you want to insert a background, click the Format menu, point to Sheet, and then click Background. Select the picture you want to use as a background, and then click Insert.

You can use groups to affect multiple worksheets. Click a sheet tab, press and hold Shift, and click another sheet tab to group worksheets. Control-click a grouped sheet tab, and then click Ungroup Sheet on the shortcut menu.

Copy a Worksheet

1. Click the sheet tab of the worksheet you want to copy.

   TIMESAVER *Press and hold the ⌘ key while you drag a sheet name to copy a worksheet.*

2. Click the **Edit** menu, and then click **Move or Copy Sheet**.

3. If you want to copy the sheet to another open workbook, click the **To book** drop-down, and then select the name of that workbook. The sheets of the selected workbook appear in the Before Sheet list.

   TROUBLE? *If the workbook you want to copy to does not show up in the To Book drop-down list, you must first open the workbook.*

4. Click a sheet name in the Before Sheet list. Excel inserts the copy to the left of this sheet.

5. Select the **Create a copy** check box.

6. Click **OK**.

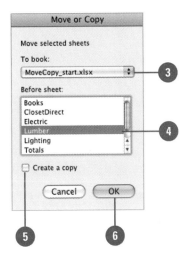

Did You Know?

You can copy or move a sheet to a different workbook. You must first open the other workbook, and then switch back to the workbook of the sheet you want to copy or move.

You can use the Create a copy check box to move a worksheet. Clear the Create a copy check box in the Move or Copy dialog box to move a worksheet rather than copy it.

Hiding or Unhiding a Worksheet

Not all worksheets should be available to everyone. You can keep sensitive information private without deleting it by hiding selected worksheets. For example, if you want to share a workbook with others, but it includes confidential employee salaries, you can simply hide a worksheet. Hiding worksheets does not affect calculations in the other worksheets; all data in hidden worksheets is still referenced by formulas as necessary. Hidden worksheets do not appear in a printout either. When you need the data, you can unhide the sensitive information.

Hide or Unhide a Worksheet

1. Click the sheet tab you want to hide.

2. Click the **Format** menu, point to **Sheet**, and then click the command you want.

   ◆ **Hide**.

   ◆ **UnHide**, select the worksheet you want to unhide, and then click **OK**.

   TIMESAVER *Control-click the sheet you want to hide, and then click Hide.*

Click to Unhide a worksheet

Hiding and Unhiding a Column or Row

Not all the data on a worksheet should be available to everyone. You can hide sensitive information without deleting it by hiding selected columns or rows. For example, if you want to share a worksheet with others, but it includes confidential employee salaries, you can simply hide the salary column. Hiding columns and rows does not affect calculations in a worksheet; all data in hidden columns and rows is still referenced by formulas as necessary. Hidden columns and rows do not appear in a printout either. When you need the data, you can unhide the sensitive information.

Hide a Column or Row

1. Click the column or row header button of the column or row you want to hide. (Drag to select multiple header buttons to hide more than one column or row.)

2. Click the **Format** menu, point to **Column** or **Row**, and then click **Hide**.

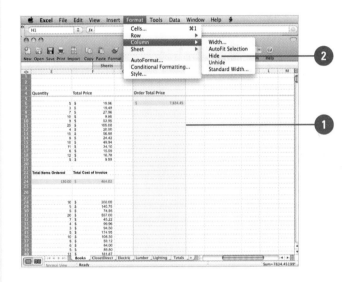

Unhide a Column or Row

1. Drag to select the column or row header buttons on either side of the hidden column or row.

2. Click the **Format** menu, point to **Column** or **Row**, and then click **Unhide**.

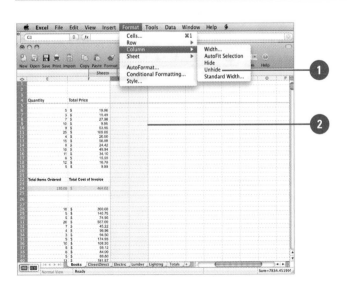

Inserting a Column or Row

You can insert blank columns and rows between existing data, without disturbing your worksheet. Excel repositions existing cells to accommodate the new columns and rows and adjusts any existing formulas so that they refer to the correct cells. Formulas containing absolute cell references will need to be adjusted to the new columns or rows. When you insert one or more columns, they insert to the left. When you add one or more rows, they are inserted above the selected row.

Insert a Column or Row

① Click to the right of the location of the new column you want to insert.

To insert a row, click the row immediately below the location of the row you want to insert.

② Click the **Insert** menu, and then click **Columns** or **Rows**.

③ To adjust formatting, click the **Insert Options** button, and then click a formatting option.

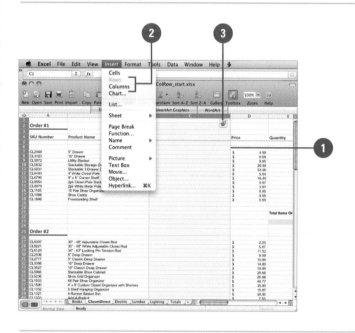

Insert Multiple Columns or Rows

① Drag to select the column header buttons for the number of columns you want to insert.

To insert multiple rows, drag to select the row header buttons for the number of rows you want to insert.

② Click the **Insert** menu, and then click **Columns** or **Rows**.

③ To adjust formatting, click the **Insert Options** button, and then click a formatting option.

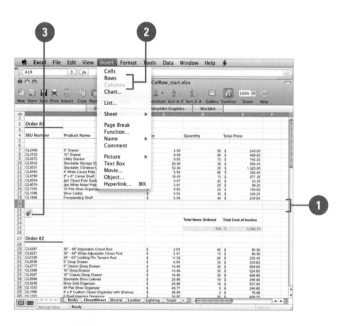

Deleting a Column or Row

At some point in time, you may want to remove an entire column or row of data from a worksheet rather than deleting or editing individual cells. You can delete columns and rows just as easily as you insert them. Formulas will need to be checked in your worksheet prior to deleting a row or column, especially when referencing absolute cell addresses. Remaining columns and rows move to the left or up to join the other remaining data.

Delete Columns or Rows

1 Select one or more column header buttons or row header buttons that you want to delete.

2 Click the **Edit** menu, and then click **Delete**.

Did You Know?

You can re-check your formulas. When deleting columns or rows that are referenced in a formula, it is important to adjust your formula for recalculations.

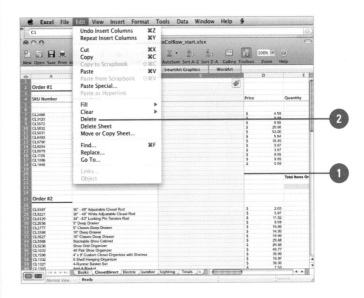

Adjusting Column Width and Row Height

You've entered labels and values, constructed formulas, and even formatted the cells, but now some of your data isn't visible; the value displays as ##### in the cell. Also, some larger-sized labels are cut off. You can narrow or widen each column width to fit its contents and adjust your row heights as needed. As you build your worksheet, you can change the default width of some columns or the default height of some rows to accommodate long strings of data or larger font sizes. You can manually adjust column or row size to fit data you have entered, or you can use AutoFit to resize a column or row to the width or height of its largest entry.

Adjust Column Width or Row Height

1. Click the column or row header button for the first column or row you want to adjust.

2. If you want, drag to select more columns or rows.

3. Do either of the following:

   ◆ **Column Width.** Click the **Format** menu, point to **Column**, and then click **Width**.

   ◆ **Row Height.** Click the **Format** menu, point to **Row**, and then click **Height**.

   TIMESAVER *Control-click the selected column(s) or row(s), and then click Column Width or Row Height.*

4. Type a new column width or row height in points.

5. Click **OK**.

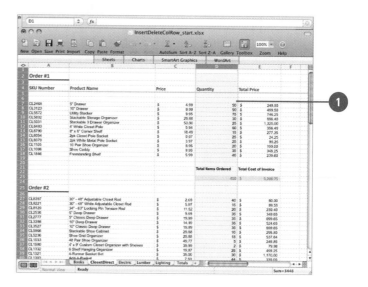

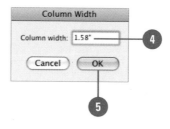

Did You Know?

What is a point? A point is a measurement unit used to size text and space on a worksheet. One inch equals 72 points.

Adjust Column Width or Row Height Using the Mouse

1 Position the mouse pointer on the right edge of the column header button or the bottom edge of the row header button for the column or row you want to change.

2 When the mouse pointer changes to a double-headed arrow, click and drag the pointer to a new width or height.

Did You Know?

You can change the default column width. Click the Format menu, point to Column, click Standard Width, type a column width in points, and then click OK.

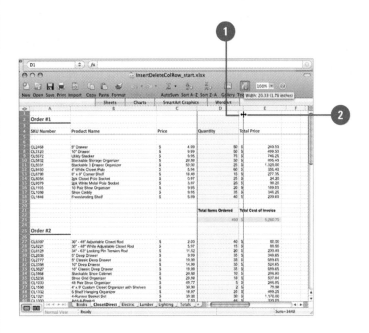

Change Column Width or Row Height Using AutoFit

1 Position the mouse pointer on the right edge of the column header button or the bottom edge of the row header button for the column or row you want to change.

2 When the mouse pointer changes to a double-headed arrow, double-click the mouse.

◆ You can also click the **Format** menu, point to **Column**, and then click **AutoFit Selection**.

◆ You can also click the **Format** menu, point to **Row**, and then click **AutoFit**.

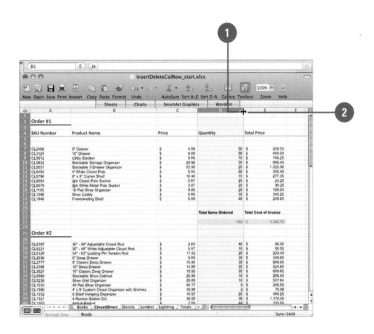

Splitting a Worksheet into Panes

If you are working on a large worksheet, it can be time consuming and tiring to scroll back and forth between two parts of the worksheet. You can split the worksheet into four panes and two scrollable windows that you can view simultaneously but edit and scroll independently using the Split bar. As you work in two parts of the same worksheet, you can resize the window panes to fit your task. Drag the split bar between the panes to resize the windows. No matter how you display worksheets, Excel's commands and buttons work the same as usual.

Split a Worksheet into Panes

1. Select the row, column, or cell location where you want to split a worksheet into panes.

   A column or row selection creates two panes, while a cell selection creates four panes.

2. Point to the Split bar at the top of the vertical scroll bar or at the right end of the horizontal scroll bar.

3. When the cursor changes, drag the Split bar down or left to the place you want.

   ◆ To split a worksheet into four pane, click the **Window** menu, and then click **Split**.

4. To remove the split, click the **Window** menu, and then click **Remove Split**.

Worksheet split into four panes

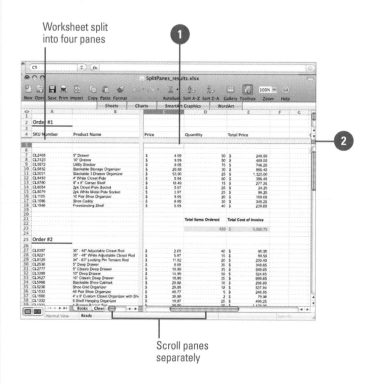

Scroll panes separately

Did You Know?

You can search for a value or data in a cell, and then replace it with different content. Click the cell or cells containing content you want to replace. Click the Edit menu, click Replace, specify the values or data you want to find and replace, and then click the appropriate Find or Replace buttons.

Freezing and Unfreezing a Column or Row

Large worksheets can be difficult to work with, especially on low-resolution or small screens. If you scroll down to see the bottom of the list, you can no longer see the column names at the top of the list. Instead of repeatedly scrolling up and down, you can temporarily set, or **freeze**, those column or row headings so that you can see them no matter where you scroll in the list. When you freeze a row or column, you are actually splitting the screen into one or more panes (window sections) and freezing one of the panes. You can split the screen into up to four panes and can freeze up to two of these panes. You can edit the data in a frozen pane just as you do any Excel data, but the cells remain stationary even when you use the scroll bars; only the unfrozen part of the screen scrolls. When you freeze a pane, it has no effect on how a worksheet looks when printed.

Freeze and Unfreeze a Column or Row

1. Click the **View** menu, and then click **Normal**.

2. Select the column to the right of the columns you want to freeze, or select the row below the rows you want to freeze.

   To freeze both, click the cell to the right and below of the column and row you want to freeze.

3. Click the **Window** menu, and then click **Freeze Panes**.

   When you freeze a pane horizontally, all the rows **above** the active cell freeze. When you freeze a pane vertically, all the columns to the **left** of the active cell freeze.

4. To unfreeze a column or row, click the **Window** menu, and then click **Unfreeze Panes**.

Showing and Hiding Workbook Elements

When you open a new or existing workbook, Excel displays a standard set of elements, such as the Formula Bar, Headings (columns and rows), Gridlines, and Ruler, which is available in Page Layout view. If you need a little more display room to see your data or you want to see how your data looks without the gridlines, you can quickly select or clear view settings on the Data menu in Excel to show or hide these elements.

Show or Hide Workbook Elements

◆ **View menu.** Click the **View** menu, and then click the element you want to show or hide.

   ◆ **Ruler.** In Page Layout view, the horizontal and vertical rulers.

   ◆ **Formula Bar.** The bar at the top of the screen.

◆ **View Preferences.** Click the **Excel** menu, click **Preferences**, click the **View** icon, and then select the check boxes with the options you want to show or hide. Some of the common options include:

   ◆ **Show gridlines.** The gray outline around cells.

   ◆ **Show row and column headings.** The column (letters) and row (numbers) headings.

Did You Know?

You can view a workbook in full screen without menus and toolbars. Click the View menu, and then click the Full Screen. To exit Full Screen view, click Close Full Screen.

Formula bar　　　No ruler

No gridlines or headings

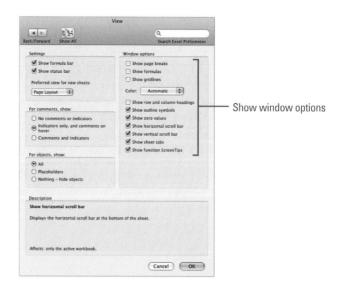

Show window options

Building a Worksheet with Excel

9

Introduction

Once you enter data in a worksheet, you'll want to add formulas to perform calculations. Microsoft Excel can help you get the results you need. Formulas can be very basic entries to more complex ones. The difficulty of the formula depends on the complexity of the result you want from your data. For instance, if you are simply looking to total this months sales, then the formula would add your sales number and provide the result. However, if you were looking to show this months sales, greater than $100.00 with repeat customers, you would take a bit more time to design the formula.

Because Microsoft Excel automatically recalculates formulas, your worksheets remain accurate and up-to-date no matter how often you change the data. Using absolute cell references anchors formulas to a specific cell. Excel provides numerous built-in functions to add to your worksheet calculations. Functions, such as AVERAGE or SUM, allow you to perform a quick formula calculation.

Another way to make your formulas easier to understand is by using name ranges in them. Name ranges—a group of selected cells named as a range—can help you understand your more complicated formulas. It is a lot easier to read a formula that uses name ranges, then to look at the formula and try to decipher it. Excel offers a tool to audit your worksheet. Looking at the "flow" of your formula greatly reduces errors in the calculation. You can see how your formula is built, one level at a time through a series of arrows that point out where the formula is pulling data from. As you develop your formula, you can make corrections to it.

What You'll Do

Understand Formulas and Referencing

Create and Edit Formulas

Name Cells and Ranges

Enter and Manage Names

Simplify a Formula with Ranges

Use Calculator and Formula Builder

Use Nested and Text Functions

Calculate Multiple Results

Use Lookup and Reference Functions

Summarize Data using Subtotals and Functions

Calculate Totals with AutoSum

Create and Format a List

Create Calculations in a List

Remove List Rows and Columns

Sort Data in a List

Display Parts of a List with AutoFilter

Convert Text to Columns

Create Groups and Outlines

Add Data Validation to a Worksheet

Create a Drop-Down List

Understanding Formulas

Introduction

A formula calculates values to return a result. On an Excel worksheet, you can create a formula using constant values (such as 147 or $10.00), operators (shown in the table), references, and functions. An Excel formula always begins with the equal sign (=).

A **constant** is a number or text value that is not calculated, such as the number 147, the text "Total Profits", and the date 7/22/2008. On the other hand, an **expression** is a value that is not a constant. Constants remain the same until you or the system change them. An **operator** performs a calculation, such as + (plus sign) or - (minus sign). A cell **reference** is a cell address that returns the value in a cell. For example, A1 (column A and row 1) returns the value in cell A1 (see table below).

Cell Reference Examples

Reference	Meaning
A1	Cell in column A and row 1
A1:A10	Range of cells in column A and rows 1 through 10
A1:F1	Range of cells in row 1 and columns A through F
1:1	All cells in row 1
1:5	All cells in rows 5 through 10
A:A	All cells in column A
A:F	All cells in columns A through F
Profits!A1:A10	Range of cells in column A and rows 1 through 10 in worksheet named Profits

A **function** performs predefined calculations using specific values, called arguments. For example, the function SUM(B1:B10) returns the sum of cells B1 through B10. An argument can be numbers, text, logical values such as TRUE or FALSE, arrays, error values such as #NA, or cell references. Arguments can also be constants, formulas, or other functions, known as **nested functions**. A function starts with the equal sign (=), followed by the function name, an opening parenthesis, the arguments for the function separated by commas, and a closing parenthesis. For example, the function, AVERAGE(A1:A10, B1:B10), returns a number with the average for the contents of cells A1 through A10 and B1 through B10. As you type a function, a ScreenTip appears with the structure and arguments needed to complete the function. You can also use the Insert Function dialog box to help you add a function to a formula.

Perform Calculations

By default, every time you make a change to a value, formula, or name, Excel performs a calculation. To change the way Excel performs calculations, click the Formulas tab, click the Calculation Options button, and then click the option you want: Automatic, Automatic Except Data Tables, or Manual. To manually recalculate all open workbooks, click the Calculate Now button (or press F9). To recalculate the active worksheet, click the Calculate Sheet button (or press Shift+F9).

Precedence Order

Formulas perform calculations from left to right, according to a specific order for each operator. Formulas containing more than one operator follow precedence order: exponentiation, multiplication and division, and then addition and subtraction. So, in the formula 2 + 5 * 7, Excel performs multiplication first and addition next for a result of 37. Excel calculates operations within parentheses first. The result of the formula (2 + 5) * 7 is 49.

Understanding Cell Referencing

Each cell, the intersection of a column and row on a worksheet, has a unique address, or **cell reference**, based on its column letter and row number. For example, the cell reference for the intersection of column D and row 4 is D4.

Cell References in Formulas

The simplest formula refers to a cell. If you want one cell to contain the same value as another cell, type an equal sign followed by the cell reference, such as =D4. The cell that contains the formula is known as a **dependent cell** because its value depends on the value in another cell. Whenever the cell that the formula refers to changes, the cell that contains the formula also changes.

Depending on your task, you can use **relative cell references**, which are references to cells relative to the position of the formula, **absolute cell references**, which are cell references that always refer to cells in a specific location, or **mixed cell references**, which use a combination of relative and absolute column and row references. If you use macros, the R1C1 cell references make it easy to compute row and column positions.

Relative Cell References

When you copy and paste or move a formula that uses relative references, the references in the formula change to reflect cells that are in the same relative position to the formula. The formula is the same, but it uses the new cells in its calculation. Relative addressing eliminates the tedium of creating new formulas for each row or column in a worksheet filled with repetitive information.

Absolute Cell References

If you don't want a cell reference to change when you copy a formula, make it an absolute reference by typing a dollar sign ($) before each part of the reference that you don't want to change. For example, A1 always refers to cell A1. If you copy or fill the formula down columns or across rows, the absolute reference doesn't change. You can add a $ before the column letter and the row number. To ensure accuracy and simplify updates, enter constant values (such as tax rates, hourly rates, and so on) in a cell, and then use absolute references to them in formulas.

Mixed Cell References

A mixed reference is either an absolute row and relative column or absolute column and relative row. You add the $ before the column letter to create an absolute column or before the row number to create an absolute row. For example, $A1 is absolute for column A and relative for row 1, and A$1 is absolute for row 1 and relative for column A. If you copy or fill the formula across rows or down columns, the relative references adjust, and the absolute ones don't adjust.

3-D References

3-D references allow you to analyze data in the same cell or range of cells on multiple worksheets within a workbook. A 3-D reference includes the cell or range reference, preceded by a range of worksheet names. For example, =AVERAGE(Sheet1:Sheet4!A1) returns the average for all the values contained in cell A1 on all the worksheets between and including Sheet 1 and Sheet 4.

Creating a Simple Formula

A **formula** calculates values to return a result. On an Excel worksheet, you can create a formula using values (such as 147 or $10.00), arithmetic operators (shown in the table), and cell references. An Excel formula always begins with the equal sign (=). The equal sign, when entered, automatically formats the cell as a formula entry. The best way to start a formula is to have an argument. An **argument** is the cell references or values in a formula that contribute to the result. Each function uses function-specific arguments, which may include numeric values, text values, cell references, ranges of cells, and so on. To accommodate long, complex formulas, you can resize the formula bar to prevent formulas from covering other data in your worksheet. By default, only formula results are displayed in a cell, but you can change the view of the worksheet to display formulas instead of results.

Enter a Formula

1. Click the cell where you want to enter a formula.

2. Type = (an equal sign). If you do not begin with an equal sign, Excel will display, not calculate, the information you type.

3. Enter the first argument. An argument can be a number or a cell reference.

   TIMESAVER *To avoid typing mistakes, click a cell to insert its cell reference in a formula rather than typing its address.*

4. Enter an arithmetic operator.

5. Enter the next argument.

6. Repeat steps 4 and 5 as needed to complete the formula.

7. Press Return.

   Notice that the result of the formula appears in the cell (if you select the cell, the formula itself appears on the formula bar).

   TIMESAVER *To wrap text in a cell, press Control+Enter, which manually inserts a line break.*

Formula bar

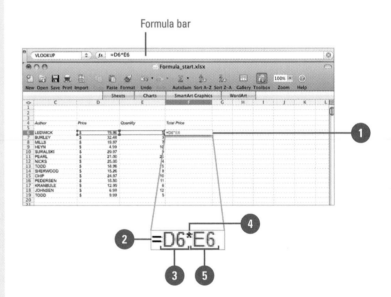

For Your Information

Understanding Order of Precedence

Formulas containing more than one operator follow the order of precedence: exponentiation, multiplication and division, and then addition and subtraction. So, in the formula 5 + 2 * 3, Excel performs multiplication first and addition next for a result of 11. Excel calculates operations within parentheses first. The result of the formula (5 + 2) * 3 is 21.

Resize, Move, or Close the Formula Bar

◆ To precisely adjust the length of the formula box, point to the bottom right corner of the formula box until the pointer changes to an arrow, and then drag left or right.

◆ To move the formula bar, point to the title bar on the left, and then drag to move it.

◆ To close the formula bar, click the **Close** button on the left. You can also click the **View** menu, and then click **Formula Bar** to open and close the formula bar.

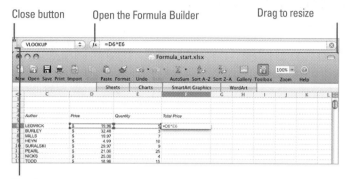

Close button   Open the Formula Builder   Drag to resize

Drag to move

Display Formulas in Cells

① Click the **Excel** menu, and then click **Preferences**.

② Click the **View** icon.

③ Select the **Show formulas** check box to show formulas or clear it to hide formulas.

④ Click **OK**.

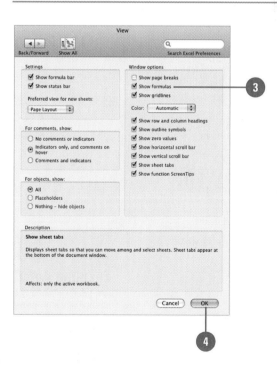

Did You Know?

Pointing to cells reduces errors. When building formulas, pointing to a cell rather than typing its address ensures that the correct cell is referenced.

You can print formulas. Display formulas in cell, click the Print button on the Standard toolbar, and then click Print.

Creating a Formula Using Formula AutoComplete

To minimize typing and syntax errors, you can create and edit formulas with Formula AutoComplete (**New!**). After you type an = (equal sign) and begin typing to start a formula, Excel displays a dynamic drop-down list of valid functions, arguments, defined names, list names, special item specifiers—including [(open bracket), , (comma), : (colon)—and text string that match the letters you type. An argument is the cell references or values in a formula that contribute to the result. Each function uses function-specific arguments, which may include numeric values, text values, cell references, ranges of cells, and so on.

Enter Items in a Formula Using Formula AutoComplete

1. Click the cell where you want to enter a formula.

2. Type = (an equal sign), and beginning letters or a display trigger to start Formula AutoComplete.

   For example, type *su* to display all value items, such as SUBTOTAL and SUM.

   The text before the insertion point is used to display the values in the drop-down list.

3. As you type, a drop-down scrollable list of valid items is displayed.

   Icons represent the type of entry, such as a function or list reference, and a ScreenTip appears next to a selected item.

4. To insert an item, click the item from the drop-down list.

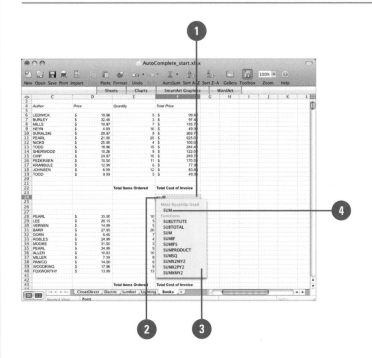

Editing a Formula

You can edit formulas just as you do other cell contents, using the formula bar or working in the cell. You can select, cut, copy, paste, delete, and format cells containing formulas just as you do cells containing labels or values. Using **AutoFill**, you can quickly copy formulas to adjacent cells. If you need to copy formulas to different parts of a worksheet, use the Clipboard.

Edit a Formula Using the Formula Bar

1. Select the cell that contains the formula you want to edit.

2. Click in the Formula bar.

   TIMESAVER *Press Control+U to change into Edit mode.*

3. If necessary, use the Home, End, and arrow keys to position the insertion point within the cell contents.

4. Use the Delete key to erase unwanted characters, and then type new characters as needed.

5. Press Return.

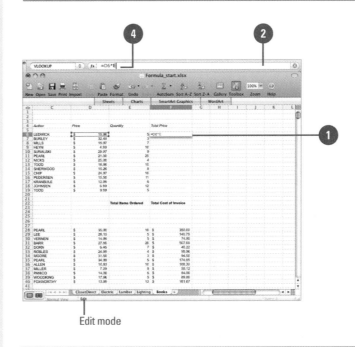

Edit mode

Copy a Formula Using AutoFill

1. Select the cell that contains the formula you want to copy.

2. Position the pointer (fill handle) on the lower-right corner of the selected cell.

3. Drag the mouse down until the adjacent cells where you want the formula pasted are selected, and then release the mouse button.

4. To change AutoFill options, click the **AutoFill Options** button, and then click **Copy Cells**, **Fill Formatting Only**, or **Fill Without Formatting**.

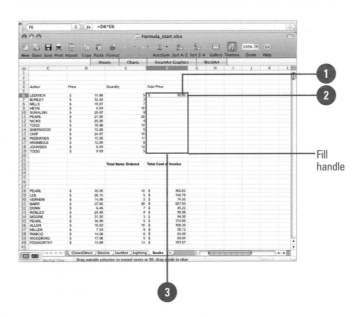

Fill handle

Naming Cells and Ranges

To make working with ranges easier, Excel allows you to name them. The name BookTitle, for example, is easier to remember than the range reference B6:B21. Named ranges can be used to navigate large worksheets. Named ranges can also be used in formulas instead of typing or pointing to specific cells. When you name a cell or range, Excel uses an absolute reference for the name by default, which is almost always what you want. You can see the absolute reference in the Refers to box in the New Name dialog box. There are two types of names you can create and use: defined name and list name. A **defined name** represents a cell, a range of cells, formula or constant, while a **list name** represents an Excel list, which is a collection of data stored in records (rows) and fields (columns). You can define a name for use in a worksheet or an entire workbook, also known as **scope**. The worksheet and formula bar work together to avoid overlapping content.

Name a Cell or Range Using the Name Box

1. Select the cell or range, or nonadjacent selections you want to name.

2. Click the Name box on the formula bar.

3. Type a name for the range.

   A range name can include up to 255 characters, uppercase or lowercase letters (not case sensitive), numbers, and punctuation, but no spaces or cell references.

   By default, names use absolute cell references.

4. Press Return. The range name will appear in the Name box whenever you select the range in the workbook.

Let Excel Name a Cell or Range

1. Select the cells, including the column or row header, you want to name.

2. Click the **Insert** menu, point to **Name**, and then click **Create**.

3. Select the check box with the position of the labels in relation to the cells.

   Excel automatically tries to determine the position of the labels, so you might not have to change any options.

4. Click **OK**.

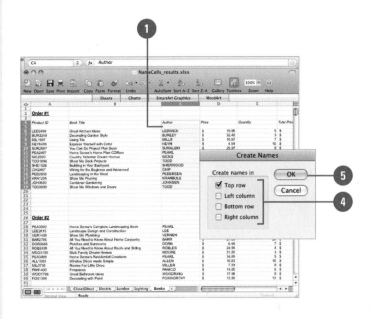

Name a Cell or Range Using the New Name Dialog Box

1. Select the cell or range, or nonadjacent selections you want to name.

2. Click the **Insert** menu, point to **Name**, and then click **Define**.

3. Type a name for the reference.

   The current selection appears in the Refer to box.

4. Click the **Collapse Dialog** button, select different cells and click the **Expand Dialog** button, or type = (equal sign) followed by a constant value or a formula.

5. Click **Add**.

6. Click **OK**.

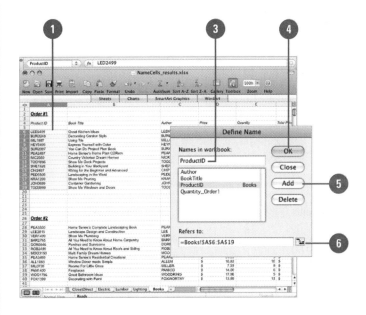

Entering Named Cells and Ranges

After you define a named cell or range, you can enter a name by typing, using the Name box, using Formula AutoComplete (**New!**), or selecting from the Use in Formula command. As you begin to type a name in a formula, Formula AutoComplete displays valid matches in a drop-down list, which you can select and insert into a formula. You can also select a name from a list of available from the Use in Formula command. If you have already entered a cell or range address in a formula or function, you can apply a name to the address instead of re-creating it.

Enter a Named Cell or Range Using the Name Box

1. Click the **Name box** drop-down on the formula bar.

2. Click the name of the cell or range you want to use.

   The range name appears in the Name box, and all cells included in the range are highlighted on the worksheet.

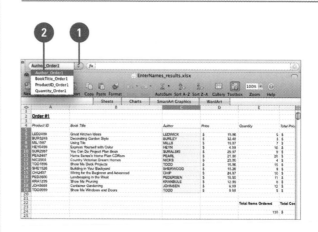

Enter a Named Cell or Range Using Formula AutoComplete

1. Type = (equal sign) to start a formula, and then type the first letter of the name.

2. To insert a name, type the first letter of the name to display it in the Formula AutoComplete drop-down list.

3. Scroll down the list, if necessary, and then select the name you want to insert it.

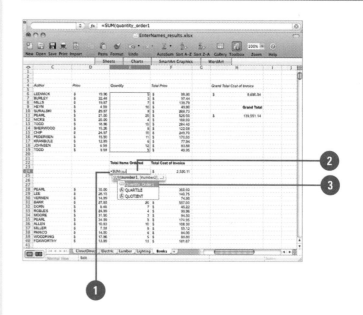

Enter a Named Cell or Range from the Use in Formula Command

1. Type = (equal sign) to start a formula.

2. Click the **Insert** menu, point to **Name**, and then click **Paste**.

3. Select a name.

4. **OK**.

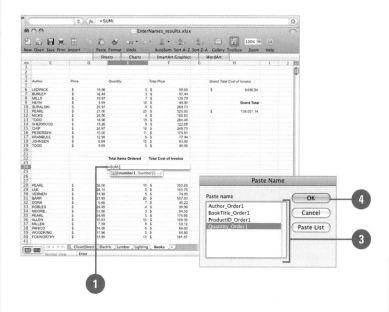

Apply a Name to a Cell or Range Address

1. Select the cells in which you want to apply a name.

2. Click the **Insert** menu, point to **Name**, and then click **Apply**.

3. Click the name you want to apply.

4. Click **OK**.

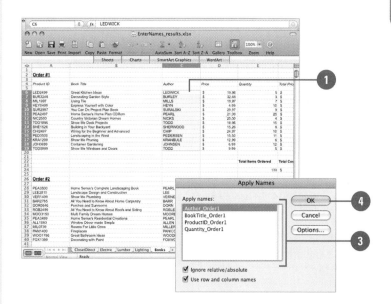

Did You Know?

Should I select the Use row and column names option? When you select this option, Excel uses the range row and column headings to refer to the range you've selected (if a cell does not have its own name, but it part of a named range).

Simplifying a Formula with Ranges

You can simplify formulas by using ranges and range names. For example, if 12 cells on your worksheet contain monthly budget amounts, and you want to multiply each amount by 10%, you can insert one range address in a formula instead of inserting 12 different cell addresses, or you can insert a range name. Using a range name in a formula helps to identify what the formula does; the formula =TotalOrder*0.10, for example, is more meaningful than =SUM(F6:F19)*0.10.

Use a Range in a Formula

1. Put your cursor where you would like the formula. Type an equal sign (=) followed by the start of a formula, such as *=SUM(*.

2. Click the first cell of the range, and then drag to select the last cell in the range. Excel enters the range address for you.

3. Complete the formula by entering a close parentheses, or another function, and then press Return.

Use a Range Name in a Formula

1. Put your cursor where you would like the formula. Type an equal sign (=) followed by the start of a formula, such as *=SUM(*.

2. Click the **Insert** menu, point to **Name**, and then click **Paste**.

3. Click the name of the range you want to insert.

4. Click **OK**.

5. Complete the formula by entering a close parentheses, or another function, and then press Return.

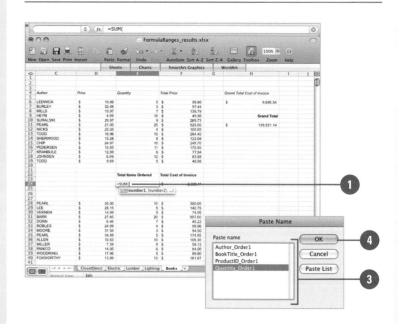

Using the Calculator

In addition to the formula bar, you can also use a special calculator in Excel to create and edit formulas. The Calculator in Excel s similar to a traditional handheld calculator with the addition of a Formula pane where you can create and edit a formula and some common functions. After you create a formula, the result, if available, appears in the Answer box. When you click OK, the formula is transferred into the destination cell on the worksheet.

Create or Edit a Formula Using the Calculator

1 Click the cell where you want to insert a formula.

2 Click the **Tools** menu, and then click **Calculator**.

The Calculator opens, displaying an equal sign (=) in the Formula pane.

3 Type directly in the Formula pane or click the buttons on the Calculator to create a formula.

◆ To insert a cell reference, click the cell or range in the worksheet.

4 Use any of the following to insert a function:

◆ **If.** Click to add a conditional text to the formula. Specify the condition to test, a true result, a false result, and then click Insert to transfer it to the Formula pane. For a text result, Excel automatically adds quotation marks.

◆ **Sum.** Click to add a Sum function to the formula. Select the range in the worksheet you want to add, and then click Insert to transfer it to the Formula pane.

◆ **More.** Click to create or edit the formula in Formula Builder.

5 Click **OK** to transfer the formula into the destination cell on the worksheet.

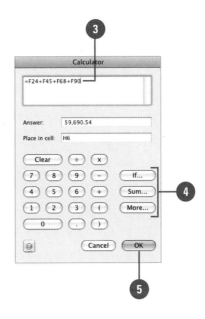

Sum function

Using the Formula Builder

Functions are predesigned formulas that save you the time and trouble of creating commonly used or complex equations. Trying to write a formula that calculates various pieces of data, such as calculating payments for an investment over a period of time at a certain rate, can be difficult and time-consuming. Formula Builder (**New!**) simplifies the process by organizing Excel's built-in formulas, called functions, into categories—such as Most Recently Used, Financial, Text, Date and Time, Lookup and Reference, Math and Trigonometry, and other functions—so they are easy to find and use. A function defines all the necessary components (also called arguments) you need to produce a specific result; all you have to do is supply the values, cell references, and other variables. You can even combine one or more functions.

Enter a Formula Using Formula Builder

1. Click the cell where you want to enter the formula.

2. Click the **Formula Builder** tab on the Toolbox.

3. Type = (equal sign) to start a formula.

4. Type or select data references and to start the formula.

5. Continue to add data references and operators.

   ◆ Type data references in the boxes.

   ◆ Click the plus (+) icon to add another data reference.

   ◆ Click the operation drop-down, and then select an operator or function.

6. When you're done, press Return to complete the formula.

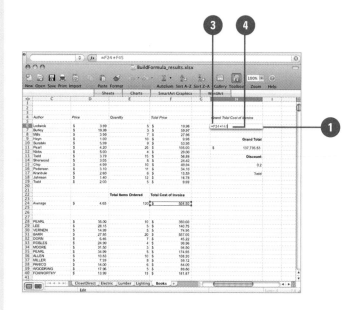

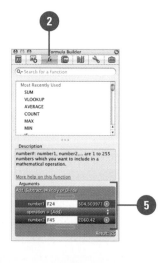

Enter a Function Using Formula Builder

1 Click the cell where you want to enter the function.

2 Click the **Formula Builder** tab on the Toolbox.

3 If you know the function you want to use, start to type the function in the Search box. As you type, possible matches appear in the list.

4 Double-click the function you want. Excel inserts the equal sign, function name, and parentheses.

◆ To find out more about a function and its arguments, read the text in the Description box.

5 Click the plus (+) icon (if necessary), and then type an argument to the function.

◆ To insert a function as an argument to the current function (known as a nested function), double-click the function name in the list. The nested function appears separately. To switch between the functions, click the up arrow icon.

As you add arguments and elements, formula Builder evaluates the data and display the current result in the bottom right corner.

6 Continue to add data references and operators, such as +, -, or *, as needed.

7 To remove an argument or element, click the minus (-) icon.

8 When you're done, press Return to complete the formula.

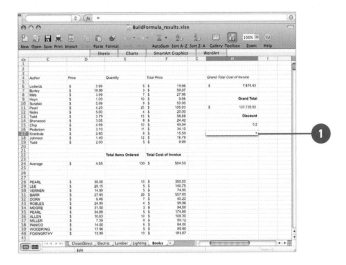

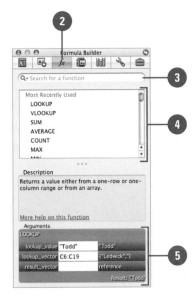

For Your Information

Inserting Placeholder Arguments

If you don't know the cell references you want to use for a function, you can insert argument names as placeholders, and then fill in the actual argument later. Press Control+Shift+A after you type the functions name. Excel uses the arguments names as arguments. For example,

=VLOOKUP(lookup_value, table_array, col_index_num, range_lookup).

Using Nested Functions

A nested function uses a function as one of the arguments. Excel allows you to nest up to 64 levels of functions. Users typically create nested functions as part of a conditional formula. For example, IF(AVERAGE(B2:B10)>100,SUM(C2:G10),0). The AVERAGE and SUM functions are nested within the IF function. The structure of the IF function is IF(condition_test, if_true, if_false). You can use the AND, OR, NOT, and IF functions to create conditional formulas. When you create a nested formula, it can be difficult to understand how Excel performs the calculations. You can use the Evaluate Formula dialog box to help you evaluate parts of a nested formula one step at a time.

Create a Conditional Formula Using a Nested Function

1. Click the cell where you want to enter the function.

2. Click the **Formula Builder** tab on the Toolbox.

3. Double-click the function you want. Excel inserts the equal sign, function name, and parentheses.

   For example, click the Logical and Reference button, and then click COUNTIF.

4. Click the plus (+) icon (if necessary), and then type an argument to the function.

5. To insert a nested function as an argument to the current function, double-click the function name in the list. The nested function appears separately. To switch between the functions, click the up arrow icon.

   For example, =COUNTIF(E6:E19), ">"&AVERAGE(E6:E19)).

6. When you're done, press Return.

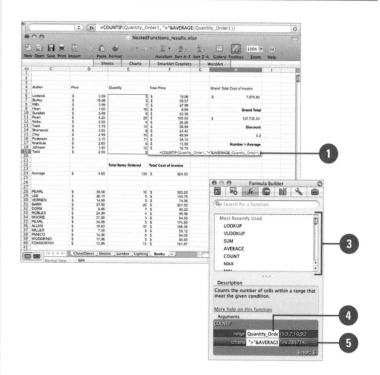

Conditional Formula Examples

Formula	Result
=AND(A2>A3, A2<A4)	If A2 is greater than A3 and less than A4, then return TRUE, otherwise return FALSE
=OR(A2>A3, A2<A4)	If A2 is greater than A3 or A2 is less than A4, then return TRUE, otherwise return FALSE
=NOT(A2+A3=24)	If A2 plus A3 is not equal to 24, then return TRUE, otherwise return FALSE
IF(A2<>15, "OK", "Not OK")	If the value in cell A2 is not equal to 15, then return "OK", otherwise return "Not OK"

Calculating Multiple Results

An array formula can perform multiple calculations and then return either a single or multiple result. For example, when you want to count the number of distinct entries in a range, you can use an array formula, such as {=SUM(1/COUNTIF(range,range))}. You can also use an array formula to perform a two column lookup using the LOOKUP function. An array formula works on two or more sets of values, known as **array arguments**. Each argument must have the same number of rows and columns. You can create array formulas in the same way that you create other formulas, except you press Control+Shift+Enter to enter the formula. When you enter an array formula, Excel inserts the formula between { } (brackets).

Create an Array Formula

① Click the cell where you want to enter the array formula.

② Type = (an equal sign).

③ Use any of the following methods to enter the formula you want.

- ◆ Type the function.

- ◆ Type and use Formula AutoComplete.

- ◆ Use the Formula Builder.

④ Press Control+Shift+Return.

{ } (brackets) appear around the function to indicate it's an array formula.

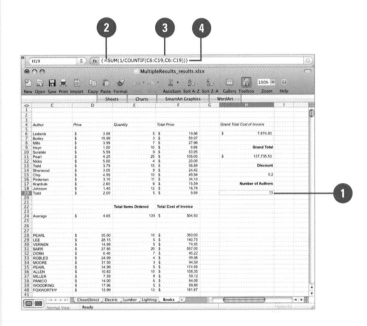

Using Lookup and Reference Functions

You can use lookup and reference functions in Excel to easily retrieve information from a data list. The lookup functions (VLOOKUP and HLOOKUP) allow you to search for and insert a value in a cell that is stored in another place in the worksheet. The HLOOKUP function looks in rows (a horizontal lookup) and the VLOOKUP function looks in columns (a vertical lookup). Each function uses four arguments (pieces of data) as shown in the following definition: =VLOOKUP (lookup_value, table_array, col_index_num, range_lookup). The VLOOKUP function finds a value in the left-most column of a named range and returns the value from the specified cell to the right of the cell with the found value, while the HLOOKUP function does the same to rows. In the example, =VLOOKUP(12,Salary,2,TRUE), the function looks for the value 12 in the named range Salary and finds the closest (next lower) value, and returns the value in column 2 of the same row and places the value in the active cell. In the example, =HLOOKUP ("Years",Salary,4,FALSE), the function looks for the value "Years" in the named range Salary and finds the exact text string value, and then returns the value in row 4 of the column.

Use the VLOOKUP Function

① Create a data range in which the left-most column contains a unique value in each row.

② Click the cell where you want to place the function.

③ Type **=VLOOKUP**(*value, named range, column,* **TRUE** *or* **FALSE**).

Or click the **Formula Builder** tab on the Toolbox, double-click **VLOOKUP** under Lookup and Reference, and then specify the function arguments.

④ Press Return.

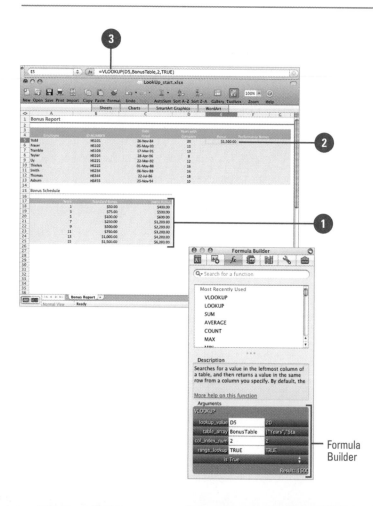

Formula Builder

Use the HLOOKUP Function

1. Create a data range in which the uppermost row contains a unique value in each row.

2. Click the cell where you want to place the function.

3. Type **=HLOOKUP**(*value, named range, row,* **TRUE** *or* **FALSE**).

   Or click the **Formula Builder** tab on the Toolbox, double-click **HLOOKUP** under Lookup and Reference, and then specify the function arguments.

4. Press Return.

Did You Know?

You can use Paste Special to copy only formulas. Select the cells containing the formulas you want to copy, click the Copy button on the Standard toolbar, click where you want to paste the data, click the Edit menu, click Paste Special, click the Formulas button, and then click OK.

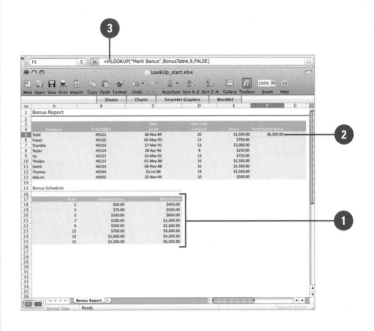

Lookup Function Arguments

Argument	Description
lookup_value	The value found in the row or the column of the named range. You can use a value, cell reference or a text string (enclosed in quotation marks).
list_array	The named range of information in which Excel looks up data.
col_index_num	The numeric position of the column in the named range (counting from the left) for the value to be returned (use only for VLOOKUP).
row_index_num	The numeric position of the row in the named range (counting from the top) for the value to be returned (use only for HLOOKUP).
range_lookup	The value returned when the function is to find the nearest value (TRUE) or an exact match (FALSE) for the lookup_value. The default value is TRUE.

Using Text Functions

You can use text functions to help you work with text in a workbook. If you need to count the number of characters in a cell or the number of occurrences of a specific text string in a cell, you can use the LEN and SUBSTITUTE functions. If you want to narrow the count to only upper or lower case text, you can use the UPPER and LOWER functions. If you need to capitalize a list of names or titles, you can use the PROPER function. The function capitalizes the first letter in a text string and converts all other letters to lowercase.

Use Text Functions

1. Create a data range in which the left-most column contains a unique value in each row.

2. Click the cell where you want to place the function.

3. Type = (equal sign), type a text function, and then specify the argument for the selected function. Some examples include:

   ◆ =LEFT(A4,FIND(" ",A4)-1)

   ◆ =RIGHT(A4,LEN(A4-FIND("*",SUBSTITUTE(A4," ","*",LEN(A4)-LEN(SUBSTITUTE(A4," ","")))))

   ◆ =UPPER(A4)

   ◆ =LOWER(A4)

   ◆ =PROPER(A4)

   Or click the **Formula Builder** tab, double-click a text function, and then specify the function arguments.

4. Press Return.

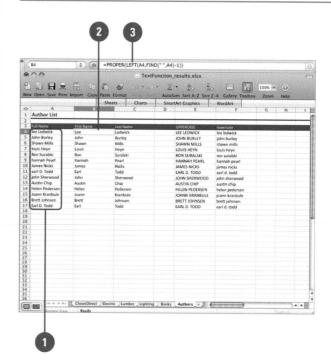

Did You Know?

You can use wildcard characters in a criteria. A question mark (?) matches any single character. An asterisk (*) matches any sequence of characters. If you want to find an actual question mark or asterisk, type a tilde (~) before the character.

274

Summarizing Data Using Subtotals

If you have a column list with similar facts and no blanks, you can automatically calculate subtotals and grand totals in a list. Subtotals are calculated with a summary function, such as SUM, COUNT, or AVERAGE, while Grand totals are created from detailed data instead of subtotal values. **Detailed data** is typically adjacent to and either above or below or to the left of the summary data. When you summarize data using subtotals, the data list is also outlined to display and hide the detailed rows for each subtotal.

Subtotal Data in a List

1. Organize data in a hierarchical fashion—place summary rows below detail rows and summary columns to the right of detail columns.

2. Select the data that you want to subtotal.

3. Click the **Data** menu, and then click **Subtotals**.

4. Click the column to subtotal.

5. Click the summary function you want to use to calculate the subtotals.

6. Select the check box for each column that contains values you want to subtotal.

7. To set automatic page breaks following each subtotal, select the **Page break between groups** check box.

8. To show or hide a summary row above the detail row, select or clear the **Summary below data** check box.

9. To remove subtotals, click **Remove All**.

10. Click **OK**.

11. To add more subtotals, use the **Subtotals** command again.

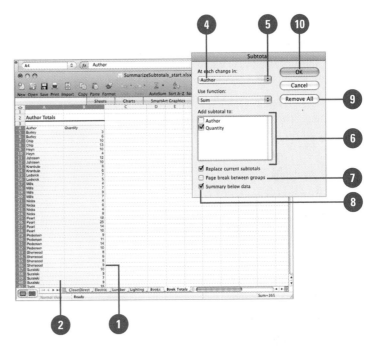

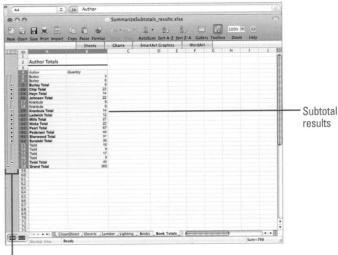

Subtotal results

Use +/- button to expand/collapse subtotals.

Summarizing Data Using Functions

You can use conditional functions, such as SUMIF, COUNTIF, and AVERAGEIF to summarize data in a workbook. These functions allow you to calculate a total, count the number of items, and average a set of numbers based on a specific criteria. You can use the SUMIF function to add up interest payment for accounts over $100, or use the COUNTIF function to find the number of people who live in CA from an address list. If you need to perform these functions based on multiple criteria, you can use the SUMIFS, COUNTIFS, and AVERAGEIFS functions. If you need to find the minimum or maximum in a range, you can use the summarizing functions MIN and MAX.

Use Summarize Data Functions

1. Click the cell where you want to place the function.

2. Type = (equal sign), type a text function, specify the argument for the selected function, and then press Return.

    Some examples include:

    ◆ =AVERAGE(D6:D19)

    ◆ ={=SUM(1/COUNTIF(C6:C19, C6:19))}

    ◆ =SUMIF(C6:C19,"Todd", Quantity_Order1)

    ◆ =SUM(Quantity_Order1)

    Or click the **Formula Builder** tab, double-click a data function, and then specify the function arguments.

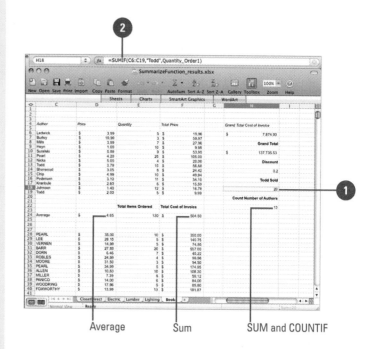

Average   Sum   SUM and COUNTIF

Did You Know?

You can use several functions to count items in a range. The COUNT function Counts the number of cells that contain numbers within the list of arguments, while the COUNTA function counts the number of cells that are not empty and the values within the list of arguments.

Calculating Totals with AutoSum

A range of cells can easily be added using the **AutoSum** button on the Standard toolbar. AutoSum suggests the range to sum, although this range can be changed if it's incorrect. AutoSum looks at all of the data that is consecutively entered, and when it sees an empty cell, that is where the AutoSum stops. You can also use AutoSum to perform other calculations, such as AVERAGE, COUNT, MAX, and MIN. Subtotals can be calculated for data ranges using the Subtotals dialog box. This dialog box lets you select where the subtotals occur, as well as the function type.

Calculate Totals with AutoSum

1. Click the cell where you want to display the calculation.

   - To sum with a range of numbers, select the range of cells you want.

   - To sum with only some of the numbers in a range, select the cells or range you want using the ⌘ key. Excel inserts the sum in the first empty cell below the selected range.

   - To sum both across and down a list of number, select the range of cells with an additional column to the right and a row at the bottom.

2. Click the **AutoSum** button arrow on the Standard toolbar, and then select an AutoSum function, such as Sum, Average, Count Numbers, Max, or Min.

3. Press Return.

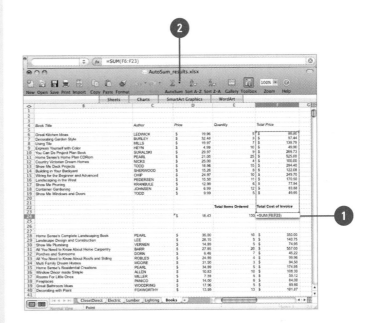

Did You Know?

You can select additional AutoFill commands. Click the Edit menu, point to Fill, and then select a fill command such as Up, Down, Left, Right, Series, or Justify.

Calculating a Conditional Sum

The Conditional Sum command in Excel totals only numbers in a column that match your criteria, which is useful when you have different types of data in the same column. Excel uses the Conditional Sum Wizard to help you select the range you want to use, which includes the column to total, the columns containing the criteria, and the column headings, and specify the criterion you want to use to complete the sum.

Calculate a Conditional Sum

1. Click the **Tools** menu, and then click **Conditional Sum**.

2. In Step 1, select the range you want to use, which includes the column to total, the columns containing the criteria, and the column headings.

3. Click **Next**.

4. In Step 2, click the drop-down, and then select the heading of the column to total.

5. Specify the first criterion by selecting a column heading and a conditional test, and type or select a value in the text box, and then click **Add** to include it. Continue to specify the criteria you want.

6. Click **Next**.

7. In Step 3, click the option you want to display only the total or the total and the criteria.

8. Click **Next**.

9. Select a cell in which to display the total and other criteria.

10. Click **Finish**.

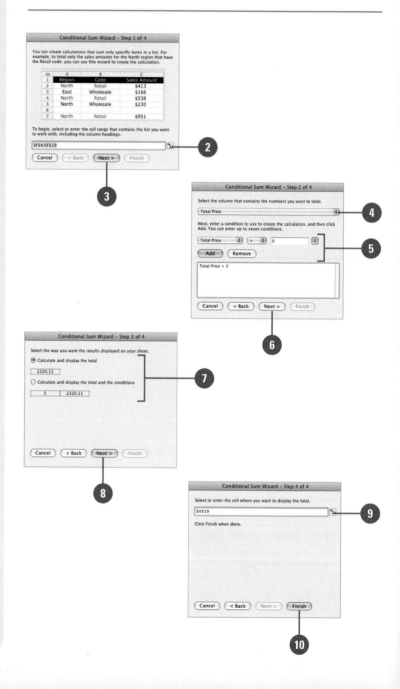

Auditing a Worksheet

In a complex worksheet, it can be difficult to understand the relationships between cells and formulas. Auditing tools enable you to clearly determine these relationships. When the **Auditing** feature is turned on, it uses a series of arrows to show you which cells are part of which formulas. When you use the auditing tools, **tracer arrows** point out cells that provide data to formulas and the cells that contain formulas that refer to the cells. A box is drawn around the range of cells that provide data to formulas.

Trace Worksheet Relationships

1 Click the **Tools** menu, point to **Auditing**, and then click **Show Auditing Toolbar**.

The Formula Auditing toolbar opens, displaying buttons for tracing formula relationships.

2 Use any of the following options:

◆ Click the **Trace Precedents** button to find cells that provide data to a formula.

◆ Click the **Trace Dependents** button to find out which formulas refer to a cell.

◆ Click the **Trace Error** button to locate the problem if a formula displays an error value, such as #DIV/0!.

◆ Click the **Remove Precedent Arrows**, **Remove Dependent Arrows**, or **Remove All Arrows** button to remove precedent and dependent arrows.

3 If necessary, click **OK** to locate the problem.

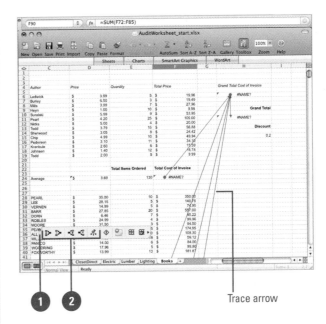

Trace arrow

Correcting Calculation Errors

When Excel finds a possible error in a calculation, it displays a green triangle in the upper left corner of the cell. If Excel can't complete a calculation it displays an error message, such as "#DIV/0!". You can use the Error smart tag to help you fix the problem. In a complex worksheet, it can be difficult to understand the relationships between cells and formulas. Auditing tools enable you to clearly determine these relationships. When the Auditing feature is turned on, it uses a series of arrows to show you which cells are part of which formulas. When you use the auditing tools, tracer arrows point out cells that provide data to formulas and the cells that contain formulas that refer to the cells. A box is drawn around the range of cells that provide data to formulas.

Review and Correct Errors

1. Select a cell that contains a green triangle in the upper left corner.

2. Click the **Error Smart Tag** button.

3. Click one of the troubleshooting options (menu options vary depending on the error).

   ◆ To have Excel fix the error, click one of the available options specific to the error.

   ◆ To find out more about an error, click **Help on this error**.

   ◆ To locate the error, click **Trace Error**.

   ◆ To remove the error alert, click **Ignore Error**.

   ◆ To fix the error manually, click **Edit in Formula Bar**.

   ◆ To modify error checking options, click **Error Checking Options**.

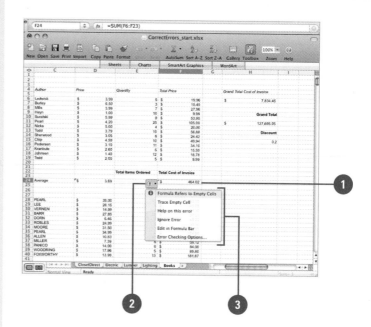

Did You Know?

You can check for errors in the entire worksheet. Click the Tools menu, and then click Error Checking.

Correcting Formulas

Excel comes with a tool called Error checker to help you find and correct problems with formulas. Excel uses an error checker in the same way Microsoft Word uses a grammar checker. The Error checker uses certain rules, such as using the wrong argument type, a number stored as text or an empty cell reference, to check for problems in formulas.

Set Error Checking Options

1. Click the **Excel** button, and then click **Preferences**.

2. Click the **Error Checking** icon.

3. Select the **Enable background error checking** check box.

4. Point to an error checking rule option to display a description of the rule.

5. Select the error checking rules check boxes you want to use.

6. Click **OK**.

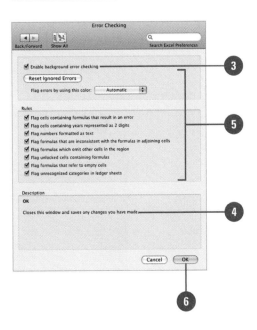

Correct Errors

1. Open the worksheet where you want to check for errors.

2. Click the **Tools** menu, and then **Error Checking**.

   The error checker scans the worksheet for errors, generating the Error Checker dialog box every time it encounters an error.

3. If necessary, click **Resume**.

4. Choose a button to correct or ignore the problem.

5. If necessary, click **Close**.

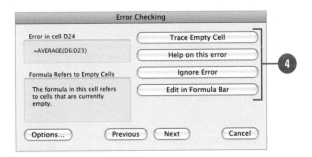

Creating a List

With its grid-like structure, Excel works well to create and manage lists. To create a list in Excel, you can enter data on worksheet cells, just as you do on any other worksheet data, but the placement of the field names and range must follow these rules: (1) Enter field names in a single row that is the first row in the list (2) Enter each record in a single row (3) Do not include any blank rows within the range (4) Do not use more than one worksheet for a single range. You can enter data directly in the list. Don't worry about entering records in any particular order; Excel tools can organize an existing list alphabetically, by date, or in almost any order you can imagine. If you also use Office 2007 for Windows, lists are called tables.

Create a List

① Do one of the following to start the list:

- ◆ **Create a list in a new worksheet.** Click the **File** menu, click **Project Gallery**, select the **Blank Document** category, click the **List Wizard** icon, and then click **Open**.

- ◆ **Create a list in an existing worksheet.** Click a starting cell, click the **Insert** menu, and then click **List**.

- ◆ **Convert existing data into a list.** Click a cell within the range, click the **Insert** menu, and then click **List**.

- ◆ **Create a list from scratch.** Click a starting cell, click the **Insert** menu, and then click **List**.

② In Step 1 of the List Wizard, select one of the following options for the data source:

- ◆ **None.** Creates a list from scratch.

- ◆ **In an open workbook.** Creates a list from an existing data range.

- ◆ **External data source.** Imports data from an external source (with ODBC drivers). Click **Get Data** to navigate to the data file.

① Convert existing data into a list

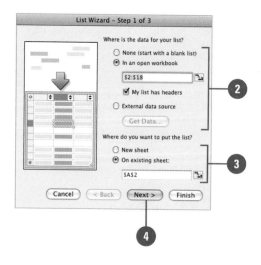

3 Click the **New sheet** or **On existing sheet** option to specify where you want to start the list.

Enter values or use the **Collapse Dialog** button to select a starting cell.

4 Click **Next**.

5 In Step 2, do one of the following to create the list:

◆ **Create a list from existing data.** Select each column, select a data type, edit the column name, and click **Modify** to make the change.

◆ **Create a list from scratch.** Enter each column name, select a data type, and click **Add**.

6 Click **Settings** to set formatting, conditional formatting, or validation options for the selected field.

7 Click **Next**.

8 In Step 3, name the list, and specify whether you want to use AutoFormat style and show a totals row.

9 Click **Finish**.

Your list appears along with the LIst toolbar, which you can use to modify the list, and even convert the list back to normal data.

Did You Know?

You can move a list. Point to the edge of the list, when the cursor changes, drag the list to a new location. You can also select the list and use Copy and Paste commands on the Standard toolbar.

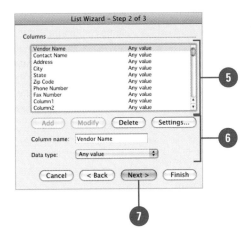

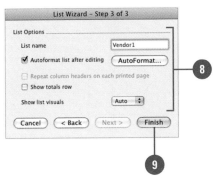

Data list

List toolbar

Entering and Editing Data in a List

After you create a list, you can enter and edit data in the list using the same techniques to enter and edit data in a normal worksheet. However, Excel also gives you another way with the use of forms. If you have a lot of data to enter, you can use a form to make it easier. You can enter new records, navigate from record to record, edit existing records, or delete records. A record is a collection of fields from a list. For example, name, address, city, state, and zip are individual fields that make up a record.

Enter and Edit Data in a List

1 Do one of the following to add data to a list:

◆ **On the worksheet.** In the worksheet column for the list, type data into each cell. You can use Tab or Shift Tab to move to the next or previous cell.

◆ **Create a new record on the worksheet.** Enter data in a row marked with an asterisk (*) at the bottom of the list.

◆ **In a form.** Click the **Data** menu or click the **List** button on the List toolbar, and then click **Form**. Use the form to enter or edit the data.

◆ **Create a record in a form.** In the form, click **New**.

2 To delete a list row, select a cell in the row, click the **Edit** menu, and then click **Delete Row**.

◆ You can also click the **List** button on the List toolbar, point to **Delete**, and then click **Row**.

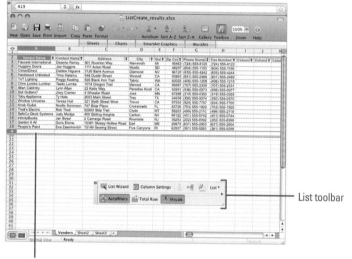

List toolbar

Click to create a new record on the worksheet

1 of 16 — Data form

Did You Know?

You can delete or clear a data list. Select the list, and then press Delete to delete the entire list. Select the list, click the Edit menu, point to Clear, and then click Clear Contents.

Formatting a List

In addition to using standard formatting options on the Formatting Palette tab—such as bold, italic, font, size, color, borders, and shading—to format a list, you can also use a AutoFormat style. AutoFormat allows you to quickly format a list starting from a list style, which you can further modify.

Apply an AutoFormat Style to a List

1 Select a cell or range in the list to which you want to apply an AutoFormat.

2 Click the **Format** menu, and then click **AutoFormat**.

   TIMESAVER *Click the AutoFormat button on the List toolbar.*

3 Select the list style you want from the Table format list.

4 To apply other formatting options, click **Options**.

5 Click **OK**.

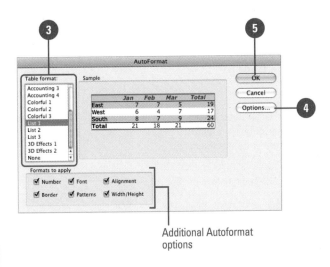

Additional Autoformat options

AutoFormat applied to a list

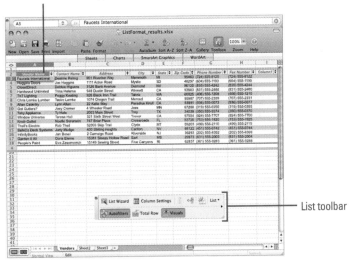

List toolbar

Did You Know?

You can copy cell formats with Format Painter. Select the cell or range whose formatting you want to copy, double-click the Format Painter button on the Standard toolbar, select the cells you want to format, and then click the Format Painter button.

You can print an Excel list. Click a cell within the list, click the File menu, click Print, click the List option, and then click OK.

You can get a complete look of the list. To hide the frame around the list so you can fully view the list, click the Visuals button on the List toolbar.

Working with Lists

After you create a list, you can sort the entries, add new entries, and display totals. You can insert rows anywhere in a list or add rows at the bottom of the list. To add a blank row at the end of the list, select any cell in the last row of the list, and then press Return, or press Tab in the last cell of the last row. If you no longer need the data in list form, you can convert the list back to normal Excel data. Selecting list rows and columns is different than selecting worksheet rows and columns. Selecting cells is the same. You delete rows and columns in a list the same way you delete rows and columns in a worksheet.

Insert or Delete a Row or Column

1. Click a cell in the list where you want to insert or delete a row or column. To insert or delete multiple rows or columns, select more than one row or column.

2. To insert a row or column, click the **Insert** menu, and then click **Rows** or **Columns**.

   ◆ You can also click the **Insert Column** or **Insert Row** button on the List toolbar.

3. To delete rows or columns, click the **Edit** menu, and then click **Delete Row** or **Delete Column**.

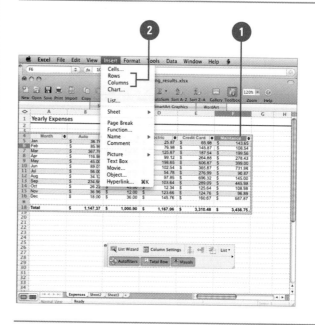

Select Rows and Columns

◆ **Column.** Click the top edge of the column header or the column in the list to select column data.

◆ **Row.** Click the left border of the row.

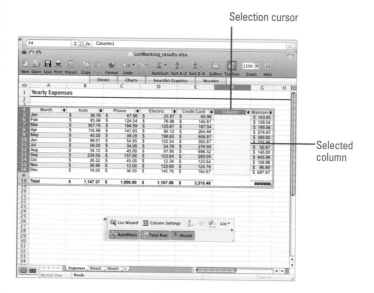

Selection cursor

Selected column

Modify Column List Settings

1. Double-click the column header for the column you want to change.

   ◆ You can also select a cell, and then click the **Column Settings** button on the List toolbar.

2. Specify the any of the following column setting options:

   ◆ **Column name.** Edit the column name for the list.

   ◆ **Data type.** Select a data type for the list.

   ◆ **Formatting.** Click **Formatting** to change cell formatting options for the list.

   ◆ **Conditional Formatting.** Click **Conditional Formatting** to add criteria for formatting cells in the list.

   ◆ **Option options.** Select check boxes to specify a default value or use unique values only in the list.

   ◆ **Validation.** Click **Validation** to add criteria for validating data in the list.

3. Click **OK**.

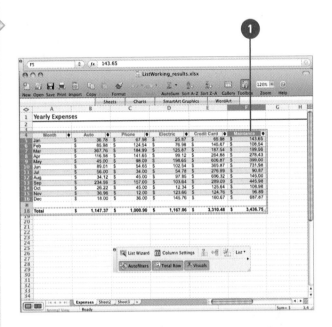

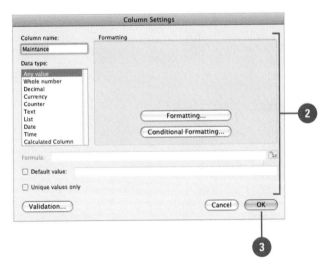

Did You Know?

You can resize a list. To resize a list column, point to the border between the list headers (pointer changes to a double-arrow), and then drag. To resize the entire list, point to the bottom right corner (pointer changes to a box with arrows), and then drag.

You can convert a list to a range. Click a cell in the list, click the List button on the List toolbar, click Remove List Manage, and then click Yes.

Sorting Data in a List

After you enter records in a list, you can reorganize the information by sorting the records. For example, you might want to sort records in a client list alphabetically by last name or numerically by their last invoice date. **Ascending order** lists records from A to Z, earliest to latest, or lowest to highest. **Descending order** lists records from Z to A, latest to earliest, or highest to lowest. You can sort the entire list or use AutoFilter to select the part of the list you want to display in the column. You can also sort a list based on one or more **sort fields**—fields you select to sort the list. A sort, for example, might be the telephone directory numerically by area code and then alphabetically by last name. If you have manually or conditionally formatted a range or list column by cell or font color or by an icon set, you can sort by these cell attributes using the Sort button.

Sort Data Quickly

1 Click the list cell with the field name by which you want to sort.

2 Click the **Sort Ascending** or the **Sort Descending** button on the Standard toolbar.

◆ You can also click the dropdown of the field, and then click **Sort Ascending** or **Sort Descending**.

Did You Know?

You can sort data with the case sensitive option. Click the list cell you want to sort by, click the Data menu, click Sort, click Options, select the Case sensitive check box, and then click OK twice.

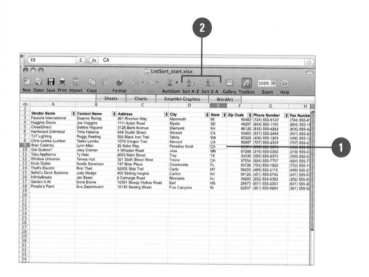

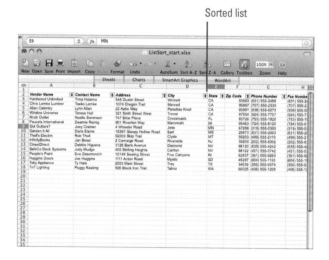

Sorted list

Sort a List Using Multiple Fields and Attributes

1. Click anywhere within the list range.

2. Click the **Data** menu, and then click **Sort**.

3. Click the **Sort by** drop-down, and then select a sort field.

4. Click the **Ascending** or **Descending** option.

5. If you want to sort by other fields, click the **Then by** drop-down, select a sort field, and then click the **Ascending** or **Descending** option.

6. Click **OK**.

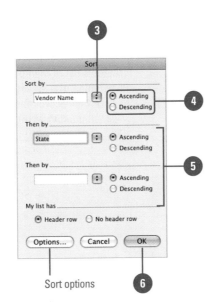

Sort options

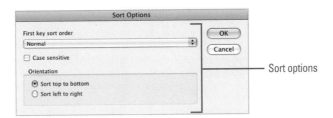

Sort options

Did You Know?

You can change the sort order for day or month. If you're sorting by day or month, you can change the sorting order to calendar order instead of alphabetic order. Click the list cell you want to sort by, click the Data menu, click Sort, click Options, click the First key sort order drop-down, select the method you want, and then click OK twice.

You can sort data in rows. If the data you want to sort is listed across a row instead of a column, click the list cell you want to sort by, click the Data menu, click Sort , click Options, and then select the Sort left to right check box, and then click OK twice.

Sort results

Displaying Parts of a List with AutoFilter

Working with a list that contains numerous records can be difficult—unless you can narrow your view of the list when necessary. For example, rather than looking through an entire inventory list, you might want to see records that come from one distributor. The **AutoFilter** feature creates a list of the items found in each field, which is useful in PivotTables. You select the items that you want to display in the column (that is, the records that meet certain criteria). Then you can work with a limited number of records.

Display Specific Records Using AutoFilter

1. Click anywhere within the list range.

2. Click the **Data** menu, point to **Filter**, and then click **AutoFilter**.

   TIMESAVER *Click the Autofilters button on the List toolbar.*

3. Click the field drop-down for which you want to specify search criteria.

4. Select the item that records must match in order to be included in the list.

5. To use built-in filters, select a filter option, such as Show Top 10 or Custom Filter.

6. Repeat steps 3 through 5, as necessary, to filter out more records using additional fields.

   The drop-down displays an icon indicating the field is filtered.

7. To clear a filter, click the drop-down of the field, and then click **Show All**.

   ◆ To clear all filters in a worksheet and redisplay all rows, click the **Data** menu, point to **Filter**, and then click **Show All**.

8. To turn off AutoFilter, click the **Data** menu, point to **Filter**, and then click **AutoFilter** to clear it.

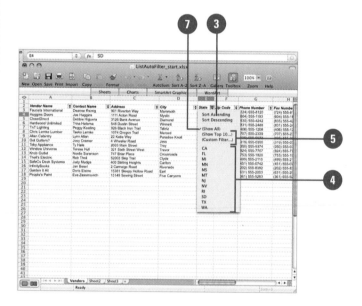

Filtered results

Creating Custom Searches

There are many times you'll want to search for records that meet multiple criteria. For example, you might want to see out-of-stock records of those orders purchased from a particular distributor. Using the AutoFilter feature and the Custom command, you can create complex searches. You can use **logical operators** to measure whether an item in a record qualifies as a match with the selected criteria. You can also use the **logical conditions** AND and OR to join multiple criteria within a single search. The result of any search is either true or false; if a field matches the criteria, the result is true. The OR condition requires that only one criterion be true in order for a record to qualify. The AND condition, on the other hand, requires that both criteria in the statement be true in order for the record to qualify.

Create a Custom Search Using AutoFilter

1. Click anywhere within the list range.

2. Click the drop-down next to the first field you want to include in the search.

3. Click **Custom Filter** to enable the command (a check mark appears).

4. Click the **Field** drop-down (on the left), and then select a logical operator.

5. Click the drop-down (on the right), and then select a field choice.

6. If you want, click the **And** or **Or** option.

7. If you want, click the drop-down (on the left), and then select a logical operator.

8. If you want, click the drop-down (on the right), and then select a field choice.

9. Click **OK**.

The drop-down displays an icon indicating the field is filtered.

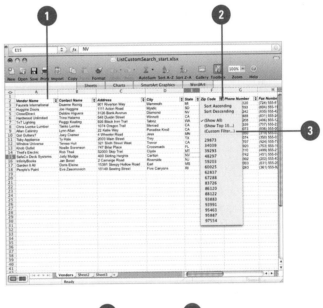

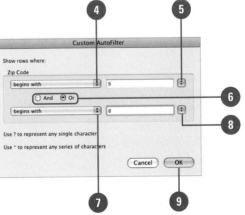

Creating Calculations in a List

You can quickly total data in a list using the Total Row option. When you display a total row at the end of the list, a drop-down list appears for each total cell along with the word *Total* in the leftmost cell. The drop-down list allows you to select a function to perform a calculation. If the function you want is not available in the drop-down list, you can enter any formula you want in a total row cell. If you're not using a total function, you can delete the word *Total*.

Total the Data in a List

1. Click a cell in a list.

2. Click the **Total Row** button on the List toolbar.

   The total row appears as the last row in the list and displays the word *Total* in the leftmost cell.

3. Click the cell in the column for which you want to calculate a total, and then click the drop-down list arrow.

4. From the drop-down list, select the function you want to use to calculate the total.

   TIMESAVER *Enter a formula in the row directly below a list without a total row to create a total row without the word Total.*

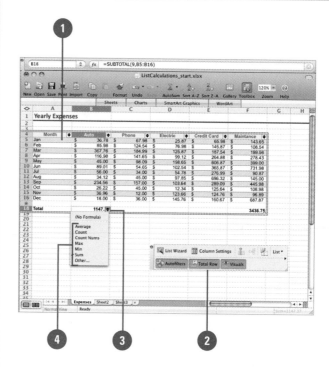

Did You Know?

You can create a calculated column.
A calculated column uses a single formula that adjusts for each row in a list. To create a calculated column, click a cell in a blank list column, and then type a formula. The formula is automatically filled into all cells of the column. Not every cell in a calculated column needs to be the same. You can enter a different formula or data to create an exception.

Converting Text to Columns

The Convert to Columns Wizard helps you separate simple cell contents into different columns. For example, if a cell contains first and last names, you can use the Convert to Columns Wizard to separate first and last name into different columns. The wizard uses the delimiter—such as a tab, semicolon, comma, space, or custom—to determine where to separate the cell contents into different columns; the wizard options vary depending on the delimiter type. For example, the cell contents *Julie, Kenney* uses the comma delimiter.

Convert Text to Columns

1. Select the range you want to covert to columns.

2. Click the **Data** menu, and then click **Text to Columns**.

3. In Step 1, click the **Delimited** or **Fixed Width** option.

4. Click **Next**.

5. In Step 2, select the delimiter type you want to use, and then clear the other check boxes.

   The wizard options vary depending on the selected delimiter.

6. Click **Next**.

7. For the Fixed Width option, click to set a column width, and then click **Next**.

8. In Step 3, click a column in the Data preview box, and then click the **Text** option, and then repeat this for each column you want.

9. Click the **Collapse Dialog** button, select a new destination for the separated data, and then click the **Expand Dialog** button.

10. Click **Finish**.

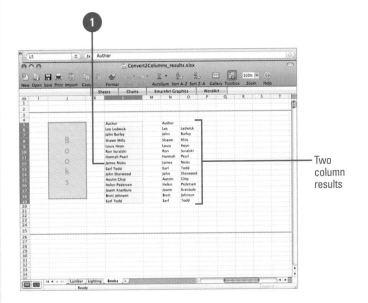

Two column results

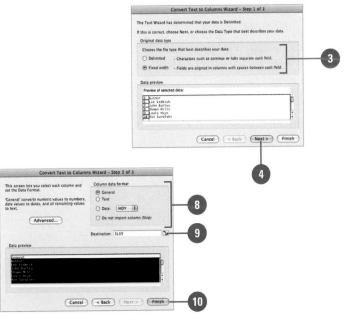

Creating Groups and Outlines

A sales report that displays daily, weekly, and monthly totals in a hierarchical format, such as an outline, helps your reader to sift through and interpret the pertinent information. In outline format, a single item can have several topics or levels of information within it. An outline in Excel indicates multiple layers of content by displaying a plus sign (+) on its left side. A minus sign (-) indicates that the item has no contents, is fully expanded, or both.

Create an Outline or Group

1 Organize data in a hierarchical fashion—place summary rows below detail rows and summary columns to the right of detail columns.

2 Select the data that you want to outline.

3 To create an outline, click the **Data** menu, point to **Group and Outline**, and then click **AutoOutline**.

4 To create a group, click the **Data** menu, point to the **Group and Outline**, and then click **Group**. Click the **Rows** or **Columns** option, and then click **OK**.

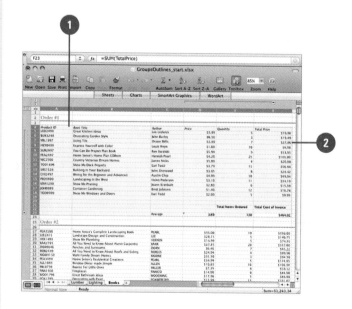

Work an Outline or Group

◆ Click a plus sign (+) to expand an outline level; click a minus sign (-) to collapse an outline level.

Did You Know?

You can ungroup outline data. Select the data group, click the Data menu, point to Group and Outline, and then click Ungroup, click the Rows or Columns option, and then click OK.

You can clear an outline. Select the outline, click the Data menu, point to Group and Outline, and then click Clear Outline.

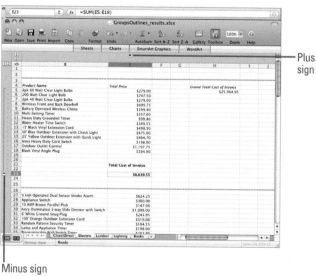

Plus sign

Minus sign

Adding Data Validation to a Worksheet

Worksheet cells can be adjusted so that only certain values can be entered. Controlling how data is entered decreases errors and makes a worksheet more reliable. You might, for example, want it to be possible to enter only specific dates in a range of cells. You can use **logical operators** (such as equal to, not equal to, less than, or greater than) to set validation rules. When invalid entries are made, a message—developed and written by you—appears indicating that the entry is in violation of the validation rules. The rule set will not allow data to flow into the cell.

Create Validation Rules

1. Select the range you want covered in the validation rules.

2. Click the **Data** menu, and then click **Validation**.

3. Click the **Settings** tab.

4. Click the **Allow** drop-down, and then select a value type.

   Options vary depending on the Allow value type you select.

5. Click the **Data** drop-down, and then select a logical operator.

6. Enter values or use the **Collapse Dialog** button to select a range for the minimum and maximum criteria.

7. Click the **Input Message** tab, and then type a title and the input message that should be displayed when invalid entries are made.

8. Click the **Error Alert** tab, and then select an alert style, type a title, and error message.

9. Click **OK**.

10. To view invalid data, click the **Circle Invalid Data** on the Formula Auditing toolbar. To clear the circles, click **Clear Validation Circles** on the Formula Auditing toolbar.

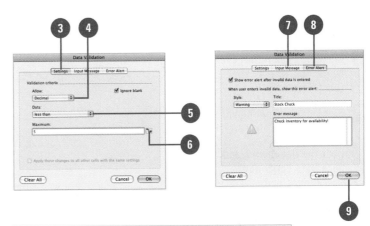

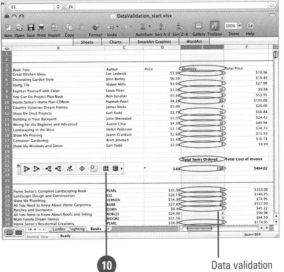

Data validation

Creating a Drop-Down List

Entering data in a list can be tedious and repetitive. To make the job easier, you can create a drop-down list of entries you define. This way you get consistent, accurate data. To create a drop-down list, create a list of valid entries in a single column or row without blanks, define a name, and then use the List option in the Data Validation dialog box. To enter data using a drop-down list, click the cell with the defined drop-down list, click the drop-down, and then click the entry you want.

Create a Drop-Down List

1. Type entries in a single column or row without blanks in the order you want.

2. Select the cell range, click the **Name** box, type a name, and then press Return.

3. Select the cell where you want the drop-down list.

4. Click the **Data** menu, and then click Data **Validation**.

5. Click the **Settings** tab.

6. Click the **Allow** drop-down, and then click **List**.

7. Enter values or use the **Collapse Dialog** button to select a range of valid entries.

8. Click the **Input Message** tab, and then type a title and the input message that should be displayed when invalid entries are made.

9. Click the **Error Alert** tab, and then select an alert style, type a title, and error message.

10. Click **OK**.

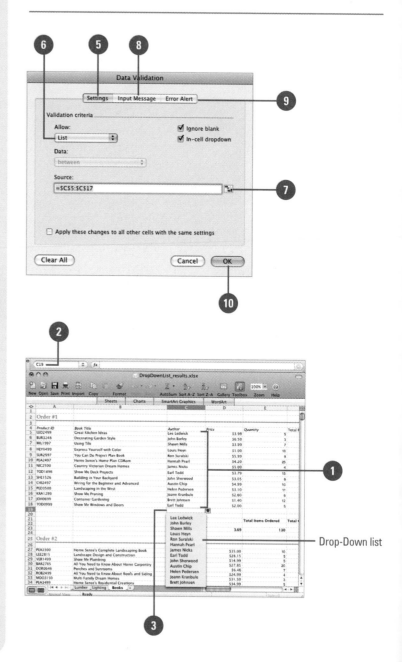

Drop-Down list

Designing a Worksheet with Excel

Introduction

Microsoft Excel offers several tools for making your worksheets look more attractive and professional. Without formatting, a worksheet can look like a sea of meaningless data. To highlight important information, you can change the appearance of selected numbers and text by adding dollar signs, commas, and other numerical formats.

When your Microsoft Excel worksheet is completed, you can preview and print its contents. You can insert page breaks to control what you print on each page. You can change the orientation of the page from the default of portrait (vertical) to landscape (horizontal). This is helpful when you have wide or multiple columns that would look better on one page. You can also adjust your margins to better fit the worksheet on the page. After you make layout adjustments you can add headers and footers on the page in Page Layout view, which lets you focus on how your worksheet is going to look when you print it. Headers are typically a descriptive title about your worksheet or workbook. Footers can include date printed, page numbers, or other company related information. Excel provides options to set the print area and customize what you want to print. For example, you might want to print a different range in a worksheet for different people. After you set the print area, you can choose to print your worksheet. The Print dialog box allows you to customize all the options and more, and then you can send your worksheet or entire workbook to the printer.

Formatting Numbers

You can change the appearance of the data in the cells of a worksheet without changing the actual value in the cell. You can apply **numeric formats** to numbers to better reflect the type of information they represent—dollars, dates, decimals, and so on. For example, you can format a number to display up to 15 decimal places or none at all. If you don't see the number format you need, you can create a custom one.

Format Numbers Quickly

1 Select a cell or range that contains the number(s) you want to format.

2 Click the **Formatting Palette** tab on the Toolbox.

3 Click the **Number** panel to expand it.

4 Click the **Number Format** list arrow, and then click any of the following formats:

◆ **General.** No specific format.

◆ **Number.** 0.75

◆ **Currency.** $0.75

◆ **Accounting.** $ 0.75

◆ **Date.** 3/17/2008, Wednesday, March 17, 2008

◆ **Time.** 6:00:00 PM

◆ **Percentage.** 75.00%

◆ **Fraction.** 3/4

◆ **Scientific.** 7.50E-01

◆ **Text.** Numbers treated as text.

◆ **Special.** Zip code, phone number, or social security number.

◆ **Custom.** Use a number format code.

5 To fine-tune the format, click any of the following format buttons:

◆ **Increase Decimal.**

◆ **Decrease Decimal.**

You can apply multiple attributes to the range.

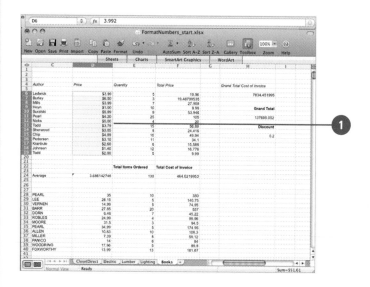

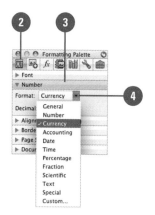

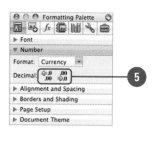

Format Numbers Quickly

1. Select a cell or range that contains the number(s) you want to format.

2. Click one of the buttons on the Formatting toolbar to apply that attribute to the selected range.

   ◆ **Currency Style.**

   ◆ **Percent Style.**

   ◆ **Comma Style.**

   ◆ **Increase Decimal.**

   ◆ **Decrease Decimal.**

   You can apply multiple attributes to the range.

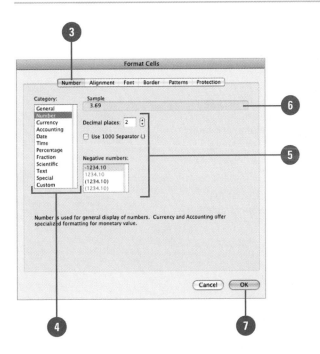

Format a Number Using the Format Cells Dialog Box

1. Select a cell or range that contains the number(s) you want to format.

2. Click the **Format** menu, and then click **Cell**.

3. Click the **Number** tab.

4. Click to select a category.

5. Select the options you want to apply.

   To create a custom format, click Custom, type the number format code, and then use one of the existing codes as a starting point.

6. Preview your selections in the Sample box.

7. Click **OK**.

Designing Conditional Formatting

You can make your worksheets more powerful by setting up conditional formatting. **Conditional formatting** lets the value of a cell determine its formatting. For example, you might want this year's sales total to be displayed in red and italics if it's less than last year's total, but in green and bold if it's more. The formatting is applied to the cell values only if the values meet the a condition that you specify. Otherwise, no conditional formatting is applied to the cell values.

Establish a Conditional Format

1. Select a cell or range you want to conditionally format.

2. Click the **Format** menu, and then click **Conditional Formatting**.

3. Select the operator and values you want for condition 1.

4. Click **Format**, select the attributes you want applied, and then click **OK**.

5. Click **Add** to include additional conditions, and then repeat steps 3 and 4.

6. Click **OK**.

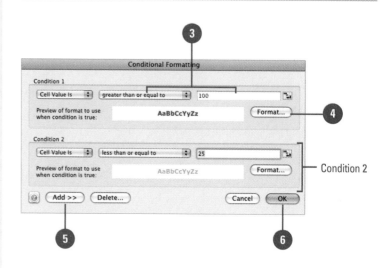

Delete a Conditional Format

1. Click the **Format** menu, and then click **Conditional Formatting**.

2. Click **Delete**.

3. Select the check box for the condition(s) you want to delete.

4. Click **OK**.

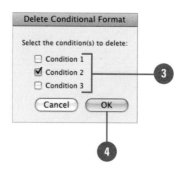

Controlling Text Flow

The length of a label might not always fit within the width you've chosen for a column. If the cell to the right is empty, text spills over into it, but if that cell contains data, the text will be truncated (that is, cut off). A cell can be formatted so its text automatically wraps to multiple lines; that way, you don't have to widen the column to achieve an attractive effect. For example, you might want the label *Interior Vanity Strips* to fit in a column that is only as wide as *Interior*. Cell contents can also be modified to fit within the available space or can be combined with the contents of other cells.

Control the Flow of Text in a Cell

1. Select a cell or range whose text flow you want to change.

2. Click the **Format** menu, and then click **Cells**.

3. Click the **Alignment** tab.

4. Click to select one or more Text Control check boxes.

   ◆ **Wrap Text** moves the text to multiple lines within a cell.

   ◆ **Shrink To Fit** reduces character size to fit within a cell.

   ◆ **Merge Cells** combines selected cells into a single cell.

5. Click **OK**.

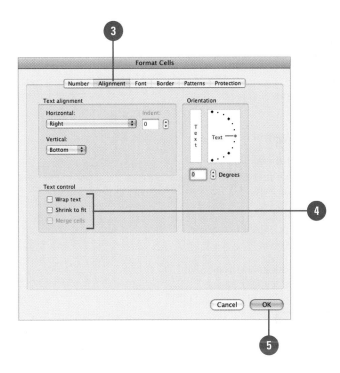

Did You Know?

You can paint a format. When you paint a format using the Format Painter button on the Standard toolbar, the fill colors and patterns get copied too.

Changing Data Alignment

When you enter data in a cell, Excel aligns labels on the left edge of the cell and aligns values and formulas on the right edge of the cell. **Horizontal alignment** is the way in which Excel aligns the contents of a cell relative to the left or right edge of the cell; **vertical alignment** is the way in which Excel aligns cell contents relative to the top and bottom of the cell. Excel also provides an option for changing the flow and angle of characters within a cell. The **orientation** of the contents of a cell is expressed in degrees. The default orientation is 0 degrees, in which characters are aligned horizontally within a cell.

Change Alignment Using the Format Dialog Box

1. Select a cell or range containing the data to be realigned.

2. Click the **Format** menu, and then click **Cells**.

3. Click the **Alignment** tab.

4. Click the **Horizontal** drop-down or the **Vertical** drop-down, and then select an alignment.

5. Select an orientation. Click a point on the map, or click the **Degrees** up or down arrow.

6. If you want, select one or more of the Text Control check boxes.

7. Click **OK**.

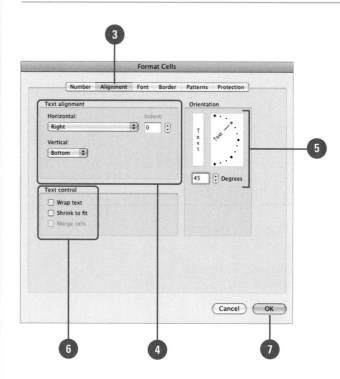

Did You Know?

You can use the Format Cells dialog box to select other alignment options. Many more alignment options are available from the Format Cells dialog box, but for centering across columns and simple left, right, and center alignment, it's easier to use the Formatting toolbar buttons.

Change Alignment

① Select a cell or range containing the data to be realigned.

② Click the **Formatting Palette** tab on the Toolbox.

③ Click the **Alignment and Spacing** panel to expand it.

④ Use any of the following alignment buttons:

◆ To align cell contents horizontally, click the **Align Left**, **Center**, **Align Right**, or **Justify** button.

◆ To align cell contents vertically, click the **Top**, **Center**, **Bottom**, or **Justify** button.

◆ These buttons are also available on the Formatting toolbar.

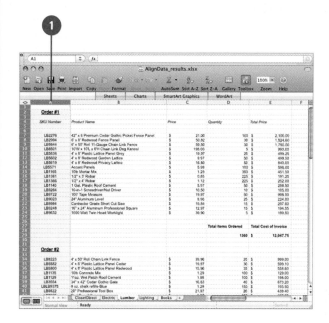

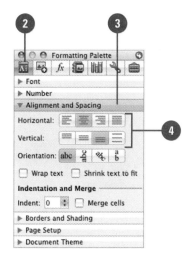

Changing Data Color

You can change the color of the numbers and text on a worksheet. Strategic use of **font color** can be an effective way of tying similar values together. For instance, on a sales worksheet you might want to display sales in green and returns in red. Or, you may want to highlight column or row headers with colored labels. Either way, using color to highlight numbers and texts makes deciphering your worksheet data easier.

Change Font Color

1. Select a cell or range that contains the text you want to change.

2. Click the **Formatting Palette** tab on the Toolbox.

3. Click the **Font** panel to expand it.

4. Click the **Font Color** button arrow, and then click a color.

   ◆ The Font Color button is also available on the Formatting toolbar.

Did You Know?

The Font Color button on the Font panel and Formatting toolbar displays the last font color you used. To apply this color to another selection, simply click the button, not the list arrow.

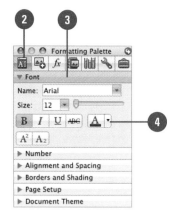

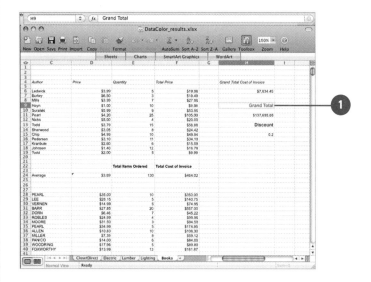

Adding Color and Patterns to Cells

You can **fill** the background of a cell with a color and a pattern to make its data stand out. Fill colors and patterns can also lend consistency to related information on a worksheet. On a sales worksheet, for example, formatting all fourth-quarter sales figures with a blue background and all second-quarter sales with a yellow background would make each group of figures easy to identify. You can use fill colors and patterns in conjunction with text attributes, fonts, and font colors to further enhance the appearance of your worksheet.

Apply Color and Patterns

1. Select a cell or range to which you want to apply colors and patterns.

2. Click the **Formatting Palette** tab on the Toolbox.

3. Click the **Borders and Shading** panel to expand it.

4. To add a color to a cell, click the **Fill Color** button arrow, and then select a color.

   ◆ The Fill Color button is also available on the Formatting toolbar.

5. To add a pattern to the cell, click the **Pattern** box, and then select a pattern and color in the palette.

Did You Know?

You can use the Format Cells dialog box to apply color and patterns.
Click the Format menu, click Cells, click the Patterns tab, select the color and pattern you want, and then click OK.

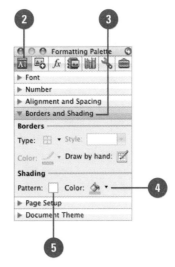

Adding Borders to Cells

The light gray grid that appears on the worksheet helps your eyes move from cell to cell. Although you can print these gridlines, sometimes a different grid pattern better emphasizes your data. For example, you might put a decorative line border around the title or a double-line bottom border below cells with totals. You can add borders of varying colors and widths to any or all sides of a single cell or range. If you prefer, you can draw a border outline or grid directly on a worksheet.

Apply or Remove a Border

1 Select a cell or range to which you want to apply a border.

2 Click the **Formatting Palette** tab on the Toolbox.

3 Click the **Borders and Shading** panel to expand it.

4 Click the **Border Type** button, and then select a border.

5 Click the **Border Color** button, and then select a color.

6 Click the **Border Style** button, and then select a border style.

◆ To remove cell borders, click **No Border**.

◆ These buttons are also available on the Formatting toolbar.

Did You Know?

You can draw a border. In the Borders and Shading panel on the Formatting Palette tab, click the Draw by hand button, use buttons on the Border Drawing toolbar, such as Draw Border, Draw Border Grid, Erase Border Line Color, and Line Style. Press Esc to exit.

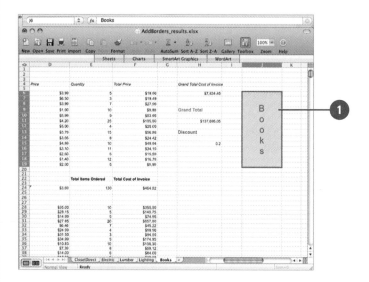

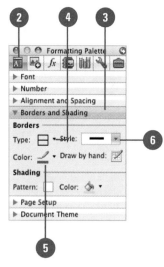

Formatting Data with AutoFormat

Formatting worksheet data can be a lot of fun but also very intensive. To make formatting data more efficient, Excel includes 18 AutoFormats. An **AutoFormat** includes a combination of fill colors and patterns, numeric formats, font attributes, borders, and font colors that are professionally designed to enhance your worksheets. If you don't select any cells before choosing the AutoFormat command, Excel will "guess" which data it should format. You can control individual elements in an AutoFormat so that not all are applied to the current worksheet. These changes are temporary; you can't permanently alter an AutoFormat.

Apply an AutoFormat

① Select a cell or range to which you want to apply an AutoFormat, or skip this step if you want Excel to "guess" which cells to format.

② Click the **Format** menu, and then click **AutoFormat**.

③ Click an AutoFormat in the list.

④ Click **Options**.

⑤ Select one or more Formats To Apply check boxes to turn a feature on or off.

⑥ Click **OK**.

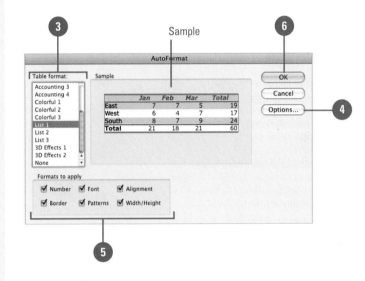

Did You Know?

You can let Excel choose the range to format. If you don't select the cells you want to apply the AutoFormat to, Excel will guess which cells you want formatted.

You can copy cell formats with Format Painter. Select the cell or range whose formatting you want to copy, double-click the Format Painter button on the Standard toolbar, select the cells you want to format, and then click the Format Painter button.

Creating and Applying Styles

A **style** is a defined collection of formats—font, font size, attributes, numeric formats, and so on—that you can store as a set and later apply to other cells. For example if you always want subtotals to display in blue 14-point Times New Roman, bold, italic, with two decimal places and commas, you can create a style that includes all these formats. If you plan to enter repetitive information, such as a list of dollar amounts in a row or column, it's often easier to apply the desired style to the range before you enter the data. That way you can simple enter each number, and Excel formats it as soon as you press Return. You can also copy styles from one workbook to another. Once you create a style, it is available to you in every workbook. Any style—whether it was supplied by Excel or created by you or someone else—can be modified.

Create a New Style

1. Select a cell or range that you want to create a style.

2. Click the **Format** menu, and then click **Style**.

3. Type the name of the new style.

4. Clear the check boxes with the options you do not want.

5. Click **Modify**.

6. Click any of the formatting tabs, and then make additional formatting changes to the style.

7. Click **OK**.

8. Click **OK**.

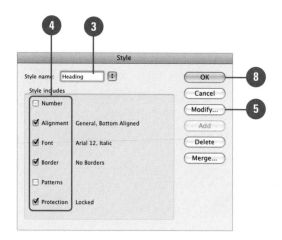

Did You Know?

You can modify a style. Click the Format menu, click Style, click the style you want to modify, click Modify, make the changes you want, and then click OK, and then click OK again.

You can delete a style. Click the Format menu, click Style, select the style you want to delete, click Delete, and then click OK.

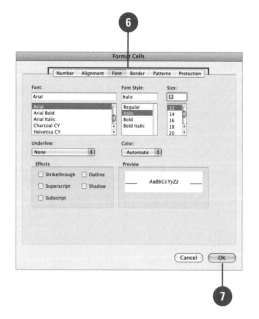

Apply a Style

1. Select a cell or range to which you want to apply a style.

2. Click the **Format** menu, and then click **Style**.

3. Click the **Style Name** drop-down, and then select the style you want to apply.

4. Click **OK**.

Merge Styles

1. Open the worksheet that contains the styles you want to merge.

2. Click the **Format** menu, and then click **Style**.

3. Click **Merge**.

4. Click the workbook that contains the styles you want to merge with the current workbook.

5. Click **OK**.

6. Click **OK**.

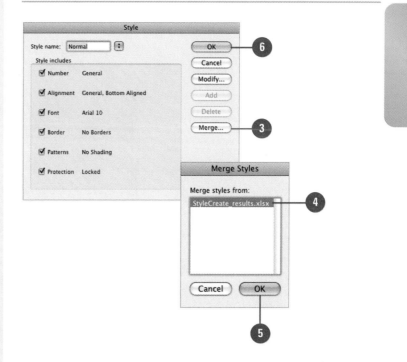

Formatting a Background

Depending on your screen size, the sheet tabs at the bottom of your workbook can be hard to view. You can add color to the sheet tabs to make them more distinguishable. If you want to add artistic style to your workbook or you are creating a Web page from your workbook, you can add a background picture. When you add a background to a worksheet, the background does not print, and it's not included when you save an individual worksheet as a Web page. You need to publish the entire workbook as a Web page to include the background.

Add or Remove a Background

1. Click the sheet tab you want to add a background to.

2. Click the **Format** menu, point to **Sheet**, and then click **Background**.

3. Select the folder with the graphic file you want to use.

4. Select the graphic you want.

5. Click **Insert**.

6. To remove the background, click the **Format** menu, point to **Sheet**, and then click **Delete Background**.

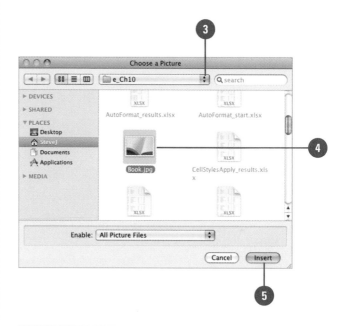

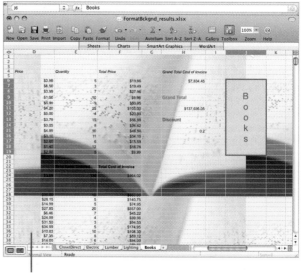

Sheet with a background picture

Inserting Page Breaks

If you want to print a worksheet that is larger than one page, Excel divides it into pages by inserting **automatic page breaks**. These page breaks are based on paper size, margin settings, and scaling options you set. You can change which rows or columns are printed on the page by inserting **horizontal** or **vertical page breaks**. In page break preview, you can view the page breaks and move them by dragging them to a different location on the worksheet.

Insert a Page Break

1. To insert a horizontal page break, click the row where you want to insert a page break.

   To insert a vertical page break, click the column where you want to insert a page break.

2. Click the **Insert** menu, and then click **Page Break**.

Did You Know?

You can remove a page break. Select the column or row next to the page break, click the Insert menu, and then click Remove Page Break. To remove all manual page breaks, click the diamond at the top left corner of the sheet, click the Insert menu, and then click Reset All Page Breaks.

You can move a page break. Click the View menu, click Normal, point to the page break, and then drag the page break line to a new location. When you move an automatic page break, it changes to a manual page break, which are not adjusted automatically by Excel.

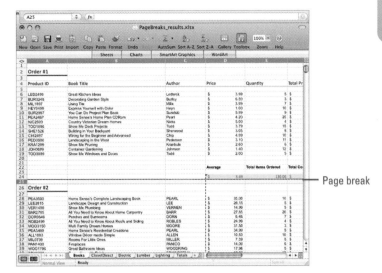

Page break

Setting Up the Page

You can set up the worksheet page to print just the way you want. With the Page Setup dialog box, you can choose the **page orientation**, which determines whether Excel prints the worksheet data portrait (vertically) or landscape (horizontally). You can also adjust the **print scaling** (to reduce or enlarge the size of printed characters), change the paper size (to match the size of paper in your printer), and resize or realign the left, right, top, and bottom margins (the blank areas along each edge of the paper). You can use the mouse pointer to adjust margins visually for the entire document in Page Layout view, or you can use the Page Setup dialog box to set precise measurements for an entire document or a specific section. Changes made in the Page Setup dialog box are not reflected in the worksheet window. You can see them only when you preview or print the worksheet.

Change Page Orientation

1. Click the **File** menu, and then click **Page Setup**.

2. Click the **Page** tab.

3. Click the **Portrait** option (the default) or click the **Landscape** option to select page orientation.

4. Click **OK**.

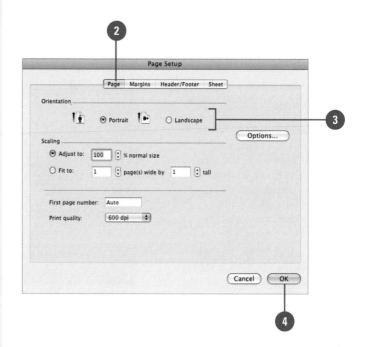

Change the Margin Settings

1. Click the **File** menu, and then click **Page Setup**.

2. Click the **Margins** tab.

3. Click the **Top**, **Bottom**, **Left**, and **Right** up or down arrows to adjust the margins.

4. Select the **Horizontally** and/or **Vertically** check boxes to automatically center your data.

5. Click **OK**.

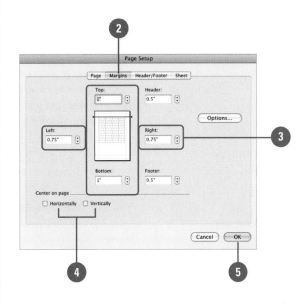

Change the Margin Using the Mouse in Page Layout View

1. Click the **Page Layout View** button.

2. Click the **View** menu, and then click **Ruler** to display it.

3. Position the cursor over the left, right, top, or bottom edge of the ruler until the cursor changes to a double arrow.

   A ScreenTip appears indicating the margin name and current position.

4. Drag to change the margin.

5. To exit Page Layout view, click the **Normal** button.

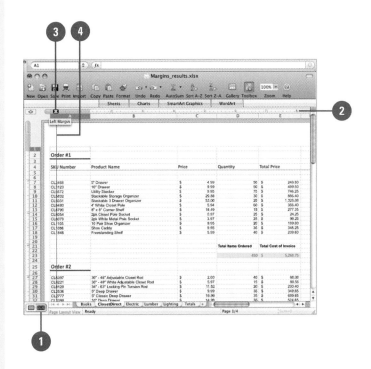

Adding Headers and Footers

Adding a header or footer to a workbook is a convenient way to make your printout easier for readers to follow. Using the Page Setup command, you can add information such as page numbers, the worksheet title, or the current date at the top and bottom of each page or section of a worksheet or workbook. Using the Custom Header and Custom Footer buttons, you can include information such as your computer system's date and time, the name of the workbook and sheet, a graphic, or other custom information.

Change a Header or Footer

① Click the **File** menu, and then click **Page Setup**.

② Click the **Header/Footer** tab.

③ If the Header box doesn't contain the information you want, click **Custom Header**.

④ Type the information in the Left, Center, or Right Section text boxes, or click a button to insert built-in header information. If you don't want a header to appear at all, delete the text and codes in the text boxes.

⑤ Select the text you want to format, click the **Font** button, make font changes, and then click **OK**. Excel will use the default font, Arial, unless you change it.

⑥ Click **OK**.

⑦ If the Footer box doesn't contain the information that you want, click **Custom Footer**.

⑧ Type information in the Left, Center, or Right Section text boxes, or click a button to insert the built-in footer information.

⑨ Click **OK**.

⑩ Click **OK**.

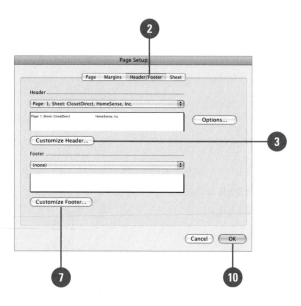

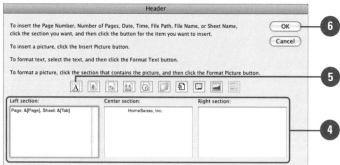

Setting the Print Area

When you're ready to print your worksheet, you can choose several printing options. The **print area** is the section of your worksheet that Excel prints. You can set the print area when you customize worksheet printing or any time when you are working on a worksheet. For example, you might want to print a different range in a worksheet for different people. In order to use headers and footers, you must first establish, or set, the print area. You can design a specific single cells or a contiguous or non-contiguous range.

Set or Clear the Print Area

1. Select the range of cells you want to print.

2. Click the **File** menu, and then point to **Print Area**.

3. Click **Set Print Area** or **Clear Print Area**.

Did You Know?

You can avoid repeating rows and columns. For best results when printing a multipage worksheet, you'll want to coordinate the print area with specified print titles so that columns or rows are not repeated on a single page.

You can add to a print area. Click the cell where you want to extend the print area, click the File menu, point to Print Area, and then click Add to Print Area.

Customizing Worksheet Printing

At some point you'll want to print your worksheet so you can distribute it to others or use it for other purposes. You can print all or part of any worksheet, and you can control the appearance of many features, such as whether gridlines are displayed, whether column letters and row numbers are displayed, or whether to include print titles, columns and rows that are repeated on each page. If you have already set a print area, it will appear in the Print Area box on the Sheet tab of the Page Setup dialog box. You don't need to re-select it.

Print Part of a Worksheet

1. Click the **File** menu, and then click **Page Setup**.

2. Click the **Sheet** tab.

3. Type the range you want to print. Or click the **Collapse Dialog** button, select the cells you want to print, and then click the **Expand Dialog** button to restore the dialog box.

4. Click **OK**.

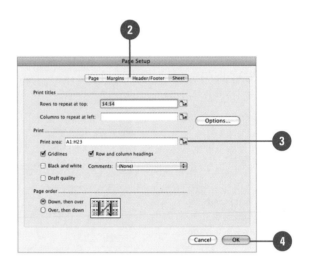

Print Row and Column Titles on Each Page

1. Click the **File** menu, and then click **Page Setup**.

2. Click the **Sheet** tab.

3. Enter the number of the row or the letter of the column that contains the titles. Or click the **Collapse Dialog** button, select the row or column with the mouse, and then click the **Expand Dialog** button to restore the dialog box.

4. Click **OK**.

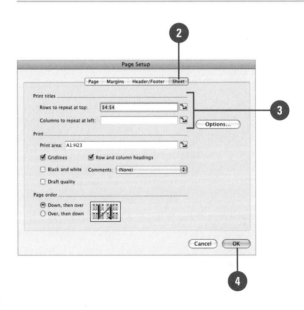

Print Gridlines, Column Letters, and Row Numbers

1. Click the **File** menu, and then click **Page Setup**.

2. Click the **Sheet** tab.

3. Select the **Gridlines** check box.

4. Select the **Row and column headings** check box.

5. Click **OK**.

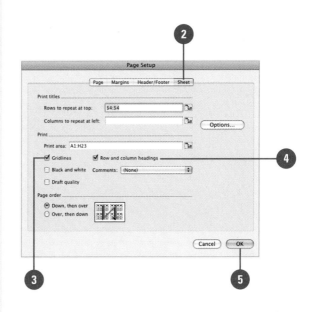

Fit Your Worksheet on a Specific Number of Pages

1. Click the **File** menu, and then click **Page Setup**.

2. Click the **Page** tab.

3. Select a scaling option.

   ◆ Click the **Adjust to** option to scale the worksheet using a percentage.

   ◆ Click the **Fit to** option to force a worksheet to be printed on a specific number of pages.

4. Click **OK**.

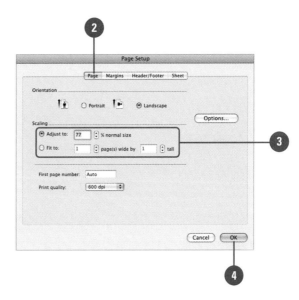

Did You Know?

You can print comments. Display the comments you want to print. Click the File menu, click Page Setup, click the Sheet tab, click the Comments drop-down, click As displayed on sheet or At end of sheet, and then click OK.

Sharing a Worksheet with Excel

11

Introduction

Creating successful documents is not always a solitary venture; you may need to share a document with others or get data from other programs before a project is complete. In Microsoft Excel, you have several methods that you can use to create a joint effort. In many offices, your co-workers (and their computers) are located across the country or the world. They are joined through networks that permit users to share information by opening each other's files and to simultaneously modify data.

Excel makes it easy for you to communicate with your teammates. Instead of writing on yellow sticky notes and attaching them to a printout, you can insert electronic comments within worksheet cells. You can also track changes within a workbook made by you and others. In addition to sharing workbooks, you can merge information from different workbooks into a single document, and you can link data between or consolidate data from different worksheets and workbooks. You can also import data from a database, including FileMaker Pro (version 5.0 - 9.0) into Excel.

If your worksheet or workbook needs to go beyond simple calculations, Excel offers several tools to help you create more specialized projects. With Excel, you can perform "what if" analysis using several different methods to get the results you want or create multiple scenarios lets you speculate on a variety of outcomes.

PivotTables are also available to pull your data together for easier viewing and reporting. The PivotTable Wizard walks you through setting up a PivotTable. Excel has some designed reports that contain layout formatting to give that extra touch to your reports.

What You'll Do

Lock and Unlock Worksheet Cells

Protect Worksheets and Workbooks

Share Workbooks

Create and Read a Cell Comment

Edit and Delete a Cell Comment

Track Changes

Compare and Merge Workbooks

Ask "What If" with Goal Seek

Create Scenarios

Export Data

Analyze Data Using PivotTable

Consolidate Data

Link Data

Get Query Data from a Database

Get Query Data from the Web

Get Data from a FileMaker Pro Database

Get Text Data

Locking or Unlocking Worksheet Cells

To prevent accidental changes to your data, you can lock worksheet cells. When you lock selected cells, you cannot make changes to them until you unlock them. When you lock cells, users can unlock the data and make changes unless you add password protection to the worksheet. For security or confidentiality reasons, you might want to hide formulas from view. If so, you can hide or unhide them using the Protection tab in the Format Cells dialog box.

Lock or Unlock Worksheet Cells

1. In Excel, select the cell or range you want to lock or unlock.

2. Click the **Format** menu, and then click **Cell**.

3. Click the **Protection** tab.

4. Select the **Locked** check box to lock the selection or clear it to unlock it.

5. Click **OK**.

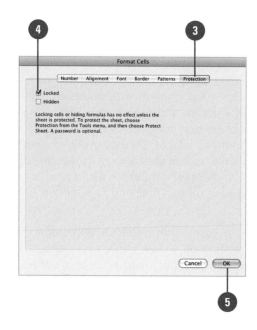

Hide or Show Formulas

1. In Excel, select the cell or range with the formulas you want to hide or show.

2. Click the **Format** menu, and then click **Cell**.

3. Click the **Protection** tab.

4. Select the **Hidden** check box to hide formulas or clear it to show formulas.

5. Click **OK**.

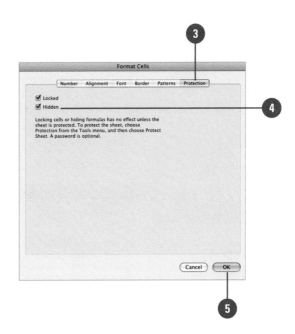

Protecting Worksheets and Workbooks

To preserve all your hard work—particularly if others use your files—protect it with a password. You can protect a sheet or an entire document. In each case, you'll be asked to supply a password, and then enter it again when you want to work on the file. Passwords are case sensitive, so be sure to supply your password as it was first entered. If you forget a password, there is no way to open the file, so it's very important to remember or write down your password(s). Keep your password in a safe place. Avoid obvious passwords such as your name, your company, or your favorite pet.

Protect a Worksheet

1. Click the **Tools** menu, point to **Protection**, and then click **Protect Sheet.**

2. Select the check boxes for the options you want protected in the sheet.

3. Type a password.

4. Click **OK**.

5. Retype the password.

6. Click **OK**.

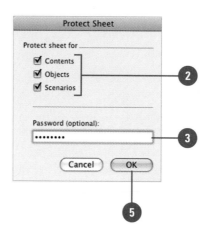

Share and Protect a Workbook

1. Click the **Tools** menu, point to **Protection**, and then click **Protect and Share Workbook.**

2. Select the **Sharing with track changes** check box.

3. Type a password.

4. Click **OK**.

5. Retype the password.

6. Click **OK**.

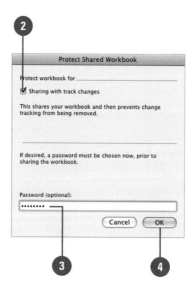

Protect a Workbook

1. Click the **Tools** menu, point to **Protection**, and then click **Protect Workbook**.

2. Select the check boxes for the options you want protected in the sheet.

   ◆ **Structure.** Select the check box to prevent users from viewing, copying, moving, or inserting worksheets. It also prevents users from recording new macros, displaying data from PivotTable reports, using analysis tools, or creating scenario summary reports.

   ◆ **Windows.** Select the check box to prevent users from moving, resizing, or closing windows.

3. Type a password.

4. Click **OK**.

5. Retype the password.

6. Click **OK**.

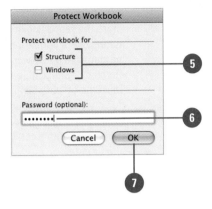

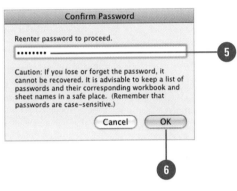

Sharing Workbooks

When you're working with others in a networked environment, you may want to share workbooks you have created. You may also want to share the responsibilities of entering and maintaining data. Sharing means users can add columns and rows, enter data, and change formatting, while allowing you to review their changes. When sharing is enabled, "[Shared]" appears in the title bar of the shared workbook. This type of work arrangement is particularly effective in team situations where multiple users have joint responsibility for data within a single workbook. In cases where multiple users modify the same cells, Office can keep track of changes, and you can accept or reject them at a later date.

Enable Workbook Sharing

1. Open the workbook you want to share.

2. Click the **Tools** menu, and then click **Share Workbook**.

4. Click the **Editing** tab.

5. Select the **Allow changes by more than one user at the same time** check box.

6. Click **OK**.

7. Click **OK** again to save your workbook.

Did You Know?

You can set file options to prompt to open as read-only. To prevent accidental changes to a document, you can display an alert requesting (not requiring) the user open the file as read-only. A read-only file can be read or copied. If the user makes changes to the file, the modifications can only be saved with a new name.

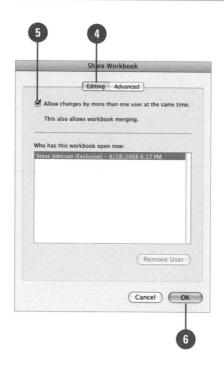

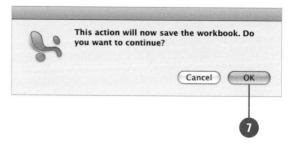

Change Sharing Options

1. Open the workbook you want to share.

2. Click the **Tools** menu, and then click **Share Workbook**.

3. Click the **Advanced** tab.

4. To indicate how long to keep changes, select one of the Track changes options, and then set the number of days, if necessary.

5. To indicate when changes should be saved, select one of the Update changes options, and then set a time internal, if necessary.

6. To resolve conflicting changes, select one of the Conflicting changes between users options.

7. Select one or both of the Include in personal view check boxes.

8. Click **OK**.

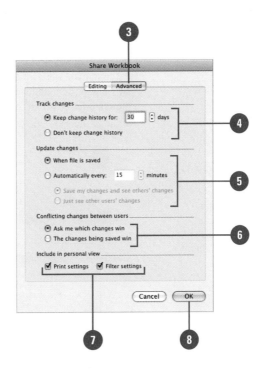

Creating and Reading a Cell Comment

Any cell on a worksheet can contain a **comment**—information you might want to share with co-workers or include as a reminder to yourself without making it a part of the worksheet. (Think of a comment as a nonprinting sticky note attached to an individual cell.) A cell containing a comment displays a red triangle in the upper-right corner of the cell. By default, comments are hidden and are displayed only when the mouse pointer is held over a cell with a red triangle.

Add a Comment

1. Click the cell to which you want to add a comment.

2. Click the **Insert** menu, and then click **Comment**.

3. Type the comment in the comment box.

4. Click outside the comment box when you are finished, or press Esc twice to close the comment box.

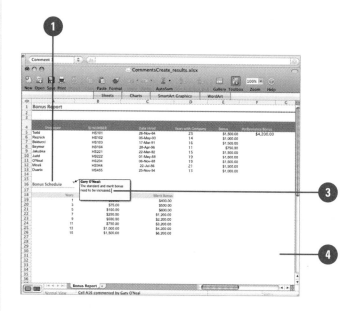

Read a Comment

1. Position the mouse pointer over a cell with a red triangle to read its comment.

2. Move the mouse pointer off the cell to hide the comment.

3. To show all comments, click the **View** menu, and then click **Comment**.

4. To navigate and work with comments using buttons on a toolbar, click the **View** menu, point to **Toolbar**, and then click **Reviewing** to display it.

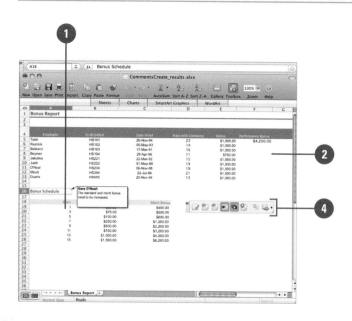

Editing and Deleting a Cell Comment

You can edit, delete, and even format cell comments just as you do other text on a worksheet. If you are working with others online, they may want to delete a comment after reading it. You might want to format certain comments to add emphasis. You can use formatting buttons—such as Bold, Italic, Underline, Font Style, Font Color, or Font Size—on the Font panel or Formatting toolbar. When you no longer need a comment, you can quickly delete it.

Edit a Comment

① Select the cell that you want to remove.

② Click the **Edit Comment** button on the Reviewing toolbar.

◆ You can also Control-click the cell containing the comment, and then click **Edit Comment**.

③ Make your changes using common editing tools, such as the Delete key, as well as the Font panel and Formatting toolbar buttons.

④ Press Esc twice to close the comment box.

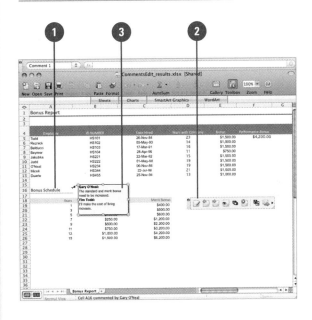

Delete a Comment

① Select the cell that you want to remove.

② Click the **Delete Comment** button on the Reviewing toolbar.

◆ You can also Control-click the cell containing the comment you want to delete, and then click **Delete Comment**.

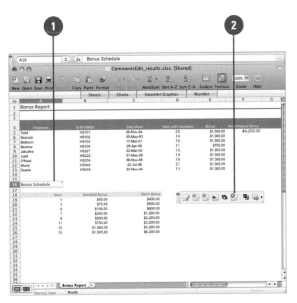

Tracking Changes

As you build and fine-tune a workbook—particularly if you are sharing workbooks with co-workers—you can keep track of all the changes that are made at each stage in the process. The Track Changes feature makes it easy to see who made what changes and when, and to accept or reject each change, even if you are the only user of a worksheet. When you or another user applies the Track Changes command to a workbook, the message "[Shared]" appears in the title bar of the workbook to alert you that this feature is active. To take full advantage of this feature, turn it on the first time you or a co-worker edits a workbook. Then, when it's time to review the workbook, all the changes will be recorded. You can review tracked changes in a workbook at any point. Cells containing changes are surrounded by a blue border, and the changes made can be viewed instantly by moving your mouse pointer over any outlined cell. When you're ready to finalize the workbook, you can review each change and either accept or reject it.

Turn On Track Changes

1. Click the **Tools** menu, point to **Track Changes**, and then click **Highlight Changes**.

2. Select the **Track changes while editing** check box.

3. Select the **When**, **Who**, or **Where** check box. Click an associated list arrow, and then select the option you want.

4. Select the **Highlight changes on screen** check box.

5. To list changes on a new worksheet, select the **List changes on a new sheet** check box.

6. Click **OK**.

7. Make changes in worksheet cells.

   Column and row indicators for changed cells appear in red. The cell containing the changes has a blue outline.

8. To view tracked changes, position the mouse pointer over an edited cell.

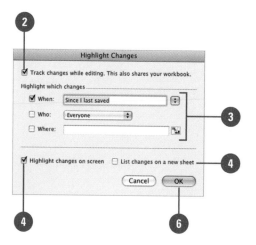

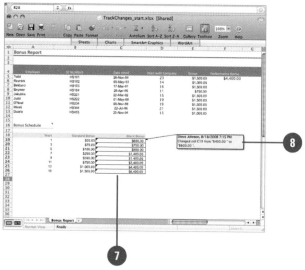

Accept or Reject Tracked Changes

1. Click the **Tools** menu, point to **Track Changes**, and then click **Accept or Reject Changes**. If necessary, click **OK** in the message box.

2. If you want, change tracking, and then click **OK** to begin reviewing changes.

3. If necessary, scroll to review all the changes, and then click one of the following buttons:

   ◆ Click **Accept** to make the selected change to the worksheet.

   ◆ Click **Reject** to remove the selected change from the worksheet.

   ◆ Click **Accept All** to make all of the changes to the worksheet after you have reviewed them.

   ◆ Click **Reject All** to remove all of the changes to the worksheet after you have reviewed them.

4. Click **Close**.

See Also

See "Protecting a Worksheets and Workbooks" on page 322 for information on protecting a shared workbook.

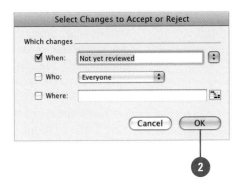

Comparing and Merging Workbooks

For one reason or another, multiple users may maintain identical workbooks. At some point, you'll want to integrate their data into one master workbook, known as the template. First, though, you need to compare the data to identify the differences between the worksheets. Excel can electronically combine the entries, which ensures the integrity of your data. When merging workbooks, all the workbooks must be identical to the file into which the data is being merged. To distribute copies of a workbook and merge the changes into the original, the workbooks must have sharing, change tracking, and change history turned on and use a different file names.

Merge Workbook Data

1 Open the shared workbook that you want to merge.

2 Click the **Tools** menu, and then click **Merge Workbooks**.

3 Click **OK** to save the workbook, if necessary.

4 Select the files you want merged with the active file.

To select more than one workbook to merge, press and hold Control, and then click other files.

5 Click **OK**.

6 Click the **Save** button.

7 Click the **Tools** menu, point to **Track Changes**, and then click **Accept or Reject Changes**.

8 Select the **When** check box, click the list arrow, and then click Not Yet Reviewed.

9 Clear the **Who** and **Where** check boxes.

10 Click **OK**.

11 Click the buttons to accept or reject changes, and then click **Close**.

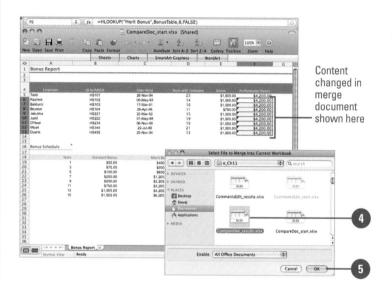

Content changed in merge document shown here

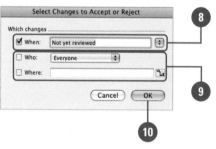

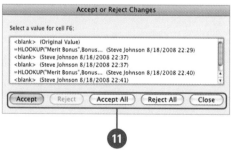

330

Asking "What If" with Goal Seek

Excel's powerful functions make it easy to create powerful formulas, such as calculating payments over time. Sometimes, however, being able to make these calculations is only half the battle. Your formula might tell you that a monthly payment amount is $2,000, while you might only be able to manage a $1,750 payment. **Goal Seek** enables you to work backwards to a desired result, or goal, by adjusting the input values.

Create a "What-If" Scenario with Goal Seek

① Click any cell within the list range.

② Click the **Tools** menu, and then click **Goal Seek**.

③ Click the **Set Cell** box, and then type the cell address you want to change.

You can also click the **Collapse Dialog** button, use your mouse to select the cells, and then click the **Expand Dialog** button.

④ Click the **To Value** box, and then type the result value.

⑤ Click the **By Changing Cell** box, and then type the cell address you want Excel to change.

You can also click the **Collapse Dialog** button, use your mouse to select the cells, and then click the **Expand Dialog** button.

⑥ Click **OK**.

⑦ Review the goal seek status, and then click **OK**.

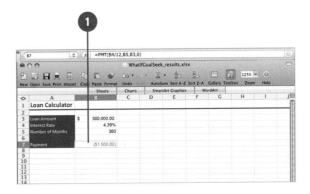

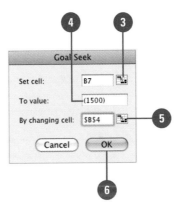

Creating Scenarios

Because some worksheet data is constantly evolving, the ability to create multiple scenarios lets you speculate on a variety of outcomes. For example, the marketing department might want to see how its budget would be affected if sales decreased by 25 percent. Although it's easy enough to plug in different numbers in formulas, Excel allows you to save these values and then recall them at a later time. The ability to create, save, and modify scenarios means a business will be better prepared for different outcomes to avoid economic surprises.

Create and Show a Scenario

1. Click the **Tools** menu, and then click **Scenarios**.

2. Click **Add**.

3. Type a name that identifies the scenario.

4. Type the cells you want to modify in the scenario, or click the **Collapse Dialog** button, use your mouse to select the cells, and then click the **Expand Dialog** button.

5. If you want, type a comment.

6. Click **OK**.

7. Type values for each of the displayed changing cells.

8. Click **OK**.

9. Click **Close**.

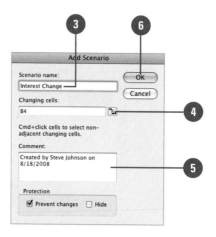

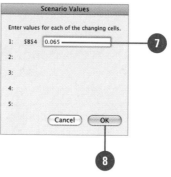

Did You Know?

You can show a scenario Click the Tools menu, click Scenarios, select the scenario you want to see, click Show, and then click Close.

You can create a scenario summary report. Click the Tools menu, click Scenarios, click Summary, click the Scenario Summary option, and then click OK. A scenario summary worksheet tab appears with the report.

Use dialog box to manage scenarios

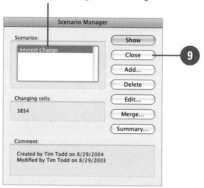

Exporting Data

In cases where you don't need the data you are using from another source to be automatically updated if the source data changes, the most expedient way to get the data is to copy and paste it. In cases where you want to copy data from one program to another, you can convert the data to a format that the other program accepts.

Export Excel Data Using Copy and Paste

1. Select the cell or range that you want to copy.

2. Click the **Copy** button on the Standard toolbar.

3. Open the destination file, or click the program's taskbar button if the program is already open.

4. Click to indicate where you want the data to be copied.

5. Click the **Paste** button on the Standard toolbar.

6. Click the **Paste Options** button, and then click the option you want.

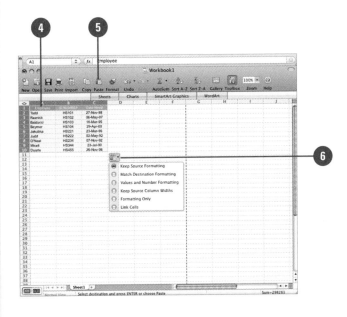

Export an Excel File to Another Program Format

1. Open the file from which you want to export data.

2. Click the **File** menu, and then click **Save As**.

3. Type a name or use the one provided.

4. Click the **Format** drop-down, and then click the file format you want.

5. Click **Save**.

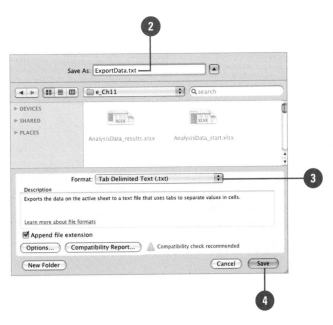

Analyzing Data Using a PivotTable

When you want to summarize information in a lengthy list using complex criteria, use the **PivotTable** to simplify your task. Without the PivotTable, you would have to manually count or create a formula to calculate which records met certain criteria, and then create a table to display that information. Once you determine what fields and criteria you want to use to summarize the data and how you want the resulting table to look, the Pivot Table Wizard does the rest. You can quickly update a PivotTable report using the PivotTable toolbar, which appears whenever a PivotTable is active. When you do want to add new data, Excel makes it easy by allowing you to drag data fields to and from a PivotTable. You can also change field settings to format a number or show the data in a different form. The field settings include functions such as Sum, Count, Average, Max, and Min.

Create a PivotTable Report

1. Click any cell within the list range.

2. Click the **Data** menu, and then click **PivotTable Report**.

3. If using the list range, click the **Microsoft Office Excel List or Database** option.

4. Click **Next** to continue.

5. If the range does not include the correct data, click the **Collapse Dialog** button. Drag the pointer over the list range, including the field names, to select a new range, and then click the **Expand Dialog** button.

6. Click **Next** to continue.

7. Click the **New sheet** option or the **Existing sheet** option, and then specify the location of the existing sheet.

8. Click **Finish**.

9. Drag fields from the Field List to areas on the PivotTable Report.

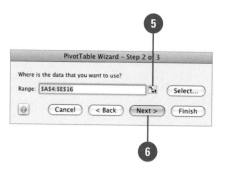

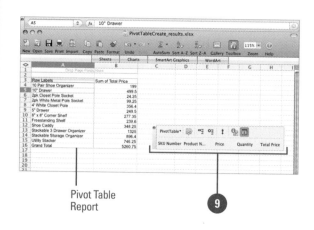

Pivot Table Report

Update a PivotTable Report

1. Make any necessary change(s) in the worksheet where your list range resides.

2. If necessary, select a different worksheet, and then click any cell in the PivotTable Report.

3. Click the **Refresh Data** button on the PivotTable toolbar, or click the **Data** menu, and then click **Refresh Data**.

4. To add or remove a field in a PivotTable, position the pointer over the field that you want to add to or remove from the PivotTable, and then drag the field on the PivotTable to add the field or drag it off the PivotTable to remove the field.

Change Field Settings in a PivotTable Report

1. Select the field you want to change.

2. Click the **Field Settings** button on the PivotTable toolbar.

3. Make the necessary changes to the field.

4. Click **OK**.

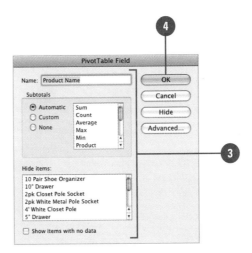

Consolidating Data

In some cases, you'll want to consolidate data from different worksheets or workbooks into one workbook, rather than simply linking the source data. For instance, if each division in your company creates a budget, you can pull together, or **consolidate**, the totals for each line item into one company-wide budget. If each divisional budget is laid out in the same way, with the budgeted amounts for each line item in the same cell addresses, then you can very easily consolidate the information without any retyping. If data in individual workbooks change, the consolidated worksheet or workbook will always be correct.

Consolidate Data from Other Worksheets or Workbooks

1. Open all the workbooks that contain the data you want to consolidate.

2. Open or create the workbook that will contain the consolidated data.

3. Select the destination range.

4. Click the **Data** menu, and then click **Consolidate**.

5. Click the **Function** list arrow, and then select the function you want to use to consolidate the data.

6. Type the location of the data to be consolidated, or click the **Collapse Dialog** button, and then select the cells to be consolidated.

Did You Know?

You can include all labels. Make sure you select enough cells to accommodate any labels that might be included in the data you are consolidating.

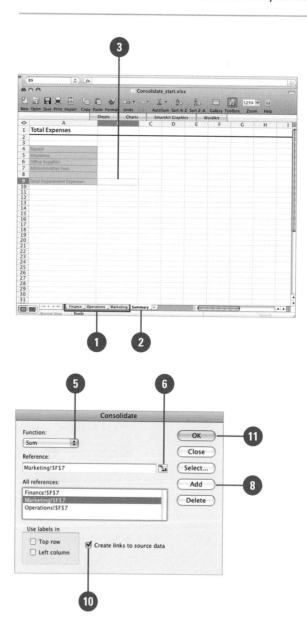

336

7 Click the **Expand Dialog** button.

8 Click **Add** to add the reference to the list of consolidated ranges.

9 Repeat steps 6 through 8 until you have listed all references to consolidate.

10 Select the **Create links to source data** check box.

11 Click **OK**.

Did You Know?

You can consolidate worksheets even if they are not laid out identically. If the worksheets you want to consolidate aren't laid out with exactly the same cell addresses, but they do contain identical types of information, select the Top Row and Left Column check boxes in the Consolidate dialog box so that Excel uses labels to match up the correct data.

You can arrange multiple documents. Use the Window menu to move between documents or to arrange them so they are visible at the same time.

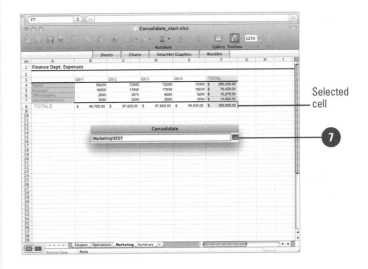

Selected cell

7

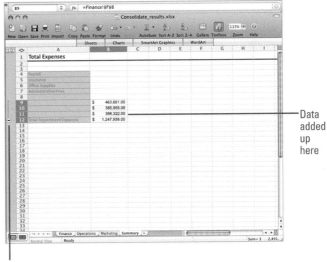

Data added up here

Click to collapse the data

Linking Data

A link can be as simple as a reference to a cell on another worksheet, or it can be part of a formula. You can link cells between sheets within one workbook or between different workbooks. Cell data to be linked is called the source data. The cell or range linked to the source data is called the destination cell or destination range. If you no longer want linked data to be updated, you can easily break a link. Create links instead of making multiple identical entries; it saves time and ensures your entries are correct.

Create a Link Between Worksheets or Workbooks

1. Select the cell or range that contains the source data.

2. Click the **Copy** button on the Standard toolbar.

3. Click the sheet tab where you want to link the data.

4. Select the destination cell or destination range.

5. Click the **Paste** button on the Standard toolbar.

6. Click the **Paste Options** button, and then click **Link Cells**.

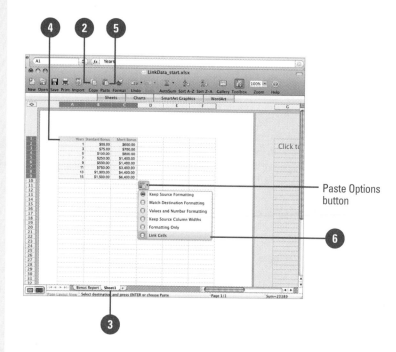

Paste Options button

Break a Link

1 Click the cell containing the linked formula you want to break.

2 Click the **Copy** button on the Standard toolbar.

3 Click the **Edit** menu, and then click **Paste Special**.

4 Click the **Values** option.

5 Click **OK**.

Did You Know?

You can include a link in a formula and treat the linked cell as one argument in a larger calculation. Enter the formula on the formula bar, and then select a cell in the worksheet or workbook you want to link. A cell address reference to a worksheet is =tab name!cell address (=Orders!A6). A cell reference to a workbook is ='[workbook name.xls]tab name'!cell address (='[Product Orders.xls]Orders'!A6).

You can arrange worksheet windows to make linking easier. To arrange open windows, click the Window menu, click Arrange, and then click the option for the window arrangement you want.

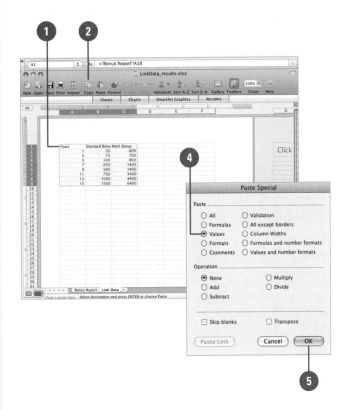

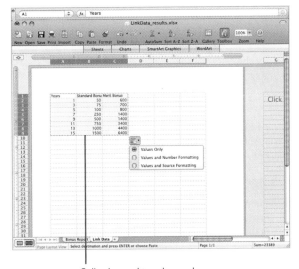

Cells changed to values only

Getting Query Data from a Database

If you have data in a database, you can use functions in Excel to retrieve data from a table in a database. To retrieve the data, you can select or create a data source, build a query to create a link to the data, and optionally, create a filter to limit the information. When you select or create a data source, you need to identify the database type and then connect to it. To build a query, you can use the Query wizard to step you through the process, or you can manually create a query the same way you do in a database. Before you can create a query, you need to first install the required ODBC (Open Database Connectivity) driver, such as ODBC for Access. You can also retrieve data from other sources. If you use the same table in a database for data, you can define and save the data source for use later.

Define a New Data Source

1. Click the **Data** menu, point to **Get External Data**, and then click **New Database Query**.

   ◆ If an alert appears indicating that no ODBC drivers are installed on your computer, click **Go to page** to display the Mactopia Web site, where you can access links to install the data source drivers you want.

2. Click the **User DSN**, **System DSN**, or **File DSN** tab.

3. Click **Add**.

4. Select a driver for the data source that you want to set up.

5. Click **Finish**.

6. Follow the wizard to create a new data source; steps vary depending on the data source.

   ◆ **Name**, **DSN Type**, **Description**

   ◆ Click **Choose**, navigate to the folder with the database you want to use, select it, and then click **Choose**.

7. Click **Continue**, and then click **Done**.

8. Click **Cancel** or select a data source, and then click **OK** to create a query.

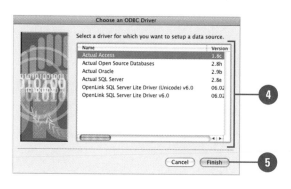

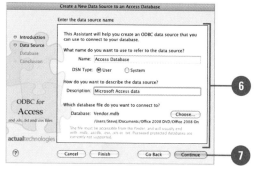

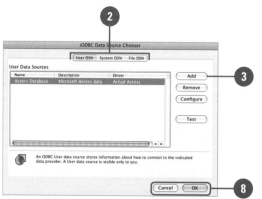

Create a Database Query

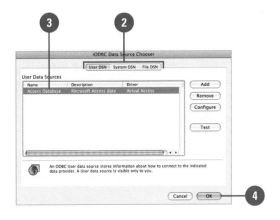

1 Click the **Data** menu, point to **Get External Data**, and then click **New Database Query**.

2 Click the **User DSN**, **System DSN**, or **File DSN** tab.

3 Click the name of the data sources you want to use.

◆ To select another database, select the source, click **Configure**, and then follow the instructions to change it.

4 Click **OK**.

5 Create the query using techniques from the data source.

In Microsoft Query for Access, for example, drag tables into Query View, select the fields from which you want to get data, and then specify the sort and filter criteria you want. Click Query View to display the data.

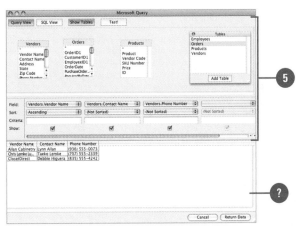

6 Click **Return Data** to continue back in Excel.

7 Click the **Existing sheet** option, and then specify a cell location, or click the **New sheet** option. If you want to create a PivotTable, click the **PivotTable report** option.

8 Click **OK**.

The data from the data source appears in your worksheet.

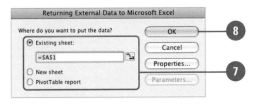

Data from the query

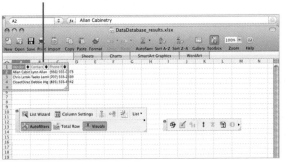

Getting Query Data from the Web

If you have data on the Web, you can retrieve it by using a query. You can create your own (see previous page) or use/modify one provided by Office 2008. The queries are located in the following folder: Microsoft Office 2008:Office:Queries. The sample queries include: MSN MoneyCentral Currencies, MSN MoneyCentral Major Indices, and MSN MoneyCentral Stock Quotes.

Import Web Data Using a Query

1. Open the workbook in which you want to insert text data.

2. Click the **Data** menu, point to **Get External Data**, and then click **Run Saved Query**.

3. Click the **Where** drop-down, and then select the folder where the query is located.

4. Select the query file you want.

5. Click **Get Data**.

6. Click the **Existing sheet** option, and then specify a cell location, or click the **New sheet** option. If you want to create a PivotTable, click the **PivotTable report** option.

7. Click **OK** to continue.

8. Enter a parameter value. To enter multiple values, separate them with commas.

9. Click **OK**.

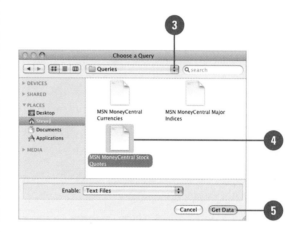

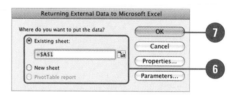

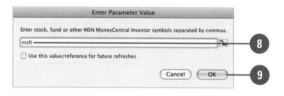

Did You Know?

You can create refreshable Web queries. If you want to analyze Web data in a worksheet, you can use the Copy and Paste commands to bring the data from a Web page into the worksheet. The Paste Options button allows you to keep the data as it is or make it refreshable on the Web. As the data changes on the Web, you can use the Refresh button to quickly update it.

Query data from the web

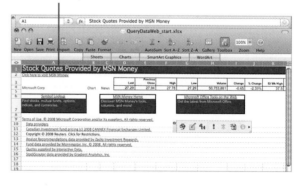

Getting Data from a FileMaker Pro Database

If you have data in a FileMaker Pro (version 5.0 - 9.0) database, you can import it directly into Excel. In addition to the database file, you must also have the appropriate version of FileMaker Pro installed on your computer along with Excel. Excel uses the FileMaker Pro Import Wizard to step you through the process of importing your data. After you complete the import, you will probably need to resort your data.

Import Data from a FileMaker Pro Database

1. Open the workbook in which you want to insert text data.

2. Click the **Data** menu, point to **Get External Data**, and then click **Import from FileMaker Pro**.

   ◆ You can also click the **File** menu, click **Import**, click the **FileMaker Pro database** option, and then click **Import**.

3. Navigate to and select the database file you want to import.

4. Click **Choose**.

   FileMaker Pro starts, the database opens, and the FileMaker Pro Import Wizard appears.

5. In Step 1, click the **Layouts** or **Tables** drop-down, select a layout or table, select each field in the Available fields list, and then click **Add** to import these fields.

6. To change the import order, click the field, and then click the up or down button.

7. Click **Next** to continue.

8. In Step 2, specify the criteria you want to filter (remove) out data from the FileMaker Pro database.

9. Click **Finish**.

10. Click the **Existing sheet** option, and then specify a cell location, or click the **New sheet** option.

11. Click **OK**.

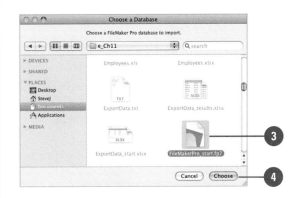

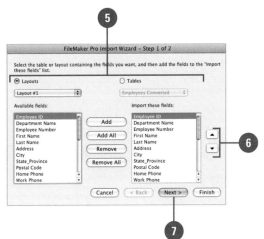

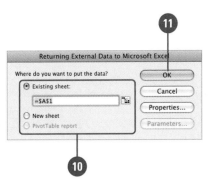

Getting Text Data

If you have data in a text file, you can either open the file using the Open command on the Office menu, or you can import the text file as an external data range using the From Text button on the Data tab. There are two commonly used text file formats to store data that you can import in Excel: Tab delimited text (.txt) and Comma separated values text (.csv). When you open a .txt file, Excel starts the Import Text Wizard. When you open a .csv file, Excel opens the file using current default data format settings.

Import a Text File

1. Open the workbook in which you want to insert text data.

2. Click the **Data** menu, point to **Get External Data**, and then click **Import Text File**.

   ◆ You can also click the **File** menu, click **Import**, click the **Text file** or CSV **file** option, and then click **Import**.

3. Click the **Enable** drop-down, and then click **Text Files** or **CSV Files**.

4. Click the **Where** drop-down, and then select the folder where the text file is located.

5. Click the text file you want to import.

6. Click **Get Data**.

7. If the file is a text file (.txt), Excel starts the Import Text Wizard. Step through the wizard (3 steps), and then click **Finish**.

8. Click the **Existing worksheet** option, and then specify a cell location, or click the **New worksheet** option.

9. Click **OK**.

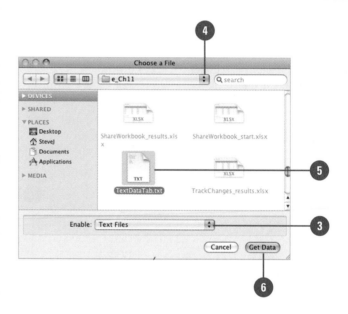

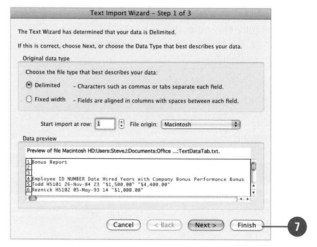

Creating a Presentation with PowerPoint

12

Introduction

When creating a new presentation, there are things to consider as you develop your content. Microsoft PowerPoint 2008 can help you with this process. There are various elements to a presentation that make good looking slides: bulleted lists, clip art, charts and diagrams, organization charts and tables, and media clips or pictures. All of these items are considered graphic objects, and are separate from the text objects that you enter. Objects can be moved from one part of a presentation to another. You can also resize, move, and delete them.

As you develop your presentation, there are a few things to keep in mind—keep the text easy to read and straight to the point, make sure it isn't too wordy, and have a balance of text and graphics. Too much text can lose your audience while too many graphics can distract their focus.

PowerPoint offers many tools to help develop your text. Using the AutoCorrect feature, text is corrected as you type. A built-in Thesaurus is always a few keystrokes away, as is a research option that allows you to look for information is available in PowerPoint or has links to the Web.

Once you've begun to enter your text, you can adjust the spacing, change the alignment, set tabs, and change indents. You can also format your text by changing the font style or its attributes such as adding color to your text. If you decide to enter text in outline form, PowerPoint offers you the Outline pane to jot down your thoughts and notes. If bulleted or numbered lists are your preference, you can enter your ideas in this format. Should you need to rearrange your slides, you can do this in various PowerPoint views.

What You'll Do

View the PowerPoint Window

Browse a Presentation

Understand PowerPoint Views

Create New and Consistent Slides

Enter and Edit Text

Resize Text While Typing

Change Character Direction

Insert and Develop an Outline

Move and Indent Text

Modify a Bulleted and Numbered List

Create Text Columns

Change Text Spacing

Rearrange Slides

Use Slides from Other Presentations

Make You Presentation Look Consistent

Control Slide Appearances, Layout and Background with Masters

Modify Placeholders

Add a Background Style

Insert, Modify and Format a Table

Create a Text Box

Viewing the PowerPoint Window

Standard Toolbar
Click to access command comments on the toolbar.

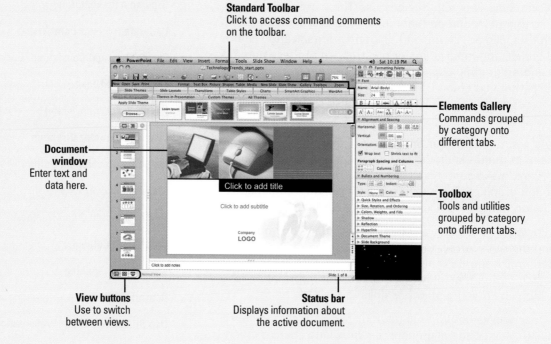

Elements Gallery
Commands grouped by category onto different tabs.

Toolbox
Tools and utilities grouped by category onto different tabs.

Document window
Enter text and data here.

View buttons
Use to switch between views.

Status bar
Displays information about the active document.

Browsing a Presentation

You might want to browse through a completed presentation to view the contents and design of each slide and to evaluate the types of slides in a presentation in several ways. When a slide doesn't fit the screen, you can change the presentation view size, or click the scroll arrows to scroll line by line or click above or below the scroll box to scroll window by window and move to another slide. To move immediately to a specific slide, you can drag the scroll box. In Slides pane, you can click the Next Slide and Previous Slide buttons, which are located at the bottom of the vertical scroll bar, to switch between slides in a presentation.

Browse Through a Presentation

◆ Click a slide miniature in the Slides pane or a slide icon in the Outline pane.

◆ Click the **Up** scroll arrow or **Down** scroll arrow to scroll line by line.

When you scroll to the top or bottom of a slide, you automatically move to the previous or next page.

◆ Click above or below the **Scroll** box to scroll window by window.

◆ Drag the **Scroll** box to move immediately to a specific slide.

As you drag, a slide indicator box appears, telling you the slide number and title.

◆ Click the **Previous Slide** or **Next Slide** button.

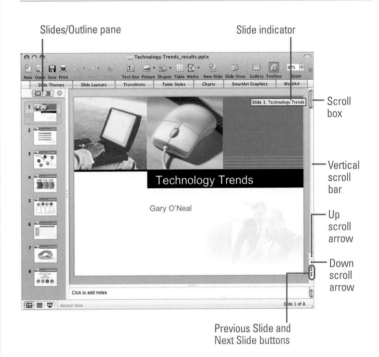

Slides/Outline pane — Slide indicator — Scroll box — Vertical scroll bar — Up scroll arrow — Down scroll arrow — Previous Slide and Next Slide buttons

Did You Know?

You can use the keyboard to browse slides. Press the Page Up or Page Down key to switch between slides. If you use these keys, the slides in the Slides pane will change also.

Understanding PowerPoint Views

To help you during all phases of developing a presentation, PowerPoint provides different views: Normal, Slide Sorter, Notes Page, Slide Show, and Presenter Tools. You can switch from one view to another by clicking a view button (Normal, Slide Sorter, and Slide Show) located on the Status bar or by using the commands on the View menu. In any view, you can use the Zoom feature on the Standard toolbar to increase and decrease the page view size and display the slide to fit the screen.

Normal view

Use the Normal view to work with the three underlying elements of a presentation—the outline, slide, and notes—each in its own pane. These panes provide an overview of your presentation and let you work on all of its parts. You can adjust the size of the panes by dragging the pane borders. You can use the **Outline pane** to develop and organize your presentation's content. Use the **Slide pane** to add text, graphics, movies, sounds, and hyperlinks to individual slides, and the Notes pane to add speaker notes or notes you want to share with your audience.

Outline pane

Use the Outline pane in Normal view to develop your presentation's content. Individual slides are numbered and a slide icon appears for each slide.

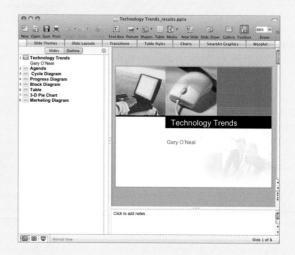

Slides pane

Use the Slides pane in Normal view to preview each slide. Click the slide you want to view. You can also move through your slides using the scroll bars or the Previous Slide and Next Slide buttons. When you drag the scroll box up or down on the vertical scroll bar, a label appears that indicates which slide will be displayed if you release the mouse button.

Notes Pages View

Use the Notes Pages view or the Notes pane in Normal view to enter notes for each slide in your presentation. The notes for each slide appear in Presenter Tools view when you deliver your presentation.

Slide Sorter view

Use the Slide Sorter view to organize your slides, add actions between slides—called slide transitions—and apply other effects to your slide show. The Animations tab helps you add slide transitions and control your presentation. When you add a slide transition, you see an icon that indicates an action will take place as one slide replaces another during a show. If you hide a slide, you see an icon that indicates the slide will not be shown during the presentation.

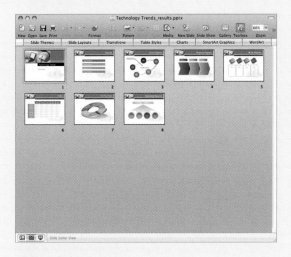

Slide Show view

Slide Show view presents your slides one at a time. Use this view when you're ready to rehearse or give your presentation. To move through the slides, click the screen, or press Return to move through the show.

Presenter Tools view

Presenter Tools view allows you to present your slides on one monitor, such as a big screen, while you control your presentation on another monitor, such as a laptop, by tracking your time and displaying notes that only you can see. Use this view when you're ready to rehearse or give your presentation.

Creating New and Consistent Slides

Creating consistent looking slides makes it easier for your audience to follow and understand your presentation. PowerPoint provides a gallery of slide layouts (**New!**) to help you position and format slides in a consistent manner. A slide layout contains **placeholders**, such as text, chart, table, or SmartArt graphic, where you can enter text or insert elements. When you create a new slide, you can apply a standard layout or a custom layout of your own design. You can also apply a layout to an existing slide at any time. When you change a slide's layout, PowerPoint keeps the existing information and applies the new look.

Insert a New Slide

1. In Normal view, display the slide before where you what to insert.

2. Click the **Slide Layouts** tab on the Elements Gallery.

3. Click the **Insert new slide** option.

   TIMESAVER *Click the New Slide button on the Standard toolbar to insert a standard slide.*

4. In the Slide Layout gallery, click the slide layout you want to use.

   ◆ You can click the arrows on the right to display more layouts.

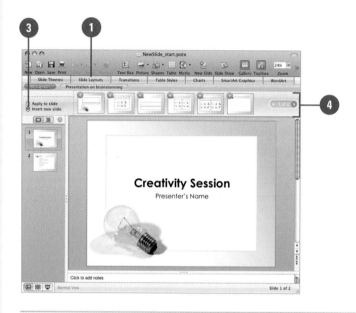

Apply an Layout to an Existing Slide

1. In Normal view, display the slide you want to change.

2. Click the **Slide Layouts** tab on the Elements Gallery.

3. Click the **Apply to slide** option.

4. In the Slide Layout gallery, click the slide layout you want to use.

   ◆ You can click the arrows on the right to display more layouts.

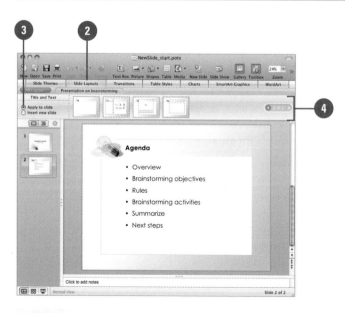

Enter Information in a Placeholder

◆ For text placeholders, click the placeholder, and then type the text.

◆ For other objects, click the icon in the placeholder, and then work with the accessory that PowerPoint starts.

Layout Placeholder

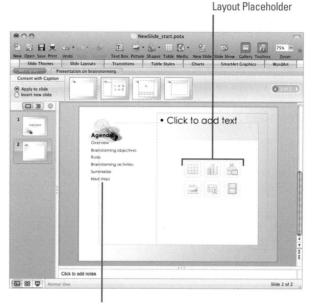

A placeholder is a border that defines the size and location of an object.

Slide Layout Placeholders

Placeholder	Description
Title	Enter title text
Bulleted	Enter bulleted list
Table	Inserts a table
Chart	Inserts a chart
Clip Art	Inserts a picture from the Clip Organizer
Picture	Inserts a picture from a file
SmartArt (**New!**)	Inserts a diagram, chart, or other graphics
Movie	Inserts a movie or video clip

Working with Objects

Once you create a slide, you can modify any of its objects, even those added by a slide layout. To manipulate objects, use Normal view. To perform any action on an object, you first need to select it. When you select an object, such as text or graphic, the object is surrounded by a solid-lined rectangle, called a **selection box**, with sizing handles (small white circles at the corners and small white squares on the sides) around it. You can resize, move, delete, and format selected objects.

Select and Deselect an Object

◆ To select an object, move the pointer (which changes to a four-headed arrow) over the object or edge, and then click to select.

◆ To select multiple objects, press and hold Shift as you click each object or drag to enclose the objects you want to select in the selection box. Press ⌘+A to select all objects on a slide.

◆ To deselect an object, click outside its border.

◆ To deselect one of a group of objects, press and hold Shift, and then click the object.

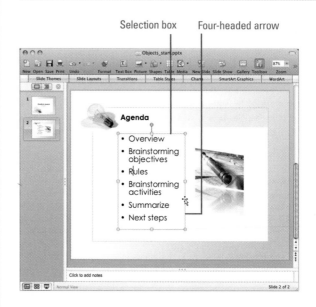

Selection box   Four-headed arrow

Resize an Object

1 Move the pointer over a sizing handle.

2 Drag the sizing handle until the object is the size you want.

TIMESAVER *Use the Shift and Option keys while you drag. The Shift key constrains an edge; the Option key maintains a proportional edge; and the Shift and Option keys together maintains a proportional object.*

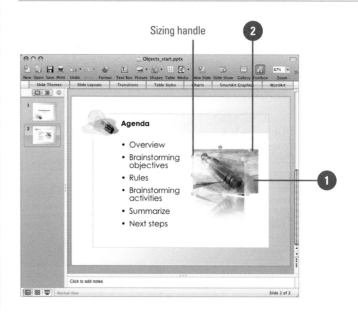

Sizing handle

Move or Copy an Object

◆ **Using the mouse.** To copy, press and hold Option while you drag. Move the pointer (which changes to a four-headed arrow) over the object, and then drag it to the new location. For unfilled objects, drag the border. You can move or copy an object in a straight line by pressing Shift as you drag the object.

◆ **Using the keyboard.** To move, click the object, and then press the arrow keys to move the object in the direction you want.

◆ **Using the keyboard shortcuts.** To cut an object from a slide, select the object and then press ⌘+X. To copy an object, select the object, and then press ⌘+C. To paste an object on a slide, press ⌘+V.

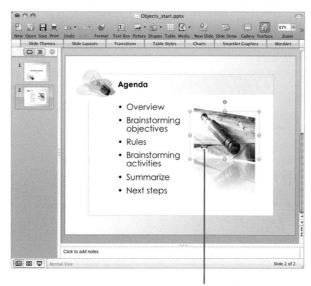

Use the four-headed arrow to drag the object to a new location

Delete an Object

① Click the object you want to delete.

② Press Delete.

Did You Know?

You can use the Tab key to select hard-to-click objects. If you are having trouble selecting an object that is close to other objects, click a different object and then press Tab until you select the object you want.

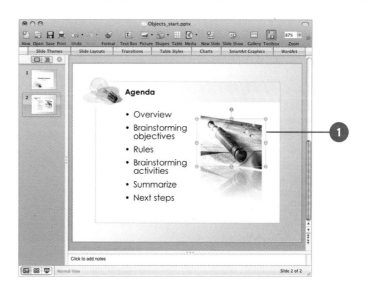

Entering and Editing Text

In Normal view, you can type text directly into the text placeholders. A **text placeholder** is an empty text box. The insertion point (the blinking vertical line) indicates where text will appear when you type. To place the insertion point into your text, move the pointer over the text. The pointer changes to an I-beam to indicate that you can click and then type. When a selection box of dashed lines appears, your changes affect only the selected text. When a solid-lined selection box appears, changes apply to the entire text object. You can move, copy, or delete existing text; replace it with new text; and undo any changes you just made.

Enter Text into a Placeholder

1. In Normal view, click the text placeholder if it isn't already selected.

2. Type the text you want to enter.

3. Click outside the text object to deselect it.

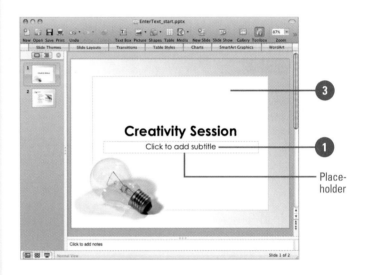

Insert Text

1. Click to place the insertion point where you want to insert the text.

2. Type the text.

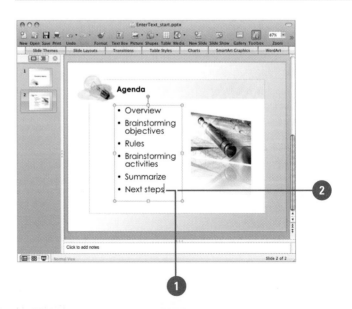

Enter Text in a Bulleted or Numbered List

1. In Normal view, click the bulleted text placeholder.

2. To switch to a numbered list, click the **Bullets and Numbering** panel to expand it, if necessary, and then click the **Numbering** button.

3. Type the first item.

4. Press Return.

   ◆ To increase the list level, press Tab or click the **Increase List Level** button.

   ◆ To decrease the list level, press Shift+Tab, or click the **Decrease List Level** button.

5. Type the next item.

6. Repeat steps 4 and 5 until you complete the list.

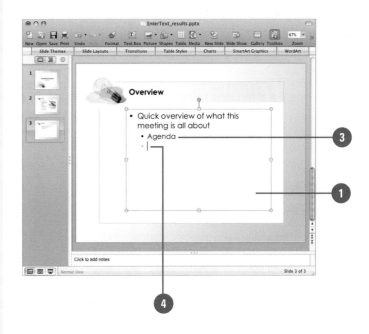

Select and Modify Text

1. Position the mouse pointer to the left of the text you want to highlight.

2. Drag the pointer over the text— just a few words, a few lines, or entire paragraphs, and then release the mouse button.

3. Modify the text the way you want.

   ◆ To delete text, press Delete.

   ◆ To replace text, type your new text.

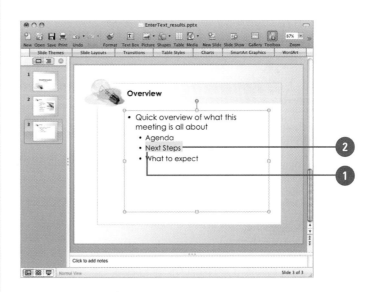

Resizing Text While Typing

If you type text in a placeholder, PowerPoint uses AutoFit to resize the text, if necessary, to fit into the placeholder. The AutoFit Text feature changes the line spacing—or paragraph spacing—between lines of text and then changes the font size to make the text fit. The AutoFit Options button, which appears near your text the first time that it is resized, gives you control over whether you want the text to be resized. The AutoFit Options button displays a menu with options for controlling how the option works. You can also display the AutoCorrect dialog box and change the AutoFit settings so that text doesn't resize automatically.

Resize Text as You Type

1. If the AutoFit Options box appears while you type, click the **AutoFit Options** button to select an option, or continue typing and PowerPoint will automatically adjust your text to fit.

2. If you click the AutoFit Options button, click the option you want to fit the text on the slide.

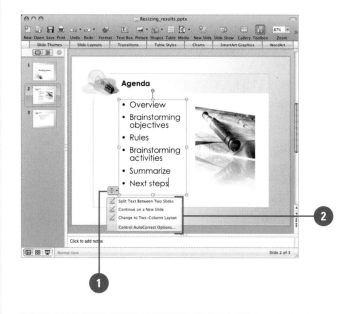

Turn Off AutoFit

1. Click the **PowerPoint** menu, and then click **Preferences**.

2. Click the **AutoCorrect** icon.

3. Click the **AutoFormat As You Type** tab.

4. Clear the **AutoFit body text to placeholder** check boxes.

5. Click **OK**.

Changing Character Direction

Sometimes changing the direction of text on a slide creates a unique or special effect that causes the audience to remember it. In PowerPoint, you can rotate all text in an object 90 and 270 degrees or stack letters (**New!**) on top of one another to create the look you want. For a more exact rotation, which you cannot achieve in 90 or 270 degree increments, you can drag the green rotate lever at the top of an object to rotate it to any position. This is useful when you want to change the orientation of an object, such as the direction of an arrow.

Quickly Change Character Direction

1. Select the text you want to format.

2. Click the **Formatting Palette** tab on the Toolbox.

3. Click the **Alignment and Space** panel to expand it.

4. Click one of the following buttons:

   - **Horizontal** to align text normally across the slide from left to right.

   - **Rotate all text 90°** to align text vertically down the slide from top to bottom.

   - **Rotate all text 270°** to align text vertically down the slide from bottom to top.

   - **Stacked** to align text vertically down the slide one letter on top of another.

5. Select additional options, such as alignment, direction or resize shape to fit text.

   - **Wrap text.** Select to wrap text in the text box.

   - **Shrink text to fit.** Select to reduce text size to fit in the current size of the text box.

6. If necessary, resize text box.

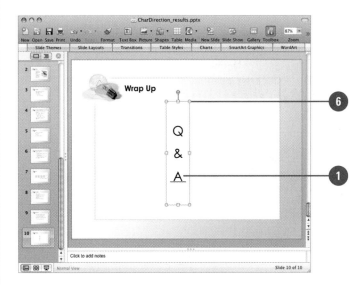

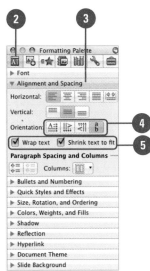

Inserting and Developing an Outline

Outlining your content is a great way to create a presentation. You can outline and organize your thoughts right in PowerPoint or insert an outline you created in another program, such as Microsoft Word. If you prefer to develop your own outline, you can create a blank presentation, and then type your outline in the Outline pane of Normal view. As you develop an outline, you can add new slides and duplicate existing slides in your presentation. If you already have an outline, make sure the document containing the outline is set up using outline heading styles. When you insert the outline in PowerPoint, it creates slide titles, subtitles, and bulleted lists based on those styles.

Enter Text in the Outline Pane

1. In the Outline pane of Normal view, click to place the insertion point where you want the text to appear.

2. Type the title text you want, pressing Enter after each line.

   To indent right a level for bullet text, press Tab before you type. Press Shift+Tab to indent left a level.

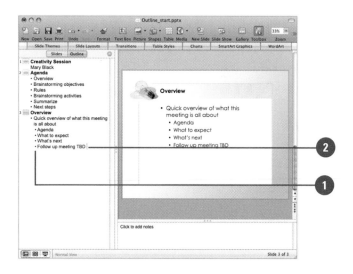

Add a Slide in the Outline Pane

1. In the Outline pane of Normal view, click at the end of the slide text where you want to insert a new slide.

2. Press Option+Return, or click the **New Slide** button on the Standard toolbar.

Did You Know?

You can delete a slide. In the Outline or Slides pane or in Slide Sorter view, select the slide you want to delete. Press Delete, or click the Edit menu, and then click Delete Slide.

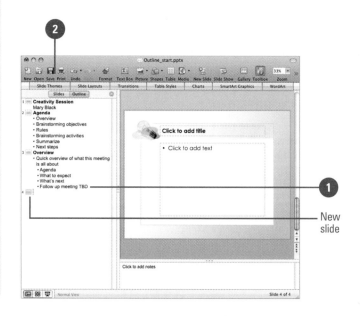

New slide

Duplicate a Slide

1. In the Outline pane of Normal view, click the slide you want to duplicate.

   TIMESAVER *To select slides in a sequence, click the first slide, hold down the Shift key, and then click the last slide. To select multiple slides, use the Control key.*

2. Click the **Edit**, and then click **Duplicate**, or Control-click the selected slide, and then click **Duplicate Slide**.

   The new slide appears directly after the slide duplicated.

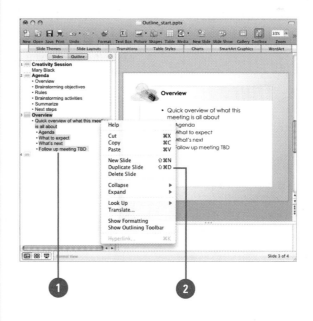

Insert an Outline from Another Program

1. In the Outline pane of Normal view, click the slide after which you want to insert an outline.

2. Click the **Insert** menu, point to **Slides From**, and then click **Outline File**.

3. Locate and select the file containing the outline you want to insert.

4. Click **Insert**.

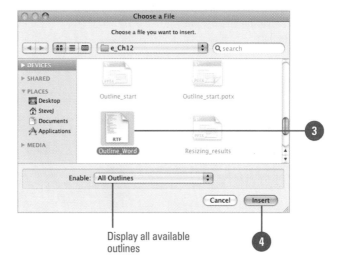

Display all available outlines

Did You Know?

You can open an outline from another program in PowerPoint. Click the Open button on the Standard toolbar, click the Enable drop-down, click All Outlines, and then double-click the outline file you want to open.

Moving and Indenting Text

Body text on a slide typically contains bulleted text, which you can indent to create levels. You can indent paragraphs of body text up to five levels. In an outline, these tools let you demote text from a title, for example, to bulleted text. You can view and change the locations of the indent markers within an object with text using the ruler. You can set different indent markers for each paragraph in an object (**New!**). The ruler includes default tab stops at every inch; when you press the Tab key, the text moves to the next tab stop, which you can change.

Change the Indent Level

1. In Normal view (Outline pane or slide), click the paragraph text or select the lines of text you want.

2. Click the **Formatting Palette** tab on the Toolbox.

3. Click the **Bullets and Numbering** panel to expand it.

4. Click the indent level option you want:

   ◆ Click the **Increase List Level** button to move the line up one level (to the left).

   ◆ Click the **Decrease List Level** button to move the line down one level (to the right).

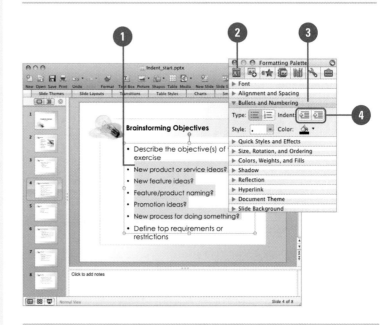

Display or Hide the Ruler

1. In Normal view, click the **View** menu, and then click **Ruler**.

Rulers

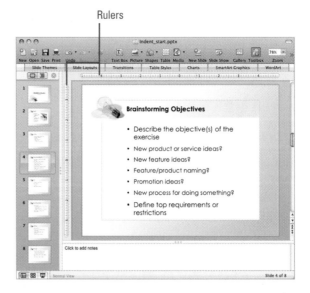

Change the Indent

1. Display the ruler.

2. Select the text for which you want to change the indentation.

3. Change the indent level the way you want.

◆ To change the indent for the first line of a paragraph, drag the first-line indent marker.

◆ To change the indent for the rest of the paragraph, drag the left indent marker.

◆ To change the distance between the indents and the left margin, but maintain the relative distance between the first-line and left indent markers, drag the rectangle below the left indent marker.

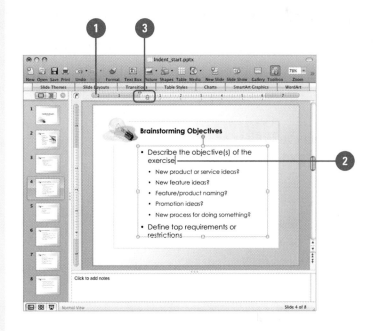

Set or Remove a Tab

1. Click the paragraph or select the paragraphs whose tabs you want to modify. You can also select a text object to change the tabs for all paragraphs in that object.

2. If necessary, click the **View** menu, and then click **Ruler** to display the ruler.

3. Click the **Tab** button at the left of the horizontal ruler until you see the type of tab you want.

4. Click the ruler where you want to set the tab.

5. To remove a tab, drag it off of the ruler.

◆ To move the tab, drag it to a new location on the ruler.

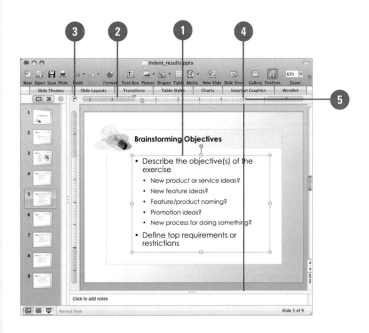

Modifying a Bulleted and Numbered List

When you create a new slide, you can choose the bulleted list slide layout to include a bulleted list placeholder. You can customize the appearance of your bulleted list in several ways, including symbols or numbering. You also have control over the appearance of your bullets, including size and color. You can change the bullets to numbers or pictures. You can also adjust the distance between a bullet and its text using the PowerPoint ruler.

Add and Remove Bullets or Numbering from Text

① Select the text in the paragraphs in which you want to add a bullet.

② Click the **Formatting Palette** tab on the Toolbox.

③ Click the **Bullets and Numbering** panel to expand it.

④ Click the **Bullets** or **Numbering** button.

⑤ To change the style, click the **Style** drop-down, and then select a style.

⑥ To remove the bullet or numbering, select the text, and then click the **Bullets** or **Numbering** button.

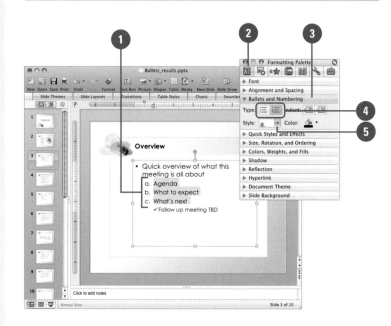

Change the Distance Between Bullets and Text

① Select the text you want to indent.

② If the ruler isn't visible, click the **View** menu, and then click **Ruler**.

③ Drag the indent markers on the ruler.

◆ **First-line Indent.** The top upside down triangle marker indents the first line.

◆ **Hanging Indent.** The middle triangle marker indent second line and later.

◆ **Left Indent.** The bottom square marker indent entire line.

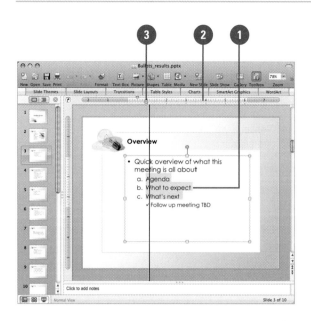

Change the Bullet or Number Character

① Select the text or text object whose bullet character you want to change.

② Click the **Format** menu, and then click **Bullets and Numbering**.

③ Click the **Bulleted** or **Numbered** tab.

④ Click one of the predefined styles or do one of the following:

◆ Click the **Custom bullet** drop-down, click **Picture**, and then click the picture you want to use for your bullet character.

◆ Click the **Custom bullet** drop-down, click a symbol or click **Character**, and then click the character you want to use for your bullet character.

⑤ To change the bullet or number's color, click the **Color** drop-down, and then select a color.

⑥ To change the bullet or number's size, enter a percentage in the Size box.

⑦ Click **OK**.

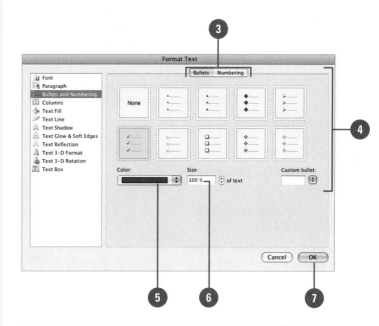

Did You Know?

You can select bulleted or numbered text. Position the mouse pointer over the bullet or number next to the text you want to select; when the pointer changes to the four-headed arrow, click the bullet.

You can use the mouse to increase or decrease list level text. Move the mouse pointer over the bullet you want to increase or decrease, and then when it changes to a four-headed arrow, drag the text to the left or right.

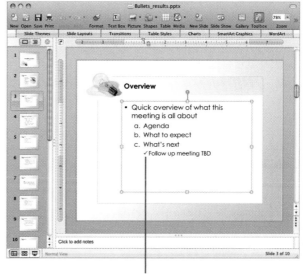

Bullet change

Creating Text Columns

Like Microsoft Word, PowerPoint can now create text columns (**New!**) within a text box. You can quickly transform a long list of text into a two, three, or more columns. After you create text columns, you can change the spacing between them to create the exact look you want. If you want to return columns back to a single column, simply change a text box to one column.

Create Text Columns

1. Select the text box.

2. Click the **Formatting Palette** tab on the Toolbox.

3. Click the **Alignment and Spacing** panel to expand it.

4. Click the **Columns** button, and then select the number of columns you want from 1 to 4.

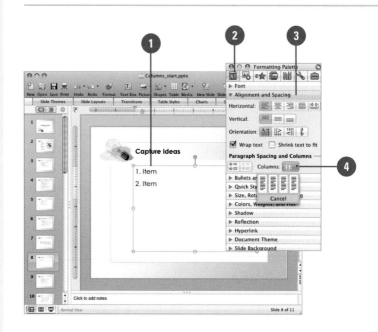

Create Multiple Text Columns and Adjust Column Spacing

1. Select the text box.

2. Click the **Format** menu, and then click **Columns**.

3. Click the **Number of columns** up and down arrow, or enter a specific number.

4. Click the **Spacing between columns** up and down arrow, or enter a specific size.

5. Click **OK**.

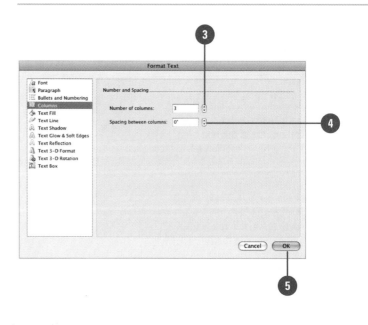

Changing Text Spacing

PowerPoint enables you to control the way text lines up on the slide. You can align text horizontally to the left or right, to the center, or to both left and right (justify) in a text object. You can also align text vertically to the top, middle, or bottom within a text object. In addition to vertical text alignment in a text object, you can also adjust the vertical space between selected lines and the space before and after paragraphs. You set specific line spacing settings before and after paragraphs in points. A **point** is equal to about 1/72 of an inch (or .0138 inches) and is used to measure the height of characters. Points are typically used in graphics and desktop publishing programs.

Adjust Line Spacing Quickly

1. Select the text box.

2. Click the **Formatting Palette** tab on the Toolbox.

3. Click the **Alignment and Spacing** panel to expand it.

4. Click the paragraph spacing option you want:

   ◆ Click the **Increase Paragraph Spacing** button to move paragraph spacing up.

   ◆ Click the **Decrease Paragraph Spacing button** to move paragraph spacing down.

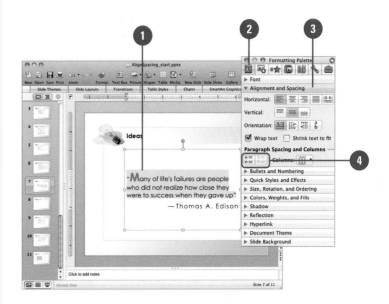

Adjust Line Spacing Exactly

1. Select the text box.

2. Click the **Format** menu, and then click **Paragraph**.

3. Click the **Before** or **After** up or down arrows to specify a setting.

4. Click the **Line Spacing** drop-down, and then select a setting.

   If you select Exactly or Multiple, specify at what spacing you want.

5. Click **OK**.

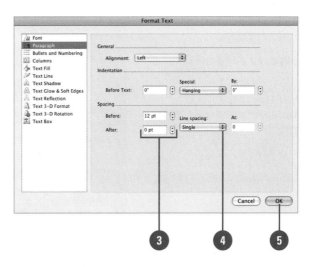

Rearranging Slides

You can instantly rearrange slides in Outline or Slides pane in Normal view or in Slide Sorter view. You can use the drag-and-drop method or the Cut and Paste buttons to move slides to a new location. In the Outline pane, you can also collapse the outline to its major points (titles) so you can more easily see its structure and rearrange slides, and then expand it back.

Rearrange a Slide in Slide Pane or Slide Sorter View

1. Click **Slides** pane in Normal view or click the **Slide Sorter View** button.

2. Select the slide(s) you want to move.

3. Drag the selected slide to a new location.

   A vertical bar appears where the slide(s) will be moved when you release the mouse button.

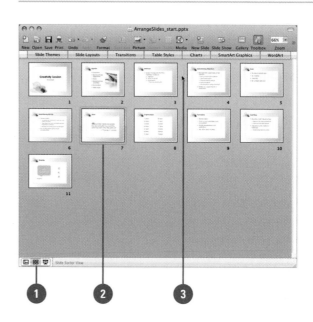

Move a Slide Using Cut and Paste

1. In the Outline or Slides pane or in Slide Sorter view, select the slide(s) you want to move.

2. Click the **Edit** menu, and then click **Cut**.

   The Clipboard task pane might open, displaying items you have cut or copied.

3. Click the new location.

4. Click the Edit menu, and then click **Paste**.

Rearrange a Slide in the Outline Pane

1. In the Outline pane in Normal view, select the slide(s) icons you want to move.

   TIMESAVER *To select slides in a sequence, click the first slide, hold down the Shift key, and then click the last slide. To select multiple slides, use the Control key.*

2. Drag the selected slide up or down to move it in Outline pane to a new location.

   A vertical bar appears where the slide(s) will be moved when you release the mouse button.

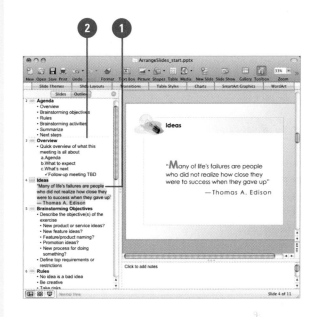

Collapse and Expand Slides in the Outline Pane

1. In the Outline pane in Normal view, select the slide text you want to work with.

2. Do any of the following:

   - To collapse selected or all slides, click the **Collapse** or **Collapse All** button on the Outlining toolbar.

     A horizontal line appears below a collapsed slide in Outline view.

   - To expand selected or all slides, click the **Expand** or **Expand All** button on the Outlining toolbar.

   TIMESAVER *Double-click a slide icon in the Outline pane to collapse or expand it.*

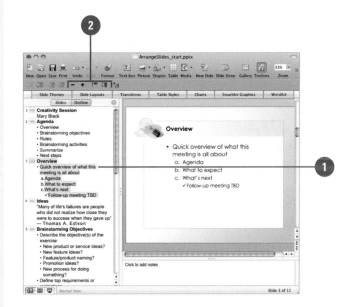

Using Slides from Other Presentations

To insert slides from other presentations in a slide show, you can open the presentation and copy and paste the slides you want, or you can use the **Slide Finder** feature. With Slide Finder, you don't have to open the presentation first; instead, you view a **miniature** of each slide in a presentation, and then insert only the ones you select. With Slide Finder, you can also create a list of favorite presentations for use in future slide shows.

Insert Slides from Another Presentation

1. Click the **Insert** menu, point to **Slides From**, and then click **Other Presentation**.

2. Click the **Insert all slides** or **Select slides to insert** option.

   If you selected Insert all slides, all the slides are inserted into your presentation. If you selected Select slides to insert,

3. Locate and select the file you want.

4. Click **Insert**.

5. Select the slides you want to insert.

   ◆ To insert just one slide, click the slide, and then click **Insert**.

   ◆ To insert multiple slides, click each slide you want to insert, and then click **Insert**.

   ◆ To insert all the slides in the presentation, click **Insert All**.

   ◆ To keep the slide design, select the **Keep design of original slides** check box. Clear the check box to use the slide design of the active presentation.

6. When you're done, click **Close**.

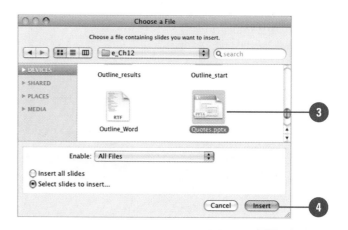

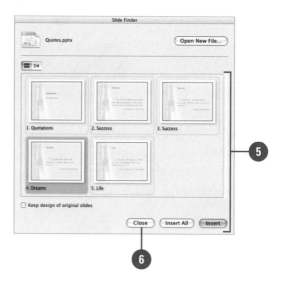

Making Your Presentation Look Consistent

Each PowerPoint presentation comes with a set of **masters**: slide, notes, and handout. A master controls the properties of each corresponding slide or page in a presentation. For example, when you make a change on a slide master, the change affects every slide. If you place your company logo, other artwork, the date and time, or slide number on the slide master, the element will appear on every slide.

Each master contains placeholders and a theme (New!) to help you create a consistent looking presentation. A placeholder provides a consistent place on a slide or page to store text and information. A theme provides a consistent look, which incorporates a color theme, effects, fonts, and slide background style. Placeholders appear on the layouts associated with the master. The notes and handout masters use one layout while the slide master uses multiple layouts. Each master includes a different set of placeholders,

which you can show or hide at any time. For example, the slide master includes master title and text placeholders, which control the text format for every slide in a presentation, while the handout master includes header, footer, date, page number, and body placeholders. You can modify and arrange placeholders on all of the master views to include the information and design you want.

You can also view and make changes to a master—either slide, notes, or handout—in one of the master views, which you can access using the Master submenu on the View menu. When you view a master, the Master toolbar appears, which allows you to insert new master pages and layout along with other master page elements, such as titles and footers. The Master toolbar also includes a Close Master button, which returns you to the view you were in before you opened the master.

Slide Master view

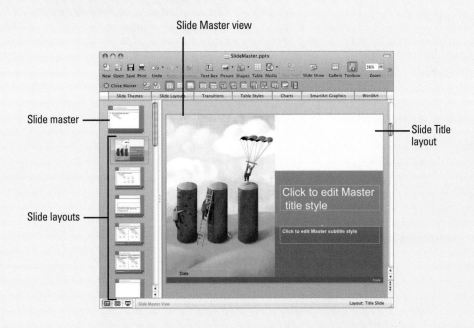

Slide master

Slide layouts

Slide Title layout

Controlling Slide Appearance with Masters

If you want an object, such as a company logo or clip art, to appear on every slide in your presentation, place it on the **Slide Master**. All of the characteristics of the Slide Master (background color, text color, font, and font size) appear on every slide. However, if you want an object to appear on a certain slide type, place it on a slide layout (**New!**) in Slide Master view. The Master toolbar contains several buttons to insert masters, layouts, and placeholder. You can create unique slides that don't follow the format of the masters. You can also arrange the placeholders the way you want them.

Include an Object on Every Slide or Only Specific Slides

1. Click the **View** menu, point to **Master**, and then click **Slide Master**.

    TIMESAVER *Hold down the Shift key, and then click the Normal View button.*

2. Add the objects you want to a slide master or slide layout, and then modify its size and placement.

    ◆ **Slide master.** Includes object on every slide.

    Slide master is the top slide miniature in the left column.

    ◆ **Slide layout.** Includes object only on the specific layout.

3. Click the **Close Master** button on the Master toolbar.

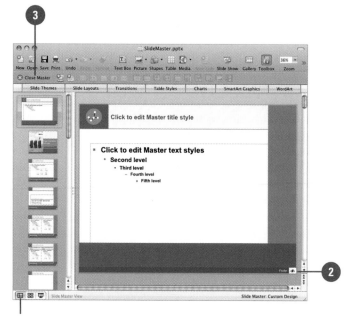

Hold down the shift key and click to display Slide Master view

Did You Know?

You can rename a slide master. Select the slide master you want to rename in Slide Master view, click the Edit menu, click Rename Slide Master, type a new name, click Rename, and then click the Close Master button on the Master toolbar.

Insert a New Slide Master

1. Click the **View** menu, point to **Master**, and then click **Slide Master**.

2. Click the **Insert New Master** button on the Master toolbar.

   The new slide master appears at the bottom of the left pane.

3. Click the **Close Master** button on the Master toolbar.

   The new slide master and associated layouts appears in the Add Slide and Layout galleries at the bottom (scroll down if necessary).

Did You Know?

You can delete a slide master. Select the slide master you want to delete in Slide Master view, press Delete (or click the Edit menu, click Delete Slide Master), and then click the Close Master button on the Master toolbar.

New slide master
and layouts

Controlling a Slide Layout with Masters

Each slide master includes a standard set of slide layouts (**New!**). If the standard layouts don't meet your specific needs, you can modify one to create a new custom slide layout, or insert and create a new custom slide layout from scratch. You can use the toolbar in Slide Master view to help you create a custom slide layout. In the Master Layout group, you can show and hide available placeholders or insert different types of placeholders (**New!**), such as Content, Text, Picture, Chart, Table, SmartArt Graphic, Media, and Clip Art.

Insert a New Slide Layout

1. Click the **View** menu, point to **Master**, and then click **Slide Master**.

2. Select the slide master in the left pane in which you want to associate a new layout.

3. Click the **Insert New Layout** button on the Master toolbar.

   The new slide layout appears at the end of the current slide layouts for the slide master.

4. Click the **Close Master** button on the Master toolbar.

Did You Know?

You can delete a slide layout. Select the slide layout you want to delete in Slide Master view, press Delete (or click the Edit menu, click Delete Slide Layout), and then click the Close Master button on the Master toolbar.

You can rename a slide layout. Select the slide layout you want to rename in Slide Master view, click the Edit menu, click Rename Layout, type a new name, click Rename, and then click the Close Master button on the Master toolbar.

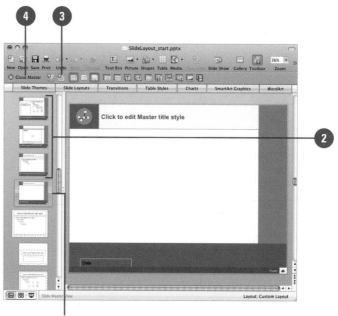

New slide layout

Create a New Slide Layout from an Existing One

1. Click the **View** menu, point to **Master**, and then click **Slide Master**.

2. Select the slide layout you want to use, click the Edit menu, and then click **Duplicate**.

   The duplicate layout appears below the original one.

3. Click the **Edit** menu, and then click **Rename Layout**.

4. Type a new layout name.

5. Click **Rename**.

6. Click the **Close Master** button on the Master toolbar.

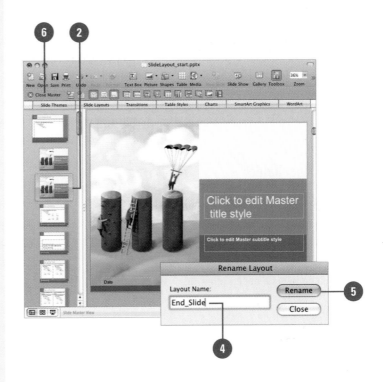

Insert a Placeholder

1. Click the **View** menu, point to **Master**, and then click **Slide Master**.

2. Select the slide layout to which you want to insert a placeholder.

3. Click the button on the Master toolbar for the placeholder you want to insert.

   The placeholder buttons include Title, Vertical Title, Footers, Content, Vertical Content, Text, Vertical Text, Table, Chart, SmartArt Graphic, Clip Art, Picture, and Media.

4. On the slide, drag to create a placeholder the size you want on the slide layout.

5. Click the **Close Master** button on the Master toolbar.

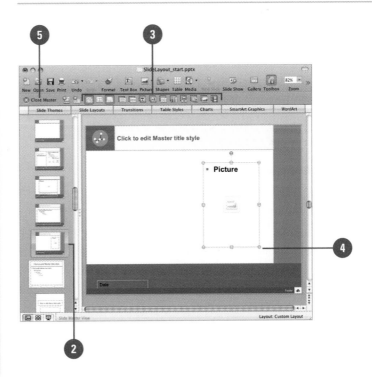

Modifying Placeholders

Each PowerPoint master comes with a different set of standard placeholders. The slide master comes with Title and Footer placeholder, while the handouts master comes with Header, Footer, Date and Time, and Page Number placeholders. If a master doesn't contain the information you need, you can modify it by reshowing the placeholders. After you display the placeholders you want, you can insert content—such as header or footer text—and format it like any other text box with the look you want. For example, you can format placeholder text using Quick styles, WordArt styles and Font and Paragraphs tools.

Reshow a Placeholder

1. Click the **View** menu, point to **Master**, and then click the master view (**Slide Master**, **Handout Master**, or **Notes Master**) you want to change.

   If a master item has been removed from the master, you can reshow it again.

2. If you're in Slide Master view, select the slide master or slide layout you want to change.

3. Use buttons on the Master toolbar, or click the **Insert** menu, point to **Master Placeholders**, and then select the command for the placeholder you want to reshow.

   IMPORTANT *If the command is grayed out, the placeholder item is already on the master.*

   - **Slide Master.** Select the Title, Date and Time, Footer, Slide Number, or Body.
   - **Handout Master.** Select the Date and Time, Header, Footer, or Page Number.
   - **Notes Master.** Select the Date and Time, Header, Footer, Page Number, Slide Image, or Body.

4. Click the **Close Master** button on the Master toolbar.

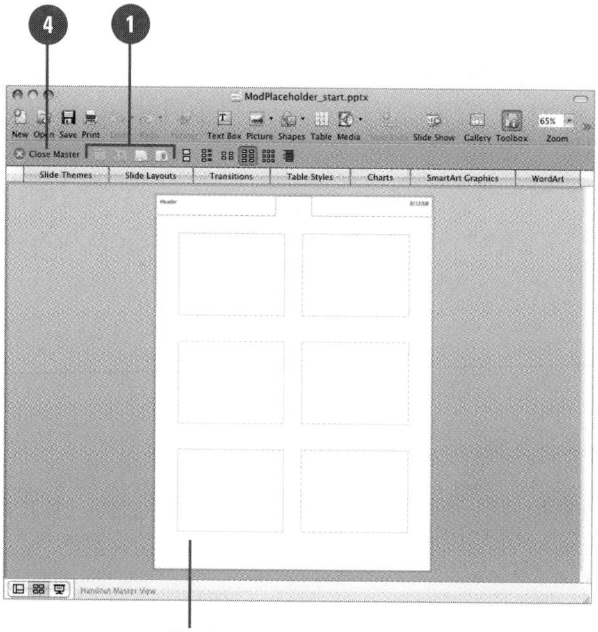

Handout Master view

Modify and Format Placeholders

① Click the **View** menu, point to **Master**, and then click the master view (**Slide Master**, **Handout Master**, or **Notes Master**) you want to change.

② If you're in Slide Master view, select the slide master or slide layout you want to change.

③ Select the placeholder you want to change.

④ To add information to a placeholder, such as a header or footer, click the text box to insert the I-beam, and then type the text you want.

⑤ To format the placeholder, use the formatting tools on the Formatting Palette tab or Formatting toolbar.

◆ Use tools in the **Font** panel and **Alignment and Spacing** panel to modify the selected placeholder.

◆ Use tools in the **Quick Styles and Effects** panel to apply Quick Styles, Shadows, Glows, Reflections, 3D- Effects, or Text Transformations to the selected placeholder.

◆ Use **WordArt** on the Elements Gallery to apply text styles to the selected placeholder.

⑥ To delete the placeholder, press the Delete key.

⑦ Click the **Close Master** button on the Master toolbar.

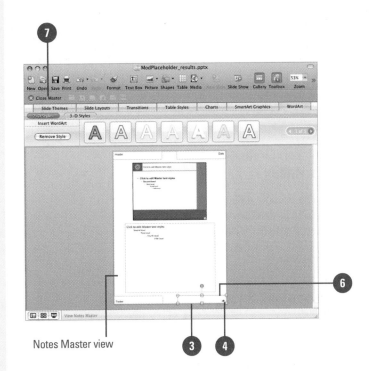

Notes Master view

Controlling a Slide Background with Masters

You may want to place an object onto most slides, but not every slide. Placing the object on the slide master saves you time. Use the Insert tab to help you insert objects. Once an object is placed on the slide master, you can hide the object in any slide you want. You can even choose to hide the object on every slide or only on specific ones. If you select the slide master in Slide Master view, you can hide background graphics on all slides. If you select a slide layout, you can hide them on the selected layout.

Hide Master Background Objects on a Slide

1. Click the **View** menu, point to **Master**, click **Slide Master**, and then select the slide master (for all slides) or slide layout (for specific slides) you want to hide background objects.

2. Click the **Formatting Palette** tab on the Toolbox.

3. Click the **Slide Background** panel to expand it.

4. Select the **Hide Background Graphics** check box.

5. Click the **Close Master** button on the Master toolbar.

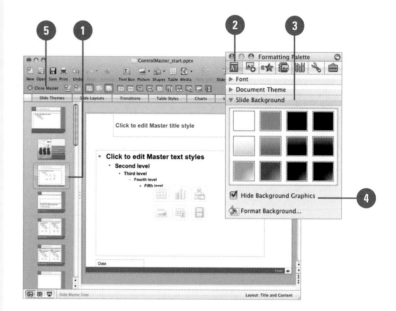

Did You Know?

You can hide background graphic or object on a single slide. Display the slide in Normal view, and then select the Hide Background Graphics check box in the Slide Background panel.

See Also

See "Making Your Presentation Look Consistent" on page 369 for information on master pages in PowerPoint.

For Your Information

Adding Background Graphics

You can add background graphics. To add graphics, such as pictures, shapes, or media, click the View menu, point to Master, and then click a master view. To insert a picture or media, click the Picture or Media button on the Standard toolbar, select a command, select the file, and then click Insert. To insert a shape, click the Shapes button on the Standard toolbar, point to a shape category, select a shape, and then draw the shape on the master. When you're done, click the Close Master button on the Master toolbar.

Adding a Background Style

In PowerPoint, you can add a background style to your presentation. A **background style** is a background fill made up of different combinations of theme colors (**New!**). When you change a presentation theme, the background styles change to reflect the new theme colors and backgrounds. You can add a background style to a master or layout in Master view or a single slide in Normal view.

Add a Background Style

1. Display a single slide in Normal view or a slide master or layout in Slide Master view.

   ◆ **Slide.** In Normal view, display the slide you want to change.

   ◆ **Slide master or slide layout.** Click the **View** menu, point to **Master**, click **Slide Master**, and then select the slide master or slide layout you want to change.

2. Click the **Formatting Palette** tab on the Toolbox.

3. Click the **Slide Background** panel to expand it.

4. Click the style you want from the gallery to apply it to the selected slide, slide master (and all its slides), or slide layout.

5. To add/change a color, picture, texture, or gradient, click **Format Background**.

> ### Did You Know?
>
> **You can reset the slide background back to white.** Display a single slide in Normal view or a slide master or layout in Slide Master view, click the Formatting Palette tab, click the Slide Background panel, and then click the Style 1 (white in the upper-left corner).

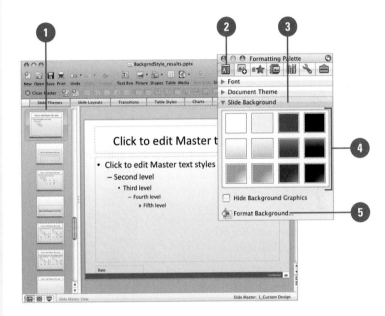

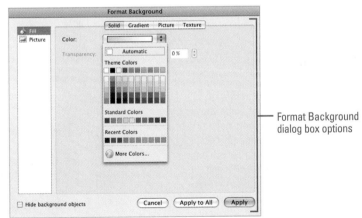

Format Background dialog box options

Inserting a Table

A **table** neatly organizes information into rows and columns. The intersection of a column and row is called a **cell**. Enter text into cells just as you would anywhere else in PowerPoint, except that pressing the Tab key moves you from one cell to the next. PowerPoint tables behave much like tables in Word. You can insert tables by specifying a size, or drawing rows and columns to create a custom table. If you like to use Microsoft Excel worksheets, you can also insert and create an Excel table in your presentation.

Insert a Table Quickly

1. In Normal view, display the slide to which you want to add a table.

2. Click the **Table** button, and then drag to select the number of rows and columns you want, or click **Insert** menu, click **Table**, enter the number of columns and rows you want, and then click **OK**.

3. Release the mouse button to insert a blank grid in the document.

   A table appears with the most recently used table style.

   The Tables Styles tab on the Elements Gallery appears, displaying all tables styles.

4. When you're done, click outside of the table.

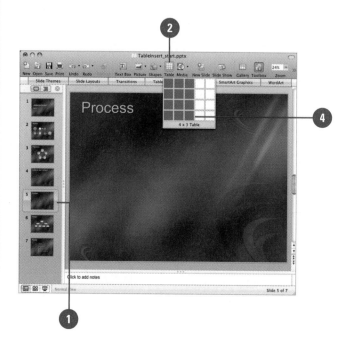

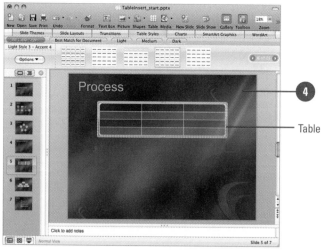

Table

Did You Know?

You can draw a custom table. In Normal view, display the slide you want, click the View menu, point to Toolbars, click Tables and Borders, click the Draw button on the toolbar, drag the table size you want, and then drag horizontal lines to create rows and vertical lines to create columns. When you're done, click outside the table.

Adding a Quick Style to a Table

Instead of changing individual attributes of a table, such as shape, border, and effects, you can quickly add them all at once with the Table Styles gallery on the Elements Gallery. The Table Style gallery (**New!**) provides a variety of different formatting combinations. In addition to applying one of the preformatted table from the Table Style gallery, you can also create your own style by shaping your text into a variety of shapes, curves, styles, and color patterns.

Add a Quick Style to a Table

1. Click the table you want to change, or select the cells you want to modify.

2. Click the **Table Styles** tab on the Elements Gallery.

3. Click a tab to narrow down the list of styles: All Table Styles, Best Match for Document, Light, Medium, or Dark.

4. Click the scroll up or down arrows to see additional styles.

5. Click the style you want from the gallery to apply it to the selected table.

   ◆ If you don't select a table or cell, PowerPoint prompts you to specify a number for columns and rows to insert a new table.

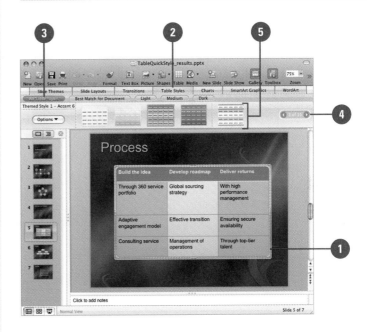

Modifying a Table

After you create a table or begin to enter text in one, you might want to add more rows or columns to accommodate the text you are entering in the table. PowerPoint makes it easy for you to format your table. You can change the alignment of the text in the cells (by default, text is aligned on the left of a cell). You can also modify the appearance and size of the cells and the table.

Insert and Delete Columns and Rows

① Click in a table cell next to where you want the new column or row to appear.

② Click the **Table** panel on the expand it.

③ Select any of the following row and column options on the Table panel:

◆ **Insert columns or rows.** Click the **Insert Table** button, and then select an insert column or row command.

◆ **Delete columns or rows.** Click the **Delete Table** button, and then select a delete column or row command.

◆ **Distribute columns or rows.** Select the columns or rows you want, and then click the **Distribute Columns Evenly or Distribute Rows Evenly** button.

◆ **Align cells, columns or rows.** Select the cells, columns, or rows you want, click the **Align** button, and then select an alignment command.

◆ **Merge cells.** Select the cells you want, click the **Merge** button.

◆ **Split cells.** Select the cell you want, click the **Split** button, specify the number of columns and rows, and then click **OK**.

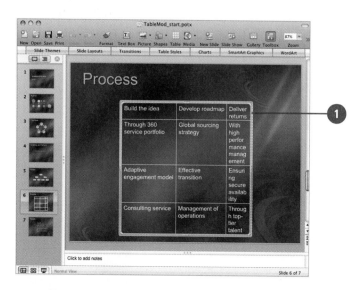

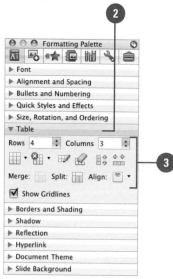

Change Cells Margins and Table Sizes

1. Select the text you want to align in the cells, rows, or columns.

2. Click the **Format** menu, and then click **Table**.

3. To set a specific size for the table, click **Size**, and then specify a height and width. To keep the size proportional, select the **Lock Aspect Ratio** check box.

   ◆ To resize the table manually, drag a corner or middle resize handle.

4. To change margins, click **Text Box**, and then specify the internal margin: **Left**, **Right**, **Top**, and **Bottom**.

5. Click **OK**.

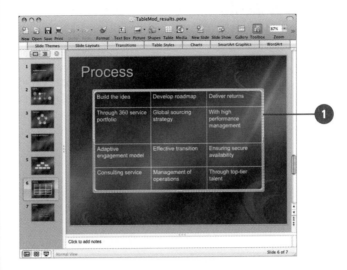

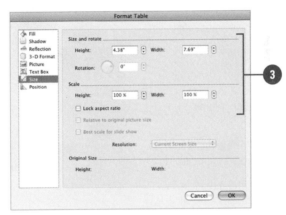

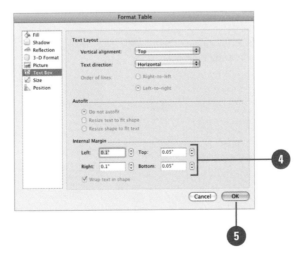

Formatting a Table

When you create a table, you typically include a header row or first column to create horizontal or vertical headings for your table information. You can use Table Quick Style options (**New!**), such as a header or total row, first or last column, or banded rows and columns, to show or hide a special row and column formatting. The Total Row option displays a row at the end of the table for column totals. The Banded Row or Banded Column option formats even rows or columns differently from odd rows or columns to make a table easier to view. You can also insert a picture into a table to create a more polished look.

Format Table Columns or Rows

① Click the table you want to change.

② Click the **Table Styles** tab on the Elements Gallery.

③ Click **Options** on the Table Styles tab, and then select any of the following row and column options:

◆ **Header Row** to format the top row of the table as special.

◆ **Total Row** to format the bottom row of the table for column totals.

◆ **First Column** to format the first column of the table as special.

◆ **Last Column** to format the last column of the table as special.

◆ **Banded Rows** to format even rows differently than odd rows.

◆ **Banded Columns** to format even columns differently than odd columns.

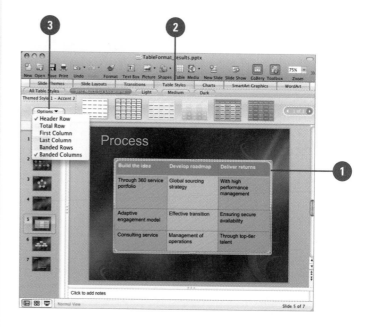

Inserting Special Characters

PowerPoint comes with a host of symbols and special characters for every need. Insert just the right one to keep from compromising a document's professional appearance with a hand-drawn arrow («) or missing mathematical symbol (å). You can insert symbols by using the Object Palette on the Toolbox. If you can't find the symbol you're looking for, you can also use the Special Characters command on the Edit menu to find other characters.

Insert Special Characters

1. Click the document where you want to insert a symbol or character.

2. Click the **Edit** menu, and then click **Special Characters**.

3. To see other symbols, click the **View** drop-down, and then click a new language type.

4. Click the **by Category** tab.

5. Click a category in the left pane.

6. Click a symbol or character.

7. Click the triangle next to Character Info or Font Variation to display more content related to the symbol or character.

8. To add this symbol or character to your favorites, click the **Actions** button, and then click **Add to Favorites**.

   ◆ You can click the Favorites tab to access it.

9. Click **Insert**.

10. Click the **Close** button.

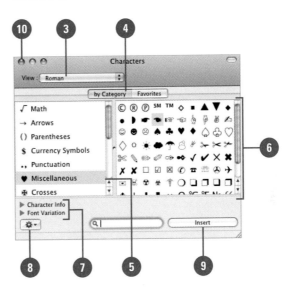

Creating a Text Box

Usually you use the title and bulleted list placeholders to place text on a slide. However, when you want to add text outside one of the standard placeholders, such as for an annotation to a slide or shape text, you can create a text box. Text boxes appear in all views and panes, except in the Outline pane. When you place text in a shape, the text becomes part of object. You can format and change the object using Font options, as well as Shape and WordArt styles. You can also adjust the text margins with a text box or a shape to create the look you want.

Create a Text Box

1. In Normal view, click the **Text Box** button on the Standard toolbar.

2. Perform one of the following:
   - To add text that wraps, drag to create a box, and then start typing.
   - To add text that doesn't wrap, click and then start typing.

3. To delete a text box, select it, and the press Delete.

4. Click outside the selection box to deselect the text box.

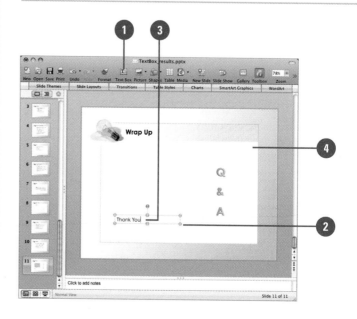

Wrap and Adjust Text Margins

1. Select an object with text.

2. Click the **Format** menu, and then click **Shape**.

3. In the left pane, click **Text Box**.

4. Select the **Wrap text in shape** check box.

5. Use the Internal margin **up** and **down** arrows to change the left, right, top, and bottom slides of the shape.

6. Click **OK**.

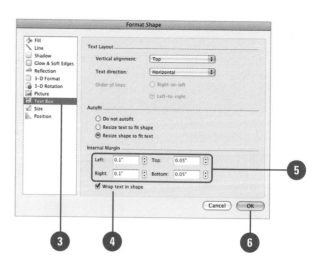

Delivering a Presentation with PowerPoint

13

Introduction

When you're done preparing your slide show, it's time to consider how to show it to your audience. Microsoft PowerPoint 2008 gives you several ways to give and share your presentations. When you are presenting the show in person, you can use PowerPoint's slide navigation tools to move around your presentation. You can move forward and backward or move to a specific slide by using various navigation keys on the keyboard and on-screen Slide Show tools.

As you're presenting your slide show, you can highlight key ideas by using the mouse as a pointer or pen/highlighter. By annotating your slide show, you can give extra emphasis on a topic or goal for your audience. Annotations can be saved as enhancements to your presentation for later. If you are presenting a slide show using a second monitor or projection screen, PowerPoint includes the tools you need to properly navigate the display equipment.

If you are taking your presentation to another site, you might not need the entire PowerPoint package. Rather than installing PowerPoint on the sites' computer, you can pack your presentation into one compressed file, storing it on a CD. Once you reach your destination, you can expand the compressed file onto your client's computer and play it, regardless of whether that computer has PowerPoint installed.

What You'll Do

Change Page Setup Options

Add Animation

Use Specialized Animation

Coordinate Multiple Animations

Add Slide Timings

Create Slide Transitions

Record a Narration

Insert Movies and Sounds

Set Movie and Sound Play Options

Set Up a Slide Show

Create a Custom Slide Show

Start and Navigate a Slide Show

Use View Presenter Tools

Annotate a Slide Show

Save a Presentation as a Movie

Save a Presentation as a Slide Show

Prepare Handouts and Speaker Notes

Add Comments to a Presentation

Add a Footer and Header

Insert the Date, Time and Slide Numbers

Print a Presentation

Changing Page Setup Options

Before you print a presentation, you can use the Page Setup dialog box to set the proportions of your presentation slides—standard and wide screen (**New!**)—and their orientation on the page. You can also control slide numbering in the Number Slides From box. For a new presentation, PowerPoint opens with default slide page settings: on-screen slide show, landscape orientation, and slides starting at number one. Notes, handouts, and outlines are printed in portrait orientation.

Control Slide Size

1 Click the **File** menu, and then click **Page Setup**.

2 Click the **Slides sized for** drop-down.

3 Click the size you want.

- ◆ **On-Screen Show** for slides that fit computer monitor with ratios of 4:3 (standard), 16:9 (wide screen HDTV's) (**New!**), or 16:10 (wide screen laptops) (**New!**).

- ◆ **Letter Paper** for slides that fit on 8.5-by-11-inch paper.

- ◆ **Ledger Paper** for slides that fit on 11-by-17-inch paper.

- ◆ **A3 Paper**, **A4 Paper**, **B4 (ISO) Paper**, or **B5 (ISO) Paper** for slides that fit on international paper.

- ◆ **35mm Slides** for 11.25-by-7.5-inch slides.

- ◆ **Overhead** for 10-by-7.5-inch slides that fit transparencies.

- ◆ **Banner** for 8-by-1-inch slides that are typically used as advertisements on a Web page.

- ◆ **Custom** to enter the measurements you want in the width and height boxes.

4 To orient your slides, notes, handouts, and outline, click the **Portrait** or **Landscape** option.

5 Click **OK**.

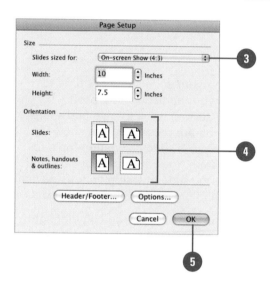

For Your Information

Using Portrait and Landscape Together

In PowerPoint, you can have only one slide orientation in a presentation. However, if you want to use portrait and landscape slide orientation in the same presentation, you can do it by creating a link between two presentations. For best results, place both presentations in the same folder on your computer. First, you create a link from the first presentation to the second presentation, and then create a link from the second presentation back. See "Creating a Hyperlink" on page 484 for instructions on creating a link to another presentation.

Adding Animation

You can use animation to introduce objects onto a slide one at a time or with animation effects. For example, a bulleted list can appear one bulleted item at a time, or a picture can fade in gradually. The easiest way to apply animation is to use buttons on the Custom Animation tab on the Toolbox. You can also design your own customized animations, including those with your own special effects and sound elements.

Apply a Standard Animation Effect to Text or an Object

1. Select the text or object you want to animate.

2. Click the **Custom Animation** tab on the Toolbox.

3. Click an Add Effect button (**Add Entrance Effect**, **Add Emphasis Effect**, **Add Exit Effect**, or **Add Media Effect**).

4. Click the animation you want.

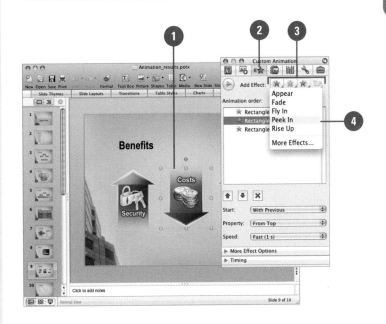

Preview an Animation

1. In Normal view, display the slide containing the animation you want to preview.

2. Click the **Custom Animation** tab on the Toolbox.

3. Select the animation you want.

4. Click the **Play** button.

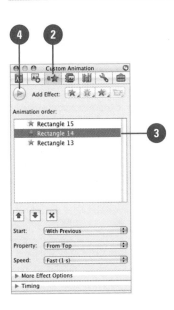

Did You Know?

You can view a slide's animation quickly in Slide Sorter view. In Slide Sorter view, click a slide's animation icon to view the animation.

Using Specialized Animations

Using specialized animations, you can apply animations specific to certain objects. For example, for a text object, you can introduce the text on your slide all at once or by word or letter. Similarly, you can introduce bulleted lists one bullet item at a time and apply different effects to older items, such as graying the items out as they are replaced by new ones. You can animate charts by introducing chart series or chart categories one at a time.

Animate Text

① In Normal view, select the text object you want to animate.

② Click the **Custom Animation** tab on the Toolbox.

③ Click an Add Effect button, and then choose an effect from the animation list.

④ Click the **Text Animations** panel to expand it.

⑤ Click the **Animate Text** drop-down, and then click the effect you want.

⑥ Click the **Play** button.

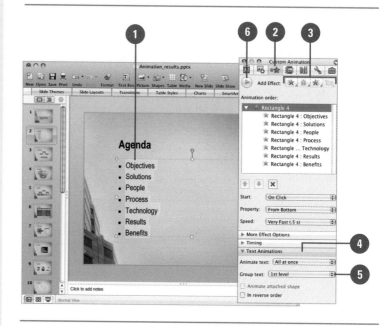

Animate Bulleted Lists

① In Normal view, select the bulleted text you want to animate.

② Click the **Custom Animation** tab on the Toolbox.

③ Click an Add Effect button, and then choose an effect from the animation list.

④ Click the **Text Animations** panel to expand it.

⑤ Click the **Group text** drop-down, and then click at what paragraph level bulleted text will be animated.

⑥ Click the **Play** button.

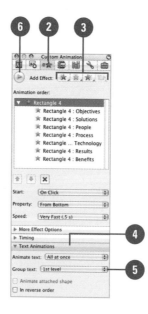

Dim Text After Its Animated

1. In Normal view, select the text you want to animate.

2. Click the **Custom Animation** tab on the Toolbox.

3. Click an Add Effect button, and then choose an effect from the animation list.

4. Click the **More Effect Options** panel to expand it.

5. Click the **After Animation** drop-down, and then click the dim text color or option you want. Click **Don't Dim** to remove the effect.

6. Click the **Play** button.

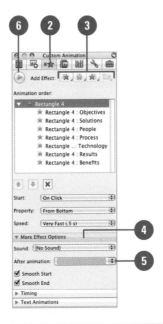

Animate Chart Elements

1. In Normal view, select the chart you want to animate.

2. Click the **Custom Animation** tab on the Toolbox.

3. Click an Add Effect button, and then choose an effect from the animation list.

4. Click the **Chart Animation** panel to expand it.

5. Click the **Group Chart** drop-down, and then click the order you want to introduce chart elements.

6. Select the **Start animation by drawing the chart background** check box to animate the chart background first.

7. Click the **Play** button.

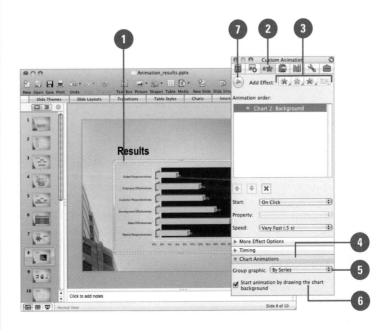

Coordinating Multiple Animations

The Custom Animation task pane helps you keep track of your presentation's animations by listing all animated objects in a single location. Use these lists if your slides contain more than one animation, because they help you determine how the animations will work together. For example, you can control the animation of each object, the order each object appears, the time between animation effects, and remove unwanted animations.

Add Multiple Animation Effects to Slide Objects

1. In Normal view, select the slide object you want to animate.

2. Click the **Custom Animation** tab on the Toolbox.

3. Click an Add Effect button, and then choose an effect from the animation list.

4. Click the **Start**, **Direction**, or **Speed** drop-down, and then select the option you want.

5. Repeat Steps 1 through 4 to create multiple animation effects.

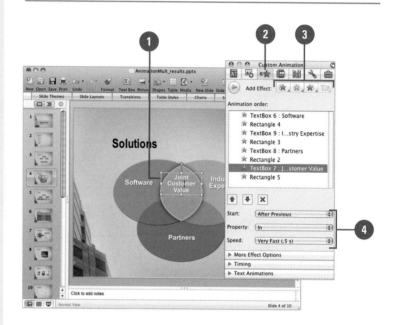

Modify the Animation Order

1. In Normal view, select the slide object you want to animate.

2. Click the **Custom Animation** tab on the Toolbox.

3. In the Animation Order list, select the animation you want to move.

   ◆ If a triangle appears next to an animation, click it to expand the animation associated with the object.

4. Click the **Re-Order Up** or **Down** arrow button.

5. Click the **Play** button.

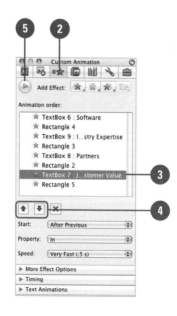

Set Time Between Animations

1 In Normal view, select the slide object you want to animate.

2 Click the **Custom Animation** tab on the Toolbox.

3 Click the **Start** drop-down, and then click **After Previous**.

4 Click the **Timing** panel to expand it.

5 Use the **Delay** arrows to select the number of seconds between this animation and the previous event.

Remove an Animation

1 In Normal view, select the slide object you want to change.

2 Click the **Custom Animation** tab on the Toolbox.

3 In the Animation Order list, select the animation you want to remove.

4 Click the **Delete** button.

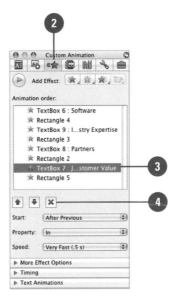

Did You Know?

You can add sound to an animation. In Normal view, select the slide object you want to add a sound, click the Custom Animation tab on the Toolbox, select the animation you want, click the More Effect Options panel to expand it, click the Sound drop-down, and then select a sound or click Other Sound to insert your own.

Adding Slide Timings

Use PowerPoint's timing features to make sure that your presentation is not too long or too fast. You can specify the amount of time given to each slide or use Rehearse Timings, which ensures that your timings are legitimate and workable. By rehearsing timings, you can vary the amount of time each slide appears on the screen. If you want the timings to take effect, make sure the show is set to use timings in the Set Up Show dialog box.

Set Timings Between Slides

① Click the slide(s) to which you want to set slide timings.

◆ You can select slide(s) in the Slides pane in Normal view or in Slide Sorter view.

② Click the **Transitions** tab on the Elements Gallery.

③ Click **Options** on the Transitions tab.

④ Select the **Automatically after X seconds** check box.

⑤ Enter the time (in seconds) before the presentation automatically advances to the next slide after displaying the entire slide.

⑥ Click **Apply**.

◆ To apply the settings to all slides in your presentation, click **Apply to All**.

Did You Know?

You can use the mouse to control slide timings. In Slide Show View, a mouse click always advances a slide, even if the set timing has not elapsed, and holding down the mouse button prevents a timed transition from occurring until you release the mouse button.

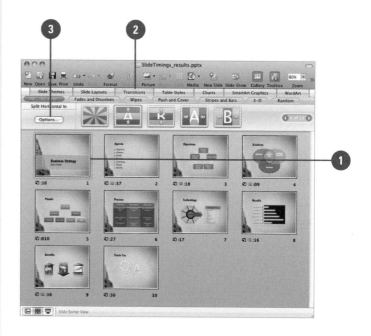

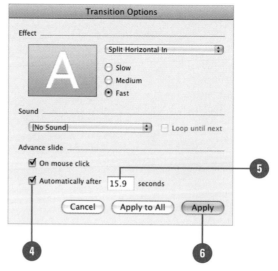

Create Timings Through Rehearsal

1 Click the **Slide Show** menu, and then click **Rehearse Timings**.

2 As the slide show runs, rehearse your presentation by clicking or pressing Return to go to the next transition or slide.

3 When you're done, click **Yes** or **No** to accept the timings.

4 Click **Yes** or **No** to review and edit individual timings in Slide Sorter view.

5 To test timings, start the slide show and note when the slides advance too quickly or too slowly.

Edit Timings

1 Click the **Slide Sorter View** button.

2 Click the slide whose timing you want to change.

3 Click the **Transitions** tab on the Elements Gallery.

4 Click **Options** on the Transitions tab.

5 Enter a new value in the Seconds box.

6 Click **Apply**.

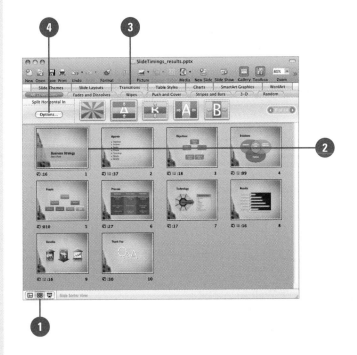

Rehearsal timing

Creating Slide Transitions

If you want to give your presentation more visual interest, you can add transitions between slides using the Elements Gallery (**New!**). For example, you can create a fading out effect so that one slide fades out as it is replaced by a new slide, or you can have one slide appear to push another slide out of the way. You can also add sound effects to your transitions, though you need a sound card and speakers to play them. When you add a transition effect to a slide, the effect takes place between the previous slide and the selected slide.

Specify a Transition

1 In Normal view, click the **Slides** tab in the Slides pane.

2 Click the slide(s) to which you want to add a transition effect.

3 Click the **Transitions** tab on the Elements Gallery.

4 Click a category tab to display the type of transition style you want.

5 Click the transition effect you want.

◆ You can click the arrows on the right to display more styles.

6 To remove a slide transition, click the **No Transition** style.

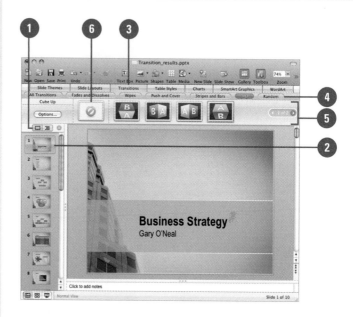

Apply a Transition to All Slides in a Presentation

1 Click the **Transitions** tab on the Elements Gallery.

2 Click **Options** on the Transitions tab.

3 Click the **Transition** drop-down, and then select a transition.

4 Click the **Slow**, **Medium**, or **Fast** option.

5 Click **Apply to All**.

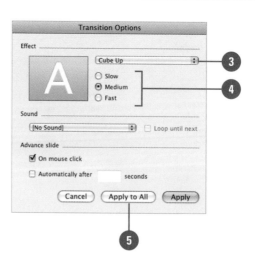

Recording a Narration

If you are creating a self-running presentation, you might want to add a narration to emphasize the points you make. PowerPoint lets you record your own narration as you rehearse your slide show. You can record a narration before you run a slide show, or you can record it during the presentation and include audience comments. As you record the narration, you can pause or stop the narration at any time. When you play back a narration, the recording is synchronized with the presentation, including all slide transitions and animations. You can also delete a voice narration, as with any other PowerPoint object. You will need a microphone and a computer with a sound card to record the narration.

Record a Narration

1 Click the **Slide Show** menu, and then click **Record Narration**.

2 Click the **Sound input device** drop-down, and then select a device with a microphone.

3 Click the **Input source** drop-down, and then select an input device.

4 If necessary, select the **Link narrations** check box to insert the narration as a linked object.

◆ Click **Set** to specify a folder where you want to store the linked narrations.

5 Click **Record**.

6 Speak clearly into the microphone and record your narration for each slide.

To pause or resume the narration, Control-click anywhere on the screen, and then click Pause Narration, or Resume Narration.

7 Click **Yes** or **No** when prompted to save slide timings along with your narration.

8 Click **Yes** or **No** to review and edit individual timings in Slide Sorter view.

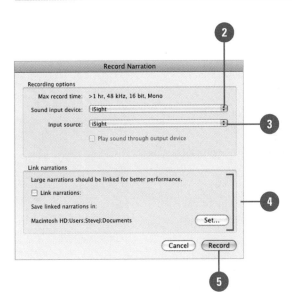

Inserting Movies and Sounds

You can insert movies or sounds into a presentation by inserting them from the Clip Art task pane or a file. Movies can be either animated pictures—also known as animated GIFs, such as cartoons—or they can be digital videos. Movies and sounds are inserted as objects. When you insert a sound, a small icon appears representing the sound. PowerPoint supports the following audio file formats (AIFF, AU, MP3, WAV, WMA), and video file formats (ASF, AVI, MPG or MPEG, WMV).

Insert a Movie or Sound from a File

1. Click the **Media** button on the Standard toolbar.

2. Click **Insert Movie** or **Insert Sound and Music**.

3. Locate and select a movie or sound file.

4. Click **Choose** (movie) or **Insert** (sound).

5. When a message is displayed, do one of the following:

   To play the media clip automatically when you go to the slide, click **Automatically**.

   To play the media clip only when you click it, click **When Clicked**.

6. To play a movie or sound, double-click it, and then click the **Play** button, if necessary.

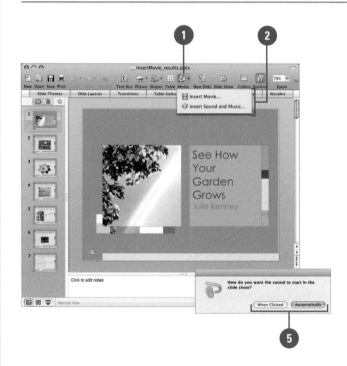

Did You Know?

You can record and insert a sound. Click the Insert menu, point to Sound and Music, click Record Sound, type a name for the sound, select an input device, click the Record button, record a sound, and then click the Stop button. Click Play to hear it. When you're done, click Save.

Setting Movie and Sound Play Options

After you insert movie, sound, or CD audio objects, you can set play options to determine how they will play back. You can change settings so they play continuously or just one time. Movies and sounds can play in either Normal view or Slide Show view. You can also view and play movies using the full screen. PowerPoint supports the following audio file formats (AIFF, AU, MP3, WAV, WMA), and video file formats (ASF, AVI, MPG or MPEG, WMV, QuickTime). To play sound and movies, you need to have the appropriate media player, such as QuickTime, installed on your computer, which you can download from the Web. You can download QuickTime at *www.quicktime.com*.

Change Movie or Sound Play Options

1. Click the movie object you want to change options.

2. Click the **Custom Animations** tab on the Toolbox.

3. Click the **Media Options** panel to expand it.

4. Change the available movie or sound settings: **After current slide** or **After X slides**, **Hide while not playing**, or **Rewind after playing**.

5. Click the **Formatting Palette** tab.

6. Click the **Movie** or **Sound** panel to expand it.

7. Change the available movie or sound settings: **Play**, **Volume**, **Play Full Screen** (Movie), **Hide During Slide Show**, **Loop Until Stopped**, **Rewind After Playing** (Movie), or **Show Controller** (Movie).

Did You Know?

You can movie options in preferences. Click the PowerPoint menu, click Preferences, click the General icon, click Movie Options, select the options (Size and quality, Media settings, and Save) you want, and then click OK twice.

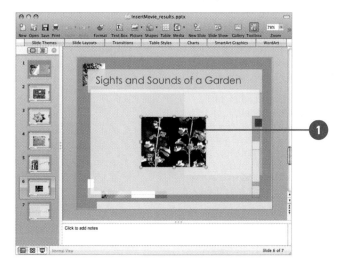

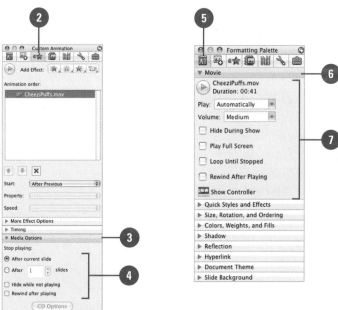

Setting Up a Slide Show

PowerPoint offers several types of slide shows appropriate for a variety of presentation situations, from a traditional big-screen slide show to a show that runs automatically on a computer screen at a conference kiosk. When you don't want to show all of the slides in a PowerPoint presentation to a particular audience, you can specify only a range of slides to show, or you can hide individual slides. You can also save a presentation to open directly into Slide Show view or run continuously.

Set Up a Show

1 Click the **Slide Show** menu, and then click **Set Up Slide Show**.

2 Choose the show type you want.

- ◆ Click the **Presented by a speaker (full screen)** option to run a full screen slide show.

- ◆ Click the **Browsed by an individual (window)** option to run a slide show in a window and allow access to some PowerPoint commands.

- ◆ Click the **Browsed at a kiosk (full screen)** option to create a self-running, unattended slide show for a booth or kiosk.

3 Select or clear the following show options check boxes:

- ◆ **Loop continuously until 'Esc'.** Select to replay the slide show again until you stop it.

- ◆ **Show without narration.** Select to not play narration.

- ◆ **Show without animation.** Select to not play animation.

- ◆ **Show scrollbar.** Select to display the scroll bar.

4 Select the **Manually** or **Using timings, if present** option, where you can advance the slides manually or automatically.

5 Click **OK**.

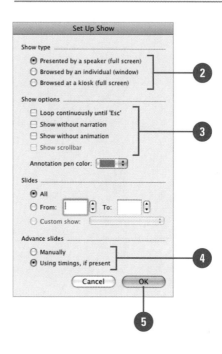

Show a Range of Slides

① Click the **Slide Show** menu, and then click **Set Up Slide Show**.

② Click the **From** option.

③ Enter the first and last slide numbers of the range you want to show.

④ Click **OK**.

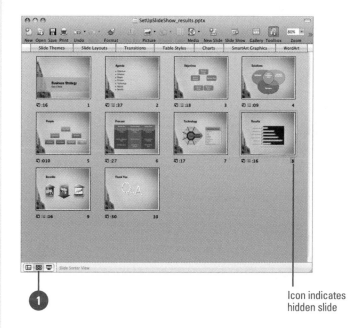

Icon indicates hidden slide

Hide Slides

① In Slide Sorter view or Normal view, select or display the slide you want to hide.

② Click the **Slide Show** menu, and then click **Hide Slide**.

The slide number in the Slide pane or Slide Sorter view appears with circle and a line through it.

③ To show a hidden slide, click it, click the **Slide Show** menu, and then click **Hide Slide** again.

Did You Know?

You can run a slide show continuously. Open the presentation you want to run, click the Slide Show menu, click Set Up Show, select the Loop Continuously Until 'Esc' check box, and then click OK.

Creating a Custom Slide Show

If you plan to present a slide show to more than one audience, you don't have to create a separate slide show for each audience. Instead, you can create a custom slide show that allows you to specify which slides from the presentation you will use and the order in which they will appear. You can also edit a custom show which you've already created. Add, remove, and rearrange slides in a custom show to fit your various needs.

Create a Custom Slide Show

1. Click the **Slide Show** , and then click **Custom Slide Show**.

2. Click **New**.

3. Type a name for the show.

4. Click the slide(s) you want, and then click **Add**. To remove a slide, select it in the Slides in custom show list, and then click **Remove**.

5. Click **OK**.

6. Click **Edit** to modify the selected custom slide show, or click **Remove** to delete the selected one.

7. Click **Close**.

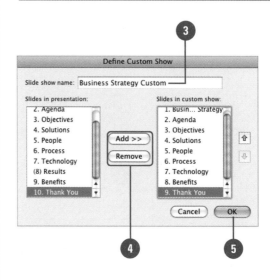

Show a Custom Slide Show

1. Click the **Slide Show** , and then click **Custom Slide Show**.

2. Click the custom slide show you want to run.

3. Click **Show**.

Did You Know?

You can print a custom show. Click the File menu, click Print, click the Custom Show option, click the Slide Show drop-down, select a custom show, and then click Print.

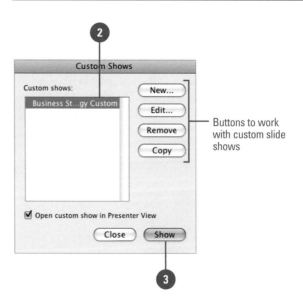

Buttons to work with custom slide shows

Starting and Navigating a Slide Show

Once you have set up your slide show, you can start the show at any time. In Slide Show view, you advance to the next slide by clicking the mouse button, pressing the Spacebar, or pressing Return. In addition to those basic navigational techniques, PowerPoint provides keyboard shortcuts that can take you to the beginning, the end, or any particular slide. You can also use the navigation commands on the shortcut menu or Slide Show button. If your Mac comes with an Apple Remote, you can use it to deliver and navigate through your slide show (**New!**).

Start and Navigate a Slide Show

1 Click the **Slide Show** menu, and then click **View Slide Show**.

> **TIMESAVER** *Click the Slide Show View button on the Status bar or press ⌘+Return to start a slide show quickly from the current slide.*

2 Move the mouse pointer to display the Slide Show button.

> **TIMESAVER** *Control-click a slide to display a shortcut menu.*

3 Click the **Slide Show** button (bottom left corner), and then select commands to move to the next or previous slide, or navigate the slide show, or end the show.

> **TIMESAVER** *Press Esc to stop a slide show.*

After a period of inactivity during a normal full-screen slide show, PowerPoint hides the pointer and Slide Show button.

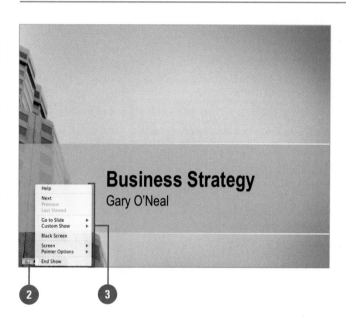

Did You Know?

You can set Slide Show options. Click the PowerPoint menu, click Preferences, click the View icon, select the slide show and pop-up toolbar check box options you want (Slide Show Navigation, Pop-up menu on Control+mouse click toolbar, or End with black slide), and then click OK.

Slide Show View Shortcuts

Action	Result
Mouse click, press Return, or Left arrow	Moves to the next slide
Press Delete or Right arrow	Moves to the previous slide
Press Page Up or Down	Moves to the previous or next slide
Press Home or End	Moves to the first or last slide in the show
Enter a slide number when and press Return	Moves to the slide number you specified you press Return
Press B	Displays a black screen; press again to return
Press W	Displays a white screen; press again to return
Press Esc	Exits Slide Show view

Annotating a Slide Show

When you are presenting your slide show, you can turn your mouse pointer into a pen tool to highlight and circle your key points. If you decide to use a pen tool, you might want to set its color to match the colors in your presentation. When you are finished, you can turn the pen back to the normal mouse pointer. Mark ups you make on a slide with the pen tool during a slide show can be saved with the presentation, and then turned on or off when you re-open the presentation for editing.

Use a Pen During the Slide Show

① In Slide Show view, move the mouse to display the Slide Show button.

② Click the **Slide Show** button, point to **Pointer Options**, and then click a pointer option.

◆ **Automatic** hides the pointer until you move the mouse.

◆ **Hidden** makes the pointer invisible throughout the presentation.

◆ **Arrow** makes the pointer appear and function as an arrow.

◆ **Pen** makes the pointer a pen, which you can draw on the screen with during the slide show.

TIMESAVER *Press* ⌘+A *and* ⌘+P *to switch between pointer and pen..*

◆ **Pen Color** select a pen ink color.

③ Drag the mouse pointer to draw on your slide presentation with the pen.

④ To remove ink, click the **Slide Show** button, point to **Screen**, and then click **Erase Pen**.

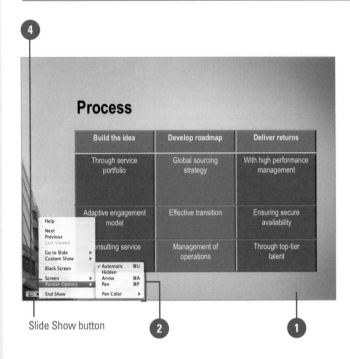

Slide Show button

Using Presenter Tools

Presenter tools allow you to present your slides on one monitor, such as a big screen, while you control your presentation on another monitor, such as a laptop, that only you can see. You can track your time, skips slides, view slide notes, and preview the next slide. Presenter tools are useful when you're ready to rehearse or give your presentation. Before you can use presenter tools, you need to set up two monitor using Displays in System Preferences. Presenter tools appear on your primary monitor (the one with the menu bar), and the audience view appears on your secondary monitor.

Use Presenter Tools

1. Click the **Slide Show** menu, and then click **View Presenter Tools.**

2. In presenter tools, use any of the following tools:

   - **Elapsed time** shows you the current presentation time.

   - **Audience view** shows you the slide show that the audience sees.

   - **Notes pane** shows you notes for the current slide in Audience view.

   - **Up Next** shows you the next slide that the audience sees in Audience view.

   - **Thumbnails** contains all the slides in the presentation. Click a thumbnail to skip all others and display it.

   - **Left and Right Arrows** allow you to navigate to the previous or next slide. You can also click the slide in Audience view to go to the next one.

3. If you want to display a help screen with keyboard shortcuts, click **Help**, and then click **OK** to close it.

4. When you're done, click **End** to close presenter tools.

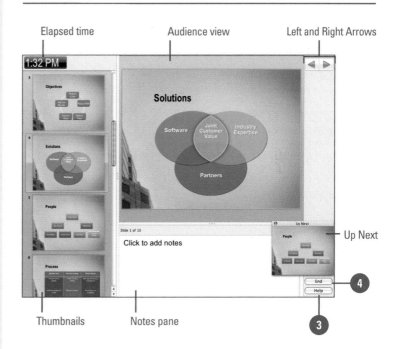

Elapsed time   Audience view   Left and Right Arrows

Up Next

Thumbnails   Notes pane

Saving a Presentation as a Movie

If you want to run your presentation on a computer that doesn't have PowerPoint 2008 installed, you can save your presentation as a PowerPoint movie with the .MOV extension, which you can play with the QuickTime Player. The QuickTime Player is available to download for free at the Apple web site at *www.apple.com*. Before you save your presentation as a movie, you can set movie options, such as Optimization, Show movie player controls, Move dimensions, Background soundtrack, and Slide transitions. The QuickTime Player doesn't support all PowerPoint slide show features, so your slide show may run differently. For example, some transitions play differently and animation effects don't play at all.

Save a Presentation as a Movie

1. Click the **File** menu, and then click **Save as Movie**.

2. Click the **Where** drop-down, and then select the location where you want to store the movie.

3. Type a name for the movie.

4. Click **Movie Options**.

5. Click the **Movie Settings** tab.

6. Select from the following movie options:

   ◆ **Optimization.** Select an option to optimize the movie for size, smooth playback, or quality.

   ◆ **Movie dimensions.** Select the screen size option that works best for your playback computer.

   ◆ **Slide transitions.** Select an option to follow slide show settings for slide transitions or not to use them.

   ◆ **Background soundtrack.** Select an option to select a soundtrack from a file or not to use one.

   ◆ **Loop Movie.** Select the check box to repeat the movie when it's done.

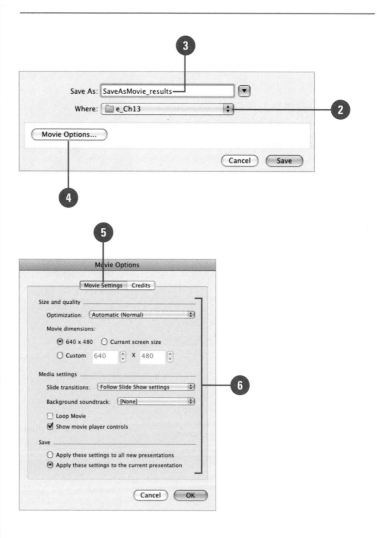

- ◆ **Show movie player controls.** Select the check box to show the movie player controls when the movie plays using the QuickTime Player.

- ◆ **Save.** Select an option to apply these settings to all new presentations or the current presentation.

7 Click the **Credits** tab.

8 Enter the information you want for the credits.

9 Click **OK**.

10 Click **Save**.

11 To play the movie using QuickTime, double-click the movie icon in the Finder, and then use the movie player controls and navigation buttons to run the movie.

The QuickTime Player needs to be installed on your computer in order to play the PowerPoint movie. You can download a free version of the QuickTime Player from the Apple web site at *www.apple.com* or from the QuickTime web site at *www.quicktime.com*.

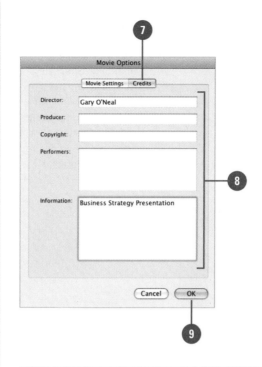

Working Together

Sending Presentation Text to a Word Document

You can send presentation text directly to a Word document. Only th title and bulleted text box based on a layout gets sent to Word. The rest of the presentation text remains in PowerPoint. Title text for a slide becomes a Heading 1 style in a Word document, while a first level of indented text becomes a heading 2 style, and so on. To send slide text to a Word document, click the File menu, point to Sent To, and then click Microsoft Word.

Saving a Presentation as a Slide Show

When you're giving a professional slide show presentation, you might not want your audience to see you start it from PowerPoint. Instead, you can save a presentation as a PowerPoint Show to open directly into Slide Show view. You can use the Save As dialog box to save a presentation as a PowerPoint Show (.ppsx) or PowerPoint Macro-Enabled (.ppsm). After you save a presentation as a PowerPoint Show file, you can create a shortcut to it on your desktop and then simply double-click the PowerPoint Show file to start it directly in Slide Show view.

Save a Presentation as a PowerPoint Show

1. Click the **File** menu, and then click **Save As**.

2. Type a presentation show file name.

3. Click the **Where** drop-down, and then select the location where you want to save the file.

4. Click the **Format** drop-down, and then click **PowerPoint Show (.ppsx)** or **PowerPoint Macro-Enabled Show (.ppsm)**.

5. Click **Save**.

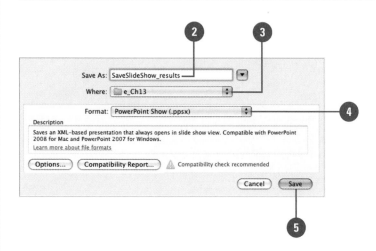

Did You Know?

You can save slides as pictures. Click the File menu, click Save as Picture, type a name for the pictures, select the location where you want to save the pictures, and then select a format for the pictures. Click Options to select save settings, such as current slide or all slides, resolution, and compression, and then click OK. When you're done, click Save.

Working Together

Saving a Presentation to iPhoto

In addition to saving a presentation as a movie, you can also save a presentation as a series of slides to an iPhoto album (**New!**), which you can sync and playback in a video iPod. Open the presentation you want to use, click the File menu, point to Send To, click iPhoto, enter a name for the new album that stores the images, select a format from the Format drop-down, click the All or Selected option, and then click Send to iPhoto.

Preparing Handouts

Prepare your handouts in the Print dialog box, where you can specify what to print. You can customize your handouts by formatting them in the handout master first, using the formatting and drawing tools. You can also add a header and footer to include the date, slide number, and page number, for example. In the Print dialog box, you can choose to print one, two, three, four, six, or nine slides per page.

Format the Handout Master

1. Click the **View** menu, point to **Master**, and then click **Handout Master**.

2. Click the button with how many slides you want per page.

3. To add a background style, click the background, click the **Slide Background** panel to expand it, and then click a style.

4. Use the formatting tools on the Formatting Palette tab or Formatting toolbar to format the handout master placeholders.

5. If you want, add objects to the handout master that you want to appear on every page, such as a picture or a text object.

6. Click the **Close Master** button on the Master toolbar.

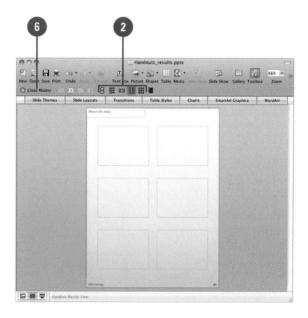

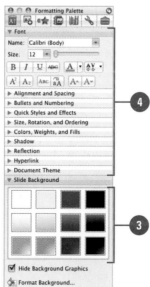

Did You Know?

You can add headers and footers elements to create consistent handouts. If the Handout Master doesn't have header or footer elements, you can click the Header, Footer, Date and Time and Page Number buttons on the Master toolbar to add them.

Preparing Speaker Notes

You can add speaker notes to a slide in Normal view using the Notes pane. Also, every slide has a corresponding **notes page** that displays a reduced image of the slide and a text placeholder where you can enter speaker's notes. Once you have created speaker's notes, you can reference them as you give your presentation, either from a printed copy or from your computer. You can enhance your notes by including objects on the notes master.

Enter Notes in Normal View

1. Click on the slide for which you want to enter notes.

2. Click to place the insertion point in the Notes pane, and then type your notes.

Did You Know?

You can view more of the Notes pane. To see more of the Notes pane in Normal view, point to the top border of the Notes pane until the pointer changes to a double-headed arrow, and then drag the border until the pane is the size you want.

Enter Notes in Notes Page View

1. Switch to the slide for which you want to enter notes.

2. Click the **View** menu, and then click **Notes Page**.

3. If necessary, click the **Zoom** list arrow on the Standard toolbar, and then increase the zoom percentage to better see the text you type.

4. Click the text placeholder.

5. Type your notes.

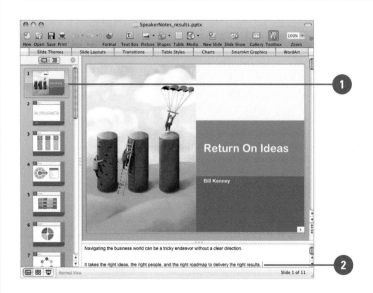

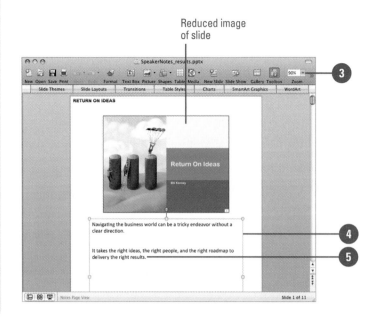

Reduced image of slide

Format the Notes Master

① Click the **View** menu, point to Master, and then click **Notes Master**.

② To add a background style, click the background, click the **Slide Background** panel to expand it, and then click a style.

③ Use the formatting tools on the Formatting Palette tab or Formatting toolbar to format the handout master placeholders.

④ If you want, add objects to the notes master that you want to appear on every page, such as a picture or a text object.

⑤ Click the **Close Master** button on the Master toolbar.

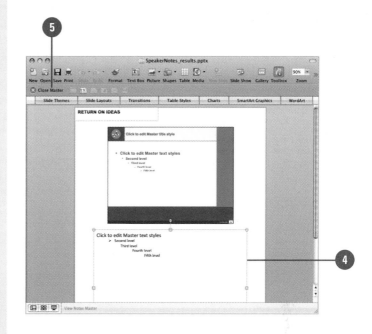

Did You Know?

Why don't the objects on the Notes master appear in the Notes pane in Normal view? The objects that you add to the Notes master will appear when you print the notes pages. They do not appear in the Notes pane of Normal view or when you save your presentation as a Web page.

You can add headers and footers elements to create consistent notes pages. If the Notes Master doesn't have body, slide image, header, or footer elements, you can click the Header, Footer, Date and Time Page Number, Body, and Slide Image buttons on the Master toolbar to add them.

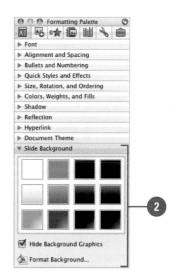

Adding Comments to a Presentation

When you review a presentation, you can insert comments to the author or other reviewers. **Comments** are like electronic adhesive notes tagged with your name. They typically appear in yellow boxes in PowerPoint. You can use comments to get feedback from others or to remind yourself of revisions you plan to make. A comment is visible only when you show comments using the Show Comments button and place the mouse pointer over the comment indicator. You can attach one or more comments to a letter or word on a slide, or to an entire slide. When you insert a comment, PowerPoint create a comment thumbnail with your initials and a number, starting at 1, and a comment box with your user name and date. When you're reviewing a presentation, you can use the Show Comment/Hide Comments button on the Reviewing toolbar or View menu to show and hide comments.

Insert a Comment

1. Click the slide where you want to insert a comment or select an object.

2. Click the **Insert** menu, and then click **Comment**.

3. Type your comment in the comment box or pane.

4. Click outside the comment box.

Did You Know?

You can move a comment. Drag it to a new location on the same slide.

My reviewer initials and name are incorrect. You can change them in PowerPoint preferences. Click the PowerPoint menu, click Preferences, click the Advanced icon, enter your User name and Initials in the boxes provided, and then click OK.

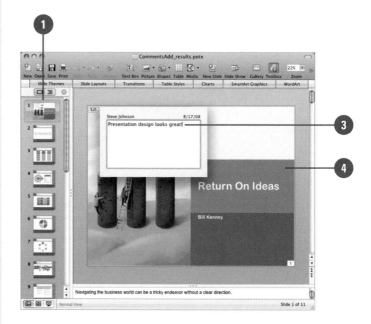

Read a Comment

1. Click the **View** menu, point to **Toolbars**, and then click **Reviewing**.

2. Click the **Show Comments** button to show all comments.

   The Show Comments button toggles to Hide Comments.

3. Click the comment box.

4. Read the comment.

5. Click the **Previous** or **Next** button to read another comment.

6. To edit a comment, click to select it, click the **Edit** button on the Reviewing toolbar, make your changes, and then click outside the comment box.

Did You Know?

You can delete a comment. Click the comment to select it, and then press Delete or click the Delete Comment button on the Reviewing toolbar. To delete all comments in a presentation, click the Delete All button on the Reviewing toolbar.

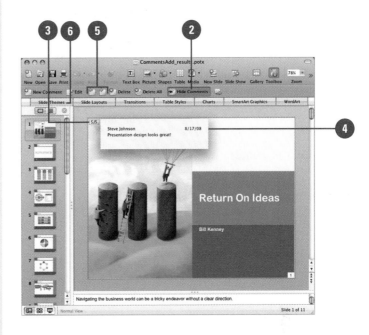

Next comment

Adding a Header and Footer

Headers and footers appear on every slide. You can choose to not have them appear on the title slide. They often include information such as the presentation title, slide number, date, and name of the presenter. Use the masters to place header and footer information on your slides, handouts, or notes pages. Make sure your header and footer don't make your presentation look cluttered. The default font size is usually small enough to minimize distraction, but you can experiment by changing their font size and placement to make sure.

Add a Header and Footer

1. Click the **View** menu, and then click **Header and Footer**.

2. Click the **Slide** or **Notes and Handouts** tab.

3. Enter or select the information you want to include on your slide or your notes and handouts.

4. To not include a header and footer on the title slide, select the **Don't show on title slide** check box.

5. Click **Apply** to apply your selections to the current slide (if available), or click **Apply to All** to apply the selections to all slides.

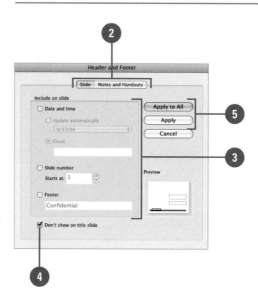

Change the Look of a Header or Footer

1. Click the **View** menu, point to **Master**, and then click the master view (**Slide Master**, **Handout Master**, or **Notes Master**) with the master you want to change.

2. Make the necessary changes to the header and footer like any other text box. You can move or resize them or change their text attributes.

3. Click the **Close Master** button on the Master toolbar.

Make changes to the header and footer

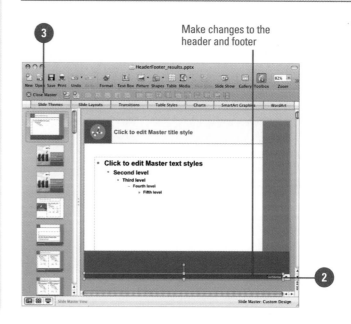

Inserting the Date and Time

You can insert the date and time into your presentation. For example, you might want today's date to appear in a stock market quote. You can insert the date and time on every slide, notes page or handout, or only on a specific slide. To insert the date and time on every page, you place it in a placeholder on the slide master. To insert the date and time only on a specific page, you insert it in a text box on the slide you want. You can set the date and time to automatically update to your computer's clock or stay fixed until you change it.

Insert the Date and Time on a Specific Slide

① Display an individual slide in Normal view.

② Click to place the insertion point in the text object where you want to insert the date and time.

③ Click the **Insert** menu, and then click **Date and Time**.

④ Click the date or time format you want.

⑤ To have the date and time automatically update, select the **Update automatically** check box.

⑥ Click **OK**.

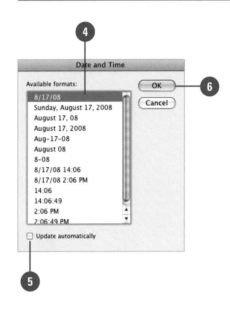

Insert the Date and Time on Slides, Notes, and Handouts

① Click the **Insert** menu, and then click **Date and Time**.

② Click the **Slide** or **Notes and Handouts** tab.

③ Click the **Date and time** check box.

④ Click the **Update automatically** or **Fixed** option, and then specify or select the format you want.

⑤ Click **Apply** to apply your selections to the current slide, or click **Apply to All** to apply the selections to all slides.

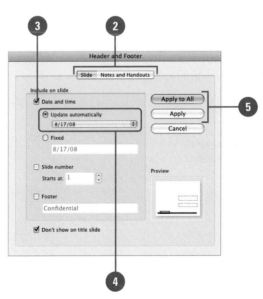

Inserting Slide Numbers

You can insert slide numbers into the text of your presentation. When you insert slide numbers, PowerPoint keeps track of your slide numbers for you. You can insert slide numbers on every slide or only on a specific slide. To insert a slide number on every page, you place it in a placeholder on the slide master. In the Slide Master view, PowerPoint inserts a code <#> for the slide number. When you view slides in other views, the slide number is shown. To insert a slide number only on a specific page, you insert it in a text box on the slide you want. You can even start numbering with a page number other than one. This is useful when your slides are a part of a larger presentation.

Insert Slide Numbering on a Slide, Notes, or Handout Master

1. Click the **View** menu, point to **Masters**, and then select a master.

2. For Slide Master view, select the slide master or slide layout in the left pane in which you want to insert a slide number.

   If the slide already contains a placeholder with the <#> symbol, which indicates slide numbering, you don't need to continue.

3. Click to place the insertion point in the text object where you want to insert the current slide number.

4. Click the **Insert** menu, and then click **Slide Number**.

   The <#> symbol appears in the text.

5. Click the **Close Master** button on the Master toolbar.

Did You Know?

Insert slide numbers on slides, notes, and handout using the default placeholder. Click the Insert menu, click Insert Slide Number, click the Slide or Notes and Handouts tab, select the Slide number check box, specify a start number, and then click Apply or Apply to All.

Insert Slide Numbering on a Specific Slide

1. Click to place the insertion point in the text object where you want to insert the current slide number.

2. Click the **Insert** menu, and then click **Slide Number**.

   The current slide number is inserted into the text box.

   TROUBLE? *If you don't place the insertion point, the Header and Footer dialog opens.*

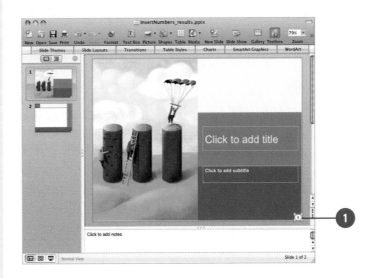

Start Numbering with a Different Number

1. Insert the slide number if you need one on the slide or slide master.

2. Click the **Insert** menu, and then click **Slide Number**.

3. Click the **Slides number** check box, and then enter a starting number.

4. Click **Apply** to apply your selections to the current slide, or click **Apply to All** to apply the selections to all slides.

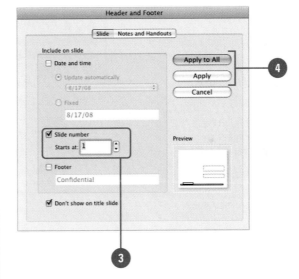

Printing a Presentation

You can print all the elements of your presentation—the slides, outline, notes, and handouts—in either color or black and white. PowerPoint makes it easy to print your presentation; it detects the type of printer that you choose—either color or black and white—and then prints the appropriate version of the presentation. When you print an outline, PowerPoint prints the presentation outline as shown in Outline view. What you see in the Outline pane is what you get on the printout. PowerPoint prints an outline with formatting according to the current view setting. Set your formatting to display only slide titles or all of the text levels, and choose to display the outline with or without formatting.

Print a Presentation

1. To print an outline, format your outline the way you want it to be printed in Outline pane.

   ◆ Display only slide titles or all text levels.

   ◆ Display with or without formatting. Control-click the outline, and then click **Show Formatting**.

2. Click the **File** menu, and then click **Print**.

3. Click the **Print What** drop-down, and then click what to print.

4. Select options for **Slide Show**, **Output**, **Scale to Fit Page**, **Print Hidden Slides**, and **Frame Slides**.

5. To view a quick preview, select the **Show Quick Preview** check box, and then click the **Previous** and **Next** buttons.

6. Click **Print**.

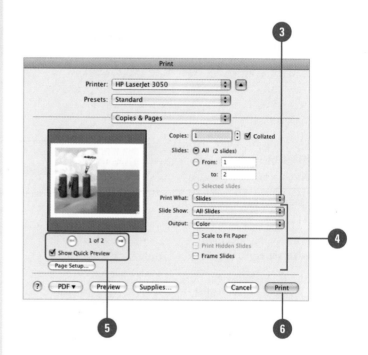

Did You Know?

You can preview slides in grayscale. If you are using a black and white printer, you can preview your color slides in grayscale in print preview to verify that they will be legible when you print them. Click the View menu, and then click Grayscale.

Communicating with Entourage

14

Introduction

Microsoft Entourage 2008 takes managing and organizing your daily routine to a new level. Its updated look gives you a larger viewing area and easier access to the tools that you want to use. You can customize its features so that they are seamlessly interwoven as you move from your electronic mail to your calendar to your notes to your journal.

Managing your personal communications and information has become an intricate and important aspect of everyday life at the workplace and at home. With Entourage, you can store, track, and manage all your information and communications in one place. You can track your appointments, meetings, and tasks on your Calendar and store information, including phone numbers, addresses, e-mail addresses, about all your business associates, family, and friends in your Contacts list. Use Notes to write reminders to yourself and Tasks to record your daily or weekly to-do list, checking them off as you complete them. Of course, one of the most important parts of your day is communicating, and Entourage provides the tools that help you address all your electronic communications needs.

What You'll Do

View the Entourage Window

Prepare for Entourage

Set Up an Account

Change Views

View Items and Folders

Create and Sort Contacts

Create a Contact Group

Create and Address an E-Mail Message

Format Message Text

Attach a File to a Message

Create a Signature

Flag, Categorize, and Delete Messages

Send, Receive, and Read Messages

Reply to and Forward a Message

Find and Filter Messages

Manage and Organize Messages

Reduce Junk E-Mail

Archive Messages

Send and Receive Instant Messages

Create a News Server Account

Read and Post a News Message

Customize Toolbars in Entourage

Viewing the Entourage Window

View. Click one of the view buttons—Mail, Address Book, Calendar, Notes, Tasks, or Project Center—to work in that view.

Toolbar. The toolbar provides buttons you click to quickly execute commands. The buttons on this toolbar change depending on the current view.

Favorites bar. The Favorites bar (**New!**) is a customizable place to provide shortcut buttons to frequently visited places, such as Inbox, or Calendar.

Folder list. The Folder list displays the contents of the folder, such as Inbox, you select for each account. In Entourage, you store information in folders and the folder you use depends on the Entourage item you are using. At the bottom of the Folder list is a special folder, such as Mail Views, that contains custom views which display the specified information. Click the triangle to expand or collapse a folder.

Message list. In Mail view, the Message list displays message headers for the selected mail folder in the Folder list.

Preview pane. The Preview pane gives you a greater area for reading your e-mail messages without having to scroll to view them.

Mini Calendar. The Mini Calendar allows you to quickly view your schedule for a specific date or range of dates. Click the arrows to switch months or the dot to view the current month.

Search box. Using the Spotlight search engine, the Search box allows you to locate items with certain text in a specified folder.

Quick Filter. The Quick Filter applies your rules and settings to narrow down the list of items shown in any view.

Status bar. The Status bar displays program status information, including progress, selection, and send & receive time.

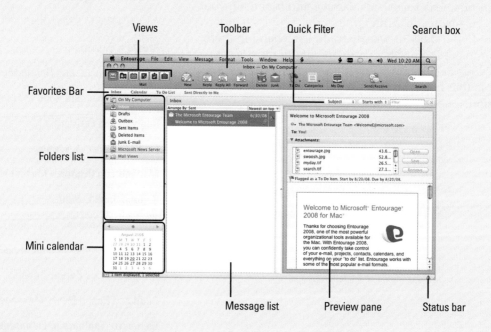

Views   Toolbar   Quick Filter   Search box

Favorites Bar

Folders list

Mini calendar

Message list   Preview pane   Status bar

Preparing for Entourage

Entourage is Microsoft's personal information manager and electronic mail (e-mail) software for handling incoming and outgoing e-mail messages.

To use Entourage as your personal information management (PIM) and e-mail tool, you need to be connected to the Internet or a network. Through this connection, you can take full advantage of the e-mail, scheduling, and contact capabilities of Entourage. Before you start Entourage for the first time, you need to know about the different types of connections and e-mail servers you can use with Entourage.

You can use Entourage on a standalone computer or one that is part of a network of computers, also called a **local area network (LAN)**. When you connect your standalone or networked computer to the Internet so you can communicate electronically, your computer becomes part of a worldwide network. You need two things to establish a connection to the Internet: a physical connection and an **Internet service provider (ISP)**.

Options for physical connections include a modem via a phone line (also called a dial-up network connection), a cable broadband modem, or a **digital subscriber line (DSL)** connected directly to your computer or through a LAN. Your options for an ISP, however, are numerous and vary greatly, both in cost and features, and depend upon the type of physical connection you choose. ISPs can include your local telephone or cable company, or a company, such as MSN or AOL (American Online), that provides only Internet access service.

The ISP provides the names of your incoming and outgoing **e-mail servers**, which collect and store your e-mail until you are ready to retrieve or send it. If you are using a modem, your ISP provides the phone number and modem settings needed to establish an Internet connection.

If you are working on a LAN that uses its own mail server, such as Microsoft Exchange Server, to send and receive e-mail, your network administrator provides all the information that you need for establishing a connection. However, you still need to set up your Entourage Profile with the Exchange mail connector. You will need the Exchange Server name from your system administrator.

Once you establish your connection, you can send and receive e-mail, or you can communicate using instant messaging, participating in a chat room, or subscribing to a newsgroup.

There are several different types of e-mail accounts that you can use with Entourage: POP3, IMAP, and HTTP:

- **Post Office Protocol 3 (POP3)** is a common e-mail account type provided by ISPs. Messages are downloaded from the e-mail server and stored on your local computer.

- **Internet Message Access Protocol (IMAP)** is similar to POP3 except that messages are stored on the e-mail server.

- **Hypertext Transfer Protocol (HTTP)** is a common type of Web e-mail account. Messages are stored, retrieved, and displayed as individual Web pages. Hotmail is an example of an HTTP e-mail account.

Setting Up an Account

When you start Entourage for the first time, what you see depends on whether you installed Entourage as a new program or as an upgrade. In either case, a setup wizard appears to step you through the process of setting up a profile and an e-mail service. A profile is a collection of all the data necessary to access one or more e-mail accounts and address books. A **service** is a connection to an e-mail server where you store and receive e-mail messages. Before you use Entourage, the Auto Account Setup tries to configure the account for you. All you need to do is specify your e-mail account name and password. If Entourage is unable to complete the account set up, you can manually enter account information, including the names of the incoming and outgoing e-mail servers, which you need to get from your ISP. If you installed Entourage as an upgrade, Entourage 2008 uses existing settings.

Set Up an Account in Entourage

1. Start Entourage.

2. Click the **Tools** menu, click **Accounts**, click the **Mail** tab, click the **New** button, and then click **Mail**.

   ◆ The first time you start Entourage, the Account Setup Assistant wizard automatically appears, displaying the Set Up a Mail Account screen.

3. Enter your e-mail address in the form name@domain, such as perspection1@mac.com.

4. If this account is for an Exchange Server, select the **My account is on an Exchange server** check box.

5. Click the **right arrow** button to continue.

   Entourage tries to determine the account type and establish the related settings.

6. If Entourage fails to determine the account type, enter the information requested.

7. Click the **right arrow** button to continue.

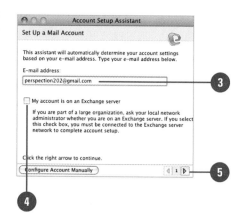

8 In the Verify and Complete Settings screen, enter (or verify) your name, the account ID and password, incoming and outgoing mail servers.

You can get incoming and outgoing mail server information from your ISP or company).

◆ To save your password, select the **Save password in Mac OS X Keychain** check box. If you clear the check box, Entourage prompts for the password each time you connect.

9 Click the **right arrow** button to continue.

10 In the Verify Setting screen, click **Verify My Settings** to make sure your settings are correct.

11 When the test is successful, click the **right arrow** button to continue.

12 In the Setup Complete screen, enter a name for the account, and then select final options you want.

13 Click **Finish**.

Did You Know?

You can change account settings. In the Accounts window, double-click the account name, change the settings you want on the different tabs, and then click OK.

You can delete an account. In the Accounts window, select the account you want to delete, and then click the Delete button on the toolbar.

You can select a default account. If you have multiple accounts, you need to make one the default, or main account. In the Accounts window, select the account, and then click the Make Default button on the toolbar.

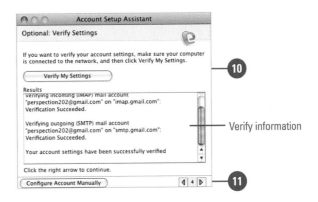

Verify information

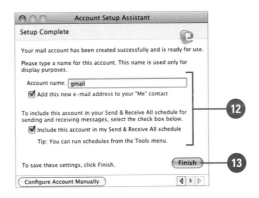

Changing Views

The View buttons on the toolbar are designed to display more of what you need to see in a simple and straightforward layout. When you click an Entourage view button, the entire Entourage window transforms to provide a clear, uncluttered view of your Mail, Address Book, Calendar, Notes, Tasks, and Project Center. In addition to the View buttons, you can also access the views using the Go To submenu on the View menu. The View menu also allows you to show and hide program elements, such as Quick Filter, Favorites bar, and Folder list. If you prefer the Preview pane in a different location, you can display it on the right (default) or below the Message list. If you like the Toolbox (**New!**) in Word, Excel, and PowerPoint, you can use it in Entourage too. It only contains the Scrapbook, Reference Tools, and Object Palette tabs.

Change Views

◆ **View buttons**. On the left side of the toolbar, click a view button: **Mail**, **Address Book**, **Calendar**, **Notes**, **Tasks**, and **Project Center**.

◆ **View menu**. Click the **View** menu, point to **Go To**, and then click **Mail**, **Address Book**, **Calendar**, **Notes**, **Tasks**, and **Project Center**.

◆ **Show or hide elements**. Click the **View** menu, and then click one of the following:

◆ **Show Quick Filter** or **Hide Quick Filter**.

◆ **Show Favorites Bar** or **Hide Favorites Bar**.

◆ **Show Folder List** or **Hide Folder List**.

◆ **Show Quick Filter** or **Hide Quick Filter**.

◆ **Toolbox**. Click the **Tools** menu, point to **Toolbox**, and then click **Object Palette**, **Reference Tools**, or **Scrapbook**.

◆ **Preview pane**. Click the **View** menu, point to **Preview Pane**, and then click **On Right**, **Below List**, or **None** (hides it).

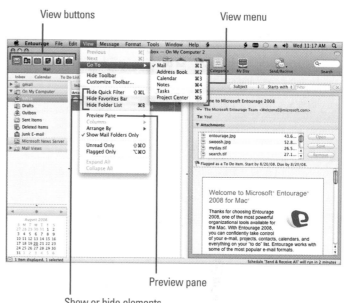

View buttons

View menu

Show or hide elements

Preview pane

Viewing Items and Folders

When you use Entourage, you work with views. The main views in Entourage are Mail, Address Book, Calendar, Notes, Tasks, and Project Center. Within those views, Entourage stores related items in folders. For each of these views, you can choose how to display the items and folders in which you stored the items. You can use a special folder, such as Mail Views, that contain custom views which display the specified information. For example, in Mail view, you can select a folder to display Sent Items, or Junk E-mail, or select a view to display items due today, high priority, flagged for follow up, or received today.

View an Item or Folder

1. Click a view button on the toolbar to switch to that Entourage view.

2. Click the **View** menu, and then click **Show Folder List** to display it, if necessary.

3. Click a triangle next to an item or folder to expand/collapse it.

4. Click the view you want to apply or a folder in the Folder list.

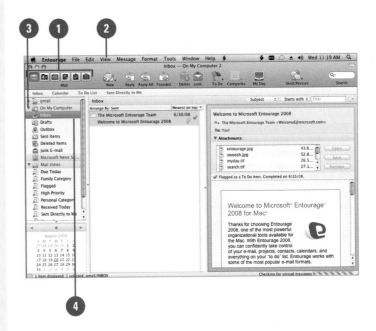

Did You Know?

You can add or remove a folder to the Favorites bar. In the Folder list, drag the folder you want to the Favorites bar. To remove an item from the Favorites bar, drag the shortcut name off the Favorites bar.

You can show or hide the Favorites bar. Click the Mail button on the toolbar, click the View menu, and then click Show Favorites Bar or Hide Favorites Bar.

Creating a Contact

A contact is a person or company with whom you want to communicate. One contact can have several mailing addresses, various phone and fax numbers, e-mail addresses, and Web sites. You can store all this data in the Address Book folder along with more detailed information, such as job titles, and birthdays. When you create a contact you also create an Electronic Business Card (vCards), which you can customize and share with others as an attachment or as part of your signature. When you double-click a contact, you open a dialog box in which you can edit the detailed contact information. You can also directly edit the contact information from within the Address Book folder. If you send the same e-mail message to more than one person, you can group contacts together into a distribution list.

Import Contacts in the Address Book

1 Click the **File** menu, and then click **Import**.

2 In the Begin Import screen, select an import option:

- ◆ **Entourage information from an archive or earlier version.** Select to import contacts from a back up or earlier version.

- ◆ **Information from another application.** Select to import from Apple Mail or Qualcomm Eudora.

- ◆ **Contacts or messages from a text file.** Select to import contracts from a text file (tab- or comma delimited, or as an MBOX file; an Entourage data storage format). Export contracts in other e-mail programs or databases into a text file for import here.

3 Click the **right arrow** button to continue.

Screens vary depending on the option you selected.

4 Follow the screens and provide information to complete the import, which includes an import program, data file, and data types.

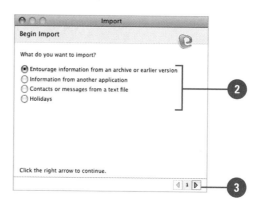

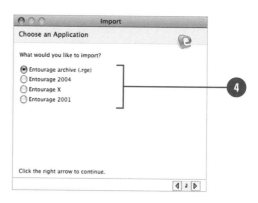

Create or Modify a Contact

1. Click the **Address Book** button on the toolbar.

2. Click the **New** button to create, or double-click an existing contact to edit a contact.

   ◆ In Mail view, you can also Control-click a message header or an vCard, and then click **Add Sender To Address Book**. If the option is grayed out, the address already exists in the Address Book.

3. Type as much information as you know about the contact.

   ◆ For a new contact, click **More** to expand the dialog box.

4. Click a tab to select the type of information you want to enter or edit.

5. Click the **File** menu, and then click **Save**.

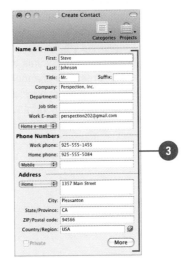

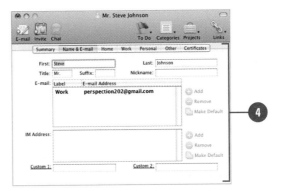

Did You Know?

You can delete a contact. Click Address Book button on the toolbar, select the contacts you want to delete, click the Delete button on the toolbar or press Delete, and then click Delete to confirm the deletion.

You can use a Global Address List with Microsoft Exchange. The Global Address list is a special address book that allows you to search for and get information about all Microsoft Exchange users.

For Your Information

Working with Electronic Business Cards

Instead of having to retype contact information into Address Book, you can send and receive contact information in the form of an Electronic Business Card (vCard) as a file (.vcf) attachment in an e-mail message. To add a vCard to the Address Book, open the e-mail message in Mail view, display the attachment in the Attachments pane, and then double-click the vCard attachment file. If necessary, click Open to display the contact information in a new contact. Enter any further information you want, click the File menu, and then click Save. To e-mail a vCard, select one or more contracts in Address Book, click the Contact menu, and then click Forward as vCard. In the new e-mail with the vCard attachment, enter address and body of the message, and then click Send.

Sorting Contacts

Entourage allows you to sort contacts in any view and by any field, either in ascending order (A to Z) or descending order (Z to A). You can sort contacts by a specific field or by a column header appearing at the top of the view's table (Name, Company, Categories, Projects, and so on). When sorted in a view, the contacts maintain the same view, but their order has changed. It's also possible to generate multi-layered sorts within a sort by adding more fields to the sort. For example, you might want to sort contacts by their company names first and then alphabetically by their last names.

View and Sort Contacts

① Click the **Address Book** button on the toolbar.

② Click the **View** menu, point to **Columns**, and then select the item names that you want to display.

A check mark on the menu indicates the column is currently shown, while no check mark indicates the column is not shown.

③ Click a column head in the table format view to sort by that column.

The triangle in the column head indicates the direction of the sort. If the triangle points down, the column sorts ascending order (A to Z). If the triangle points up, the column sorts in descending order (Z to A).

④ Click the column head again to re-sort in ascending or descending order.

Indicates contacts sorted by name in descending order

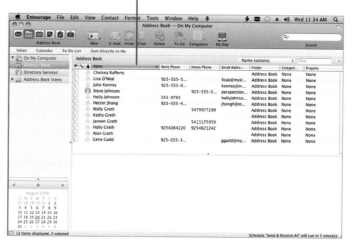

Did You Know?

You can find a contact quickly. Click Address Book on the toolbar, and then start typing the name of the contact you want to find in the Search box. The contact that best matches the text is displayed.

For Your Information

Printing Contacts

You can use the Print command in Address Book to print one contact, selected contacts, or all contacts in phone list or address book format. In Address Book, select the contacts you want to print (only for a partial list), click the File menu, click Print, specify the general print settings you want, click the Print drop-down, select what you want to print (Selected Contacts, All Contacts, or Flagged Contacts), click the Style drop-down, select a print format (Address Book or Phone List), click Layout to specify the contact information you want, and then click Print.

Creating a Contact Group

A contact group is a collection of contacts usually grouped together because of a specific task or association and then identified by one name. You can use a contact group in your e-mail messages, task requests, and other contact groups. When you address an e-mail message using a contact group, you are sending the message to everyone whose address is included in the list. Because a contact group often contains many names, it provides a faster, more efficient way to address an e-mail message to multiple recipients.

Create a Contact Group

1. Click the **Address Book** button on the toolbar.

2. Click the **New** button arrow on the toolbar, and then click **Group**.

   ◆ You can also click the **File** menu, point to **New**, and then click **Group**.

3. Type the name for the contact group.

4. Click the **Add** button on the toolbar.

5. Type the contact's name or e-mail address.

   A drop-down list appears with matching names from Address Book.

6. Select a person from the list, or type the complete e-mail address for the person.

   Add as many contacts to the group as you want.

7. Select the **Don't show addresses when sending to the group** check box to prevent the display of group member's e-mail addresses.

8. Click the **File** menu, and then click **Save**.

9. When you're done, click the **Close** button.

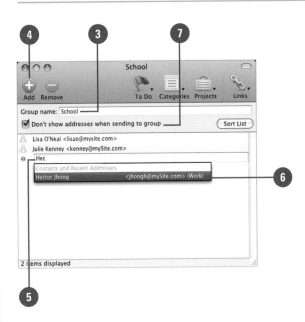

Creating and Addressing an E-Mail Message

When you create an e-mail message, the untitled message window opens with all the tools you need to communicate electronically. Your first step is addressing the message. You must identify who will receive the message or a copy of the message. For each recipient, you enter an e-mail address. You can enter the address manually by typing it in the To or Cc box, or you can select an address from your list of contacts. If you enter multiple addresses, you must separate the addresses with a semicolon (;). You can type a semicolon after each recipient's e-mail address, or you can just press Return after a recipient's address. Addressing a new message also means indicating the purpose of the message by entering a subject. Try to indicate the intent of the message as briefly and clearly as possible.

Create and Address an E-Mail Message

1. Click the **Mail** button on the toolbar to display the Inbox folder.

2. Click the **New** button on the toolbar.

3. Specify the e-mail address of each recipient you want to use:

   ◆ Enter the e-mail address of each recipient. As you type, Entourage displays a list with matching names and addresses. If the address you want appears in a list, click the name to use it.

   ◆ Click the **Address Book** button, and then drag contacts to the To box. You can also drag contacts to the Cc (carbon copy) or Bcc (blind carbon copy) boxes.

4. To check addresses for sendability, click the **Check Names** button.

5. Type a subject that indicates the purpose of the message.

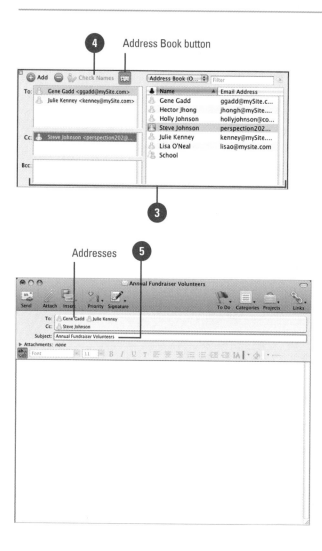

Address Book button

Addresses

Write a Message and Check Spelling

1 In the message window, click in the message body area.

2 Type the content of your message.

3 Control-click any word that appears with a red wavy underline to display a list of suggested corrections, and then click a suggested word to replace the error, or click another option.

4 To check spelling, click the **Tools** menu, click **Spelling**, and then use the Spelling dialog box to ignore or change words in the message.

- ◆ To select a spelling language to use, click the **Tools** menu, point to **Spelling Language**, and then select a language.

5 To insert research, use thesaurus or dictionary, translate text, click the **Tools** menu, click **Thesaurus** to open the Reference tab on the Toolbox, and then use the panels to find the right word or definition you want.

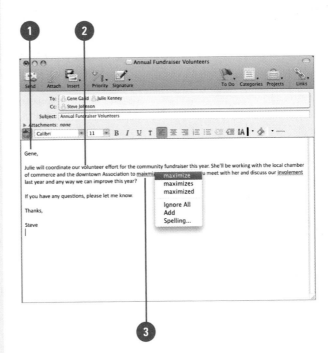

Did You Know?

You can automatically check spelling before you send a message. Click the Entourage menu, click Preferences, click Spelling, select the Always check spelling before queuing outgoing messages check box, and then click OK.

See Also

See "Checking Spelling" on page 46 for information on the Spelling dialog box..

Formatting Message Text

You can specify a file format for message text. The Plain Text format is one that all e-mail programs recognize, but it doesn't support text formatting. The HTML format allow text formatting, but are not always supported. However, most programs that don't recognize HTML, convert the message to plain text. When you use HTML, you can use tools, such as bold, italicize, and underline text to help draw the reader's attention to key words and emphasize the meaning of your message. With Word as the Entourage e-mail editor, you can take advantage of Word's formatting features when you write the text of your e-mail messages. In additional to message text, you can also insert other content, including pictures, sound, and movies. However, media files can dramatically increase the size of an e-mail, which can cause transmission problems when you send it.

Format the Message Text

1. Create or open the message you want to change.

2. Click the **Use HTML** button on the toolbar to format the message in HTML or plain text.

   When the button is pushed, the message format is HTML. When it's not, the message format is plain text.

3. If you selected HTML, use the tools on the toolbar to format the message text and background.

4. To insert media in ann HTML message, click the **Insert** button on the toolbar, and then click **Picture**, **Background Picture**, **Sound**, or **Movie**.

Did You Know?

You can specify the file format for all messages. Click the Entourage menu, click Preferences, click Compose, click the Mail Format drop-down, select HTML or Plain Text, and then click OK.

2 Plain text

2 HTML **4**

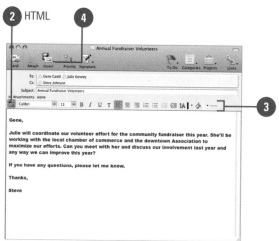

Attaching a File to a Message

You can also add an attachment to your e-mail messages. An attachment can be a file, such as a document or a picture. When you add an attachment to a message, an attachment icon appears under the Subject box in the Attachment pane, identifying the name and size of the attachment. Although you can add multiple attachments to a message, you should limit the number and size of the attachments. The size of the attachment affects the time it takes to send the message. The larger the attached file, the longer it takes to send. If an attached file is too large, the message might not be sent. After you send the message with the attachment, which appears with a paper clip icon, message recipients can double-click the attachment icon to open and view the file.

Attach a File to a Message

1. Create or open the message you want to change.

2. Click the triangle next to Attachments to open the Attachment pane, and then click **Add**

   ◆ You can also click the **Attach** button on the toolbar.

3. Navigate to the folder that contains the file.

4. Click the file you want to attach.

5. Click **Open**.

6. To remove a file attachment, select the attachment file in the Attachment pane, and then click **Remove**.

7. Click the bar under the Attachments pane to display an options window.

   ◆ Click the **Any computer (AppleDouble)** option or one for a specific computer type.

   ◆ Select the **Compress in ZIP** format to compress the file

   ◆ Select or clear **Append file name extensions** and **send attachments to Cc and Bcc recipients** check boxes.

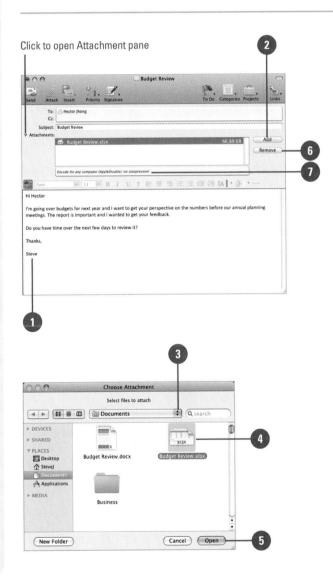

Click to open Attachment pane

Creating a Signature

If you type the same information at the end of each e-mail message that yo create, then you can automate that task by creating a signature. A signature can consist of both text and pictures. You can customize your signature with a variety of formatting styles, such as font type, size and color. For example, for your personal correspondence you can create a signature that includes a closing, such as Best Regards and your name; for business correspondence, you can create a signature that includes your name, address, job title, and phone and fax numbers. You can even include a logo image, sound or movie. You can create as many signatures as you want.

Create and Insert a Signature

1 Click the **Tools** menu, click **Signatures**.

2 Click the **New** button on the toolbar.

3 Type a name for the new signature.

4 Type your signature text.

5 Select the signature text, and then use formatting buttons to customize the text.

6 Click the **File** menu, and then click **Save**.

7 Click the **Close** button in the Signature window.

8 Select the check boxes for the signatures you want to randomly insert in a message.

9 Click the **Close** button in the Signatures window.

10 To insert a signature in a message, create or open a message, click the **Signature** button on the toolbar, and then select the signature name you want.

◆ To remove a signature, click the **Signature** button on the toolbar, and then click **None**.

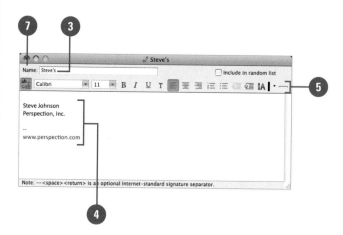

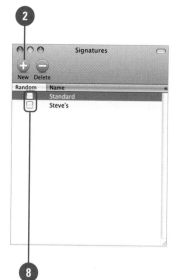

Setting Message Delivery Priorities

When you send a message, you can set message delivery options to help you track and manage it. You can specify the level of importance, highest, high, normal (the default), low, and lowest. If you need a recipient to follow up on an e-mail, you can set a follow up flag or reminder. You can specify when the follow up flag or reminder is due, today, tomorrow, this week, next week, or a specific date. When the To Do item is finished, you can mark it as complete.

Set Importance and Follow Up Options

1. Create or open the message you want to change.

2. To set an importance level, click the **Priority** button on the toolbar, and then select the priority level you want:

   ◆ **Highest**.

   ◆ **High**.

   ◆ **Normal**.

   ◆ **Low**.

   ◆ **Lowest**.

3. To set a follow up option, click the **To Do** button arrow, and then select the option you want:

   ◆ **Today, Tomorrow, This Week, Next Week**.

   ◆ **No Due Date** or **Choose Date**.

   ◆ **Add Reminder**.

   ◆ **Mark as Complete**.

   ◆ **Clear To Do Flag**.

Sending Messages

When you click the Send button, Entourage connects to the e-mail server, and moves the message to the Outbox folder, which sends your message to its recipient and checks the server for incoming mail. You can also send and check for messages from one or more accounts by clicking the Send button on the toolbar or using the Send & Receive submenu on the Tools menu. If you need customization, you can set send and receive options. If security is an issue, you can encrypt message contents, or add a digital signature. An encrypted message requires only recipient with the proper software key to decode and read the message, while a digitally signed message assures the message came from the sender. Before you can use these security options, you need to obtain a certificate, also known as a digital ID, from an authorized issuer, such as VeriSign (*www.verisign.com*).

Send a Message

1. Create a new message, or open an existing message saved in the Drafts folder.

2. Click the **Send** button on the toolbar.

   ◆ You can also click the **Tools** menu, point to **Send & Receive**, and then click **Send & Receive All**, **Send All**, or an account name.

   The message is sent to the Outbox folder. If you're working offline, Entourage waits to automatically send the message until you reconnect. Click the **Entourage** menu, and then click **Work Offline** to deselect it.

Set Message Delivery Options

1. Click the **Tools** menu, and then click **Accounts**.

2. Click the **Mail** tab, and then double-click the account you want to change.

3. Click the **Account Settings** tab.

4. Select the **Include this account in my "Send & Receive All" Schedule** check box.

5. Click the **Options** tab, and then set options to select a default signature, and work with the mail server.

6. Click the **Advanced** tab, and then set options to select folders to store messages and specify when to delete messages.

7. Click **OK**.

8. Click the **Close** button.

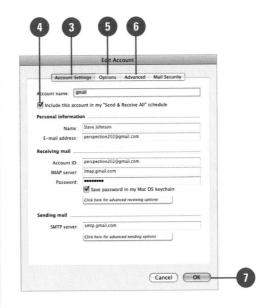

Set Security Options

1. Click the **Tools** menu, and then click **Accounts**.

2. Click the **Mail** tab, and then double-click the account you want to change.

3. Click the **Mail Security** tab.

4. To specify a certificate, click **Select** at the top.

5. To select a certificate to use for encryption, click **Select** at the bottom.

6. Select the check boxes with the delivery options you want for digital signing and encryption.

7. Click **OK**.

8. Click the **Close** button.

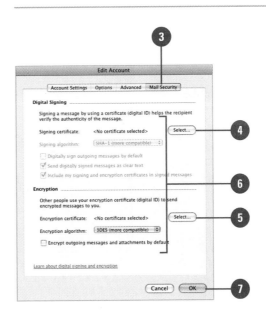

Receiving and Reading Messages

Messages that have been sent to you are stored on your e-mail server until Entourage retrieves them. By default, Entourage retrieves your mail at regular intervals. You can also retrieve your messages between scheduled retrieval times by clicking the Send & Receive button. When a message is retrieved, its message header appears in the Entourage Inbox. Click the message header to display the contents of the message in the Preview pane, which increases the area for reading your e-mail. If you receive a message that contains an attachment, you can open, save, or remove it.

Receive and Read Messages

1. Click the **Send/Receive** button on the toolbar. If a message arrives when you're online, a mail alert appears above the Dock. Click the alert to open it.

2. To display a message in the Inbox, click the message header.

3. Read the contents of the message in the Preview pane.

4. If the message contains an attachment, click the triangle to open the Attachment pane, and then do any of the following:

   ◆ **Open.** Double-click the attachment file.

   ◆ **Preview.** File attachments, such as PDF and JPEG files, appear in the Preview pane.

   ◆ **Save.** Click the attachment file, click **Save**, specify a location, and then click **Save**.

   ◆ **Remove.** Click the attachment file, and then click **Remove**.

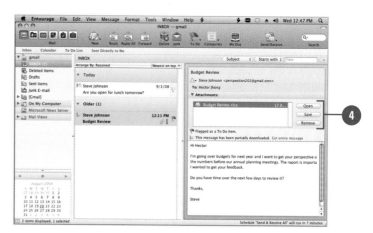

Did You Know?

You can close, open, or move the Preview pane. To move the Preview pane location, click the View menu, point to Preview Pane, and then click On Right, Below List, or None.

Check for Mail Using a Schedule

1. Click the **Tools** menu, and then click **Schedules**.

2. Click the **New** button on the toolbar.

3. Type a name for the schedule.

4. Click the **When** drop-down, click **Repeating Schedule**, and then specify a time interval.

5. Select the **Only if connected** check box to run only when you're connected to the Internet.

6. Click the **Action** drop-down, and then click **Receive Mail**, and then select an account.

7. To add more accounts, click **Add Action**, and then repeat Step 6.

8. Select the **Stay Connected** option.

9. Select the **Enable** check box.

10. Click **OK**.

11. Select the check boxes next to the schedules that you want to run.

12. To edit or remove a schedule, do the following:

    ◆ **Edit**. Double-click the schedule.

    ◆ **Remove**. Select the schedule, and then click the **Delete** button.

13. Click the **Close** button in the Schedules window.

    The Send/Receive schedule provides a way for POP or Hotmail type account to quickly get mail. If you're using an Exchange account, you don't need to do this.

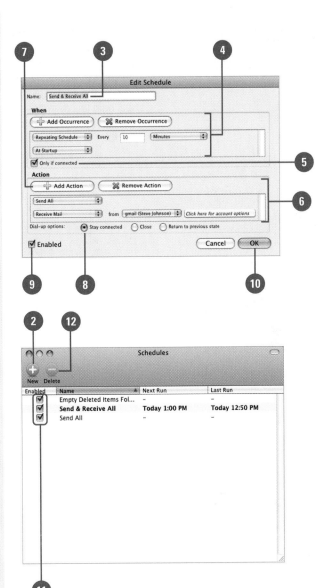

Flagging Messages

As you look through the list of messages that you have received, you might find messages that require your attention, though you don't have the time to respond when you are reading the message. To make sure you don't overlook an important message, you can click the flag icon next to the message to mark it with a To Do flag. The To Do flag icon will help jog your memory so you can respond promptly to the message. The To Do list provides an up-to-date list of messages marked with To Do flags in your mailbox.

Flag and Follow Up a Message

1. Click the **Mail** button on the toolbar.

2. Click the **Inbox** folder.

3. Scan your messages to see if any require follow up.

4. To set a follow up flag, select the messages you want, click the **To Do** button arrow on the toolbar, and then select the option you want.

   ◆ The To Do flags include: **Today**, **Tomorrow**, **This Week**, **No Due Date**, or **Choose Date**.

   ◆ To mark a follow up message as complete, select the messages you want, click the **To Do** button arrow on the toolbar, and then click **Mark as Complete**. The flag icon changes to a check mark.

   ◆ To remove a follow-up flag, select the messages you want, click the **To Do** button arrow on the toolbar, and then click **Clear To Do Flag**.

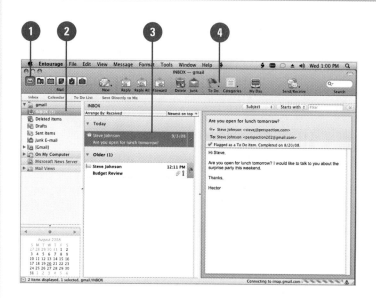

Did You Know?

You can quickly sort messages by To Do flag. Click the Arrange By header button, and then click To Do Flag Status. To toggle the sort order, click the button to the right of the Arrange By header.

Categorizing Messages By Color

When your Inbox is full of messages, sometimes it's hard to distinguish between them. To help you locate and manage related messages and other items in Entourage, you can assign a color category to e-mail, calendar, and task items. When you're working on a project, you can quickly see all related items at a glance. You can customize the color categories by name. For example, you can name the green category Finance and assign it the money related items.

Color Categorize Messages

1. Click the **Mail** button on the toolbar.

2. Click the **Inbox** folder.

3. Select the messages you want to change.

4. Click the **Categories** button arrow on the toolbar, and then click the color you want. Click **None** to remove a color.

    The first time you select a color category, a dialog box appears, asking you to name the color category.

5. To change the color categories, click the **Categories** button arrow, click **Edit Categories**, select a new color, specify a new name, save your changes, and then click the **Close** button.

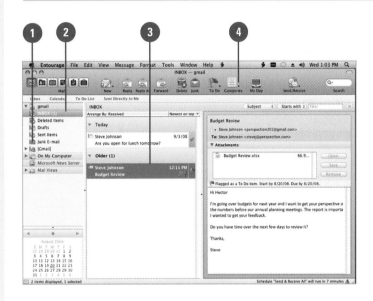

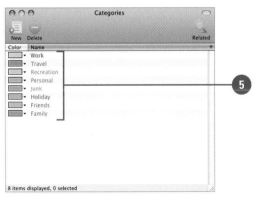

Did You Know?

You can quickly sort messages by color category. Click the Arrange By header button, and then click Categories. To toggle the sort order, click the button to the right of the Arrange By header.

Replying To and Forwarding a Message

You can respond to messages in your Inbox in two ways: you can reply to the person who sent you the message, or you can forward the message to others. Replying to a message sends a copy of the original message and new text that you type to the sender, or to both the sender and all the other original recipients. You can reply by returning a message to only the sender or to the sender and all other original recipients. The reply message recipient sees RE: and the original subject in the message header. Forwarding a message sends a message to someone who was not on the original recipient list. You can also type additional information at the start of the forwarded message before sending the message. To forward a message, you click the Forward button. The recipient sees FW: and the original subject in the message header.

Reply To a Message

1. Click the **Mail** button on the toolbar.

2. Select the message to which you want to reply.

3. Click the **Reply** button to reply to the sender only, or click the **Reply To All** button to send a message to the sender and all the recipients of the original message.

4. Type any new message text.

5. Click the **Send** button.

Subject automatically inserted with RE: added to indicate you are replying to a message

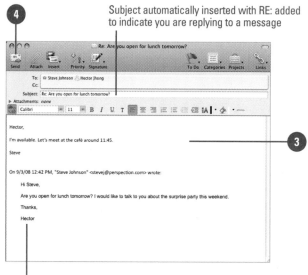

Message header and text from original message

Forward a Message

1. Click the **Mail** button on the toolbar.

2. Select the message that you want to forward.

3. Click the **Forward** button on the toolbar.

4. Enter the name(s) of the recipient(s) in the To and Cc boxes.

5. Type any new message text.

6. Click the **Send** button.

Subject automatically inserted with FW: added to indicate this is a forwarded message

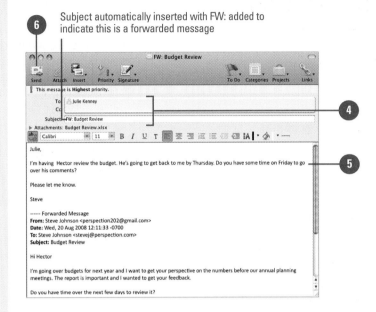

Did You Know?

Entourage sends a copy of the attachment in a forwarded message. When you forward a message, Entourage includes a copy of any attachments received with the original message.

Add an e-mail address to your contact list. Open the e-mail message, Control-click the e-mail address you want, click Add Sender To Address Book, enter any additional information, save the contact, and then click the Close button.

You can forward a message as an attachment. In Mail view, open the message you want to forward, Control-click the message, click Forward as Attachment, and then click the Send button.

For Your Information

Redirecting a Message

If your receive an e-mail message by mistake, you can redirect to the right recipient. Redirecting an e-mail message to the right recipient in this case works better than forwarding it. When you redirect a message, you cannot change the message and the e-mail appears to the recipient to have come from the original sender and any replies go to the original sender. To redirect a message, select the message in Mail view, click the Message menu, click Redirect, enter or select addresses you want, and then click the Send button.

Organizing Messages in Folders

Although Entourage provides the Inbox folder, this folder will become cluttered with messages unless you decide how you want to handle the messages that you have read. Some messages will be deleted immediately; others you will reply to or forward. With the exception of the deleted messages, all messages will remain in the Inbox until you move them elsewhere. To organize the messages you want to keep, you can create folders and move messages between the folders.

Create a New Folder

1. Click the **Mail** button on the toolbar.

2. Click the **Inbox** folder.

3. Click the **File** menu, point to **New**, and then click **Folder** or **Subfolder**.

4. Type a new name for the folder.

5. Click **Create**.

6. To rename or move a folder in the Folder list, do the following:

   ◆ **Rename.** Click the folder name, edit the name, and then press Return.

   ◆ **Move.** Drag the folder name to another location in the Folder list.

Did You Know?

You can save a mail message as a file. Click the mail message you want to save, click the File menu, click Save As, type a new file name, click the Format drop-down, select a file type, and then click Save.

Sort items within a folder. If available, click a column button to sort items in the folder by that column in either ascending or descending order.

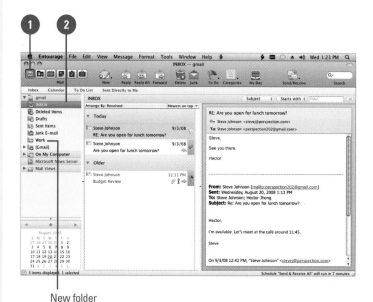

New folder

Delete a Folder

1. Select the folder you want to delete.

2. Click the **Edit** menu, and then click **Delete Folder**.

   ◆ You can also press Delete or Control-click the folder, and then click **Delete Folder**.

3. Click **Delete** to confirm the deletion.

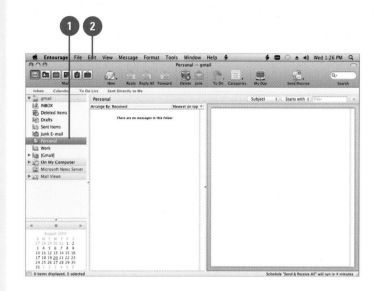

Move a Message to a Folder

1. Display the folder that contains the message you want to move.

2. Select the messages that you want to move.

3. Drag the message to a folder in the Folders list.

   ◆ You can also click the **Message** menu, point to **Move To**, click **Choose folder**, select a folder, and then click **Move**.

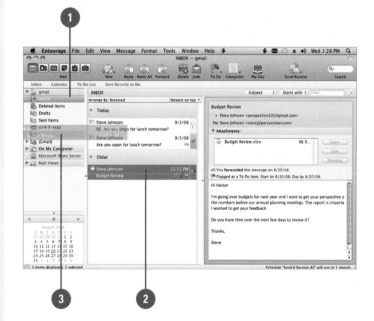

Managing Messages with Rules

Entourage provides a way to organize messages in folders using specific criteria, known as **rules**, that you set. For example, you can create a rule to automatically move, categorize, forward, and delete messages. You can color-code the messages that you send to or receive from particular contacts for quick and easy recognition.

Manage Messages Using Rules

1. Click the **Tools** menu, and then click **Rules**.

2. Click the **New** button on the toolbar.

3. Type a name for the rule.

4. Specify the search criterion you want to use for the rule.

   ◆ To add more search criterion, click **Add Criterion**. To remove one, click **Remove Criterion**.

5. Specify the action you want to take when the criterion is met.

   ◆ To add more actions, click **Add Action**. To remove one, click **Remove Action**.

6. Select the **Do not apply other rules to messages that meet these criteria** check box to only apply the rule to new messages.

7. Select the **Enable** check box.

8. Click **OK**.

9. Select the check boxes next to the rules that you want to run.

10. To edit or remove a rule, do the following:

    ◆ **Edit.** Double-click the rule.

    ◆ **Remove.** Select the rule, and then click the **Delete** button.

11. Click the **Close** button in the Rules window.

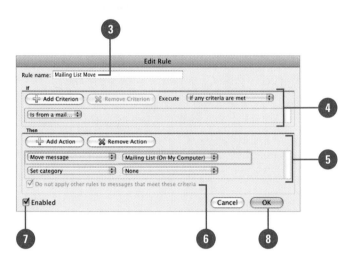

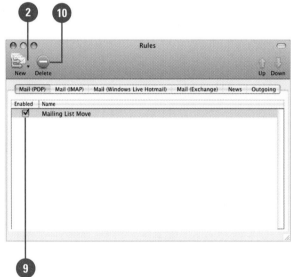

Searching with Spotlight

With Spotlight preferences (**New!**) enabled (the default) in Entourage, you can use Spotlight to search for e-mail, calendar events, tasks, contacts, and other Entourage items. Spotlight is conveniently located on the right side of the menu bar on your Mac screen. You can identify Spotlight by the blue icon with a magnifying glass. Spotlight performs a live search of your Home folder on your computer using the information you know. As you type in Spotlight, a menu appears displaying a list of everything Spotlight can find to match what you've typed so far.

Search with Spotlight

1 Click the **Spotlight** (magnifying-glass) icon on the right side of the menu bar or press ⌘+Space.

2 In the Spotlight field, start to type what you want to find. To find a specific phrase, place quotes around it. For example, "Apple Computer."

IMPORTANT *Spotlight only recognizes the beginnings of words.*

As you type, a menu begins to display a list of everything Spotlight can find to match what you've typed so far. As you continue to type, the list changes.

3 To open an item on the menu, click the item or use the arrow keys to scroll down the list, and then press Return.

4 To clear or stop a search, click the **Close** button (x) in the Spotlight field.

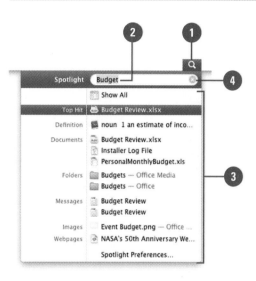

Did You Know?

You can enable Spotlight. Click the Entourage menu, click Preferences, click Spotlight in the left pane, select the Include Entourage items in Spotlight search results check box, and then click OK.

Finding and Filtering Messages

By using the Quick Filter in your Inbox, you can easily and quickly locate one particular piece of e-mail among what may be hundreds of stored messages. If you know that the message contains a specific word or phrase in its title, contents, or properties, you can conduct a search using that word or phrase as the criteria. If you assign categories to your messages, you can locate them searching by category. You can use a filter to view only the items that meet the conditions you have defined. For example, you can filter your messages so the only ones that appear are those that you flagged as high priority or have categorized as business items.

Find a Message Using Quick Filter

1. Select the folder in the Folder list with the items you want to filter.

2. Click the first drop-down on the Quick Filter bar, and then select a filter type, such as Subject, From, To, Category is, or Project is.

   Depending on your selection, additional drop-down menus or a text box appears.

3. Specify the search criteria you want. As you enter criteria, Entourage displays the results.

4. To redisplay all your items, click the **Clear** button on the Quick Filter bar.

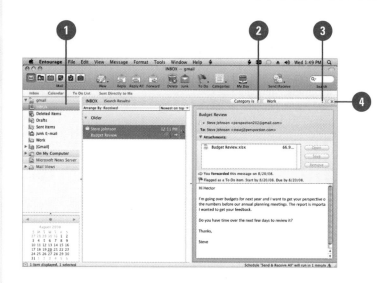

Did You Know?

***You can create an Out of Office message** (New!).* If you have a Microsoft Exchange account, you can have Entourage reply to message automatically when you're out of the office. You can now schedule your Out of Office times in advance, so you don't forget to turn it off. Click the Tools menu, click Out of Office Assistant, and then follow the instructions.

Perform a Basic and Advanced Search

1. Click in the Search box, and then type the search text.

   ◆ To use a recent search, click the magnifying glass drop-down, and then select the text.

2. To narrow down or expand the search, click a button on the Search bar.

3. To perform an advanced search, click the plus (+) button, and then do the following:

   ◆ Click the first drop-down on the Search bar, and then select a match option.

   ◆ Specify the search criteria you want. As you enter criteria, Entourage displays the results.

   ◆ To add a criterion, click the plus (+) button to its right.

   ◆ To remove a criterion, click the minus (-) button to its right.

4. To redisplay all your messages, click the **Clear** button on the Search bar.

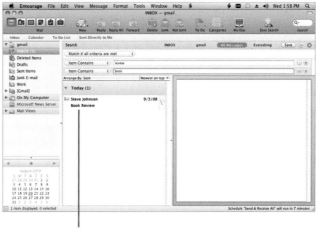

Narrowed results

Using Search Folders

Entourage's search folders are another way that Entourage makes managing mail easier. Search folders are not like the folders that you create or even like the Entourage default folders. Search folders store information about your messages, without having to move the messages to a specific folder. There are several search folders already created: Flagged, which displays the message you flag; Unread, which displays the unread mail you have accumulated. You can also create a search folder for the messages that meet your specific criteria.

Use a Search Folder

1 In any view, click the triangle next to a Search Folder, such as Mail Views, Calendar Views, or Notes Views.

2 Click the saved search you want to use.

Did You Know?

You can retrieve mail messages from the Deleted Items folder. Items remain in the Deleted Items folder until you empty it. To retrieve mail messages from the Deleted Items folder, click Deleted Items folder in the Folder list. Drag an item to the Inbox or to any other folder icon in the Folder list.

You can empty the Deleted Items folder. To empty the Deleted Items folder and permanently delete its contents, Control-click Deleted Items in the Folders list, click Empty Deleted Items, and then click Yes to confirm the deletion.

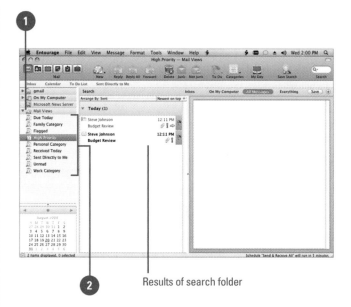

Results of search folder

Customize a Search Folder

1. In any view, click the triangle next to a Search Folder, such as Mail Views, Calendar Views, or Notes Views.

2. Control-click the saved search, and then click **Edit Saved Search**.

3. Make the changes you want.

4. Click the **Save Search** button on the toolbar.

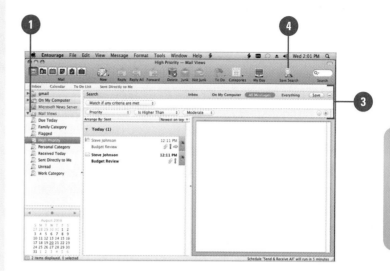

Create a Search Folder

1. Click the view button where you want to save the search.

2. Click the **File** menu, point to **New**, and then click **Saved Search**.

3. Click the first drop-down, and then select a match option.

4. Specify the search criteria you want. As you enter criteria, Entourage displays the results.

5. To add or remove a criterion, click the plus (+) or minus (-) button to its right.

6. To redisplay all your messages, click the **Clear** button on the Search bar.

7. Click the **Save Search** button on the toolbar, type a name, and then click **OK**.

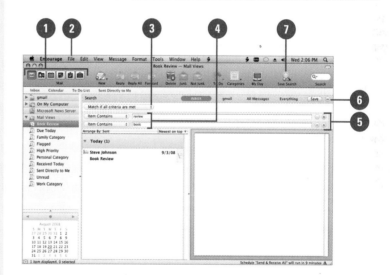

Creating a Mailing List

A mailing list allows members to send and receive messages to/from all subscribers of the list. If you want to hold forum discussions to convey information and ask questions over e-mail, a mailing list is a good way to go. You can set up and manage a mailing list using the Mailing List Manager. The main disadvantage of using a mailing list is the increased number of e-mails you receive from members of the list. To help you manage the number of e-mails, you can have mailing list e-mails automatically moved into a separate folder and delete your own sent copies.

Create and Manage a Mailing List

① Click the **Tools** menu, and then click **Mailing List Manager**.

② Click the **New** button on the toolbar.

③ Click the **Mailing List** tab.

④ Type a name for the mailing list.

⑤ Specify an address for the list, and then specify where to store messages to and from the list.

⑥ Click the **Advanced** tab, and then set options to determine what to do with messages.

⑦ Click **OK**.

⑧ To edit or remove a schedule, do the following:

  ◆ **Edit.** Double-click the list.

  ◆ **Remove.** Select the list, and then click the **Delete** button.

⑨ Click the **Close** button.

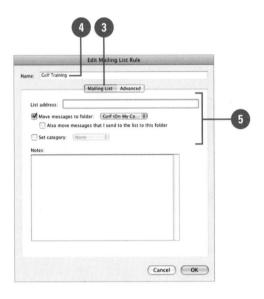

Deleting Messages

As your Inbox gets full and harder to manage, you can quickly delete messages you no longer need. When you delete a message, it's not permanently deleted from your computer. The message is placed in the Deleted Items folder, where it stays until you empty it. The Deleted Items folder works like the Trash Can icon on the Desktop. If you delete a message by mistake, you can move it out of the Deleted Items folder to restore it. If you don't want to delete your messages just in case you might need to reference them later, you can archive them or move them to other another folder.

Delete Messages

1. Click the **Mail** button on the toolbar.

2. Click the **Inbox** folder.

3. Select the message you want to delete.

4. To delete the message, click the **Delete** button or press Delete.

5. To restore a deleted message, click the **Deleted Items** folder in the Folders List, and then drag the message to another folder, such as the Inbox.

6. To permanently delete all messages, Control-click the Deleted Items Folder, and then click **Empty Delete Items**.

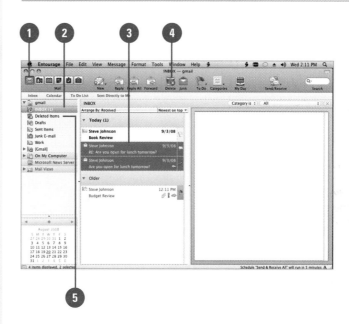

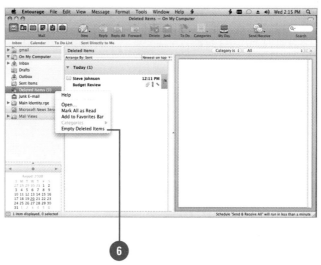

Reducing Junk E-Mail

You can have Entourage handle junk e-mail for you. You can specify what should be considered junk e-mail and how Entourage should handle that e-mail (**New!**). You can ensure that e-mail from certain addresses or domains, which might seem to be junk e-mail, but is actually from a person or site you want. If you create a contact for an individual in Address Book, e-mails from the person are not classified as junk. You can also make sure that the mail you send isn't treated as junk e-mail. If Entourage detects a phishing message (a technique criminals use to trick user into revealing personal information) with links to a specious Web site, a warning alert appears.

Reduce Junk E-Mail and Spam

① Click the **Mail** button on the toolbar.

② Click the **Tools** menu, and then click **Junk E-mail Protection**.

③ Click the **Level** tab.

④ Select the level of junk e-mail protection you want: **None**, **Low**, **High**, or **Exclusive**.

⑤ Select the **Delete messages from the Junk E-mail folder older than X days** check box, and then specify the number of days you want.

⑥ Click the **Safe Domains** tab, and then specify the messages from the addresses or domains that should not be be treated as junk mail.

⑦ Click the **Blocked Senders** tab, and then specify the messages from addresses or domains that should not be junk e-mail.

⑧ Click **OK**.

Did You Know?

You can deal with junk mail as it arrives. If you receive a message that is junk mail, select the message, click the Message menu, and then click Mark as Junk.

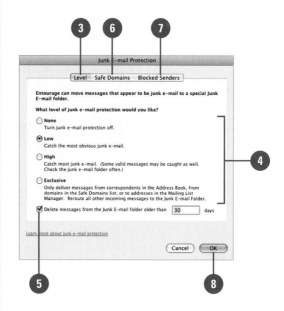

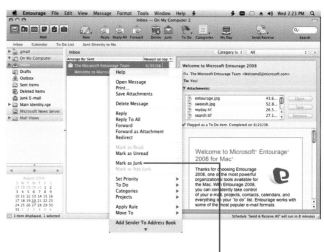

Control-click a message and then click Mark as Junk

Archiving Messages

You can archive information in Entourage by exporting selected items using the Export wizard to an archive file (.RGE) or copying message folders onto the Desktop. When you drag a folder from Entourage onto the Desktop, the messages in the folder are converted into the MBOX file format. After you archive messages, you can import them back into Entourage by dragging the message folder onto a folder in the Folder list, or by using the Import command on the File menu. The imported folder appears as a subfolder within the destination folder.

Archive Messages

1. Click the **File** menu, and then click **Export**.

2. In the Export screen, select options to specify which the items you want to include in the archive.

3. Click the **right arrow** button to continue.

4. In the Delete Archived Items? screen, specify whether you want to keep the items in Entourage after the archive or delete them.

5. Click the **right arrow** button to continue.

6. Type a name for the archive file, select a location, and then click **Save**.

7. Click **Done**.

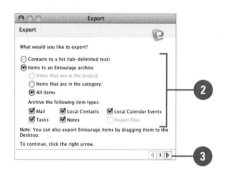

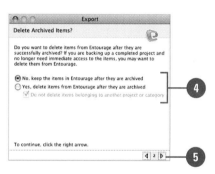

Did You Know?

You can copy a message folder onto the Desktop. Click the Mail button on the toolbar, select the folder in the Folder list, and then drag it onto the Desktop. Entourage creates a back up of all the message in the folder in the MBOX format. If the backed up folder contains subfolders, they are not included in the back up. Each folder needs to be dragged separately onto the Desktop.

Sending and Receiving Instant Messages

Entourage can identify contacts in an e-mail message who also use Microsoft Messenger, an instant messaging service. An **instant message (IM)** is an online typewritten conversation in real time between two or more contacts over the Internet. Instant messages require both parties to be online, and the communication is instantaneous. Before you can send and receive instant messages, you need to get an account with the instant messenger service. When you display an e-mail message in the Preview pane, or open a message in Entourage from an IM contact, online status indicator appears next to the sender's name. When you click the online status, Entourage displays a menu with options sign in to Messenger, and send an instant message. Entourage needs to be your default e-mail program and you must be signed in to your corporate account in Messenger. After you start a conversation with someone, you can add others to the conversation.

Start an Instant Message from Entourage

1 Open a message from a contact signed into Instant Messenger.

2 Click the online status indicator.

3 Click **Send Instant Message**.

◆ You can also click **Sign in to Microsoft Messenger** to sign in and use Messenger.

A Conversation window opens to begin a conversation with your contact.

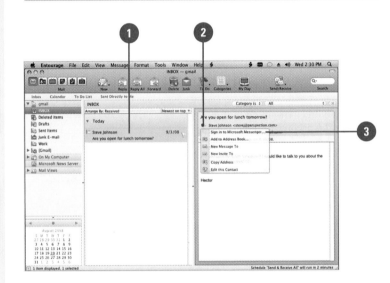

Did You Know?

You can change your online status anytime. Click the File menu, point to My Status, and then click the status you want: Online, Busy, Be Right Back, Away, On The Phone, Out To Lunch, or Appear Offline.

You can close Windows Messenger while you are signed in. Click the Close button. Windows Messenger continues to run in the background as long as you are signed in.

Send and Receive Instant Messages

1. If necessary, double-click the contact to whom you want to send an instant message in Messenger.

2. In the Conversation window, type the message.

   The text wraps to another line to fit in the window; however, if you want to start a new line of text, press Shift+Enter.

3. To add another person to the conversation, click the **Invite someone to this conversation** button, and then double-click a contact.

4. Click **Send** or press Return.

5. Wait for a reply.

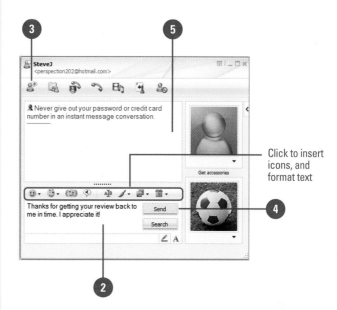

Click to insert icons, and format text

Did You Know?

You can send an e-mail from Messenger. In Messenger, click the Actions menu, point to Send Other, and then click Send an E-mail Message.

You can quickly switch back to Entourage. In Messenger, Click the File menu, point to Go To, and then click My E-mail Inbox. Entourage needs to be your default e-mail program, and your e-mail address cannot be from MSN or Hotmail, which opens your browser.

Creating a News Server Account

A **newsgroup** is an electronic forum where people from around the world with a common interest can share ideas, ask and answer questions, and comment on and discuss any subject. Before you can participate in a newsgroup, you must select a news server. A **news server** is a computer located on the Internet, which stores newsgroup messages, also called articles, on different topics. You need to get the name of the news server and possibly an account name and password. If you're not sure where to get one, perform a Web search for public news servers. When you add a news server account to Entourage, it retrieves a list of newsgroups available on that server. Often this list is quite lengthy. Once you select a newsgroup, you can view its contents. If you like the newsgroup, you can create a link to subscribe to it.

Create a News Server Account

1. Click the **Tools** menu, and then click **Accounts**.

2. Click the **New** button arrow on the toolbar, and then click **News**.

3. Select a mail account, and then enter an organization name for use in posts.

4. Click the **right arrow** button to continue.

5. Enter the news server or IP address. For example, msnews.microsoft.com provides access to the Microsoft News Server.

6. If the server requires a user name and password, select the **My news server requires me to log on** check box.

7. Click the **right arrow** button to continue.

8. Enter an account ID and password. Select the **Save password in my Mac OS keychain** check box to save your information.

9. Click the **right arrow** button to continue.

10. Enter an account name, and then click **Finish**.

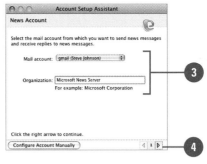

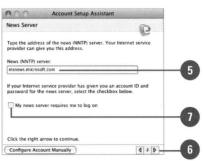

Reading and Posting a News Message

You can read new newsgroup messages after you retrieve them. Newsgroup messages appear in the Preview pane, just as e-mail messages do. To view a newsgroup message in the Display pane, click the title of the message in the Preview pane. If the Expand Indicator appears to the left of a newsgroup message, then the message contains a conversation thread. A conversation thread consists of the original message on a particular topic along with any responses that include the original message. To read the responses, click to display the message titles, then click the title of the message you want to read. To hide all the responses to a conversation thread, click the Collapse Indicator to the left of a newsgroup message. Icons appear next to the news messages to indicate whether a conversation thread is expanded or collapsed, and whether or not it has been read.

Read and Post a News Message

1. Click the **Mail** button on the toolbar.

2. Click the news server in the Folders list.

3. If this is the first time you're opening the news server, click **Receive** to get a list of newsgroups.

4. To subscribe to a list, select the newsgroup, and then click the **Subscribe** button on the toolbar.

   ◆ To narrow down the newsgroup list, click the **View** menu, and then click **Subscribed Only**. Click the command again to view the entire list.

5. Select the newsgroup that you want to view in the Folders list.

6. Select and read different messages in the newsgroup. Use the Search box to narrow down the Message list.

7. Click the **New** button to create a new message, or click the **Reply** or **Reply All** button to respond to a message. Fill in the message, and then click the **Send** button.

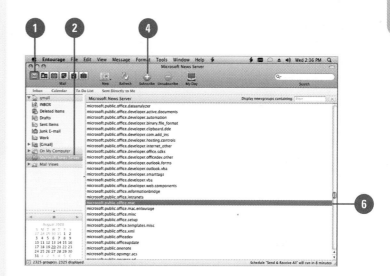

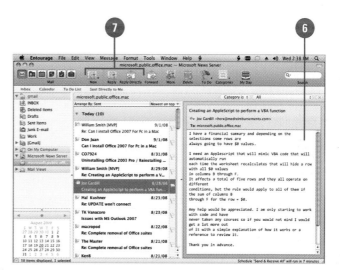

Customizing Toolbars in Entourage

Entourage uses toolbar on almost every window. Each toolbar contains different set of buttons depending on the view or features provided by Entourage. Each toolbar is independent of the other, which means you can customize them individually (**New!**). For example, the Task window doesn't include the Save, which is something you'll use a lot. You can use the Customize Toolbar command on the View menu to quickly drag and drop the Save button into the toolbar. You can also customize how the buttons appear on the toolbar. If you don't want to show a toolbar, you can hide it. The changes you make to one toolbar will not affect another.

Customize Toolbars in Entourage

1. Open the window with the toolbar that you want to change.

2. Click the **View** menu, and then click **Customize Toolbar**.

3. Drag the buttons you want into the toolbar, or drag the default set into the toolbar.

4. To further customize the toolbar, do any of the following:

   ◆ Click the **Show** drop-down, and then select a toolbar display: **Icon & Text**, **Icon Only**, or **Text Only**.

   ◆ Select the **Use Small Size** check box to reduce the size of the toolbar buttons.

5. Click **Done**.

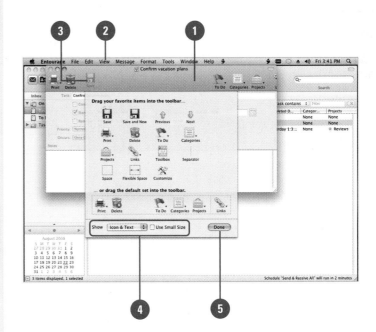

Did You Know?

You can show and hide individual toolbars in Entourage. Open the window with the toolbar you want to show or hide, click the View menu, and then click Show Toolbar or Hide Toolbar.

Managing Information with Entourage

15

Introduction

Microsoft Entourage 2008 provides an easy and efficient way to track and organize all the information that lands on your desk. You can use Entourage tools for your personal information management needs. With Entourage, you can organize and manage your day-to-day information, from e-mail and calendars to contacts and tasks. It's easy to share information with others, and organize and view your schedule and communications in one place.

Using the Calendar feature, you can manage your time by doing much more than circling dates. Among its many features, the Entourage Calendar lets you schedule **Appointments** (dates that are noted with data referring to that day's activity and do not require attendance by other individuals) and **Events** (an appointment that lasts 24 hours or more). Entourage also allows you to share your calendar with others. In Entourage, you view the schedules of your coworkers before you schedule meetings or appointments so that you can determine when all the people in your group are free at the same time.

You can use Entourage to create a to-do list and assign the items on the list to others as needed from Tasks. Rather then cluttering your desk or obscuring your computer with sticky pad notes, use Notes to jot down your immediate thoughts, ideas, and other observations. To help organize and locate information, Entourage allows you to group, sort, and filter items.

Viewing the Calendar

The **Calendar** is an electronic version of the familiar paper daily planner. You can schedule time for completing specific tasks, meetings, vacations, holidays, or for any other activity with the Calendar. You can change the Calendar to show activities for the Day, Work Week (five business days), Week (all seven days), or Month. In Day/Week/Month view, the Calendar is split into two sections: the Appointment area and the Mini Calendar. The Appointment area serves as a daily planner where you can schedule activities by the day, work week, full week, or month. Appointments are scheduled activities such as a doctor's visit, and occupy a block of time in the Appointment area. Events are activities that last 24 hours or longer, such as a seminar, and do not occupy blocks of time in your calendar. Instead, they appear in a banner at the beginning of a day.

Open and Change the Calendar View

1. Click the **Calendar** button on the toolbar.

2. You can change the Calendar view in several ways.

   ◆ Click the **Calendar** menu, and then click the view option you want.

   ◆ Click one of the **Calendar** view buttons (**Day**, **Work Week**, **Week**, or **Month**) in Calendar view.

   ◆ Click the left arrow or right arrow on the mini calendar to change the current month, or click the circle to display the current day.

   ◆ Click a date on the mini calendar to view that day's schedule. The date highlighted in red is today's date.

   ◆ Drag the mini calendar to view a specific range of dates (up to 6 weeks). You can drag the right edge of the Views pane to display a pair of mini calendars.

3. View and work with tasks associated with the current Calendar view.

Calendar view buttons

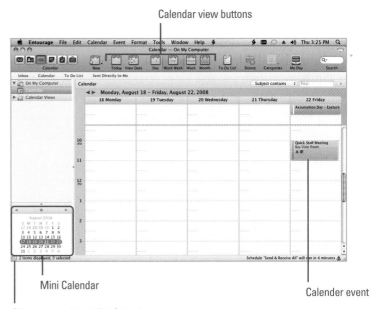

Mini Calendar

Click to show/hide Mini Calendar

Calender event

Customizing the Calendar

As with other folders in Entourage, you can customize Calendar to suit your needs. One way to customize the Entourage Calendar is to change the work week settings. For example, if you are in the medical field and you work three twelve-hour shifts a week, Wednesday through Friday, you might want to change the work week in your Calendar to reflect this. You can change the days included in the work week, the start day of the work week, the start and end times of the work day, the first week of the work year, and the default time zone.

Customize the Calendar View

① Click the **Entourage** menu, and then click **Preferences**.

② In the left pane, click **Calendar**.

③ Click the **First day of week** drop-down, and then select the day of the week you want to start the week.

④ Click the Calendar work week and work hours options you want to customize.

⑤ Click the **Default time zone for new user events** drop-down, and then select a time zone.

⑥ Click **OK**.

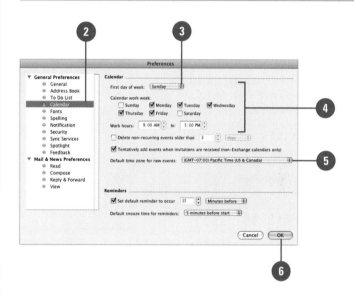

Did You Know?

You can save your Calendar as a Web page. Switch to Calendar view, click the File menu, click Save as Web Page, select the duration and publishing options you want, enter a title and file name, and then click Save. Once the Calendar is published, you can open the file in a Web browser.

For Your Information

Adding and Removing Holidays

The default Calendar in Entourage doesn't include holidays. However, if you want them, you can import them using the Import wizard. Click the File menu, click Import, click the Holiday option, click the right arrow to continue, select the holidays that you want to use (including religious and country-specific holidays), click the right arrow to continue, and then click Finish. To remove holidays, click the Edit menu, click Advanced Search, set the search criteria to Category, Is and Holiday to select the holiday set you want to remove or edit, select the holidays you want to delete, click the Delete button on the toolbar, and then click Delete to confirm it.

Scheduling an Appointment and Event

In Entourage, an **appointment** is any activity you schedule that doesn't include other people or resources. An **event** is any appointment that lasts one or more full days (24-hour increments), such as a seminar, a conference, or a vacation. You can mark yourself available (free or tentative) or unavailable (busy or out of the office) to others during a scheduled appointment or an event. You enter appointment or event information in the same box; however, when you schedule an event, the All-day event check box is selected.

Schedule an Appointment

1. Click the **Calendar** button on the toolbar.

2. Drag the time of the appointment in the Appointment area. An Office Reminder window appears. Click the **Close** button to exit it.

   ◆ You can also click the **File** menu, point to **New**, and then click **Calendar Event**.

3. Type a name for the appointment, and then press Return.

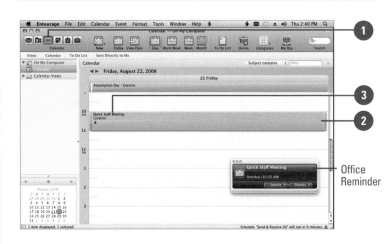

Office Reminder

Include Appointment Details

1. In Calendar view, double-click a block of time or an appointment.

2. Add or change the subject, location, start and end times, and any notes, as necessary.

3. Click the **Occurs** drop-down, and then select the occurrence time. If the event occurs more than once, click **Edit** to set recurring options.

4. To set a reminder, select the **Reminder** check box, and then specify a reminder time.

5. To add travel time, select the **Travel time** check box, and then specify a time.

6. Click the **File** menu, click **Save**, and then click the **Close** button.

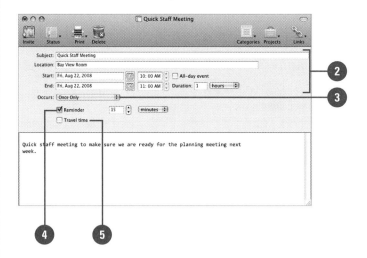

Schedule an Event and Include Details

① Click the **Calendar** button on the toolbar.

② Click the top of the day in the Appointment area.

③ Type a description of the event, and then press Return.

④ Double-click the event.

The All-day event check box is selected.

⑤ Add or change the subject, location, start and end times, and any notes, as necessary.

⑥ Click the **Occurs** drop-down, and then select the occurrence time. If the event occurs more than once, click **Edit** to set recurring options.

⑦ To set a reminder, select the **Reminder** check box, and then specify a reminder time.

⑧ To add travel time, select the **Travel time** check box, and then specify a time.

⑨ To add a color category, click the **Categorize** button, and then click a color category.

⑩ Click the **File** menu, click **Save**, and then click the **Close** button.

Did You Know?

You can mark yourself available or unavailable to others. In the Event window, click the Status button on the toolbar, click Busy, Free, Tentative, or Out of Office.

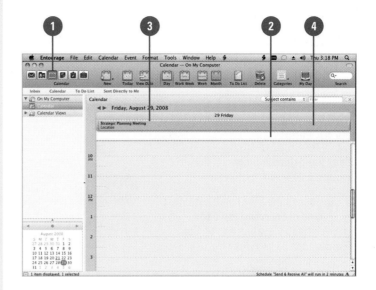

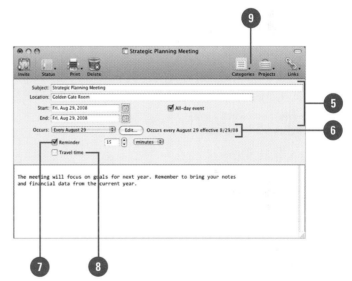

Modifying or Deleting an Event

After you create an appointment or event in Entourage, you can change it by quickly dragging the scheduled event to a new day and time in the calendar, or by double-clicking it to change event details, including recurring events. If an event gets cancelled, you can quickly delete it. If you have old non-recurring events on the calendar, you can set a Calendar preference to automatically delete them based on a specific time interval.

Modify an Event

1. Click the **Calendar** button on the toolbar.

   ◆ To change the scheduled date or time of an event, you can drag it to a new location on the calendar.

2. Double-click the event.

3. If this is a recurring event, select an option to open the entire series of events or just the individual event, and then click **OK**.

4. Make the event option changes you want.

5. Click the **File** menu, click **Save**, and then click the **Close** button.

Did You Know?

You can create an event in another time zone. Click the Calendar button, click the New button, type the event information, click the Event menu, point to Time Zone, and then click the time zone you want.

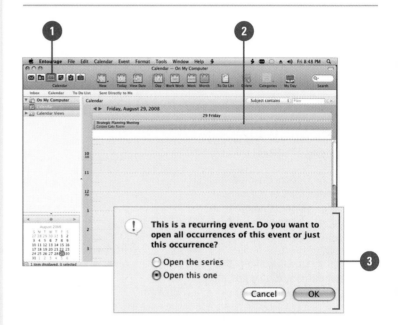

Delete an Event

① Click the **Calendar** button on the toolbar.

② Select the event you want to delete.

③ Press Delete or click the **Delete** button on the toolbar.

④ Do one of the following:

◆ If this is a one-time event, click **Delete**.

◆ If this is a recurring event, select an option to delete the entire series of events or just the individual event, and then click **OK**.

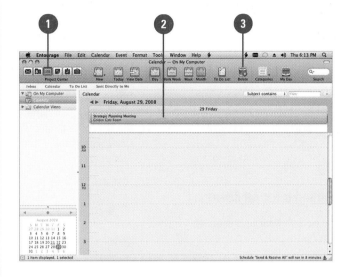

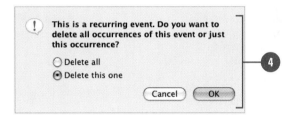

Did You Know?

You can delete old calendar events automatically. Click the Entourage menu, click Preferences, click Calendar, select the Delete non-recurring events older than X check box, specify a time interval, and then click OK.

You can change your availability status. With a Microsoft Exchange account, Entourage shows you as Busy during an event unless you change the status to Free using the Status button in the Event window.

Responding to Reminders

When you create or edit an event, you can set up a reminder to appear when based on a time interval. When the date and time for the reminder takes place, the Office Reminder window appears—even if an Office program isn't running—displaying options to dismiss the reminder, dismiss all reminders, snooze the reminder for a short period of time, open the item, or do nothing. Office Reminder is a stand-alone Office related program that works with Entourage to remind you about upcoming events and tasks. As with any stand-alone program, when the Office Reminder window appears, its icon also appears on the Dock. The number in the clock icon indicates the current number of reminders.

Set a Reminder for an Event

1. Click the **Calendar** button on the toolbar.

2. Double-click the event that you want to set a reminder.

3. If this is a recurring event, select an option to open the entire series of events or just the individual event, and then click **OK**.

4. Select the **Reminder** check box, , and then specify a reminder time.

5. Click the **File** menu, click **Save**, and then click the **Close** button.

Did You Know?

You can turn Office Reminders sound on and off. In the Office Reminders program, click the Office Reminders menu, click Turn On Sounds or Turn Off Sounds.

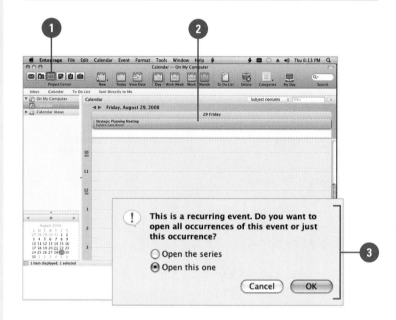

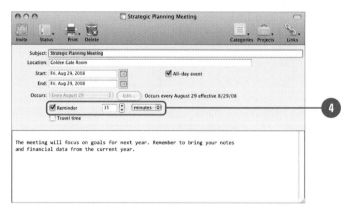

Responding to a Reminder

1. At the designated date and time, the Office Reminder window appears.

2. Do one of the following:

   ◆ **Complete.** Select the **Complete** check box to indicate the task is done or clear it to leave the task as incomplete.

   ◆ **Dismiss.** Click **Dismiss** to remove the reminder.

   ◆ **Dismiss All.** Click and hold **Dismiss**, and then click **Dismiss All** to remove all listed reminders.

   When you dismiss a reminder, the event remains on the calendar and not removed.

   ◆ **Snooze.** Click **Snooze** to display the reminder again in the specified time.

   ◆ **Open the item.** Double-click the document name in the reminder to open and edit the item.

   ◆ **Do nothing.** Click the **Close** button to exit the Office Reminder window.

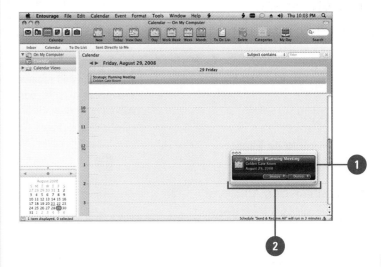

Inviting Others to an Event

Scheduling a meeting involves more than setting up an event. It also entails inviting people outside your organization to meet and discuss a subject. When you schedule an event using Entourage you are sending a special kind of e-mail message—a message request. Each invited attendee and the person responsible for the resource that you may have requested receive a message request. It is to this message that the invitee must respond. Entourage sends event invitations in the iCalendar format (.ICS), which is also supported by Microsoft Outlook.

Invite Others to an Event

1. Click the **Calendar** button on the toolbar.

2. Double-click the event that you want to invite others to.

3. If this is a recurring event, select an option to open the entire series of events or just the individual event, and then click **OK**.

4. Click the **Invite** button on the toolbar.

   ◆ If you have a Microsoft Exchange account, click the **Scheduling** tab to check invitees availability. To keep an event private, select the **Private** check box.

5. In the address pane, specify the contacts that you want to send an invitation to the event, and then close the pane.

   ◆ If you have multiple accounts, select the account from which you want to send the invitation.

6. Add or change the subject, location, start and end times, as necessary.

7. Enter a message in the body of the invitation.

8. If you decide not to send the invitation, click the **Cancel Invite** button on the toolbar.

9. Click the **Send** button to send the e-mail invitation.

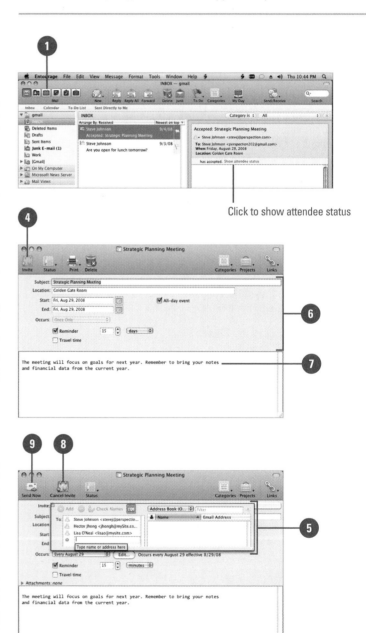

Click to show attendee status

Responding to Event Requests

When you receive an event or meeting request it appears in your Inbox such as any message would. The difference is when you view the message you can also view your calendar to see where the event is scheduled. Once you are sure whether or not you can attend the event, then you use the Accept button or the Decline button at the top of the request e-mail. If you are not sure, you use the Tentative button. When you accept or tentatively accept a request, the event is added to your calendar. A message is sent to the sender of the event request with your response.

Accept or Decline an Event Request

1. Display your Inbox, and then double-click the e-mail with the meeting request.

   If the message arrives when you're online, a mail alert appears above the Dock. Click the alert to open it.

2. In the e-mail message, click a button to response to the event request: **Accept**, **Decline**, or **Tentative**.

3. Select a response option: **Yes, with comments**, **Yes, without comments**, or **No**.

   Options vary depending on the e-mail program.

4. Click **OK**.

5. If prompted, type a message that explains your response, and then click the **Send** button.

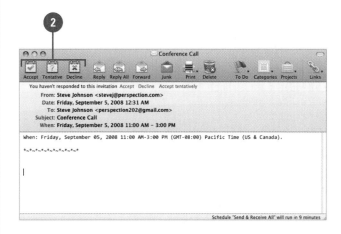

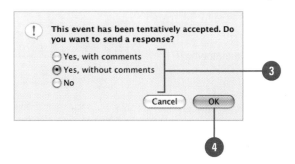

Did You Know?

You can tentatively add events automatically. Click the Entourage ment, click Preferences, click General, select the Tentatively add events when invitations are received check box, and then click OK.

Updating and Canceling Event Requests

Planning events can be a difficult task when you have to coordinate multiple schedules, schedules that often change with little or no notice. You can use the Calendar to reschedule or cancel meetings. You can send an event update request, or cancel the event. When you send attendees an updated event request, the attendee receives an e-mail message, the original event is deleted, and the new event time is added to his/her Calendar. If you send a cancellation notice about the event, the event is deleted from the attendees' Calendars.

Update a Event Request

1. Click the **Calendar** button on the toolbar, and then double-click the scheduled event.

2. Make the changes you want to the event, such as date or time.

3. To invite others, click the **Invite list**, add more contacts, and then close the address pane.

4. To change invitee status, click **View attendee status**, select contact, delete it or change the response, and then close it.

5. Click the **Send** button, select an update option, and then click **OK.**

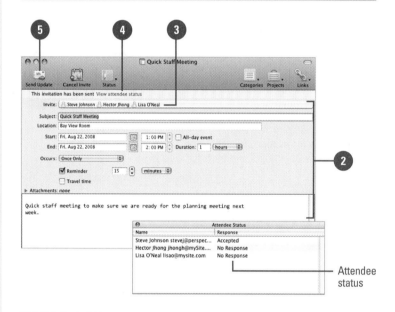

Attendee status

Cancel a Event Request

1. Click the **Calendar** button on the toolbar, and then double-click the scheduled event.

2. Click the **Cancel Invite** button on the toolbar.

3. Select a cancelation option: **Yes, with comments, Yes, without comments,** or **No.**

4. Click **OK**.

5. If prompted, type a message that explains your response, and then click the **Send** button.

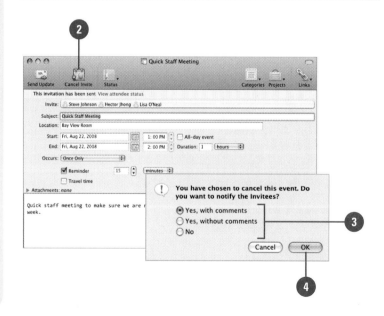

Creating and Updating Tasks

You can quickly create a simple task by name only using the create a task box on the To-Do List pane (**New!**) in Calendar view or a more detailed task using the New button on the toolbar in Tasks view. The Task window allows you to set a Due Date (the date by which the task must be completed), Start Date, the Priority, and select the Reminder check box to have a reminder window open the morning of the due date. You can type additional information about the task in the Notes area at the bottom of the window.

Create or Update a Task

1. Click the **Tasks** button on the toolbar.

2. Click the **New** button on the toolbar to create a new task, or double-click an existing one to update it.

3. Type a name for the task.

4. Select the **Start Date** and **Due Date** check boxes, and then specify dates for both.

   ◆ To quickly set a due date, click the **To Do button** arrow on the toolbar, and then select an option, such as **Today**, **Next Week**, or **No Due Date**.

5. To set a reminder, select the **Reminder** check box, and then select a date and time.

6. Click the **Priority** drop-down, and then select a priority level.

7. Click the **Occurs** drop-down, and then select the occurrence time. If the event occurs more than once, click **Edit** to set recurring options.

8. Click in the Notes area, and then type information about the task.

9. Click the **File** menu, click **Save**, and then click the **Close** button.

Task

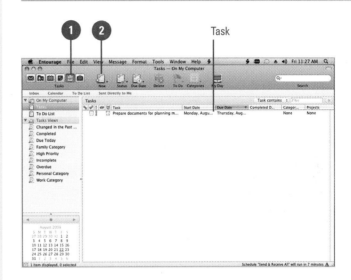

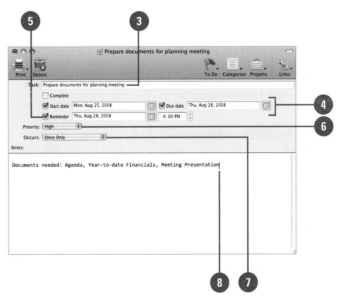

Creating a To Do List Item

In addition to creating tasks, you can also create To Do List items (**New!**). You create a To Do List item by simply setting a follow-up flag with the To Do button or flag icon for an e-mail message in Mail view or a contact in Address Book. From the To Do button, you can select a due date: Today, Tomorrow, This Week, Next Week, or Choose Date. If you don't know the due date, you can select No Due Date. When you work in Calendar view, you can display and create tasks and To Do List items in the To Do List pane. At the bottom of the To Do List pane is a text box you can use to create a simple task or a To Do List item.

Create a To Do List Item

1. Select the e-mail message in Mail view or contact in Address Book that you want to set as a to do item.

2. Click the **To Do** button arrow on the toolbar, and then select an due date option.

   ◆ You can also click the flag icon or the Address Book to create a To Do List item.

   Entourage adds the item as a new To Do List item.

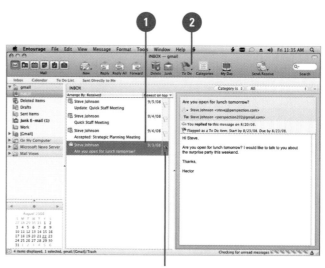

Click the flag icon to create a To Do List item

Create a To Do List Item in the Calendar

1. Click the **Calendar** button on the toolbar

2. Click the **To Do List** button on the toolbar.

   A list of all current tasks and To Do List items appear in the To Do List pane.

3. Click in the box at the bottom of the To Do List pane, and then type a task name.

4. Press Return to create a task, or click the **Action** button, and then select a To Do due date option.

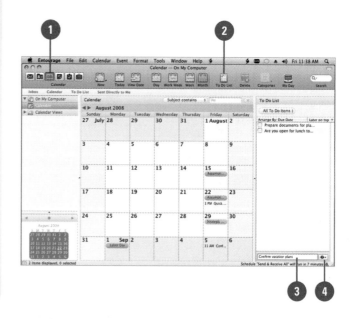

Viewing Tasks and To Do List Items

You can display tasks and To Do Lists in a variety of views. In the Tasks view, you can use the Folder list to quickly display tasks or To Do Lists (**New!**). After you display the items you want in Tasks view, you can use menu commands to filter the list or column headings to sort the list. When you work in Calendar view, you can display and create tasks and To Do List items in the To Do List pane. At the bottom of the To Do List pane is a text box you can use to create a simple task or a To Do List item.

Change Tasks Views

① Click the **Tasks** button on the toolbar.

② In the Folder list, click **Tasks** or **To Do List**.

TIMESAVER *Click the To Do List in the Favorites Bar.*

③ You can view tasks and To Do items several ways.

◆ **Filter To Do List items.** Click the **View** menu, and then click **Incomplete Items**, **Completed Items**, or **All To Do Items**.

◆ **Filter tasks.** Click the **View** menu, and then click **Incomplete Tasks**, **Completed Tasks**, or **All Tasks**. You can also use the **Status** button on the toolbar.

◆ **Filter due date.** Click the **Due Date** button, and then select a date option.

◆ **Sort items.** Click any column heading in the list except the first one.

◆ **Tasks Views.** Expand Tasks Views in the Folder list, and then select a search folder to display items that meet the criteria.

◆ **To Do List pane.** Click the **Calendar** button on the toolbar, click the **To Do List** on the toolbar.

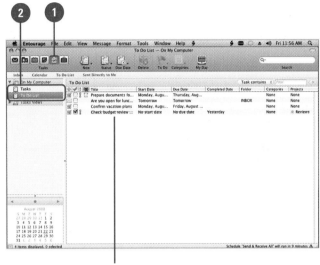

Completed item

Managing Tasks and To Do List Items

As you work with tasks, you'll want to keep your Tasks folder updated to reflect the status of each task. One obvious tactic is to mark each task as completed once you've finished the task. To do this, you open the Task window and then select the Complete check box. Once you've marked a task as complete, it appears in Tasks view with a line through it. Some tasks are jobs that you need to complete on a regular basis. In this case, you can make a task recurring. Recurring tasks have a small icon with two circling arrows in Tasks view.

View and Mark a Task or To Do List Item as Completed

1. Click the **Tasks** button on the toolbar.

2. To view only certain tasks or To Do List items, do any of the following:

   ◆ To view only incomplete items in the list, click the **Status** button on the toolbar, and then click **Incomplete**.

   ◆ To view items by due date, click the **Due Date** button on the toolbar, and then click **Due Today** or **Due This Week**.

   ◆ To view all items, click the **View** menu, and then click **All Tasks** or **All To Do Items**.

3. In the Status column for the task or To Do List item, select the **Complete** check box.

   ◆ To edit the item and mark it complete, double-click the item, and then select the **Complete** check box. Click the **File** menu, click **Save**, and then click the **Close** button.

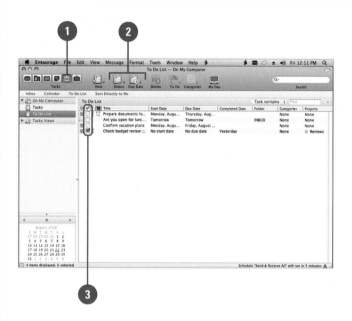

Instance Name

See Also

See "Creating and Updating Tasks" on page 471 for information on editing tasks.

Creating and Modifying Notes

Notes in Entourage are electronic versions of paper sticky notes. Notes replace the random scraps of paper on which you might jot down reminders, questions, thoughts, ideas, or directions. Like the popular sticky notes, you can move an Entourage note anywhere on your screen and leave it displayed as you work. Any edits you make to a note are saved automatically. The ability to color-code, size, categorize, sort, or filter notes makes these notes even handier than their paper counterparts. When you open a new Note window in Entourage, you simply type text to create a note. The first paragraph becomes the note name in the Notes folder. Entourage inserts the date and time that you created the note for your reference.

Create or Modify a Note

1. Click the **Notes** button on the toolbar.

2. Click the **New** button on the toolbar to create a new note, or double-click an existing one to update it.

3. Type a name for the notes.

4. Type your note.

5. Format the notes using buttons on the Formatting toolbar.

6. Click the **File** menu, click **Save**, and then click the **Close** button.

Did You Know?

You can delete a note. Select the note or notes you want to delete, and then press Delete, or click the Delete button on the toolbar, and then click Delete to confirm it.

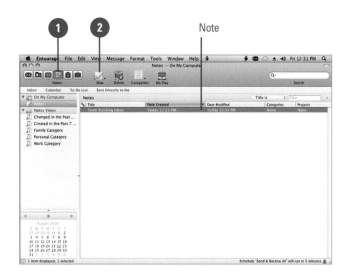

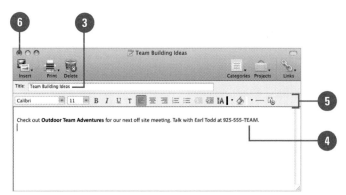

Using My Day

My Day (**New!**) is a stand-alone Office related program that allows you to display upcoming events and tasks from Entourage. In fact, you don't need to have Entourage or any other Office program running to use My Day. You can start My Day from the Finder or within Entourage. If you want My Day to always be running, you can set a preference option to start My Day after your computer starts up.

Start or Quit My Day

◆ In Entourage, click the **My Day** button on the toolbar, or click the **Window** menu, and then click **My Day**.

◆ Double-click the My Day icon located in the Microsoft Office 2008/Office folder.

◆ Click the **My Day** menu, and then click **Quit My Day** to exit the program.

Click to customize Entourage Today

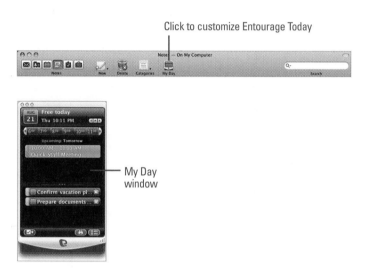

My Day window

Customize My Day to Start Automatically

1 Start My Day.

2 Click the **My Day** menu, and then click **Preferences**.

3 Click the **General** icon.

4 Select the **Open after computer logon** check box.

5 Click **OK**.

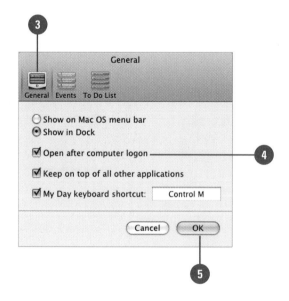

Viewing the My Day Window

Date. The My Day window (**New!**) displays the current date in the upper left corner.

Day and time. The My Day window displays the current day and time along with the time until the next event or task. Click the Date to go to a specific date.

View other dates. Click the View buttons to view the events and tasks for other dates. Click the left and right arrows to go back and forth between dates, or click the bullet (between the arrows) to display today's date.

Time line. Click arrows on the timeline to view events and tasks for the selected time slot.

Calendar events, tasks, and To Do items. These items appear in the middle area of the My Day window. You can double-click an item to open it.

Print. Click to print a list of events, tasks, and To Do items for the selected date.

New Task. Click to open a pane in My Day to create a note. Click the New Task button again to close the pane.

Preferences. Click to customize the way you work with the My Day program.

Run Entourage. Click to start Entourage.

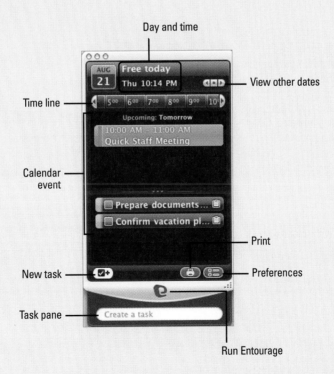

Day and time

View other dates

Time line

Calendar event

Print

New task

Preferences

Task pane

Run Entourage

Synchronizing Entourage with an iPod

If you have an iPod, iPod Touch, or iPhone, you can enable Sync Services in Entourage to synchronize your Entourage Address Book and Calendar event with data in the Apple Address Book and iCal. When you connect your iPod, iPod Touch, or iPhone to your Mac, iTunes starts and synchronizes data with the current settings. After you change the synchronization settings for Entourage, iTunes synchronizes Entourage data with the Apple Address Book and iCal on the devices.

Enable Sync Services

① Click the **Entourage** menu, and then click **Preferences**.

② In the left pane, click **Sync Services**.

③ Select the **Synchronize contacts with Address Book and .Mac** check box.

④ Select the **Synchronize events and tasks with iCal and .Mac** check box.

⑤ Click **OK**.

⑥ If prompted, click a synchronization option to merge Entourage data with Address Book and iCal data, replace Entourage data with the Address Book and iCal data, or replace the Address Book and iCal data with the Entourage data.

⑦ Click **OK**.

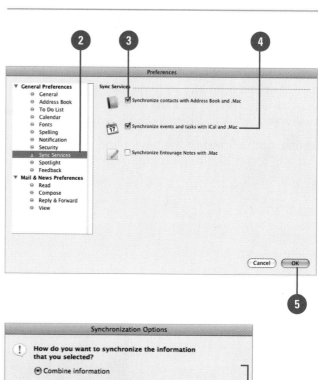

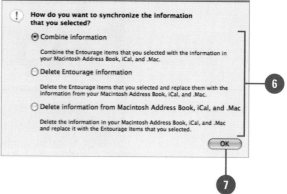

Synchronize Entourage Data with an iPod, iPod Touch, or iPhone

1 Connect your iPod or iPhone to your Mac.

iTunes starts and performs a synchronization with the current settings.

2 In the Devices list, select your device, and then click the **Info** or **Contacts** tab.

3 In the Calendars area, select the **Sync iCal calendars** check box, click the **All calendars** or **Selected calendars** option, and then select the check boxes for the calendars you want to sync as needed.

4 In the Contacts area, select the **Sync Address Book contacts** check box, click the **All contacts** or **Selected groups** option, and then select the check boxes for the contact groups you want to sync as needed.

5 Click **Apply**.

iTunes performs a new synchronization with the new settings. These setting remain in effect until you change them.

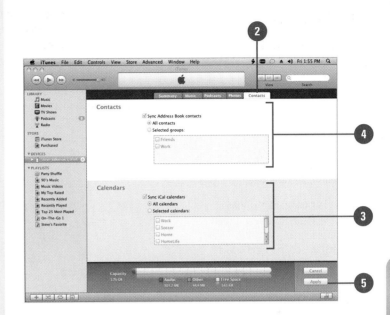

Printing Items from Entourage

You can print any item in Entourage. You can click the Print command on the File menu to print the selected item using the default print settings. The default or preset printing style is different for each view depending on what type of information you are printing. Printing options change depending on the item and view. There are different printing options available in table, calendar, and card views. If you have already printed an item and want to print it again, you can use the Print One Copy command.

Print an Item or View

1. Click the item you want to print.

2. If necessary, click the **File** menu, point to **Page Setup**, and then click a print style (styles differ depending on the item you choose), and then click **OK**.

3. Click the **File** menu, and then click **Print**.

   ◆ To print a single copy without the Print dialog box, click the **File** menu, and then click **Print One Copy**.

   Printing options change depending on the item and view.

4. If necessary, click the **Printer** drop-down, and then select a printer.

5. Click the **Print** drop-down, and then select what you want to print.

6. If available, click the **Style** drop-down, and then select a print style.

7. Click **Layout**, select the specific items that you want to print, and then click **OK**.

8. Specify print options or a print range. Options vary depending on the item you selected.

9. Click **Print**.

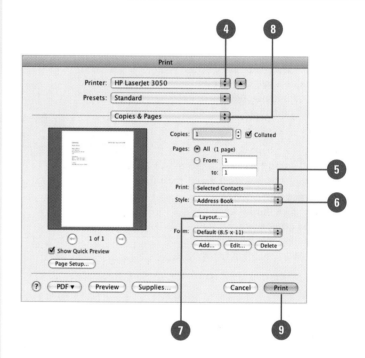

Publishing Office Documents on the Web

16

Introduction

Web pages are multimedia documents that provide information and contain links to other documents on the Internet, an intranet, a local network, or a hard disk. These links—also called hyperlinks—are highlighted text or graphics that you click to follow a pathway from one Web page to another. Incorporating hyperlinks within your Office documents adds an element of connectivity to your work. Web pages are based on **Hypertext Markup Language (HTML)**—a simple coding system used to format Web pages. A browser program, such as Microsoft Internet Explorer, interprets these special codes to determine how a certain Web page should be displayed. Different codes mark the size, color, style, and placement of text and graphics as well as which words and graphics should be marked as hyperlinks and to what files they link.

Web technology is available for all your Microsoft Office programs. Office provides you with the tools you need to create and save your documents as a Web page and to publish it on the Web. Office makes it easy to create a Web page without learning HTML. Saving your Office documents in HTML format means you can use most Web browsers to view them. By saving your Office documents as Web pages, you can share your data with others via the Internet. You can also preview how your document will look as a Web page in your Office program or in your browser. Office uses HTML as a companion file format; it recognizes the .html filename extension as accurately as it does those for its own Office programs (.docx, .xlsx, and .pptx).

What You'll Do

Open a Web Page

Preview a Web Page

Create a Hyperlink

Add Hyperlinks to Slide Objects

Change Web Page Options

Save a Web Page

Save Slides as Web Graphics

Create a PDF Document

Send a Document Using E-Mail

Opening a Web Page

After saving an Office document as a Web page, you can open the Web page, an HTML file. This allows you to quickly and easily switch from HTML to the standard Office program format and back again without losing any formatting or functionality. For example, if you create a formatted chart in an Excel workbook, save the workbook file as a Web page, and then reopen the Web page in Excel, the chart will look the same as the original chart in Excel. Excel preserves the original formatting and functionality of the workbook.

Open an Office Document as a Web Page

1. Click the **File** menu, and then click **Open**.

2. Click the **Enable** drop-down, and then click **All Readable Documents**.

   ◆ Click **Web Pages** (Word and Excel) to narrow down the list of files.

3. Click the **Where** drop-down, and then select the folder where the file is located.

4. Click the Web file.

5. Click **Open**.

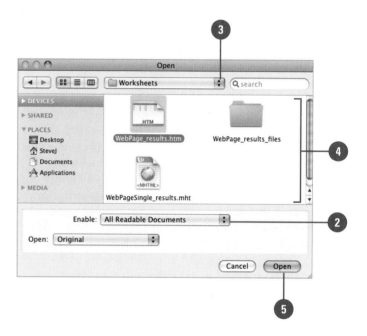

Previewing a Web Page

You can view any Office document as if it were already on the Web by previewing the Web page. By previewing a file you want to post to the Web, you can see if there are any errors that need to be corrected, formatting that needs to be added, or additions that need to be made. Just as you should always preview a document before you print it, you should preview a Web page before you post it. Previewing the Web page is similar to using the Print Preview feature before you print a document. This view shows you what the page will look like once it's posted on the Internet. You do not have to be connected to the Internet to preview a document as a Web page.

View an Office Document as a Web Page

① Open the Web file you want to view as a Web page.

② Click the **File** menu, and then click **Web Page Preview**.

Your default Web browser starts and displays the Web page.

③ Quit your Web browser, and then return to the Office program.

Did You Know?

Web addresses and URLs mean the same thing. Every Web page has a Uniform Resource Locator (URL), or Web address. Each URL contains specific parts that identify where a Web page is located. For example, the URL for Perspection's Web page is: *http://www.perspection.com/index.htm* where "http://" shows the address is on the Web, "www.perspection.com" shows the computer that stores the Web site, and "index.htm" is a Web page on the Web site.

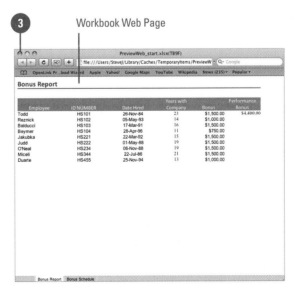

Workbook Web Page

Creating a Hyperlink

With instant access to the Internet, your documents can contain links to specific sites so you and anyone else using your documents can access Web information. You can create a **hyperlink**—a graphic object or colored, underlined text that you click to move (or jump) to a new location (or destination). The destination can be in the same document, another file on your computer or network, or a Web page on your intranet or the Internet. When you point to hyperlinked text or an object, the cursor changes to a pointing hand to indicate it's a hyperlink. To connect to the linked location, just click the hyperlink.

Create or Edit a Hyperlink

1. Select the text, cell, or object, such as a picture, where you want to create or edit a hyperlink.

2. Click the **Insert** menu, and then click **Hyperlink**.

   TIMESAVER *Press Ctrl+K.*

3. Click one of the tabs to specify the type of link that you want to create:

   ◆ **Web Page.** Enter the URL of the Web page that you want to link to in the Link to box. If you want to link to a specific place (anchor) within the Web page, enter the anchor name or click **Locate** to find it.

   ◆ **Document.** Click **Select**, locate the file, and then click **Open**. The path appears in the Link to box. If you want to link to a specific place (anchor) within the Web page, enter the anchor name or click **Locate** to find it.

   ◆ **E-mail Address.** Enter the e-mail address and subject. When visitors click the e-mail address, your e-mail program automatically opens with the address.

4. Type the display name for the hyperlink or use the one provided.

5. Click **OK**.

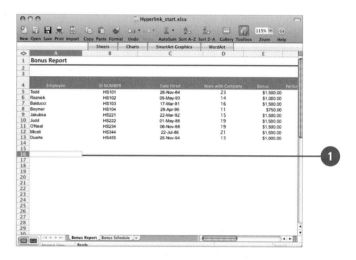

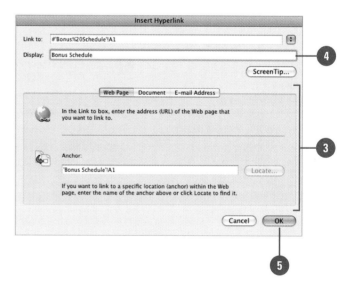

Jump to a Hyperlink

1. Click the hyperlink on your document; your cursor changes to a hand when the hyperlink is available.

   ◆ You can also Control-click the hyperlink, point to **Hyperlink**, and then click **Open in New Window**.

   Office opens the linked location. For Web addresses, Office opens your Web browser, displaying the Web page associated with the hyperlink.

Remove a Hyperlink

1. Control-click the hyperlink you want, point to **Hyperlink** (if necessary), and then click **Edit Hyperlink**.

2. Click **Remove Link**.

3. Click **OK**.

Did You Know?

You can create a custom ScreenTip for a hyperlink. Select the hyperlink you want to customize, click the Insert menu, click Hyperlink, click ScreenTip, type the ScreenTip text you want, click OK twice.

Adding Hyperlinks to Slide Objects

In PowerPoint, you can turn one of the objects on your slide into an action button so that when you click or move over it, you activate a hyperlink and jump to the new location. You can point hyperlinks to almost any destination, including slides in a presentation and Web pages on the Web. Use the Action Settings dialog box to add sound to a hyperlink. You can add a default sound such as Chime, Click, or Drum Roll, or select a custom sound from a file.

Add a Hyperlink to a Slide Object

1. In PowerPoint, click the object (not within a SmartArt graphic) you want to modify.

2. Click the **Slide Show** menu, and then click **Action Settings**.

   ◆ To draw a button, click the **Slide Show** menu, point to **Action Buttons**, select a button type, and then drag to create the button.

3. Click the **Mouse Click** or **Mouse Over** tab.

4. Click the **Hyperlink to** option.

5. Click the **Hyperlink to** drop-down, and then click a destination for the hyperlink.

6. Click **OK**.

7. Run the slide show and test the hyperlink by pointing to or clicking the object in the slide show.

Did You Know?

You can edit an action button. Select the object, click the Slide Show menu, and then click Action Settings.

You can highlight a click or mouse over. When you click or move over a hyperlink, you can highlight the object. In the Action Settings dialog box, select the Highlight click or Highlight when mouse over check box.

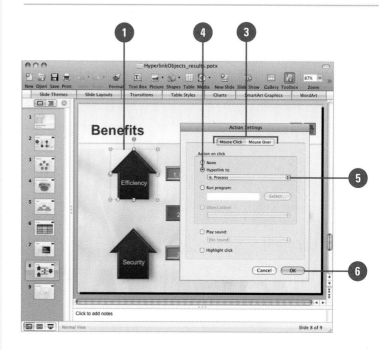

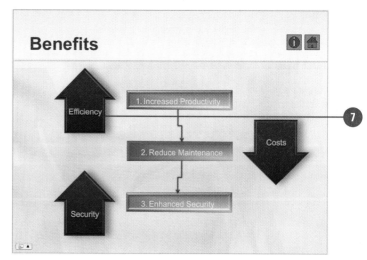

Add a Sound to a Hyperlink

1. In PowerPoint, click the object (not within a SmartArt graphic) you want to modify.

2. Click the **Slide Show** menu, and then click **Action Settings**.

   ◆ To draw a button, click the **Slide Show** menu, point to **Action Buttons**, click **Sound**, and then drag to create it.

3. Click the **Mouse Click** or **Mouse Over** tab.

4. Select the **Play sound** check box.

5. Click the **Play sound** drop-down, and then select the sound you want to play when the object is clicked during the show.

   ◆ **Custom Sound.** Or scroll to the bottom of the Play sound list, and then click **Other Sound**, locate and select the sound you want to use, and then click **OK**.

6. Click **OK**.

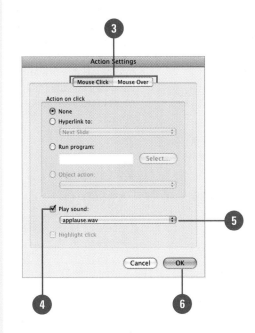

Create a Hyperlink to a Program

1. In PowerPoint, click the object (not within a SmartArt graphic) you want to modify.

2. Click the **Slide Show** menu, and then click **Action Settings**.

3. On the Mouse Click tab, click the **Run program** option, if necessary.

4. Click **Select**, and then locate and select the program you want, and then click **OK**.

5. Click **OK**.

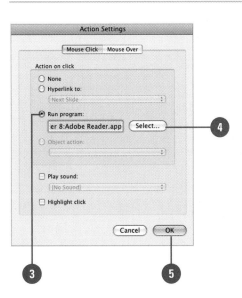

Changing Web Page Options

When you save a document as a Web page, you can change the appearance of the Web page by changing Office's Web options. You can enter a page title, add searchable keywords, and set Web options to automatically update links, use the PNG graphic format as an output format for optimization, and save the Web page with international text encoding so users on any language system are able to view the correct characters. Additional options are available depending on the Office program.

Change Web Page Options

1. Click the **Word**, **Excel**, or **PowerPoint** menu, and then click **Preferences**.

2. Click the **General** icon.

3. Click **Web Options**.

   ◆ You can also click **Web Options** in the Save as Web Page dialog box.

4. Click the **General** tab, and then enter a Web page title, and Web page keywords (separated by commas).

5. Click the **Files** tab, and then select the following options:

   ◆ Select or clear the **Update links on save** check box.

   ◆ In Word, select or clear the **Save only display information into HTML** check box.

   ◆ In PowerPoint, select or clear the **Include the original file with this Web presentation so it can be edited in PowerPoint later** check box.

6. In PowerPoint, click the **Appearance** tab, and then select the following options:

   ◆ Click the **Default view** drop-down, and then select **Normal** or **Full Screen**.

   ◆ Click the **Colors** drop-down, and then select a color scheme.

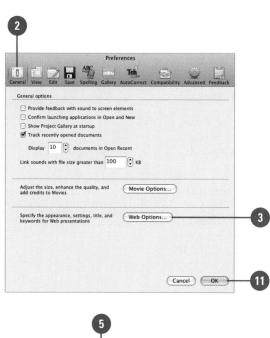

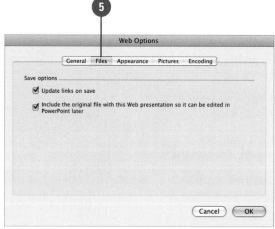

- ◆ Select or clear the **Include slide notes** check box.

- ◆ Click the **Navigation buttons** drop-down, and then select the type of buttons you want: **Graphic**, **Regular**, **Text**, or **None**.

- ◆ Click the **Button placement** drop-down, and then select the location where you want the navigation buttons: **Top**, **Bottom**, or **Floating window**.

7 Click the **Pictures** tab, and then select the following options:

- ◆ Select or clear the **Enable PNG as an output format** check box.

- ◆ In PowerPoint and Word, click the **Screen size** drop-down, select a monitor size.

    In Word, specify the **Pixels per inch** (default 72).

8 Click the **Encoding** tab, and then select the following options:

- ◆ Click the **Save this document as** drop-down, select an encoding option.

- ◆ Select or clear the **Always save Web pages in the default encoding** check box.

9 In Excel and Word, click the **Fonts** tab, and then select the character set and fonts you want used in a Browser when a font in your Web page is not specified.

10 Click **OK**.

11 Click **OK**.

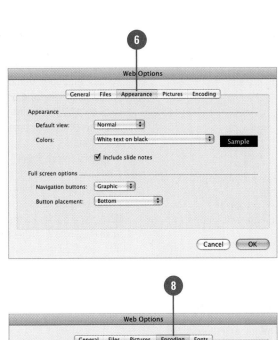

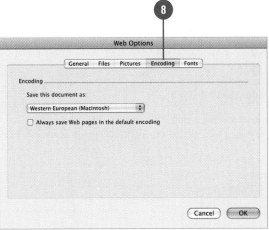

Saving a Web Page

You can place an existing Office document on the Internet for others to use. In order for any document to be placed on the Web, it must be in HTML (Hypertext Markup Language) format—a simple coding system that specifies the formats a Web browser uses to display the document. This format enables you to post, or submit information and data on a Web site for others. You don't need any HTML knowledge to save an Office document as a Web page. When you save an Office document as a Web page, you can save it using the Web Page or Single File Web Page format. The Web Page format saves the document as an HTML file and a folder that stores supporting files, such as a file for each graphic, document, and so on. Office selects the appropriate graphic format for you based on the image's content. A single file Web page saves all the elements of a Web site, including text and graphics, into a single file in the MHTML format, which is supported by Internet Explorer 4.0.1 or later.

Save an Office Document as a Web Page

1. Click the **File** menu, and then click **Save as Web Page**.

2. Type the name for the Web page.

3. Click the **Where** drop-down, and then select a location for your Web page.

4. Click the **Format** drop-down, and then click **Web Page (.htm)**.

   ◆ In Word and Excel, you can also click **Single File Web Page (.mht)**.

5. Click **Web Options** to set options for saving a Web page.

6. Select any of the following options:

   ◆ In Excel, click the **Workbook** or **Sheet**, or **Selection** option.

   ◆ In Word, click the **Save entire file into HTML** or **Save only display information into HTML** option.

7. Click **Save**.

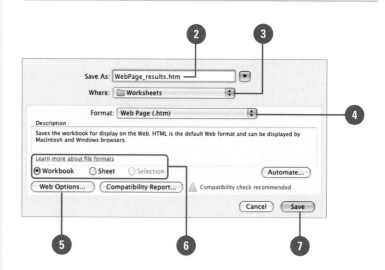

Saving Slides as Web Graphics

As you develop a Web site, you can incorporate slides from any of your PowerPoint presentations. You can save any slide in a presentation in the GIF, JPEG, or PNG Web graphic format. **Graphics Interchange Format (GIF)** is a form of compression for line drawings or other artwork. Office converts to GIF such images as logos, graphs, line drawings, and specific colored objects. **Joint Photographic Experts Group (JPEG)** is a high-quality form of compression for continuous tone images, such as photographs. Office converts to JPEG such images as photographs or other images that have many shades of colors. **Portable Network Graphics Format** is a new bit-mapped graphics format similar to GIF. You can also save slides in the TIFF or BMP format, which are not suited for the Web, yet work well in documents or printed material.

Save a PowerPoint Slide as a Web Graphic

1. In PowerPoint, display the slide you want to save as a Web graphic.

2. Click the **File** menu, and then click **Save as Pictures**.

3. Type a name for the file.

4. Click the **Where** drop-down, and then select a location for the graphic files.

5. Click the **Format** drop-down, and then click **JPEG**, **PNG**, or **GIF**.

6. Click **Options**.

7. Select the save slides as graphics files options you want:

   ◆ Click the **Save current slide only** or **Save every slide (series of graphic files)** option.

   ◆ Select the **Dots per inch (dpi)** option, and then select a dpi, or select the **Size** option, and then enter the width and height.

   ◆ To compress the files, select the **Compress graphics files** check box, and the select image quality in the drop-down.

8. Click **OK**.

9. Click **Save**.

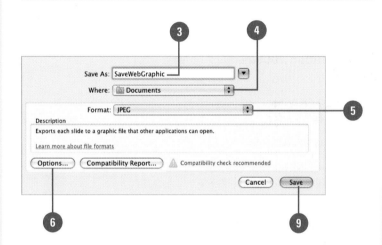

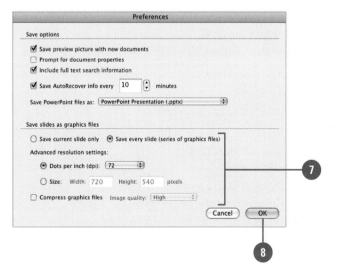

Creating a PDF Document

Portable Document Format (PDF) is a fixed-layout format developed by Adobe Systems that retains the form you intended on a computer monitor or printer. A PDF is useful when you want to create a document primarily intended to be read and printed, not modified. The reason for the success of the PDF format is Adobe's tight control over the Adobe Acrobat application (used to create PDF's), and the Acrobat Reader application (used by visitors to read PDF's). Office allows you to save a document as a PDF file (**New!**), which you can send to others for review in an e-mail. Once a PDF document is properly saved, it can be opened by virtually anyone that has Acrobat Reader, regardless of computer or operating system. And the good news is that the Reader application is a free download, just point your browser to *http://www.acrobat.com*, and then click Download Reader to obtain the latest version of the Acrobat Reader application, tailored for your specific operating system.

Save an Office Document as a PDF

1. Click the **File** menu, and then click **Save As**.

2. Type a PDF file name.

3. Click the **Where** drop-down, and then click the folder where you want to save the file.

4. Click the **Format** drop-down, and then click **PDF**.

5. Click **Save**.

6. If necessary, install Adobe Acrobat Reader and related software as directed.

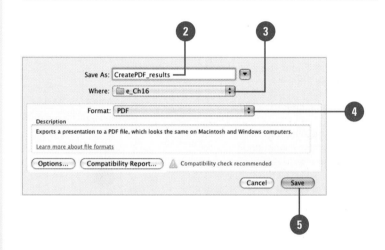

Save an Office Document as a PDF Using Print

① Open or create a document in an application.

② Click the **File** menu, and then click **Print**.

③ Click **PDF**, and then select the type of PDF you want to create:

◆ **Save as PDF.** Creates a PDF document. Enter a name, specify a location, and then click **Save**.

◆ **Fax PDF.** Creates and faxes a PDF document.

◆ **Mail PDF.** Creates and attaches a PDF document in an e-mail.

◆ **Save as PDF-X.** Creates a compacted PDF document for the Print industry. Enter a name, specify a location, and then click **Save**.

◆ **Save PDF to iPhoto.** Creates and exports a PDF document to iPhoto.

◆ **Save PDF to Web Receipts Folder.** Creates and stores a PDF document in your Web Receipts folder; great for saving Web site receipts.

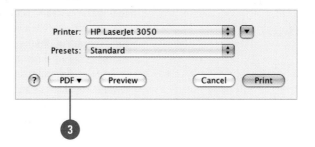

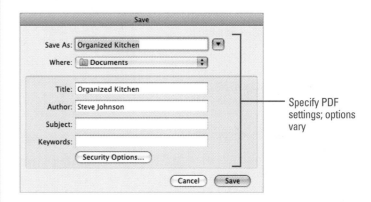

Specify PDF settings; options vary

A PDF document viewed in Acrobat Reader.

Sending a Document Using E-Mail

After you finish making changes to a document, you can quickly send it to another person for review using e-mail. Office allows you to send documents out for review as an attachment using e-mail from within the program so that you do not have to open your e-mail program. An e-mail program, such as Microsoft Entourage, needs to be installed on your computer before you begin. When you send your document out for review, reviewers can add comments and then send it back to you.

Send an Office Document Using E-Mail

1. Click the **File** menu, point to **Send To**, and then click **Mail Recipient (as Attachment)**.

   ◆ In Excel, you can also click **Mail Recipient (as HTML)**. This formats the document in HTML, which is useful when the recipient doesn't have Office.

   IMPORTANT *To complete the following steps, you need to have an e-mail program installed on your computer and an e-mail account set-up.*

   Your default e-mail program opens, such as Microsoft Entourage, with your document attached.

2. Enter your recipients and subject (appears with document name by default).

3. Enter a message for your reviewer with instructions.

4. Click the **Send** button.

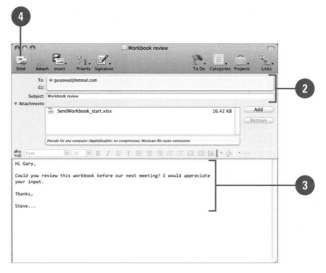

Did You Know?

You can make Entourage your default e-mail program. Open Mail, click the Mail menu, click Preferences, click the General icon, click the Default email reader drop-down, select Microsoft Entourage, and then click the Close button.

Customizing and Expanding Office

17

Introduction

Once you've become familiar with Microsoft Office 2008 and all the features it contains, you might want to customize the way you work. You can change the configuration of the menus and toolbars that you use. You can also create your own toolbar for just the commands that you use when creating your Office documents. Macros can simplify common repetitive tasks that you use regularly in Office. Macros can reside on toolbars for easy access. If a macro has a problem executing a task, Office can help you debug, or fix the error in your macro.

When you open an Office 2008 program, the Office Script menu—a scroll shaped icon—appears to the right of the Help menu. The Office Script menu provides easy access to ready-made Automator workflows and AppleScripts designed for the open Office 2008 program.

Automator is a program that lets you automate the things you frequently like to do on your Mac. You don't need to be a programmer to create automations. With Automator, all you need to do is assemble a series of actions into a workflow to complete a task. Each action performs an individual step, such as opening a file. You can create your own actions or use one of the many pre-built ones available in Automator library.

In addition to Automator, you can also use AppleScript, an English-like scripting language, to run prebuilt or custom-made scripts to automate actions performed by the computer. AppleScript lets you write your own mini applications to help with repetitious tasks.

What You'll Do

Customize Toolbars

Change Menus

Change Shortcut Keys

Work with Macros

Open a Document with Macros

Save a Document with Macros

Install and Run Office Scripts

Work with an Automator Workflow

Use Ready-Made AppleScripts

Write and Record AppleScripts

Remove Office

Customizing Toolbars

You can change the default toolbar options, such as showing the toolbar icon and text, or you can create new toolbars and customize the existing ones to maximize your efficiency. If you frequently use a toolbar, you can show it all the time and specify whether you want to dock or undock it, if available. Undocked toolbars (floating) are movable; you can drag—the vertical bar at the left edge—entire toolbars to new locations on the screen.

Change Toolbar and Menu Options

1 Click the **View** menu, and then click **Customize Toolbars and Menus**.

2 Click the **Toolbars and Menus** tab.

3 Change the options settings as necessary.

4 Click **OK**.

See Also

See "Customizing Toolbars in Entourage" on page 458 for information on change toolbars.

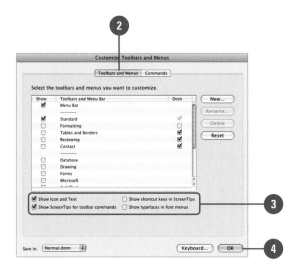

Show or Hide and Dock or Undock a Toolbar

1 Click the **View** menu, and then click **Customize Toolbars and Menus**.

2 Click the **Toolbars and Menus** tab.

3 Under the Show column, select or clear the check box next to the toolbar you want to show.

4 Under the Dock column, select or clear the check box next to the toolbar you want to show.

5 Click **OK**.

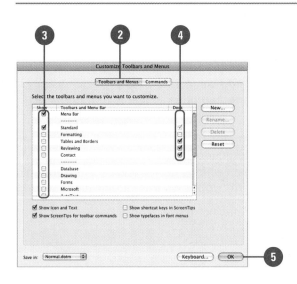

Create a Toolbar and Add Buttons to a Toolbar

1 Click the **View** menu, and then click **Customize Toolbars and Menus**.

2 Click the **Toolbars and Menus** tab.

3 Do either of the following:

- ◆ **Existing toolbar.** Double-click the toolbar to which you want to add buttons.

- ◆ **New toolbar.** Click **New**, type a toolbar name, and then click **OK**.

The toolbar is displayed.

4 Click the **Commands** tab.

5 Click a category, and then click a command.

6 Drag the command to a toolbar to add it to the toolbar or drag a button off the toolbar to remove it from the toolbar.

If the command has a button icon associated with it, that icon appears. If it doesn't, the name of the command appears.

7 Repeat steps 5 and 6 to add all the buttons you want to the toolbar, and then click the **Close** button on the toolbar.

8 Click **OK**.

Did You Know?

You can rename, delete custom toolbars. Click the View menu, click Customize Toolbars and Menus, click the Toolbars and Menus tab, select the toolbar, click Rename to rename it, or Delete to remove it, and then click OK.

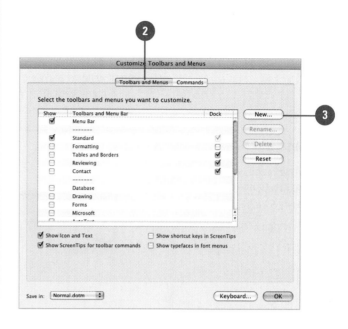

New toolbar with a button

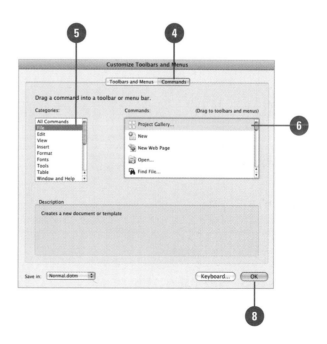

Changing Menus

You can customize the existing menu bar by adding buttons, commands, and macros that you use frequently. Adding items to the menu bar is a great way to have easy access to features without adding more buttons or toolbars. The ability to drag features from different parts of the program window makes it easy to add items to the menu bar. Imagine, having a menu with all of your most commonly used formatting, sorting, or printing commands.

Change Menus

1. Click the **View** menu, and then click **Customize Toolbars and Menus**.

2. Click the **Commands** tab.

3. Click a category, and then click a command.

4. Drag the command to a menu to add it to the menu or drag a command off the menu to remove it from the menu.

5. Repeat steps 3 and 4 to add all the commands you want to the menu.

6. Click **OK**.

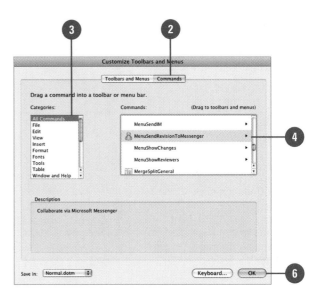

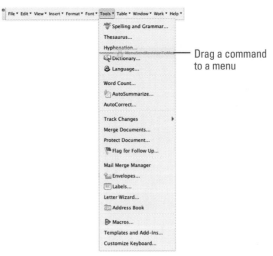

Drag a command to a menu

Changing Shortcut Keys

As you gain experience and familiarity with Office, you might find it more useful to use keyboard shortcuts for many commands rather than lifting your hands from the keyboard to use your mouse with the toolbars or menus. Most commands are assigned a default shortcut key combination, but you can edit these defaults in Word and Excel to make the most frequently used commands easier to remember, or to suit your preferences for typing speed (i.e.: some keystrokes are easier to replicate while maintaining typing speed than others).

Change Shortcut Keys

1. In Word and Excel, click the **Tools** menu, and then click **Customize Keyboard**.

   ◆ You can also click the **View** menu, click **Customize Toolbars and Menus**, and then click **Keyboard**.

2. Click the category with the command you want to change.

3. Click the command that you want to change shortcut keys.

4. Click in the **Press new keyboard shortcut** box, and then press a new keyboard shortcut.

5. Click **Assign** or **Add**.

6. To remove a keyboard shortcut, select the current keys, and then click **Remove**.

7. To reset all keyboard shortcuts back to defaults, click **Reset All**, and then click **Yes**.

8. Click **OK**.

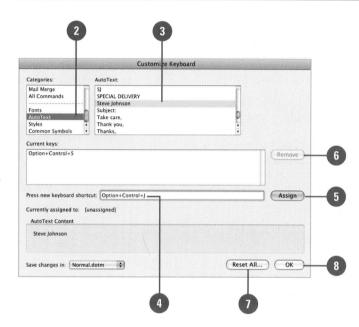

Working with Macros

If you find yourself repeating the same set of steps over and over, or if you need to add new functionality, you can use a macro. A macro is a step-by-step series of commands in script form that performs a task. You create a macro by writing a script to replay the commands you want using a programming language, such as AppleScript or Microsoft Visual Basic for Applications (VBA). Office 2004 supports AppleScript and VBA, while Office 2008 only supports AppleScript. If you have Office documents with macro-enabled VBA scripts from Office 2004 or Office 2007 for Windows, you cannot view, run, or edit them in Office 2008. However, if you have older macros from Excel 4.0 without any VBA, you can run and modify them in Excel 2008. You can store old macros for use in Excel 2008 in the following folder: Microsoft Office 2008:Office:Add-Ins. Instead of using older macros, Word 2008 provides a set of built-in macros for you to use. For example, you can accept all changes in a document, ignoring filter settings.

Run a Macro in Word

① In Word, click the **Tools** menu, and then click **Macros**.

② Click the macro you want to run.

③ Click **Run**.

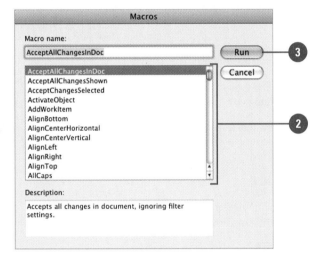

Run a Macro in Excel

1 In Excel, click the **Tools** menu, and then click **Macros**.

2 Click the **Macros in** drop-down, and then specify where the macro is stored: **This Workbook**, **All Open Workbooks**, or a specific opened workbook.

3 Click the macro you want to use.

4 To set macro options, click **Options**, specify the options you want, and then click **OK**.

5 To run the macro a step at a time, click **Step Into**.

6 To run the macro, click **Run**.

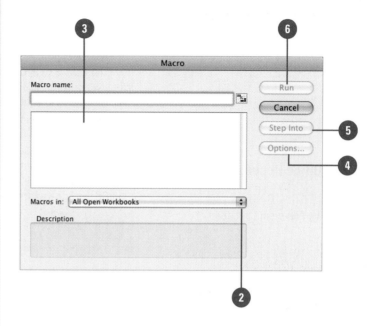

For Your Information

More About Macros in Excel

In Excel, where you store a macro determines its availability later. In the Macro dialog box, you choose to store a macro in the current workbook or all workbooks. Macros stored with the All Open Workbooks option are always available, while macros stored with the This Workbook option are only available when the document is open.

Opening a Document with Macros

When you open an Office document—created with Office 2007 for Windows or Office 2004—with a macro, VBA, or other software code, Office 2008 programs display a warning alert (**New!**) to let you know the document contains scripting code not supported by Office 2008. You have the choice to keep the code in the file for use with Office 2007 for Windows or Office 2004, remove the VBA or macro code from the file, save the macro in another macro-enabled file format, or create a new macro by using AppleScript. If you keep the code in the Office 2008, you cannot view, run, or edit the macro.

Open an Office Document with Macros

1. Click the **File** menu, and then click **Open**.

2. Click the **Where** drop-down, and then navigate to the file.

3. If necessary, click the **Enable** list arrow, and then click **All Office Documents**.

4. Click the document with macros you want to open.

5. Click **Open**.

6. In the This file contains Visual Basic macros alert, click one of the following options:

   ◆ **Keep macros.** Click **Open**.

   ◆ **Remove macros.** Click **Open and Remove Macros**.

   ◆ **Save macros.** Click **Open**. Use the topic on the next page to save the file with a macro-enabled file format.

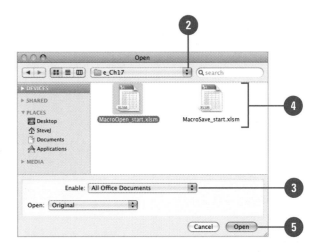

For Your Information

Open Office 2008 Files in Office 2004

Office 2008 uses a new XML file format. If you saved an Office document in 2008, but you need to open it in Office 2004, you can do it by using the Open XML Converter, which is available for download on the Microsoft Web site. To open an Office 2008 file in Office 2004, make sure Office 2004 is up-to-date with version 11.5.0, and then run the Open XML Converter program.

Saving a Document with Macros

Macros are created using Visual Basic for Applications (VBA) or AppleScript code. Office 2004 and Office 2007 for Windows support VBA, while Office 2008 supports AppleScript. If you add a macro to a document, you need to save it with a file name extension that ends with an "m" (**New!**), such as Excel Macro-Enabled Workbook (.xlsm), or Excel Macro-Enabled Template (.xltm). If you try to save a document containing a macro with a file name extension that ends with an "x" (such as .xlsx or .xltx), the Office program displays an alert message, restricting the operation. These file types are designated to be VBA code-free.

Save an Office Document with Macros

1. Click the **File** menu, and then click **Save As**.

2. Click the **Where** drop-down, and then click the folder where you want to save the file.

3. Type a file name.

4. If necessary, click the **Format** drop-down, and then select the macro format you want:

   ◆ **<Program> Macro-Enabled <File type>.** A document that contains VBA or AppleScript code.

   ◆ **<Program> Macro-Enabled Template.** A template that includes pre-approved macros.

5. Click **Save**.

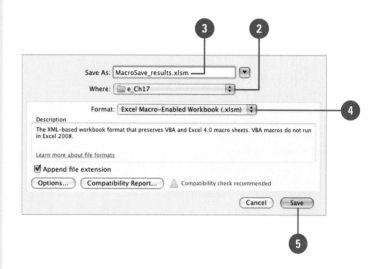

Installing and Running Office Scripts

When you open an Office 2008 program, the Office Script menu—a scroll shaped icon—appears to the right of the Help menu. The Office Script menu provides easy access to ready-made AppleScripts and Automator workflows (**New!**) designed for the open Office 2008 program. For example, you can use a sample Automator workflow to send a PDF version of a presentation in an Entourage message from PowerPoint. To add a script or workflow to the Office Script menu, copy it to the program Script Menu Items folder located in your Documents/Microsoft User Data folder.

Use Ready-Made Office Scripts

1 In an Office 2008 program on the right side of the menu bar, click the **Office Scripts** icon.

2 Point to a category.

3 Select a script option.

Some of the useful scripts include:

◆ **Send an HTML version in an Entourage message**. Sends an Web page version of an Office document in an Entourage message.

◆ **Convert text to audio and send to an iPod** (Word). Converts text to audio and send it to your iPod.

◆ **Send selected text in an Entourage message** (Word). Sends selected text in a document in an Entourage message.

◆ **Send selected content to PowerPoint or Word** (Excel). Sends selected content to PowerPoint or Word.

◆ **Combine presentations** (PowerPoint). Combines two presentation together.

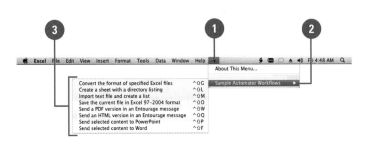

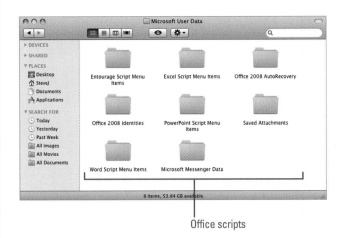

Office scripts

Working with an Automator Workflow

Automator is a program that lets you automate the things you frequently like to do on your Mac. You don't need to be a programmer to create automations. With Automator, all you need to do is assemble a series of **actions** into a workflow to complete a task. Each action performs an individual step, such as opening a file. You can create your own actions or use one of the many pre-built ones available in Automator library. The best way to learn how to create a workflow is to go through an example. Automator comes with three example workflows you can open to see what a completed one looks like.

Work with an Example Workflow

1. Open the **Applications** folder, and then double-click the **Automator** icon, click the **Custom** icon, and then click **Choose** to open Automator with a blank workflow.

2. Click the **Help** menu, and then click **Open Example Folder**.

3. Double-click the **Process Images .workflow** icon.

4. Examine the following actions in the Workflow pane:

   ◆ **Ask for Confirmation.** Displays a dialog box with information you provide for the user's benefit. You can change the button names and click the Robot icon to change it.

   ◆ **Get Specified Finder Items.** Lets you specify the files you want to process. You can use the Add or Remove buttons or drag files directly from the Finder.

   ◆ **Copy Finder Items.** Makes copies of the files to protect the originals.

   ◆ **Apply Quartz Composition Filter to Image Files.** Applies the filter to the selected image files.

   ◆ **Open Images in Preview.** Opens the specified image file in Preview.

5. To execute the workflow, click the **Run** button on the toolbar.

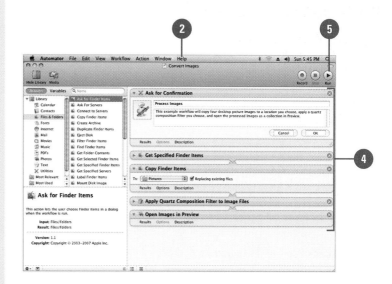

Using Ready-Made AppleScripts

You can use AppleScript right away, by working with AppleScripts created by the friendly folks at Apple. To gain access to the ready-made scripts, open the Applications folder, select the AppleScript folder, and then select Example Scripts, or do it the easy way by activating the built-in Script menu. When you activate (display) the Script menu, the Script icon appears on the right side of the menu bar and is available in the Finder and whenever you open an application. For example, you can click the Scripts icon, point to Printing Scripts, and then click Convert To PDF.

Use Ready-Made AppleScripts

1. In the Finder on the right side of the menu bar, click the **Office Scripts** icon.

2. Point to a category.

3. Select a script option.

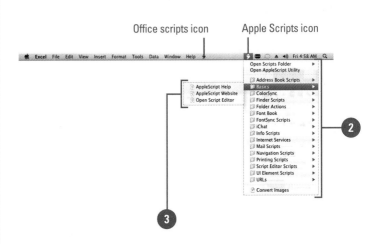

Display the Script menu

1. Open the **Applications** folder, and then open the AppleScripts folder.

2. Double-click the **AppleScript Utility** icon.

3. Select the **Show Script menu in menu bar** check box.

4. Select or clear the **Show Computer scripts** check box to show or hide library scripts.

5. Click the **top** or **bottom** option to specify where to show application scripts on the menu.

6. Click the **Close** button.

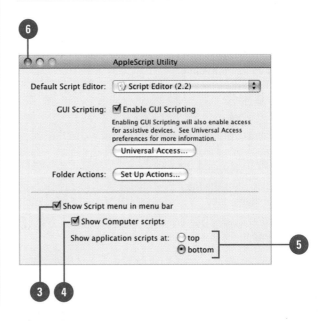

Writing and Recording AppleScripts

Anyone can write AppleScripts. All it requires is the Script Editor application available with Leopard, and knowledge of the AppleScript language. The AppleScript editor lets you type script directly into the editor window, or you can click the Record button, and then perform some Mac operation, as the editor records each step as you work. There are many places where you can go to increase your AppleScript understanding; however, point your browser to *http://www.apple.com/applescript/*, and then click the Resources link to access current resources dealing the creative techniques for AppleScript.

Write and Record AppleScripts

1. Open the **Applications** folder, point to the **AppleScript** folder, and then double-click the **Script Editor** icon.

2. Type the Script directly into the Script Editor window to create a new one or click the **File** menu, and then click **Open** to edit an existing one.

3. Click the **Record** button to record within the active script.

4. Click the **Run** button to run the active script.

5. Click the **Stop** button to stop the running of the active script.

6. Click the **Compile** button to create a version of the active script.

7. Click the **File** menu, and then click **Save**, or **Save As** to save the script using a unique name and location.

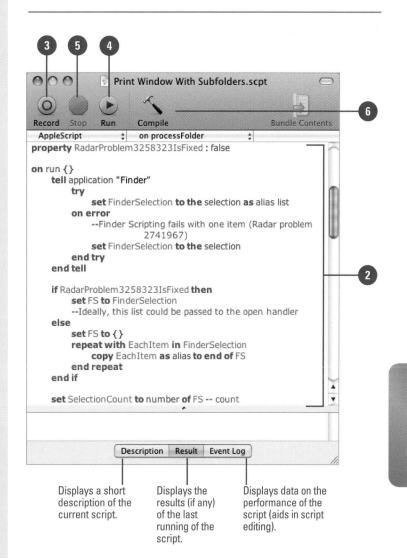

Displays a short description of the current script.

Displays the results (if any) of the last running of the script.

Displays data on the performance of the script (aids in script editing).

Removing Office

If you're having crashing problems with Office 2008 and you don't know where to turn, check out the Apple Web site at *www.apple.com* and search for some technical support. If you can't find what you need and you don't know what to do, you can remove Office 2008 from your computer and then reinstall it from your Microsoft Office 2008 for Mac installation DVD. Before you perform this task, be sure to back up all your Office documents.

Remove Office

1. In the Finder, open the **Applications** folder.

2. Double-click the **Microsoft Office 2008** folder.

3. Double-click the **Additional Tools** folder.

4. Double-click the **Remove Office** folder.

5. Double-click the **Remove Office** icon.

6. Follow the Remove Office wizard to complete the removal process.

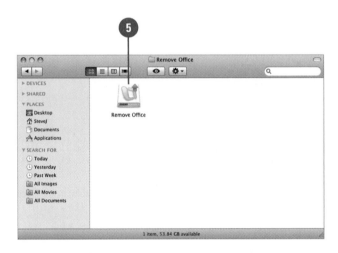

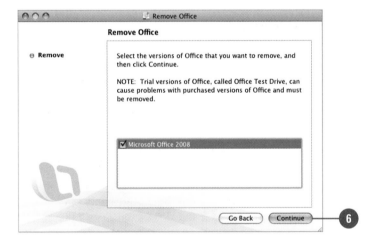

Using the Project Center

18

Introduction

The Project Center is a centralized place in Microsoft Entourage 2008 and available in Word, Excel, and PowerPoint where you can create, view, and manage Office related projects. For any project, you can add or remove project related items—such as e-mail, contacts, notes, tasks, calendar events, Scrapbook clippings, and documents.

People are the main part of any project. You can associate a contact in your Address Book with a project, so they can be a part of the process. When you create a project, Entourage also creates a new project e-mail folder where you can store and manage messages from project participants. After you create a note, task, or calendar event in Entourage or add a clipping to the Scrapbook, you can add it to a project for tracking and management purposes.

Instead of using the Project Center, you can view and manage it directly from Word, Excel, or PowerPoint by using the Project Palette tab on the Toolbox. From the Project Palette tab, you can quickly add and remove Office documents, open watch folders, enter notes, view or schedule appointments, view or flag tasks, customize and view the project information you want, and go to the Project Center.

Protecting your data is a critical part of any project. If you lose project data, it could cost you extra time and effort to re-create it. To avoid this problem, you can back up—also known as archive—a project to another location for safe keeping. If you're done with a project, you can also use the back up procedure to clear it from your hard drive.

Creating a Project

You create and manage projects in Entourage's Project Center. Entourage walks you through the creation process with the New Project Wizard. Every project has two watch folders: Entourage Project Watch folder and Finder Project Watch folder. The folders provide a place for Entourage or you to manage and work with the project files, which you can access as an alias on your desktop. In addition, you also set rules for associating e-mail messages with the project.

Create a New Project

1. Start Entourage.

2. Click the **Project Center** button on the toolbar.

3. Click the **New** button arrow on the Projects toolbar, and then click **New Project**.

   ◆ You can also click the **File** menu, point to **New**, and then click **Project**.

4. Enter a name for the project.

5. If you want to set a due date, select the **Due Date** check box, and then click the **Calendar** icon to set a date.

6. If you want a color associated with the project, click the **Color** box, and then select a color.

7. If you want to add a picture, drag and drop the image file to the Picture box.

8. Click the **right arrow** button to continue.

9. Click the **Automatically create Project Watch Folders** option to have Entourage create the watch folders, or click **Manually set Project Watch Folders option** for you to create them using the **Change** buttons.

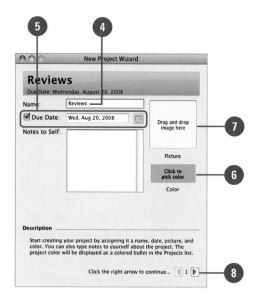

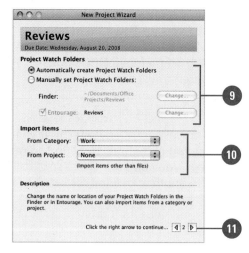

10 To import items that are assigned to an existing category or project, click the **From Category** or **From Project** drop-down, and then select a category or project from the list.

11 Click the **right arrow** button to continue.

12 Select the check boxes for the Rules for associating e-mail with the project.

- ◆ **Associate e-mail from Project contacts.** If you have project contacts, e-mail from them is automatically associated with the project.

- ◆ **Associate e-mail with the following subjects.** Enter subject keywords. If a keyword appears in a subject, e-mail from them is associated with the project.

- ◆ **Don't apply other rules to these messages.** Select to prevent other message rules from being applied to project messages.

- ◆ **Apply Rules to existing messages.** Select to use the specific rules to be a part of the project.

13 Select the **Add Project Watch Folder alias to the Desktop** check box to make easy access to project files. You can also drag new document into the folder.

14 Click the **right arrow** button to continue.

15 Read the summary.

16 Click the **right arrow** button to create the project.

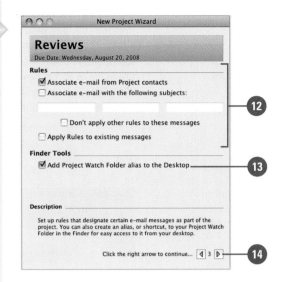

Using the Project Center

The Project Center is a centralized place in Entourage where you can manage Office related projects. In the Project Center, you can view, modify, and add project related items—such as e-mail, contacts, notes, tasks, calendar events, Scrapbook clippings, and documents—to a project. The Project Center displays a set of tabs (Overview, Schedule, Mail, Files, Contacts, Clippings, and Notes), which you can use to manage all aspects of a project.

View and Update a Project

1. In Entourage, click the **Project Center** button on the toolbar.

2. Click the project name that you want to work with in the Folders list.

3. Click the **Overview** tab.

4. Click the **Properties** button.

5. Click the tabs (**Basic**, **Add**, **Maintain**, and **Sharing**) and change the project settings you want.

6. When you're done, click **Save**.

7. Click other tabs to add or remove items from the project, or share the project with others.

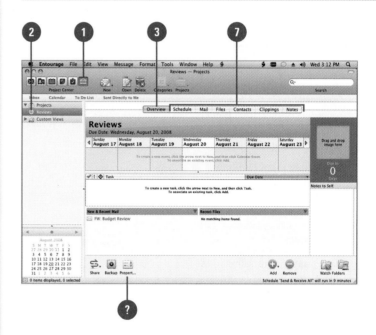

Did You Know?

You can delete a project. In the Project Center, select the project in the Folders list, click the Edit menu, click Delete Project, and then click Delete.

You can customize the information in the Overview tab. In the Project Center, click the Overview tab, and then click the triangle (on the right side of the grey heading bar) for the project-related sections at the bottom, and then select an option from the list to display the information you want.

Adding and Removing Project Contacts

People are the main part of any project. You can associate a contact in your Address Book with a project, so they can be a part of the process. Before you can associate a contact with a project, the participant needs to be a contact in your Address Book. If you no longer want a contact to be a part of a project, you can remove them. When you remove a contact from a project, the contact remains in your Address Book unless you delete it instead of removing it. The Delete commands delete the contact from the Address Book. Since you are a key participant in your projects, you forget to include yourself as a contact.

Add and Remove Project Contacts

1. In Entourage, click the **Project Center** button on the toolbar.

2. Click the project name that you want to work with in the Folders list.

3. Click the **Contacts** tab.

4. Click the **Add** button.

   ◆ You can also click the **Add** button on the Overview or Schedule tab, and then click **Contacts**.

5. Select the contacts from your Address Book, and then click **Add**.

   ◆ To select multiple contacts, ⌘-click each item.

6. To remove contacts, select the contacts you want to remove, and then click the **Remove** button.

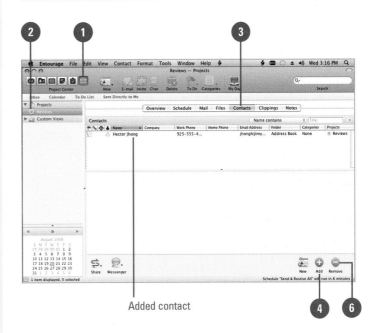

Added contact

Did You Know?

You can add and remove contacts from the Address Book. In the Entourage Address Book, select the contact, click the Edit menu, point to Projects, and then click the project name to toggle it on (add) or off (remove). To remove a contact from all projects, click None.

Adding and Removing E-mail Messages

Projects typically revolve around e-mail. Having a central place to view all project related e-mail message can greatly enhance and simplify project management and follow up. When you create a project, Entourage also creates a project e-mail folder in the Folders list where you can store and manage messages from project participants. You can add e-mail messages to a project from the Mail tab in the Project Center or from Mail view in Entourage. If you no longer need an e-mail message, you can quickly remove it from the project.

Add and Remove Project E-mail Messages

1. In Entourage, click the **Project Center** button on the toolbar.

2. Click the project name that you want to work with in the Folders list.

3. Click the **Mail** tab.

4. Click the **Add** button.

5. Select an e-mail folder from the list, select one or more messages, and then click **Add**.

   ◆ To select multiple messages, ⌘-click each item.

6. To remove messages from a project, select the messages you want to remove, and then click the **Remove** button.

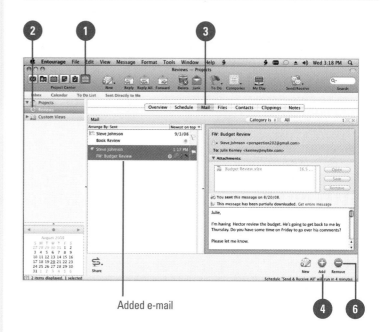

Added e-mail

Did You Know?

You can add and remove e-mail messages from Mail view. Switch to Mail view, and then drag (move) or Option-drag (copy) a message header into the project folder in the Folders list. You can also select the message, click the Edit menu, point to Projects, and then click the project name to toggle it on (add) or off (remove).

Adding Notes, Tasks, Events, or Clippings

After you create a note, task, or calendar event in Entourage or add a clipping to the Scrapbook, you can add it to a project for tracking and management purposes. You can add notes, tasks, calendar events, or clippings to a project from the Notes or Schedule tab in the Project Center or from the Notes, Tasks, or Calendar view. So, where ever you happen to be working in Entourage, you can quickly add notes, tasks, events, or clippings to a project.

Add and Remove Project Notes, Tasks, Events, or Clippings

1. In Entourage, click the **Project Center** button on the toolbar.

2. Click the project name that you want to work with in the Folders list.

3. Click the **Notes** or **Schedule** tab.

4. Click the **Add** button, and then click **Note**, **Task**, **Event**, or **Clipping**.

   ◆ You can also click the **New** button to create and add a new note, task, or event.

5. Select the note, tasks, event, or clipping you want, and then click **Add**.

6. To remove a note, task, event, or clipping, select the item, and then click the **Remove** button.

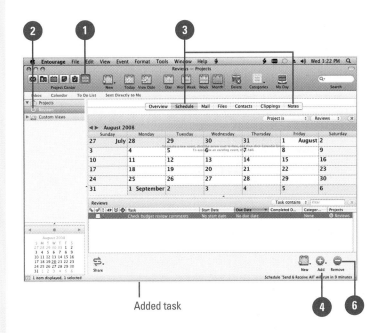

Added task

Did You Know?

You can add notes, tasks, and events in other views in Entourage. In Notes, Tasks, or Calendar view, select a note, task, or event, click the Edit menu, point to Projects, and then click the project name to toggle it on (add) or off (remove).

Adding Document Files

Documents are an important part of any project. You can add a document to a project from the Project Center or from the Project Palette tab in Word, Excel, or PowerPoint. After you add a document to a project, you can open it by using the Project Center tab in the Project Gallery dialog box, the Files tab in the Project Center, or double-clicking the file icon in one of the project watch folders.

Add and Remove Project Files in Word, Excel, or PowerPoint

① In Word, Excel, or PowerPoint, click the **Project Palette** tab on the Toolbox.

② Select the project from the drop-down.

③ Click the **Add current file** button, and the click **OK** to confirm the addition.

Add and Remove Project Files in the Project Center

① In Entourage, click the **Project Center** button on the toolbar.

② Click the project name that you want to work with in the Folders list.

③ Click the **Files** tab.

④ Click the **Add** button.

⑤ Navigate to the folder where the file is located, select the file, and then click **Open**.

◆ You can also drag the file icon into the files list on the Files tab or into the Project Watch folder on the Desktop.

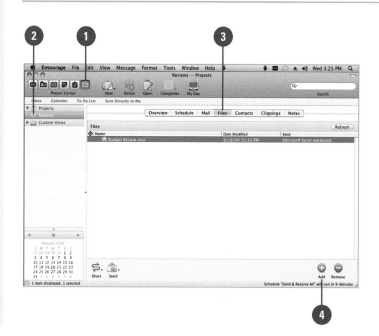

Working with Projects in Office

After you create your first project in the Project Center, you can view and manage projects from the Project Palette tab on the Toolbox in Word, Excel, or PowerPoint. From the Project Palette tab, you can quickly add and remove Office documents, open watch folders, enter notes, view or schedule appointments, view or flag tasks, customize and view the project information you want, and go to the Project Center. If you need to open a project document, you can open the file directly from the Office program or use the Project Center tab in the Project Gallery dialog box

Work with Projects in Office

1. In Word, Excel, or PowerPoint, click the **Project Palette** tab on the Toolbox.

2. Do any of the following:

   ◆ **Add or remove current document.** Click the **Add current file** or **Remove current file** button.

   ◆ **Flag a task.** Select the check box for the task to indicate it's complete. Double-click to open it in Entourage.

   ◆ **Open watch folders.** Click the **Open Entourage Project Watch Folder** or **Open Finder Project Watch Folder** button.

   ◆ **Add a note to self.** Type a note in the Notes to self box.

   ◆ **View or create a calendar appointment.** Click the **Previous Day** or **Next Day** arrow button to view an appointment, or click the **New Event** button to create one.

   ◆ **View project information.** Click the triangle, and then select the information you want to display.

3. To open a project document, click the **Project Center** tab in the Project Gallery, select the project, select the document, and then click **Open** or **Open a Copy**.

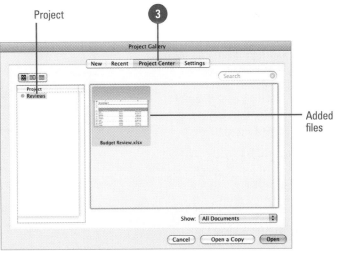

Project

Added files

Backing Up a Project

Protecting your data is a critical part of any project. If you lose project data, it could cost you extra time and effort to re-create it. To avoid this problem, you can back up—also known as archive—a project to another location for safe keeping. If you're done with a project, you can also use the back up procedure to clear it from your hard drive. You can back up all or part of a project depending on what's important to you.

Back Up a Project

1. In Entourage, click the **Project Center** button on the toolbar.

2. Click the project name that you want to work with in the Folders list.

3. Click the **Overview** tab.

4. Click the **Backup** button.

5. Select the option to specify what you want to export.

6. Select the check boxes to indicate which item types you want to export.

7. Click the **right arrow** button to continue.

8. Click the option to indicate whether to keep project items in Entourage after the back up or delete them.

9. Click the **right arrow** button to continue.

10. Type a name for the back up file or use the one provided, click the Where drop-down, select a location, and then click **Save**.

11. Click **Done**.

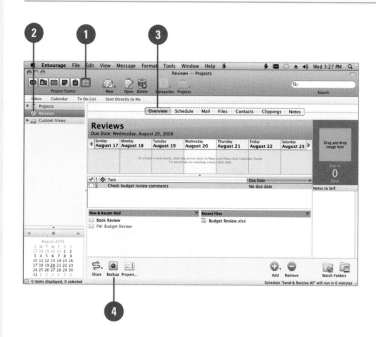

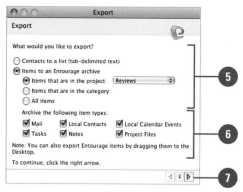

New! Features

Microsoft Office 2008

Microsoft Office 2008 provides you with the tools you need to manage your business and personal life. Each of its programs—Word, Excel, PowerPoint, and Entourage—has a special function, yet they all work together. With enhancements to the user interface, and the addition of advanced tools, Element Gallery, SmartArt graphics, Office themes and Quick Styles for text, shapes, tables, and pictures, you can accomplish a variety of tasks more easily in Office 2008.

Only New Features

If you're already familiar with Microsoft Office 2004, you can access and download all the tasks in this book with Microsoft Office 2008 New Features to help make your transition to the new version simple and smooth. The Microsoft Office 2008 New Features as well as other 2004 to 2008 transition helpers are available on the Web at *www.perspection.com.*

What's New

If you're searching for what's new in Office 2008, just look for the icon: New!. The new icon appears in the table of contents and throughout this book so you can quickly and easily identify a new or improved feature in Office 2008. The following is a brief description of each new feature and it's location in this book.

Office 2008

- ◆ **Elements Gallery (p. 10)** The Elements Gallery located below the toolbar in Word, Excel, and PowerPoint provides easy access to visual galleries where you can add SmartArt graphics, WordArt, charts, tables, and other document elements.

- ◆ **Compatibility mode (p. 14, 20-23)** When you open an Office document from Office 97-2004, Office 2008 goes into compatibility mode where it disables new features that cannot be displayed or converted well by previous versions.

- ◆ **Check compatibility (p. 14, 20-21)** The Compatibility Checker identifies the potential loss of functionality when you save an Office 2008 document in a previous venison file format.

◆ **Toolbox and Object Palette (p. 18-19, 168)** The The Toolbox provides a variety of tools organized on tabs and grouped into panels all in one central location. Some tabs are available in all of the Office programs, such as Formatting Palette, Object Palette, Scrapbook and Compatibility Report, while others are program-specific, such as Formula Builder (Excel) and Custom Animation (PowerPoint). The Object Palette provides access to shapes, clip art, symbols, and photos.

◆ **Save in XML-based file format (p. 22-25)** Office 2008 saves files in an XML (Extensible Markup Language) based file format. The XML-based format significantly reduces file sizes, provides enhanced file recovery, and allows for increased compatibility, sharing, reuse, and transportability.

◆ **Themes (p. 58-64)** A theme is a set of unified design elements that provides a consistent look for a document by using color themes, fonts, and effects, such as shadows, shading, and animations. You can use a standard theme or create one of your own.

◆ **Picture Quick Styles (p. 76)** The Picture Quick Style gallery provides a variety of different formatting combinations.

◆ **Apply a shape to a picture (p. 77)** You can now select a picture and apply a shape to it.

◆ **Picture effects (p. 78-78)** You can now change the look of a picture by applying effects, such as shadows, reflections, glow, soft edges, and 3-D rotations.

◆ **Recolor Picture Quick Styles (p. 82)** The Recolor Picture gallery provides a variety of different formatting combinations.

◆ **Text and Shape Quick Styles (p. 88-91)** You can quickly add different formatting combinations to text using WordArt Quick Styles or to a shape using Shape Quick Styles. You can also change individual styles by applying shadows, reflections, glow, soft edges, and 3-D rotations.

◆ **SmartArt graphics (p. 94-100)** SmartArt graphics allow you to create diagrams that convey processes or relationships. Office provides a variety of built-in SmartArt graphic types, including organization charts, graphical lists, process, cycle, hierarchy, relationship, matrix, and pyramid.

◆ **Microsoft Excel used to create charts (p. 101)** Office programs now use Microsoft Excel to embed and display a chart instead of Microsoft Graph.

◆ **Added chart types and effects (p. 101-103)** Office added more built-in chart layouts and styles to make charts more appealing and visually informative.

◆ **Table Quick Styles (p. 208, 379, 382)** The Table Quick Style gallery provides a variety of different formatting combinations. You can change the look of a table by applying effects, such as shadows, reflections, glow, soft edges, 3-D rotations, and transformations.

◆ **Create a PDF (p. 492-493)** You can now save a document as a PDF file, which is a fixed-layout format that retains the form you intended on a computer monitor or printer.

♦ **Macros (p. 502-503)** If you have a macro in an Office document, you need to save it with a file name extension that ends with an "m". For example, either Excel Macro-Enabled Workbook (.xlsm), or Excel Macro-Enabled Template (.xltm) for Excel. If you have Office documents with macro-enabled VBA scripts from Office 2004 or Office 2007 for Windows, you cannot view, run, or edit them in Office 2008.

♦ **Automator (p. 504)** The Office Script menu provides easy access to ready-made AppleScripts and Automator workflows designed for the open Office 2008 program.

Word 2008

♦ **Publishing Layout view (p. 135, 138, 142-145)** Publishing Layout view displays the document in a specialized view for desktop publishing. In this view, you can create professional-looking newsletters, brochures, flyers, and calendars.

♦ **Publication templates (p. 142-143)** Word provides new professionally designed publication templates.

♦ **Document Elements (p. 164-165, 214, 224)** Document Elements makes it quick and easy to add more complex parts—such as cover pages, table of contents, header, footer, and bibliographies—to a document.

♦ **Ligatures in fonts (p. 171)** Ligatures are font characters that combine two or more separate characters to improve text style and readability.

♦ **Mail Merge Manager (p. 210-2113)** The improved version of the Data Merge Manager in Word 2004 makes is easy to create letters, mailing labels, and catalogs using a step by step process.

Excel 2008

♦ **Excel 2008 Binary file format (p. 24)** In addition to the new XML-based file format, Excel also provides a new file format (BIFF12 with the extension .xls) to accommodate large or complex workbooks.

♦ **Insert worksheet (p. 241)** Click the Insert Worksheet icon at the end of the sheet tabs.

♦ **Insert preformatted sheets (p. 242-243)** From the Sheets tab in the Elements Gallery, you can select a Quick Style worksheet from a variety of categories, such as Accounts, Budgets, Invoices, Lists, Portfolios, or Reports. The Quick Style worksheets are templates with all the layout, formatting, and formulas you need to get started quickly.

♦ **Formula Builder (p. 268-269)** Formula Builder simplifies the process by organizing Excel's built-in formulas, called functions, into categories—such as Most Recently Used, Financial, Text, Date and Time, Lookup and Reference, Math and Trigonometry, and other functions—so they are easy to find and use.

◆ **Formula AutoComplete (p. 258-259, 262-263)**   You can quickly and correctly write functions with Formula AutoComplete, which detects what you type and tries to fill in the rest.

PowerPoint 2008

◆ **Slide Themes (p. 58-64, 377)**   A document theme consists of theme colors, fonts, and effects. You can quickly format an entire document with a professional look by applying a theme. When you apply a theme, the background, text, graphics, charts, and tables all change to reflect the theme. In PowerPoint, you can create your own custom theme colors, and then use them in other Office programs.

◆ **Dynamic guides (p. 126-127)**   Dynamic guides appear as you need them when you drag an object, while static guides appear when you enable them.

◆ **Slide Layout gallery (p. 350-351)**   PowerPoint provides a gallery of slide layouts to help you position and format slides in a consistent manner.

◆ **Stack letters (p. 357)**   You can now stack letters on top of one another.

◆ **Create columns (p. 364)**   You can now create text columns within a text box.

◆ **Indent markers (p. 360)**   You can now set different indent markers for each paragraph in an object.

◆ **Slide master layouts (p. 370-373)**   Each slide master includes a standard set of slide layouts. However, you can modify a slide master layout using different types of placeholders.

◆ **Wide screen slide sizes (p. 386)**   You can now set the slide size to fit computer monitor with ratios of 16:9 (wide screen HDTV's), or 16:10 (wide screen laptops).

◆ **Transition Quick Styles (p. 394)**   The Transition Quick Style gallery provides a variety of different transition effect combinations you can add between slides.

◆ **Apple Remote controls slide show (p. 401)**   If your Mac comes with an Apple Remote, you can use it to deliver and navigate through your slide show.

◆ **Send a presentation to iPhoto (p. 406)**   In addition to saving a presentation as a movie, you can also save a presentation as a series of slides to an iPhoto album, which you can sync and playback in a video iPod.

Entourage 2008

◆ **Spotlight search (p. 445)**   With Spotlight preferences enabled (the default) in Entourage, you can use Spotlight to search for e-mail, calendar events, tasks, contacts, and other Entourage items.

◆ **Out of Office (p. 446)**   If you have a Microsoft Exchange account, you can have Entourage reply to message automatically when you're out of the office. You can now schedule your Out of Office times in advance, so you don't forget to turn it off.

◆ **Junk E-mail protection (p. 452)** You can specify what should be considered junk e-mail and how Entourage should handle that e-mail. If Entourage detects a phishing message with links to a specious Web site, a warning alert appears.

◆ **Customizable toolbars (p. 458)** You can customize any toolbar in Entourage by visually dragging and dropping the buttons you want onto the current toolbar.

◆ **To Do List pane and flagging (p. 471-473)** You create a To Do List item by simply setting a follow-up flag with the To Do button or flag icon for an e-mail message in Mail view or a contact in Address Book. When you work in Calendar view, you can display and create tasks and To Do List items in the To Do List pane.

◆ **My Day (p. 476-477)** My Day is a stand-alone Office related program that allows you to display upcoming events and tasks from Entourage.

Index